AMERICA'S ASIA

Dissenting Essays on Asian-American Relations

B. Ranch

Other Pantheon Antitextbooks

THE DISSENTING ACADEMY edited by Theodore Roszak

TOWARDS A NEW PAST edited by Barton J. Bernstein

POWER AND COMMUNITY edited by Philip Green and Sanford Levinson

VINTAGE BOOKS

A DIVISION OF RANDOM HOUSE   *NEW YORK*

AMERICA'S ASIA

Dissenting Essays on Asian-American Relations

EDITED BY
Edward Friedman & Mark Selden

DEDICATION

To the furthering of the critical spirit and humanitarian purposes which informed the founding of the Committee of Concerned Asian Scholars

Introduction

ASIA IS AMERICA'S in three important ways. First, it is America's in the sense that we impose American categories to describe, evaluate, and direct Asian experience. Our cultural chauvinism might mainly provide material for humorous self-analysis were it not for the overwhelming explosion of American economic and military might throughout Asia. For Asia is America's in this second tragic sense that American power has channeled, distorted, and suppressed much that is Asia.

This book explores the dynamic and destructive interaction between American perceptions and American power in the making and unmaking of contemporary Asia. Our focus is at once Asia and America. For the investment of immense intellectual and material resources in American military adventures in Asia does more than deprive us of resources vitally needed at home. It simultaneously strengthens the very repressive tendencies in our society most prone to crush aspirations for freedom, autonomy, and equality in America.

The essays in this book suggest, moreover, that an Asia conceived in antagonistic or contemptible categories is an Asia where much that is humane, valuable, and worthy of emulation is ignored. This adds a final meaning to America's Asia. If we could change our relation to Asia we would be open to learning much from Asian peoples that could help us create a more decent and just society in the United States.

I

CONSIDER SOME OF the categories invented to judge and manipulate Asia. Of repressive oligarchies in Thailand and Indonesia, we ask: Are they good military modernizers? Of a Japan seething with burning social tension and skewed and unequal distribution, we wonder: At what rate has the annual gross national product increased? Of rural societies such as India where millions upon millions of poor tillers, tenants, and landless peasants live in hopelessness, squalor, and degradation, we ask: Have they abandoned the neutralist naïveté of a new nation to assume mature responsibilities? Definitional preoccupations reflect and project American actions in Asia. We establish the ground rules and then judge the performance. Any Asian who fails the test posed by American interests and ideology obviously needs Yankee know-how and military protection. Far from contributing to a free and independent development of new nations, our aid harnesses the economy, "security," and culture of Asian states to American power. Elites in the new Asian nations become beholden to Washington for their power and fail to respond to the urgent needs of their own poor and oppressed rural populations.

The very categories employed by American scholars, journalists, and diplomats mask the harsh realities of contemporary Asia. The essays by Dick Kagan and Leigh Kagan and Jim Peck provide the first systematic analysis of the dominant intellectual constructs which have guided America in the era of the Americanization of Asia. By examining high school textbooks on China, Leigh Kagan and Dick Kagan reveal many basic notions of the field translated into a smooth sea of English to be washed through the brains of Mr. American Citizen. China's multifaceted past and present are distorted into a simple Manichean world. A present ruthless Red menace is contrasted with a prior harmonious and beneficent Confucian tradition and the potential benefits of American-sponsored development, the supposed reality of "Free China." Such fundamental notions may bear little relation to truth, but they help to promote good consciences among men perpetrating the worst barbarisms in the name of cultural freedom and progress.

Nor is this simply a matter of talking down to high school students. The Peck essay shows that similar ideas control the discussion in the most sophisticated scholarly circles.

An ideology of modernization has carefully been constructed to play down to a null point American aggression
and exploitation and play up as a dominant motif American benevolence in assisting Asians to traverse the treach-
erous evolutionary course to the modern world. In this
worldview, revolution emerges as a menace to be crushed,
not a solution and a natural response to overwhelming
evolutionary horrors.

Our profession is limited by more than its intellectual
milieu. Its institutional development, traced by Judy Coburn, has been shaped by the Cold War and the growth
of American hegemony in Asia. How did the field grow?
Why did it grow when it did? Who provided the money and
the expertise to shape this growth? Were the products of
the scholarship and we, the people who produced them,
in the service of political and financial sources which sought
from us a very special product? Coburn shows how Asian
studies was nurtured by foundations and government to
service the growing needs of an American-dominated Asia.

The Cold War environment in which Asian studies developed is most vividly illustrated by the events of the Mc-
Carthy era. If the entire American intellectual world was
shattered at that time, few branches were more profoundly
disrupted than Asian studies whose members provided convenient scapegoats for the "loss of China." Two decades
later we are still living with the legacy of McCarthyism. A
few years ago, as America massively expanded its intervention in Vietnam, some of us suggested that the Association
for Asian Studies consider the political implications of its
activities and non-activities. We were swiftly and firmly
put down by our elders and betters whose Institute of
Pacific Relations, and in some cases professional careers,
had been destroyed or damaged by McCarthyite politics.
Many of these men had fought courageously against the
repression of the early fifties. But their defeat was overwhelming. They organized the AAS to avoid the political
vulnerability of the IPR. In the process they accepted and

perpetuated McCarthy's dicta that independent criticism has no place in scholarship and that scholars had best abjure critical, independent politics. What is a profession like in which many of the senior men who experienced the McCarthyite horror, in fear of appearing un-American, assume one must play it safe? The result has been a frozen silence by much of the profession on critical issues, while a veritable deluge of Cold War studies have been produced to tacitly or explicitly justify American Asian policy.

The essays in this book only begin to scratch the protective cover which hides the aggressive reality inherent in America's domination of much of Asia. Recently, however, a Committee of Concerned Asian Scholars has sprung up to respond to the crisis in America's Asia. This volume was in no small part stimulated by the challenge of the CCAS to investigate the relationship between knowledge and power, between intellectual creation in America and political destruction in Asia.* A number of the studies in this book were initiated in a CCAS seminar in the summer of 1968. To the regular participants in those discussions—Marianne Bastid, Herb Bix, John Dower, Tom Engelhardt, Jon Grant, Dick Kagan, Leigh Kagan, Dick Kraus, Jon Livingston, Mitch Meisner, Victor Nee, Jim Peck, John Watt, and Paul Winnacker—the editors wish to express gratitude for their incisive critical suggestions.

II

ONE OF THE striking features of American Asian scholarship has been its reiteration of Cold War myths. Long after scholars in other fields had re-examined and discarded the notion of a defensive response to Communist expansionism as inadequate for understanding America's new global posture, no similar general search for truth ruffled the calm of Asian studies. The essays of John Dower, John Gittings,

---

* A quarterly *Bulletin* of Asian history and contemporary affairs is available from CCAS at 2168 Shattuck Avenue, Berkeley, California, 94704.

Ed Friedman, Jon Mirsky, and Steve Stonefield examine these self-justifying arguments for the defensive quality of American intervention. Together their work constitutes a reinterpretation of the Cold War in Asia. The escalation of the Vietnam War in 1965 stimulated scholars such as George Kahin, John Lewis, and Franz Schurmann to expose the official lies advanced to mask American intervention in that troubled country. As the studies in this book make plain, Vietnam is no aberration. It is an integral if extremely costly link in the chain of creating and maintaining an Asian *Pax Americana*.

More than two decades ago the Occupation of Japan set the course for the militarist and anti-popular character of American intervention in Asia. John Dower explores the failure of the Occupation to live up to its promise to democratize and demilitarize Japan. With the seizure of Pacific Island bases and the "reverse course" of the Occupation, the banner of an Asian *Pax Americana* was unfurled. A decade earlier Japan had marched through Asia, bombed Pearl Harbor, and carved out an empire justified by anti-Communist politics and the promise of independence and development. That empire was brought to its knees by a combination of American technology, United States Marine human wave assaults, the fire-bombing of Tokyo, nuclear holocaust in Hiroshima and Nagasaki, and heroic efforts of guerrilla fighters in China and other parts of rural Asia. But the end of European and Japanese colonialism brought neither genuine independence nor autonomous development to the nations of "Free Asia." American military and economic power swept in to fill the void left by the departing colonial powers—achieving for America many of the dreams of empire it had denied a vanquished Japan, its rationale then as now the necessity to crush Communist aggression.

As the decade of the seventies begins, the contours of America's Asia are rapidly changing. The challenge from below of revolutionary forces in Vietnam, Laos, and elsewhere is one crucial aspect of this process. Simultaneously, the resurgence of Japanese power and the overextension of American resources has signaled the end of an era of independent American action and the beginning of close Japanese-American cooperation in controlling the future of Asia.

Friedman's essay on the armed clash between China and America in Korea further undercuts the notion of the leader of the Free World onerously but honorably assuming the burden of defending the helpless against Communist aggression. In the process he illuminates one of the central elements of Cold War politics, the origins of Sino-American confrontation. China's decision to send troops into neighboring Korea appears in a new light. After considering whether China was rational, defensive, and capable of a diplomacy of disengagement, he puts the same questions to American policy in Korea. The evidence indicates that, contrary to prevailing views of Chinese irrationality or aggressiveness, America provoked war with China.

Gittings investigates the standard American theory of the origins of the Cold War in Asia. The alleged cause lies in a master plan for revolution outlined in a speech by Zhdanov which, Walt Rostow and others claim, produced a

> more militant attitude everywhere. Guerrilla warfare on the Chinese pattern broke out in rural areas in Burma in April, 1945, and in Malaya in June; and it was resumed in the Philippines . . . in the fall of the same year.

Gittings shows that the American penchant for conspiracy theories replete with puppets and puppeteers is historical nonsense. The manipulation of the historical origins of the Cold War in Asia to pin the blame on International Communism is belied both by the fiery independent nationalist revolutions which light up the landscape of Asia, and by America's own expansion in the area. Gittings forces us to rethink the nature of revolutionary movements and their relations to foreign powers.

The Mirsky–Stonefield article explores a particular instance of the institutional and ideological factors which led America to begin a military, anti-popular course in Japan after World War II, to precipitate war with China in Korea, and aggressively assume the role of the former colonial powers throughout Southeast Asia. This is the case of Laos. Far from favoring independent, neutralist, popular governments in Laos and elsewhere, America has systematically attempted to destroy them.

Dower, Friedman, Mirsky, Stonefield, and Gittings expose the apologetics which hitherto have passed for the scholarship of the Cold War. Nonetheless, the particular relations between critical scholarship on Asia and American policy in Asia are no more obvious than the general relationship between knowledge and power. Some have argued that without the McCarthyite purge of State Department China specialists and the destruction of the Institute of Pacific Relations, America and China might not have fought in Korea, by proxy in Vietnam and Laos, on again-off again in the Formosa Straits, until it may be done once and for all with nuclear weapons. This optimistic missionary view of knowledge saving the world makes our work seem worthwhile, even vital.

Yet others insist that no amount of knowledge can change policy, that information will be used to serve predetermined, intolerable ends. Not only the contributions of scholars, but the works of Mao Tse-tung himself merely provide grist for the mill of CIA and Pentagon specialists in counter-revolutionary subversion. Consequently, American scholars of Asia would do better to study America. Armed with knowledge of the economic and political dynamics underlying American foreign policy, we might then seek to change the basic conditions which produce Vietnams and speed super-powers toward war with China.

There is much truth in the latter, pessimistic view of the relation of knowledge to power. Clearly, though the essays in this book barely begin to elucidate this problem, domestic economic and political considerations are primary determinants of foreign policy. Presidents, secretaries of state, and ambassadors employ analysts whose advice conforms with pre-established needs and dispositions. Dominant institutions and interests define those needs. Yet in significant respects all of us in the academy, the government, and the mass media, no less than the general public, are prisoners of the concepts and categories of our thinking about China, about Asia, and about American interests in Asia.

The essays in the first two sections of *America's Asia* deal with the overarching concepts which limit the possibilities open to American policy in Asia. The essays criticize pervasive myths and categories in the hope of establishing the relevance of new modes of thinking and alternatives to present policies of destruction. Admittedly, we are as prone to errors of cultural misunderstanding as the rest of our colleagues. Our hope, however, is that the examination of our profession can make us aware of how we came to be where we are and point the way to the development of new levels of understanding. Further, we hope that by consciously refusing to serve official and elite definitions of American interests in Asia we may achieve some consciousness of how those interests have defined that Asia.

This, then, is in part an attempt to discover why alternatives to present policies often seem so similar to those policies. To pose genuine alternatives we may first need genuinely different concepts. To make the world new and better it may be necessary to see the world new and better. At least the effort seems worth making. The third part of *America's Asia* is a step in that direction.

III

ARTISTS, MUSICIANS, and philosophers continually turn to Asia for inspiration. The philosophers of the Age of Enlightenment believed there was much to learn from China about social organization. But as the nineteenth-century

West turned to a massive imperialist assault on China, the Chinese people became, to our "practical" men, objects of ridicule and contempt, not alternative models to be contemplated, criticized, and, where fitting, emulated. A century later, American social scientists, generals, and politicians continue to see Asian needs in terms of American advice and aid. Whatever Asians do that is new is wrong. China provides a case in point.

When China decided over a decade ago that an essentially merit educational system should be changed because it was unjust to the majority of economically poor and culturally disadvantaged, American students of China ridiculed the Chinese effort as one which destroyed standards. Faced now with the demand of Black America for justice, America's educational system is forced to face up to the identical problem. How is America doing by comparison? Is there anything worth learning from China? Is anybody looking? We suggest that a proper approach to studying Asia would assume that major civilizations have much to learn from each other about solving humanity's fundamental problems, indeed, that wherever human beings struggle to overcome established limits, there will be much creativity and instruction for all mankind.

America is confronted with urban blight, with environmental and social problems which threaten the very existence of the American city. Would a more decentralized economy and society make sense? China thinks so. For a decade she has been trying to decentralize her cities and economy. Are any Americans looking to see what in the Chinese experience might be applied in the United States?

Is enforced retirement the best way to treat older people? Is there useful and satisfying work they still can do and perhaps do better than others? And what of more freedom for women, the need for public day-nurseries and part-time jobs? Can we learn something from the various local experiments tried in China during the commune drive and the Cultural Revolution?

American attempts to deal with the many cultural manifestations of poverty have led to the establishment of community medical clinics, even to doctors going into homes
in search of prospective patients. More than a decade ago
thousands of Chinese doctors left urban centers for the
countryside and left hospitals to enter the homes of the
poor who would not or could not go to a modern hospital.
China has devoted extraordinary efforts to bring the benefits of science to people who distrust the super-educated.
Isn't there much to learn from China?

Or is China just irrationality piled on inhumanity? The
upheavals of the Cultural Revolution, while reinforcing
certain stereotypes of China, should also make it more difficult for people to believe that concepts such as totalitarianism or monolithic Communism express the essence of
the Chinese polity. It is more than likely, however, that the
concepts that replace them will also be belittling, put-down
categories. China and revolution will be called backward,
irrational, immature, and underdeveloped, anything that
will permit America to treat and dismiss them as inferiors.

The essays in the third section of *America's Asia* represent
a different attitude toward China and revolution. John Gurley, Mark Selden, and Steve Andors treat the people they
study as subject, not object. Instead of trying to dissect and
demolish Asians, they approach the people with an open
attitude, one which is willing to learn and be changed by
interaction with the subject. By so doing they create a new
Asia for America. It is one that can be approached hopefully
and critically, not condescendingly or destructively. Focusing on the humanity of their subject, they find inspiration
and application to general human problems, to problems
Americans as well as citizens of Third World nations face
here and now.

Gurley surveys Maoist economics. He finds it differs
from the economics of Smith, Marshall, Keynes *et al*. But
instead of concluding that this makes Mao irrational and
anachronistic as economists usually do, he investigates the

value base of the new Chinese economy. The result high-lights, among other things, the positive implications of Chinese practice for an economics fundamentally concerned with distributive justice instead of gross productivity. In short, the Chinese economy has much to teach advanced industrial societies in which millions are left behind by the supposedly rational and inevitable march of a tech-nology which creates wealth at the expense of human beings and the environment.

Selden looks at the Chinese and Vietnamese revolutionary experience with an eye to the kinds of ties created among those who shared in the resistance effort. In particular he explores the role of community and participation in the effective resolution of local problems. His analysis of People's War suggests insights not only for nations strug-gling with problems of foreign domination and economic stagnation but also for a highly atomized, individuated, and alienated society like America.

Andors looks at Chinese factories. He asks whether popu-lar control can work in advanced industrial societies. He finds much in the Chinese experience instructive for reduc-ing or eliminating aspects of manipulation, hierarchy, and domination which America too readily accepts as the in-evitable price of industrialization. Yet American social scientists seldom look to China's internal development save for comic relief or to determine the impact on China's military potential. America, with all its tensions and in-humanities, is reified as realistic normality or progress incarnate. Chinese who refuse to recreate American social diseases are treated as social lepers with a bell hung round their necks warning the world against contagion from totali-tarian demons and impractical visionaries. At the very least we are forced to wonder at the parochialism which takes an American preference for individualism and technologi-cal progress over equality and community not as a reasonable choice but as reason itself. But we must go further. These essays suggest a need for fundamental reassessment of the

human and social contributions of less industrialized societies. It may be true for nation states as for business enterprises that those who feel themselves poorer and smaller
often make the daring innovations and creative break-
throughs. In some significant ways, may not the last be
first?

IV

THE ESSAYS in *America's Asia* examine the optical instruments which distort our vision of Asia and revolution. This
still leaves open the question of knowledge and power.
Would America have pushed on with democratization
during the Occupation of Japan if it believed that without
a thorough social revolution Japan would eventually re-
emerge industrially and militarily powerful, thoroughly
undemocratic and competing with the United States?
Would America have acted on behalf of revolutionaries in
China, in Vietnam, in Laos, and throughout Southeast
Asia if policy-makers understood that the alternative governments doomed peasant millions to a life without hope,
an unending cycle of poverty, ignorance, and disease? To
be truthful we cannot answer in the affirmative. Yet we
affirm the importance of the search for the whole human
truth rather than knowledge which salves the consciences
and smooths the path for men pursuing policies of destruction. We do so in the conviction that widespread acceptance
of Cold War premises by policy-makers and citizens alike
has contributed to the creation of America's Asia. In the
era of America's Asia, until we know America we cannot
understand Asia, and until fundamental changes are forthcoming in American policy, only Asian revolutions can make
Asian autonomy and independent development other than
hypocritical official myths. Challenging perceptions of ourselves and the world is a vital first step toward a more human
foreign policy and a more humane society.

April 30, 1970   —Edward Friedman and Mark Selden

Contents

AMERICA'S ASIA

Dissenting Essays on Asian-American Relations

Oh Say, *Can* You See?
American Cultural Blinders
on China

❧ *Leigh and Richard Kagan*

I · PERCEPTION OF THE ENEMY

STUDY OF CHINA often begins in high school, where students are prepared for their role as American citizens. To learn about Chinese history, they read special materials on that country prepared by educators and scholars, which are known as units. The purpose of these high school units on China is to arm future citizens for the fight to contain China and to equip them with timely rationalizations and justifications for an American strategy of domination over Asia. High school units consequently convey what their authors and publishers feel should be told to American youth about China; they in no way address themselves to historical or contemporary realities or controversies. As such, they are a propagandistic not an educational exercise; and they furnish especially fertile terrain for discovering the American distortions propagated to denature China's past and present. In short, high school units define China as the Enemy.

Study of China continues, perhaps, in college, where students are prepared for their role as American elites. To learn about Chinese civilization, they read essays and monographs written by scholars in the profession of Asian Studies. The message of these materials is more complicated and subtle than that of high school units. By breeding familiarity with the elites of traditional China and singing the praises of their cultural tradition, these scholarly works instill in their readers a lingering fondness for the abated possibility of change within China's Confucian tradition. They engender an abhorrence of China's social revolution because it is a movement of idealistic political reform which has destroyed the nature of China's institutions and her elites.

The emphasis on China's cultural present in both high school units and scholarly works is also central to the American credo of the universality of her own historical development. This credo insists that the American way of life is exportable and demonstrates this conviction by focusing on the cultural similarities between America and other countries. The emergence of this credo, which we have called culturalism, is discussed in section IV.

II · THE POLITICAL LOSS OF CHINA AND HIGH SCHOOL UNITS

THE NEED TO EXPLAIN the loss of China for America in 1949 is the impetus for high school units on China. The units' basic point is two-fold: (1) China's potential to modernize was present but miscarried because Communism cut off the rest of the time needed in order to modernize; and (2) Communism in China posed a threat to America. To demonstrate this view, a picture of traditional Chinese culture is constructed by the units in which only characteristics seen as conducive to Western-style modernization are identified as Chinese. This conception of China's proclivity for modernization is responsible for viewing twentieth-century Chinese history as an international struggle between the West and Communism.[1]

According to the units, the distinctive achievement of China's three-thousand year past was her culture. Because this culture was self-sufficient, it was capable of accommodating change within tradition. It was the stabilizing element against violent social change and for non-violent political change. As such, it was an ideal culture. As one unit asserts, "In an ideal culture all the patterns would fit together, and each one would accomplish a useful purpose. The people as a whole would find the way of living reasonably satisfying." (Ewing, p. 77) The adequacy of this culture for the Chinese instills in them all the stereotyped qualities deemed desirable.

> The Chinese believe that they have the longest history, the most civilized culture, and the best intellect of any people on earth. As a result, they are a self-confident people. . . .
> They have a fine sense of humor. . . . The Chinese are considered to be diligent and skillful . . . The Chinese have a reputation for patience . . . The Chinese are keen businessmen . . . No Chinese sees himself as an island apart from other men. He is an integral part of the history, tradition, language, and culture of China. (Swisher, pp. 9–11)

Chinese culture is characterized as permitting change within tradition, hence it is compatible with Western-style modernization. For both traditional China and Western-style modernization subscribe to gradual, non-violent political change. "The Chinese had taken some modern methods from Western culture, but they had not successfully combined the new ways with their traditional patterns. Further change was necessary." (Ewing, p. 77) The implication here being that had China been permitted to fulfill her traditional capacity to accommodate gradual political change, she would have become a modern Westernized nation. Tradition forms a barrier against radical change; its values provide "immunity against communism."[2] Conversely, only the Communists' cataclysmic destruction of Chinese culture accounts for the violent social revolution of the twentieth century. This extermination of tradition thereby becomes a criminal disruption of the natural course of Chinese history. This conviction is coarsely but forcefully expressed by the Honorable Walter H. Judd, medical missionary in China, prominent spokesman for the China Lobby and a former Minnesota Congressman:

> . . . the Chinese people are a highly civilized people. They have good manners, they are mature, and have a rich, mellow culture. They have been trained that way for centuries.
>
> Mao believes that he has to teach them instead the 'virtues' of belligerence and armed force . . . nobody is permitted to teach youth the values of that ancient civilization.[3]

Why did this ideal culture sustain self-sufficiency and political flexibility? The leaders of the country were scholars:

> The Chinese believe in education. Two thousand years ago they made education the basis for their government and society. They believed that scholars should rule the country. They established nation-wide examinations which were open to everyone. Those who passed with the highest grades became the high officials in the government. Those who failed or passed with lower grades became leaders in other areas of society. Many of them taught school. Chinese who lived then believed that knowledge of history and philosophy, and an understanding of human nature were the most important qualifications for leadership. (Swisher, p. 8)

Or again, from a more academic source: Chinese philosophers, whose central tenet was the maintenance of harmony,

> were generally members of the official class . . . always near enough to authority to promote the embodiment of their ideas in programs of action.[4]

These scholars and philosophers were pacifistic Confucians, who abjured military and violent means of bringing about reform.

This characterization by the units of China's culture gives rise to three areas of confusion and misrepresentation which permeate the high school units and the scholarly literature on Chinese culture: (1) China's cultural tradition is equated with Confucianism; (2) violent change, the military, and considerations of power, wealth, and ideology either are attributed to an aberrant development (Legalism), or simply cast out beyond the pale; (3) social and intellectual history recede from view.

The equation of China's cultural tradition with Confucianism is achieved at the expense of a true understanding of Confucianism and of Chinese social and intellectual history. The humanistic ethic of Confucius, and the "democratic" precept of Mencius, who enunciated the right to rebel against tyrannical rulers,[5] are presented as the only valid aspects of Chinese tradition. The contention that this rational strain of political thought constitutes Confucianism has often been promoted by the Nationalists and accepted by foreign observers and scholars. The belief that Confucianism means China, and that anything not Confucian is *ipso facto* not Chinese lends a false sense of continuity and unity to the Chinese character.

But violent upheaval did occur. The high school units explain it by saying that the warlike Legalists took advantage of Confucian pacifism forcibly to unite China in the third century, B.C. The "educated Chinese objected to [this] Legalistic rule" and "favored return to rule based on other philosophical systems [read Confucianism]." (Kublin, p. 53, Chapters 2 and 3 *passim*) Needless to say, Confucianism triumphed, and the Legalist dynasty fell within a generation. Such ahistorical sleight of hand ignores the intellectually and socially symbiotic relationship between Legalism and Confucianism. The facile comparison between Legalism and Communism is made. The conviction that only the Legalists and the Communists employed violent means informs a recent article in which a scholar singles out only two revolutions in China: 221, B.C.—the Legalist; and 1949, A.D.—the Communist.[6] Both are seen as alien to Chinese character. The high school unit by Fenton ends with a quotation from *Time* magazine which compares Mao's Cultural Revolution with the Legalist Ch'in (221–207, B.C.) Emperor's breach of tradition.

We are told that this non-Confucian Emperor "forcibly united most of China . . . and established a tyrannical rule that was soon swept away in civil war." (p. 338) This intimation of impending civil war lends credence to the myth that the Chinese peasant, in accordance with Mencius' dictum, eventually will rise up and destroy the alien Communist system, as he has always destroyed other non-Confucian dynasties, i.e., those of despotic and barbarian character and origin. (Armstrong, p. 27) This scenario forecloses consideration of the social origins of Confucianism, and the intellectual forces which influenced it—such as Legalism. It erects a framework within which it is impossible to comprehend the phenomenon of violent change in China.

Just as violence was anathema to Confucianism, according to the units, so was its agent, the military. China was not ruled by a militant warrior class but by educated scholar-gentry-officials. In actuality, however, every dynasty was founded by a military leader or on the strength of military might. This incontestable fact is duly noted in a recent article by a scholar who uniformly condemns the use of violence to effect social change. "The persistent historical fact is that the Chinese state has always derived its ultimate power from the army, and this has largely predetermined its authoritarian character."[7] The failure of the units, however, to acknowledge the existence of a military tradition and of a strong state neatly places the Communists outside Chinese civilization, and permits them to be named as the villains who have irrationally destroyed the pacific heritage indispensable to the survival of Confucian China.

Communist military control is seen as "anti-Chinese." The Red Army epitomizes their violation of the peasant and his innate pacifism. The specter of maniacal Red Army hordes is conjured up by the allegedly aggressive actions of the Chinese in Korea, the Straits of Taiwan, and India; and it is evoked as a potential threat to Vietnam and against the United States. The factors of foreign provocation and the largely defensive nature of China's military strategy are totally ignored. The more significant role of the Red Army as an instrument for China's modernization is absent from all discussion.

Supposedly driven by considerations of power and wealth reminiscent of Legalist intent, the Communists are depicted as having destroyed the cultural and social mainstays of Chinese civilization: the family, the social ethic of filial piety, and the peasantry. Believing that the family was its greatest competitor, the Party is said to have systematically undermined the family system so that "the needs of the state [would] have priority at all times." (Kublin, p. 208) "To increase production, the Communists tried to get women out of the home to work in the fields and factories." (Kublin, p. 209) In *China: Troubled Asian Giant,* the development of the communes is related to a methodical attack on the family: first private wealth was confiscated, then the father was deprived of his patrimony, and finally women were divested of their children. With the family gone, "the individual stands defenseless in front of the all-powerful state." Since the traditional family is presented as the social unit responsible for maintaining the "civilization of China," its abolition is tantamount to the extinction of China. Nonetheless one high school unit, clinging to belief in the indestructibility of traditional China, proposes that the attempt to give women equal rights might well "result in weakening the fabric of Chinese society, thus creating new difficulties for the [Communist] regime." (Armstrong, pp. 15, 16) For the liberation of women—and of youth—can only be an opportunistic political ploy.

The peasants reportedly have been stripped of their culture in order to work them raw for the benefit of the state. Their *raison d'être* has been violated. The "patient" (*Troubled Asian Giant,* pp. 14, 11), industrious peasant was known for his "talent to enjoy the fruits of [his] labor. Work for a Chinese is the means toward a good life, not a

compulsive end in itself [as it is in Communist China]."
(Armstrong, p. 18)

> In 1959 millions of Chinese were herded into communes to
> try to wring more food from the soil at less expense. They
> were supposed to eat, work, die, and be buried in their own
> "anthill," pooling their strength to feed the nation. (*Troubled
> Asian Giant*, p. 11)

We are told with alarm that "dams are built by hand. . . .
In one dam project, 100 million laborers were put on the
job." (Swisher, pp. 86, 89) Mass mobilization of labor is
portrayed as a tragic break in the peasants' life-style. The
implication is that once Communism is overthrown, the
"human ants" will become human beings once again. The
reality however is that the Chinese peasant for the first
time in over a hundred years is protected from the murderous floods, plagues, and droughts that prevented his
enjoyment of the fruits of his labors.

Instead of describing the realities of peasant and family
life both past and present, the units paint a picture of the
Communists' wanton destruction of hallowed institutions.
No reference is made to the bankruptcy of the family system
acknowledged by critics of *all* political persuasions since the
May Fourth movement of 1919. There is not the slightest
intimation that the tensions and inequities of the repressive
Chinese social system based on subordination of inferiors to
superiors (filial piety)—generational, intellectual, political,
sexual, etc.—were as conducive to revolution in twentieth-
century China as they had been to social control in previous
centuries.

From this travesty of the history of traditional China follows the inescapable conclusion that Chinese Communism is
alien. It is alien because it violates Chinese tradition and because it originated from and was sustained by the Soviet
Union.* Its essence is reliance on violent and disruptive

---

* Flying in the face of all evidence, Swisher states that the Red Army
which seized China in 1949 was "led by Russian officers who had just returned from the European front." (p. 54)

social change—just as the essence of Chineseness is the promotion of peaceful evolution. We have returned to our starting point. Rejection of modernization as the United States defines that process makes the Chinese Communists non-Chinese.

In edifying contrast however, American support of the Nationalists on Taiwan

> preserves the rich Chinese civilization which is being destroyed by the Chinese Communists. . . . Taiwan is the only "real" China left in the world. (Swisher, p. 100)

Taiwan is presented as a paragon of gradual change. Even its land reform was non-violent. That the elimination of political rivals, not the alteration of social values or economic relationships, was the decisive impetus for and feature of this reform is of course not mentioned by the units. The Nationalists, though utterly beholden to a foreign power, the United States, emerge as the staunch and faithful guardians of Chinese tradition. By their adherence to Western-style modernization and their commitment to gradual political and economic reform, they *ipso facto* perpetuate Chinese culture.

If Chinese culture naturally gravitates toward Western-style modernization and the violation of this process is foreign-inspired, as in the high school units, then, the transition from traditional to Communist China was a struggle between the forces of progress (the West and democracy) and of destruction (Soviet and Chinese Communism). Certain aspects of Sino-American relations, most notably, missionary activity and diplomatic policy, are trotted out to substantiate this view. Virtually dismissing nineteenth-century European missionary activity in China, the units see the United States as having assumed the burden of Christianizing China. Initial successes marked by the conversions of Sun Yat-sen, Madame Chiang K'ai-shek, the warlord Feng Yu-hsiang, and other political and international figures, strengthened the conviction that America had a special relation to China, and that without unnatural interference China would become a

Westernized state. Only the intrusion of a foreign element could interrupt the preordained outcome of this evolution. As a result, the modernization of China acquired an essentially eschatological importance. The ordeal became international, between the democratic Western-oriented Nationalists and the totalitarian Soviet-oriented Communists. The struggle thus has very little to do with China herself or with the relations between the Nationalists and the United States. Accordingly, the units supply minimal information on developments within China. Most of them move directly from Confucian to Communist China, bringing into sharper relief the contrast between the two. A serious study of the transition period might raise many questions about the nature of change in China, the effects of European and American imperialism, and the deceitful character of the Chiang–United States alliance.

In her widely used and highly regarded work, *East Asian Culture,* Ethel E. Ewing introduces the protagonists. In Hawaii, Sun Yat-sen

> got the chance to learn democratic ideas and Christian beliefs that are a part of Western democratic society. He became a Christian and resolved to work to better the condition of the Chinese. (p. 69) The story of the Chinese Communist Revolution really began outside of China—in the Soviet Union . . . Unlike the czars, the Soviet Communists had no intention of invading China. Instead, their plan was to teach Communist ideas to Chinese leaders. (p. 80)

Yet how is Christianity less of a foreign force than Communism? To re-paraphrase Ewing, did not the story of Chinese Christianity really begin outside China? The Christians did not plan to invade China either, just convert it. Why are the Christian Chinese regarded less as outsiders than the Communist Chinese? A rationale is never given in the units. History is excised not only from this bid for Sun Yat-sen. Any careful examination of the deleterious effects of the foreign missionaries on Chinese society and polity; of indigenous reforms in China since the nineteenth century;

of the rise of Chinese nationalism; of th[...]
and rural problems; and of the most signifi[...]
social movement in modern China, the May [...]
ment, would clearly indicate that the internal [...]
China were not simply concocted and manipula[...]
malevolent foreign force. The units' ahistorical app[...]
amounts to nothing less than insisting on dependency on [...]
West as the only correct course—a dependency facilitated by
the proclivity of the ideal Chinese culture to modernization,
and by the benevolence of America as its sponsor.

All the units stress the positive impact of the West on
China, and, specifically, American beneficence toward China.
Since China has profited from this contact, she should be
duly grateful. United States foreign policy, in particular, is
noted for its solicitous motivation:

> It was the United States, however that took the lead in seek-
> ing to check the threatened break-up of the Chinese Empire.
> In 1899 the American Secretary of State, John Hay, issued the
> first of his "Open Door" notes. It called on the great powers to
> support the principle of equal trading opportunity in China.
> Hay also asked the powers to stop seeking special privileges
> at the expense of China and other nations. (Kublin, p. 132)

The Open Door Policy is credited with preserving China's
sovereignty and independence. (Stavrianos, pp. 33–34;
Chang, p. 11; Kublin, p. 133)

Even the outcome of America's direct intervention in the
Boxer Rebellion (1900) was felicitous for China.

> To atone for the Boxer Uprising an indemnity of 333
> million dollars was levied on China. A few years later the
> United States turned back a large part of its share of the in-
> demnity to China. The money was used to pay for the educa-
> tion of Chinese students in America. This friendly act by the
> United States won considerable gratitude from the Chinese.
> (Bell, p. 54)

This special pleading not only ignores the rapacity of the
looting of Peking, but perpetuates the notion of America's

...osity toward China, and

...to these policies fosters
...tates as the defender of
...ica's partner in a special
...ation will accrue. History
...e United States acquired
...ern Pacific and the Philip-
...tablished at Pearl Harbor,
...ire Philippine archipelago
was colonized. Its door was closed firmly to other nations,
and its economy was subordinated to America's. The Open
Door Policy was designed to thwart the division of China by
European powers into spheres of influence and to protect the
freedom of American trade in China. It was not intended to
safeguard Chinese interests but to reinvigorate the treaty-
port system in order to counter European colonialism in
China. It is the *locus classicus* of American anti-colonial
imperialism.[8]

China is regarded in the high school units as being unique
among the nations of the world precisely because the United
States has paid special attention to her: "Few nations have
interested us for so long or touched our sympathies so deeply,
but our interest has been primarily sentimental and humanitarian rather than political or historical." (Armstrong, p. 3)
Through the American education of her westernized elites,
China received the values of Christianity and democracy
and was primed for modernization. This picture reinforces
the axiom that any Chinese unfriendly to America must
be under foreign influence; and it expresses a fundamental
proposition of American foreign policy: what is best for us
is best for them. Based as it is on fantasy, this notion en-
genders a sense of betrayal when American largesse is
spurned—as it was after the Communist victory in 1949.
It leads to the hope that when external forces are removed,
the Chinese will revert to their thankful apprenticeship
with the United States.

By avoiding the central phenomenon of imperialism, the units obviate consideration of nationalism, the major contemporary political force in Asia. This ignores the fact that solidly uniting all Chinese—Communists and Nationalists—are nationalistic feelings of anti-imperialism. Today, China's militant anti-imperialism is shared by many Asians who have been forced to endure the humiliations of direct colonial rule. Louis Fischer speaks to the point:

> I was astounded when I first went to India in 1942, how often the Russo-Japanese War of 1904–1905 came up in the conversation. It was the first time a coloured people defeated a white country, and Indians said it had stimulated their nationalism. On subsequent trips to the Orient I noted deliberate efforts to weld the consciousness of colour with the protest against poverty and the dislike of Western imperialism into an Asian mood, a sense of Asianhood.[9]

To solidify the image of Communism as an alien and international force, the high school units divorce it from its nationalistic inspiration and its vigorous defense of nationalistic goals. The Communists are depicted as cynically manipulating the peasants and posing as liberators (Stavrianos, p. 43), a maneuver eminently feasible for any well-organized group which employs "force." (Ewing, p. 82) The interaction between the people and the Party is ignored; the only possible conclusion is that the Chinese Communists came to power through the use of mendacious anti-Western propaganda, manipulative skills, insidious organizational techniques, and Soviet intrigue. The peasants and workers were mere fools and tools. The Chinese Communist Party's close relation to the Soviet Union is advanced as a given factor. But Stalin's repeated betrayal of the Communists in favor of the Nationalists, and Mao's development of his power base during World War II independent of Soviet aid are simply omitted. The Sino-Soviet Treaty of August 14, 1945, which supplied Russian military and economic aid to the Nationalists is belittled as having been "broken almost as soon as it was made." (Bell, p. 72) In reality the alliance between

China and the Soviet Union after 1949 was *not* a foregone conclusion—except in the context of overt American hostility to the new Chinese government.[10]

By the same token, the units omit nationalism from their account of the Nationalists. Their xenophobia, Chiang Kai-shek's anti-American and anti-Western policies, and his success in playing off the United States against Russia receive no mention. To admit the existence of nationalism not only would mar the picture of China's traditional culture as one striving toward a universal norm of modernization, but would also deprive the contest of its international character. Following from this omission of nationalism, the units depict the Chinese Civil War as part of a world-wide struggle between modernizing: Chiang; and communizing: Mao. They cannot concede that it may have been a battle between a culturally conservative nationalistic movement and a socially revolutionary nationalistic movement.

The refusal to deal with this history focuses the question of the Civil War in China on one man, Chiang Kai-shek: being a democratic Christian, he is China. What was good for him is likewise good for China. Conversely, to criticize him is to criticize China and to provide aid and comfort to Communism. Hyman Kublin's volume of readings reflects this commitment. In it, documents representing "The New China" from 1911 to 1949 are drawn unapologetically from Nationalist writers and sympathizers. (pp. 148–170. Stavrianos' second volume of readings provides a more balanced selection.) The inclusion of a section of Communist documents, however, is preceded by this publisher's disclaimer:

> The last section treats the Communist system imposed on China since 1949, using Communist sources and documents, and especially the writings of Mao Tse-tung. Inclusion of such material in no way implies approval of Communist ideology.[11]

Twentieth-century Chinese history thus is reduced to the problem of Communism versus anti-Communism. The focus is on which group was pro-American, not who could best solve China's problems.

The defeat of Chiang Kai-shek marked the ascendance of the Enemy. To call it by its own name, however, is to concede its legitimacy. One unit begins by putting parentheses around the "official name," thereby graphically isolating it: "Communist China (or, to use its official name, the People's Republic of China) is an immense nation by any standard." (Bell, p. 5) The "official name" is rarely used, however; the ideological exorcism, Communist or Red China, is preferred. The demonic specter of a perverted country is evoked by the units in order to justify America's stance toward China.

> It is tragic that the triumph of communism in China should have caused that great nation and the United States to become enemies. We have had a long history of friendly relations. The American people sympathize with the Chinese people's desire for a better life, and in other circumstances would gladly have helped them attain it. America is aiding other undeveloped Asian nations, such as India. But the men in power in Peking have set China on a course of opposition to the United States. Committed by their rulers to bear the double burdens of modernizing their country and building up its armaments, the Chinese people can only look forward to many years of unremitting toil and struggle. (Bell's conclusion, p. 156)

The Teaching Guide in *The Two Chinas* spells out the foreign policy implications of this tragedy:

> The Free World finds itself today faced with a Communist China that is fiercely antagonistic to it, and that has committed its vast resources to the global victory of communism by any means, becoming a nuclear power, this threat has urgent significance. (p. 2-T)

What are the characteristics of the Enemy? It is antipathetic to China's ideal culture and to Western-style modernization. China is portrayed as a country dominated by the military and by the state: all pacifism has been extinguished; the population is militaristically dragooned; and the state is authoritarian, unresponsive, the private domain of a few power-hungry men.

Control by the military is adduced by the units both externally and internally. Externally, the Chinese Communists are aggressive. "[In conclusion] there is Communist expansion in Asia—the attempt to extend Chinese power by championing Communist revolutions in other parts of Asia." (Ewing, p. 85) On her "time line of Chinese history" Ewing (p. 9) notes that since 1950, "Communist China advances against Tibet, Southeast Asia and India." We are told categorically that:

> Since 1949, the People's Liberation Army has seen action in Korea, in successive bombardments and assaults on the Offshore Islands and Taiwan, in North Vietnam, Laos, Tibet, and northern India. Although the size of the army was reduced in 1959, China is still the most militant country in the world. (Swisher, p. 90)

Internally, the regime relies solely on military power. The proof of this resides in the famous dictum: " 'Political power comes (*sic*) out of the barrel of a gun' " (Swisher, p. 90), a statement by Mao Tse-tung which appeared in 1938 in an article on the history of war in modern China. The article was a critique of the early Communist Party's exclusive reliance on political organizing which had resulted in mass slaughter of unarmed workers, peasants, and Party cadres at the hands of Chiang Kai-shek's army in 1927. Mao presented the indisputable point that during the period of warlord rule the creation of military power had been imperative in order to protect oneself and to gain power.[12]

Chiang Kai-shek's long-standing political reliance on his army is nowhere mentioned in these units. That the Nationalist Government presently maintains an army of 550,000 soldiers which imposes military rule on Taiwan and supports raids on China is omitted. For Chiang is China, reclaiming what is rightfully his.

China's growing population is seen as a major ingredient in her aggressive posture; it, along with the "area and the ambitions of its rulers are all gigantic. And China today is perhaps the biggest question mark in the future of the entire world." (Bell, p. 5) The need and desire of this population for expansion are pernicious:

> Why is the population of China worth all the West's curiosity? The answer is that population can become a powerful political weapon. The rate of population increase is especially significant. A high rate is often interpreted to mean that a country is enjoying robust economic and physical health. And for a developing nation, the illusion—if not the fact—of general prosperity is an important force in the arena of world opinion. (*Troubled Asian Giant,* p. 14)

As Dean Rusk observed in 1968, China is a potential adversary consisting of one billion people armed with nuclear weapons. It is the prototype of those hostile envious hordes of the Third World. As President Johnson remarked:

> There are three billion people in the world and we have only 200 million of them. We are outnumbered fifteen to one. If might did make right they would sweep over the United States and take what we have. We have what they want.[13]

Nowhere is the contemporary Chinese government given just credit for feeding and providing social and educational services for its people, or with eliminating the social evils endemic to their lives throughout the past century: opium traffic, prostitution, gambling, famine, plague, floods, etc. Even without massive foreign aid the Chinese government has been among the most successful in the Third World to deal effectively with the staggering problems of growth. From this perspective China is less of a threat than India—both to world peace and domestic tranquility.

The Chinese state, according to the units, is authoritarian, unrepresentative, monolithic: ". . . the power of the CCP is nearly absolute and is concentrated in the hands of a few men at the top." (*The China Giant,* p. 63) No acknowledgment—much less explanation—of the legitimacy of the Chinese government is given. The units conform to the conventional monochromatic treatment of enemy societies in their emphasis on a power elite.

If it does not represent the population, the state must control by sheer coercion (Chang) and it must warp human nature. Laborers become "ants"; students are forced into a "redness" that denies expertise and practical education. The need to balance the educational demands of expertise with the civic demands of political responsibility is not conceded. That the Chinese government might be trying to strike a new balance between zeal and professionalism is equally inadmissible.

The outcome of this rule by force places the state and the people irrevocably at loggerheads and makes the prospects for the United States—hopeful and open-ended. "Real" Chinese supposedly want what we want: material goods and democracy.

> Can you imagine a huge, modern, rapidly industrializing country like China in which there is not one privately owned automobile? No high school or college student owns a car. (Swisher, p. 87)

Nonetheless, the attraction of these goodies on the one hand, and the fortitude of the Chinese on the other hand, are so strong that even under their alien yoke they will "begin to demand the luxuries of individual liberty and popular government." (Armstrong, p. 23) The prospect of democratic forces arising within China predisposes the reader to accept, and support the legitimacy of, future American intervention in and around China. In the same way, Ithiel de Sola Pool prepares us all:

> In the nuclear age the world has become a small place. In various ways we will all become more alike, and more like America as we know it today. People everywhere want some aspects of American culture, such as automobiles, TV sets, refrigerators, and Coca-Cola.

When we come to realize that we can live in safety only in a world in which political systems of all states are democratic and pacifically oriented, the immediate lessons of Vietnam . . . recede into a dimly remembered image.

I predict that there will be a number of effective interventions in foreign crises in America's future.[14]

III · *THE LOSS OF CHINESE CULTURE AND SCHOLARLY STUDIES*

THE "LOSS" of China, the destruction of Chinese culture and the creation of a Communist nation, are the crux of high school units' approach to China. This is so not merely because of the political importance of this question in the 1950's and 1960's in the United States. Of equal importance is the orientation of the prevailing scholarship. Beginning in the 1950's, American academics rededicated themselves to an exploration and explanation of Chinese culture and civilization.* Chinese thought must be comprehended correctly this time (1953):

> A specious affinity broadcast and insisted upon can lead to more ramifying misunderstanding than a host of simple misstatements of fact. We should, at this stage of our studies and in this moment of world history, study the distinctive phenomena of Chinese thought in and for themselves. Once detached and disinterested inquiries guide us to an under-

* *Rededication* to the study of Chinese culture is indeed a key feature of recent scholarship on China. For, prior to the early fifties, the field had been marked by cultural studies of other origins and vintages, most prominently, the sinological tradition of cultural scavenging and the historical tradition of cultural and institutional continuity. The shift thus is not a volte-face, but one of emphasis and sophistication, in which tradition must be regarded as containing legacies both good: local cultural elites (Confucian and ?); and bad: state power (Legalist and Communist). In fact, for both critics and defenders of the scholarly status quo, decisive reference to the effects of the McCarthy era on Chinese Studies, specifically to the consequences of the McCarran Hearings on the Institute of Pacific Studies, is patently and only recourse to red herrings and strawmen. The tendency toward distilling all civilizations (American and European included) into cultural essences began in American scholarship early in the twentieth century.

standing of the precise ways in which Chinese thought and behavior are different from our own, we shall have gained two
indispensable requisites of intercultural understanding: a
knowledge of the roots and nature of difference, which is the
basis of tolerance, and a knowledge of the whole range and
context of Chinese thought, which must form the basis for any
search for affinities.[15]

The loss of China stands as the cardinal warning of the inadmissible consequences of the destruction of a cultural
tradition. The study of China's cultural tradition has become an act of political conservatism: dedicated to reclaiming that tradition—for ourselves and for the Chinese—it
reconstructs not a system of living ideas related to a social
structure, but fashions an instrument for the analysis of
future political change to be employed for American ends.

In 1951 the Committee on Chinese Thought of the professional Association of Asian Studies inaugurated a series
of five volumes on the role of ideas in Chinese society and
history, in order to comprehend Chinese culture and its
role in politics.[16] Apprehension of an impending world-wide
cultural conflict furnished the more sophisticated motivation for this scholarly undertaking. Intercultural encounters,
in which non-Western cultures adapt to Western values,
have engendered intellectual and political problems to
which scholars must address themselves:

> how to reconcile the competing claims of tradition and prog-
> ress; the impact of programs of technical assistance and in-
> dustrialization on preindustrial ways of life; the question as
> to the minimum of common value sufficient to make possible
> a peaceful and mutually comprehensible inter-cultural rela-
> tionship within a world community of different languages,
> religions, races, and ideologies.[17]

These volumes remain today the sole systematic undertaking within the field of Chinese Studies. Nothing of comparable scope and sophistication exists for the study of
traditional social, political or economic institutions, or for
modern Chinese history. The lop-sided distribution of the

academic work, its areas of concentration and omission, are imparted to the high school units on China. The units' concern with culture is confirmed by the scholarly world.[18]

The objective of the series on Chinese Thought is set forth by Arthur Wright:

> I suppose that the ultimate goal of all studies of Chinese thought is a characterization of Chinese thought in terms which would accurately describe and interrelate every mental production of the Chinese both past and present.[19]

A more refined definition of intellectual history is formulated by Benjamin Schwartz: "the total conscious responses of men to their situation," which include their attitudes and feelings.[20] In their attention to the operation and total comprehensibility of ideas in history, these propositions advance a construct of culture in which sheer knowledge of all thoughts, acts, and decisions renders them susceptible to control. The lesson implicit in this view is that culture is the decisive lever through which to reconstruct and manipulate society and political change.

The concept and role of culture were developed in the early years of this century. Merle Curti recounts its discovery:

> The culture, or totality of institutions, adjustments, and values binding a distinctive social group together, was recognized as molding personality and explaining variants in social behavior in the many cultures of the world. Human nature was thus seen to develop only in relation to a particular culture, and to be susceptible to change as the culture changes. The relativistic and pragmatic aspects of the culture concept which resembled rising theories in the physical sciences, promised, if fully and widely appreciated, to emancipate man from many age-old superstitions and prejudices and to provide a realistic basis for improved social relations.[21]

Study of the culture of Chinese society has focused on two phenomena: (1) the ideas within that society, intellectual history, and (2) the architects, guardians and perpetrators of ideas, the Confucian elites.

The elite cultural phenomenon of Confucianism is the subject of the volumes on Chinese thought. Collectively they arrive at a description of Confucianism in which its exponents tame the State and its power by their very reluctance to become morally or ideologically involved in politics. The elite possessed a monopoly on literacy, statecraft, and administrative skills which they brought to the legitimation and operation of the state and its power. The official was

> a scholar-gentleman, with his roots in society, sensitive to the varied complexities of individual social and family situations and adapting the law and his own behavior to suit them, accommodating himself to state power . . . but checking it simply by being what he was.

Despite "the similarity between the points of view of the bureaucrat and the throne [which] went very deep," the official stood "as a mark of the strength of the literati interest and viewpoint, able . . . to qualify the usual tendencies of a power structure."[22]

The potency of the restraining influence exerted by the scholar-official upon the state was not vouchsafed however:

> Disdained by ruthless monarchs, thwarted by palace intrigue, circumvented by eunuch power, undone by venality in their own ranks, China's bureaucrats nevertheless persisted in their efforts to infuse the politics of the realm with the principles of Confucian morality.[23]

The consequent political frustrations which beset China's scholar-officials are interpreted by American academics as having been a warning to disengage from politics *per se,* to eschew political reform of the system. The resultant degradation of Confucian politicians and delineation of spheres appropriate for elite activity are accomplished by the condemnation of Confucian institutional reformers, the Neo-Confucians of the eleventh century, and by the celebration of Confucian cultural and social activities.

Reform is castigated as folly by the volumes since it contributed to the development of state power. "Neo-Confucian idealism was in some special way ideologically conducive to despotism."[24] It had a propensity for wielding power: "the vision condemned above all else division in society . . . the emergence of separate local centers of power was never what the literati wanted." Consequently they "instinctively sided with the state" rather than with their clans, for example, and were at once "individually dependent on the throne: and collectively indispensable to it, . . . even as individuals they regularly held great power."[25]

> The Neo-Confucian visionaries wanted a utopian totalitarianism minus the trappings and sinews, the harsh reality, of power. What they got was not what they wanted. But it was what we might have expected.[26]

The inevitability of this outcome is sagaciously perceived by American China analysts because they have identified the two-fold flaw of the reformers' purpose: (1) the advocacy of moralistic idealism, and (2) its political implementation and intent to change the nature of China's institutions. Though the reformers undoubtedly were well-intentioned, their action could result only in a form of totalitarianism; for idealistic reform of society is the surest path to political totalitarianism.

The prudent Confucian sought to influence the on-going political structure. He subscribed to a persuasion,[27] a vision of perfected men living in a stable and harmonious socio-political order. A set of true and invariable norms for the conduct of life would find their perfect embodiment in the well-ordered patriarchal family, the microcosm of state and society. The values of *this* vision were "harmony, stability, and hierarchy"; they were advanced by exemplary moral suasion; and they promoted

> desirable change [which] draws society peacefully back toward the ancient moral order. Undesirable change is violent, precipitated by uncultivated men; it is a sequence of random improvisations which will lead society away from the moral order and into chaos and ruin.[28]

Confucianism managed to thrive and to endure through the extension of its temporizing influence.

The Confucian and American scholar-officials civilize the power structure with their ideas rather than reform it by their actions. Zealous social reformers are condemned, and educated political mentors are extolled. The crux of this formulation lies of course in belief in the political efficacy of the influence of ideas unaccompanied by formal political power. Its adherents pretend that it was the persuasion that affected political (and social) morality; they ignore the likelihood that the promotion of morality was but the justifying metaphor for an exploitative class and its compromised relation to state power.

Even though Confucianism is conceded to have been the point of view of a class,[29] the implications of this statement receive no treatment whatsoever in these volumes. This is not simply an intellectual oversight; it is a conceptual requirement. Since the interests of the elite and the state are assumed to be complementary, the prestige and position of the elite were obtained through its association with the state. To admit the dimension of class into this definition of the Chinese elite is to question the ascribed basis of its power and influence. This is not simply an exercise in drawing neat distinctions between the disciplines of intellectual and socio-economic history; rather, it excludes the latter altogether in order to sustain the prescription of a civilizing role for the Confucian elite vis-à-vis state power. The consequent abnegation of social, economic, and political history is felicitously amplified by the high school units.

The relationship of the Confucian elite to state power is a successful *modus operandi* only if exercised through the existing official channels and social institutions. On the one hand, "only those in public office can do anything substantial to order human society."[30] This formulation neatly proscribes any constructive extra-official political activity. In the process it eliminates responsible opposition or resistance outside the existing political structure. On the other hand, through the family and through education the elite could set the moral tenor of social and cultural life. The choice between the two spheres is construed as follows:

> Every Confucian of every generation had to choose between self-cultivation and the pursuit of power. Yet in theory the two were reconcilable: the inner cultivation of the self was seen not as an end in itself, but as a means toward ultimate self-fulfillment in the world of action.[31]

This option has been posed not by and for the Confucian literati but by and for American scholar-politicians. For it rests upon the notion that morality and politics operate in totally different spheres of life. And if they are not discrete, they ought to be, since the insinuation of the former into the latter wreaks totalitarian havoc. This was the mistake of the Neo-Confucian reformers; and this is one reason for the damnation of the Chinese Communists. Further, this perspective endorses a common role for cultural elites in China and in America—that of being a class of men whose education finds its most natural application in service to the supposedly suprapartisan state and society, and whose major activity is most effectively and persistently cultural, i.e., not political or ideological.

The primacy of culture in China studies reflects the shift from ideological to cultural concerns among American scholar-politicians.* The pronouncement in the mid- to late fifties heralding the end of ideology set the stage for a new attack against Communism, especially the Asian variety. Internal political distinctions among Free World nations became irrelevant. As long as a government opposed Communism, it was incumbent upon the United States to unite with it and support it against Communism. Anti-Communism became the criterion for cultural acceptability. It was

---

* The relationship between ideology and culture is universally one of political dynamite and intellectual tinder. Our view on this configuration is that in America, the shift from ideological to cultural concerns signaled the subsuming of ideology to culture, and yielded the phenomenon of cultural-ism (see section IV), which relegates political ideology to a position of cultural subservience within a national and global civilization.

defined by the country's participation in the American system of empire—a participation facilitated by and premised upon the preservation of the traditional culture of the country and hence the inevitable evolution toward democracy. Communism repudiated modernization—a repudiation assured by the destruction of culture and the reliance on totalitarianism. Anti-Communism was *ipso facto* pro-modernization, and modernization *ipso facto* retained culture—in fact required its maintenance. American support of politically reactionary regimes throughout Asia demonstrates this cultural conservatism. Rhee's Korea, Chiang's Taiwan and Diem's Vietnam all salvaged their indigenous culture and thus merit American support. The hope is to awaken the tendency to modernization within each culture by providing an economic base for a middle class (as in AID doctrine and W. W. Rostow's thesis), whereupon *shazam*—democracy will miraculously appear.

Focus on cultural concerns has strengthened the political influence of the American educated elites.[32] "The elitism which once glorified intellectuals as a revolutionary avant-garde now glorifies them as experts and social technicians."[33] The intellectual as expert identifies with the values and role which he has ascribed to other elites, such as the Confucian scholar-official. He is attuned to working through existing channels of the government as a political-cultural adviser, to exercise his influence upon, rather than to initiate reform of, the system. His status has been conferred through an elaborate maze of examinations culminating in a trip to the capitol, Washington, D.C. He is revered as the transmitter of an open culture—in which liberalism and conservatism harmonize to foster a democratic pluralism.

Professors Fairbank and Reischauer in the most widely respected college textbook on East Asia, describe the elite's

> public functions in the local community. . . . They were the bearers of Confucian doctrine. As learned men and often also men of wealth and political influence, they assumed responsibility for many activities which today are performed by

officials . . . they set up and supported local private schools and academies.

A list of these activities is then enumerated. The professors seek out Western counterparts:

> A partial comparison might be made in this respect with other classes that have functioned in very different societies, such as the equestrian order of ancient Rome, the modern American business class, or other non-official groups that have provided local community leadership.[34]

For the Communists, however, political commitment supersedes expertise; they have raised the position of the activist peasant or politically-oriented cadre above that of the scholar. The attack on the worst elements of elitism and bureaucratic rule, the refusal to subjugate men to machines, and the maintenance of political commitment and participation are granted no validity by the units—even in the authentic context of genuine Chinese problems. In spite of these most disconcerting tendencies, the United States can find reassurance in faith that the Chinese will return to normalcy.

> [T]he world must wait for the next generation before China is likely to have a more coherent and, hopefully less mystifying and threatening, foreign policy. In the meantime the world must also keep in mind that despite the strange behavior of its current leaders, China is a potentially great entity which must in time be integrated into the international system.[35]

If one seeks analogies, the current Chinese emphasis on moral concepts and de-emphasis of technical progress mirrors an on-going battle in Western tradition on the nature of human progress. The very existence of this debate, as waged classically by Rousseau and Turgot,[36] is disavowed by our scholar-authors. For them the conclusion is foregone: Technology lights the way, releasing us from fear and from moral concerns:

. . . How long can China and the USA, set as they are behind their respective defenses of Mao-inspired manpower and electronic super-weapons, continue to grow in population and in power and yet coexist in peace?

One answer to calm our fears is that modern technology, as it spreads, will give us common circumstances and a common view.[37]

IV · CULTURALISM

THE FACILITY with which cultural equivalents are construed coincides with an assumption of America's universal appeal. Belief that the basic problems of American society seem to have been resolved entitles this country to play a global role. The United States is a melting pot in which old and new coexist: old-fashioned ideas are gradually discredited as they prove to be outmoded; changes are made piecemeal and within tradition; and tradition forms a barrier against radical and ill-conceived ideas. Since the resolution of problems has been democratic and lawful, pragmatic and rational, this same gradualist and pluralist approach to change and to modernization is assumed by the units to be viable for all societies—regardless of the nature of their problems or of their histories. Hence America's role as model and guide for the world. Faith in "our own" historical law of change fixes the United States on the goal of modernizing the world without revolution. The Teacher's Guide for *China: Development by Force* makes the point:

> Both Nationalist China [on Taiwan] and Communist China were faced with similar problems of increasing agricultural and industrial productivity and attracting money capital. Nationalist China, however, has avoided the 'forced-savings' methods of Communist China and has used more economic planning and inducement in an effort to correct mistakes it made on the mainland. (p. 7)

The units share and promote the popular notion that rejection of the American view of the world is a threat not only to American national security but also to the American way of life. The American creed pertains not just to a political system but to a civilization. As a result, politics has become identified with culture. America does not seek annexation of territory. She is more ambitious; she wants to win "the hearts and minds of the people." She Americanizes them in order to guarantee the continuing viability of her solutions for herself and for the world. China's image of a new man (socialist man, the rejection of bourgeois man), not her economic or military capabilities, poses the ultimate threat to America's values and *raison d'être*.

Thus, two trends in current scholarship may be discerned: (1) the precedence of cultural values over political ideology and (2) the belief that tampering with a given socio-cultural system will lead to an economic and political environment conducive to the dominance of middle-class American values. This in turn will lead to a new imperialism which could be called global cultural-imperialism. Ironically, the phenomenon of culturalism has been applied by Fairbank and Reischauer to describe the cultural ethnocentricism of the Chinese.[38] Whereas primitive communication and transportation partially shielded China's neighbors from the foreign policy implications of her culturalism, modern technology now makes the world vulnerable to America's ambition. American culturalism denotes the intent to rule the world by the imposition of her values, safeguarding them when necessary by military occupation and colonialization.

The historical growth of this idea can be sketched briefly; it descends from Adam Smith through James Madison, to Walt Whitman Rostow, and the pluralists. Adam Smith argued that the only mechanism for sustaining the division of labor was a constantly growing market. A market system by definition precludes the necessity for a strong central government and allows the individual freedom of opportunity to enrich and develop his own resources. The free enterprise system establishes the prerequisites for a free political system. Adam Smith cast the same seamless imperative for political systems that he cast for the market system: freedom was indivisible—everyone had it, or no one was free.

In Federalist Paper No. 10 James Madison provided the theoretical justification for expanding the territory of a democracy. Implicitly refuting the implications of Rousseau's strictures on (American) democracy (that a pure democracy could function only within a small geographic area with a homogeneous constituency), Madison argued that the larger the territory, the more heterogeneous the interest groups, the freer the society. In sum, the greater the expanse of territory, the higher the potential for a democratic republic.[39] The shift from a democracy to a republic altered the focus from an exclusive particularistic concern (e.g., a town meeting) to an inclusive universalistic concern (e.g., a nation and a global empire).

The acceptance of Manifest Destiny dovetailed the universalistic claims of the economic system with the inclusive demands of a republic. The only way for Americans to enjoy freedom was to carry it around the world. While its instrument was economic expansion, its condition was the alteration of the internal structures of other countries in order to bring them into the domain of trade and freedom. A causal link existed between America's external economic expansion and the internal political reform of other nations. The "Open Door Policy" embodied the dual objective of opening China for trade and of training her leaders in American values, in order to guide China's development and to keep America free.

W. W. Rostow's thesis perpetuates this lunge toward globalism. He attempts to combine economic growth and political development. According to his economic taxonomy, an underdeveloped country must first create a stable (read non-Communist) government. This will then lead it to develop an economic base through the intelligent application of foreign aid and domestic investment. As the economy develops, a middle class will emerge which automatically shares the political values of the Western middle class. The authoritarian, underdeveloped state will gradually become a democratic, developed nation, and the benefits of a sound economy will make up for any political dissatisfaction.

The high school units articulate Rostow's view in discussing Taiwan under Chiang Kai-shek.

> . . . Nationalist economic planning was not patterned along the Communists' use of force. Instead, the plans were designed to induce people to do what was in their own best interest, as well as the country's. . . . Assistance has been accepted only when it has been profitable to the business, and not when the government decided it should be accepted. In short, the Nationalist government's intention has been to stimulate and guide, but not to direct and control everything as in Communist China.
>
> In summary, the economic development programs of the Nationalist government have been moderate ones. It does not intend to change the basic institutions of China . . . (Chang, pp. 64–65)

An economic miracle has occurred; private enterprise is flourishing; stability and orderliness are assured. The economy is based on "inducing people [without force] to do what is in their own best interest as well as the country's" (Chang, pp. 65, 64); it has reached "that enviable position known as 'take off.'" (Armstrong, p. 50) The units predict a transformation to a more democratic rule under the Nationalist's aegis. According to this scenario, even the Taiwanese may soon participate equally in the politics of their island. The conclusion is that the Nationalists have preserved China and are allowing the traditional culture to fulfill itself. Taiwan is now a "'showcase of Free Asia.' The high standard of living, human dignity, and national pride on Taiwan are well-known and envied by Chinese under communist rule." (Swisher, p. 100)[40] Taiwan is represented as the thriving antithesis of a contaminated Continental China.

Contemporary pluralists argue that American cultural pre-eminence is necessary for world peace. To Adam Smith's economic theory and the Federalists' political rationale for empire, they add the requirement of cultural guidance. As long as each cultural elite appears willing to abide by American ground rules, then all elites will share common values. They will non-violently promote their interests and successfully manage and overcome conflicts.

The United States, concerned with shared cultural values, stresses its allies' similarities and its enemies' incompatibilities and alien traditions. It applies one system of analysis to friends, another to foes. Competition in the American tradition is accommodated and rewarded, and abrogation of these traditions elicits the punitive responses of exclusion and of military force. In her refusal to admit China to the United Nations, America has foisted this pluralistic concept upon an international organization. In the same vein, a current view would blame the American war in Vietnam and the Sino-American conflict on the virulence of cultural differences.[41] The mission is proclaimed: make the world safe for the hegemony of American values. Countries that reject this calling are dangerously irrational and must be isolated, contained and ultimately destroyed. Lucian Pye alerts us to the quality of the apostate:

> The air of mystery which shrouds so much of Communist China is most opaque in the realm of foreign policy. Neither the imperatives of Communist doctrine nor the pragmatic calculation of natural interest seem adequate to explain either Chinese words or actions. And, moreover, it is baffling at times to find any connection between the two.*
>
> . . . The result is a disturbing make-believe quality in Peking's foreign relations. . . .
>
> From this mood and style there follows a series of substantive generalizations about Chinese foreign policy which can be listed without qualification.
>
> First, the men in Peking have almost no sensitivity for the dynamic developments taking place in American and European societies, and they still believe in the 19th-century Marxian description of capitalism.

* From *The China Giant: Perspectives on Communist China*, by C. P. Fitzgerald, *et al.*, Copyright 1967 by Scott, Foresman and Company.

Second, Peking is likely to continue to dream about "exporting" its brand of revolution, but it is not likely to do it on a grand scale. . . .

Fourth, the Chinese have staked their prestige to a large extent in Vietnam, but again they are prisoners of a situation for which they lack effective means to influence developments.[42]

The Great Wall extends not only along the northern slopes of China, but also into the minds of men. It is reconstructed year after year by teaching the children to hate, "before it's too late, before you are six or seven or eight, to hate all the people your relatives hate."[43] It is refurbished as a network of defense and a justification for murder by educating us to fear. It is impossible for us to see human beings on the other side of the Wall; it contains us with self-perpetuating stereotypes of them and of ourselves. Lu Hsün spoke of its confinement: "I am always conscious of being surrounded by a Great Wall . . . a wall that hems us in. When shall we stop reinforcing the Great Wall with new bricks?" Now!

Notes

1. This section is based on Richard Kagan's review of nine high school units on China, "A Critical Guide to Curriculum Units on China," *Intercom*, Vol. X, No. 5 (September–October, 1968), pp. 53–66. (Copies may be obtained from the National Committee on United States-China Relations, Inc., 777 United Nations Plaza, New York, New York 10017.) The units chosen for review are widely used, easily available, and especially designed for secondary school use. Among all available units on China, they were found to be the most accurate and useful to teachers. Units not chosen were judged as too intellectually obscene to review, even for an adult audience.

The authors and titles of the units reviewed (referred to in the text in abbreviated form) are:

John P. Armstrong, *Chinese Dilemma* (River Forest, Ill., Laidlaw Brothers, 1967).

Oliver Bell, *The Two Chinas* (New York, Scholastic Book Services, 1967).

Perry P. Chang, *China: Development by Force* (Glenview, Ill., Scott, Foresman & Company for Curriculum Resources, 1964).

China: Troubled Asian Giant (Columbus, Ohio, American Education Publications, 1967).

Ethel E. Ewing, *East Asian Culture* (Chicago, Ill., Rand McNally, 1967).

Edwin Fenton (gen. ed.), *Tradition and Change in Four Societies: An Inquiry Approach* (New York, Holt, Rinehart and Winston, 1968). The chapter on China is entitled, "Totalitarian Government in China," pp. 258–342. (This work was not included in Kagan's published review.)

C. P. Fitzgerald, *et al.*, *The China Giant: Perspectives on Communist China* (Glenview, Ill., Scott, Foresman & Company, 1967).

Hyman Kublin, *China*. World Regional Studies Series (Boston, Houghton Mifflin, 1968).

Leften S. Stavrianos, *China: A Culture Area in Perspective* (Boston, Allyn & Bacon, 1968).

Earl Swisher, *Today's World in Focus: China* (Boston, Ginn & Company, 1964).

2. Gunnar Myrdal, *Asian Drama* (New York, Pantheon Books, 1967), Vol. I, p. 99.

3. The Honorable Walter H. Judd, Testimony, Hearings before the Senate Committee on Foreign Relations, 89th Congress, 2nd Session on *U.S. Policy with Respect to Mainland China,* March, 1966 (Washington, D.C., U.S. Government Printing Office, 1966), pp. 462–63.

4. Arthur F. Wright, "Introduction," in Arthur F. Wright (ed.), *Studies in Chinese Thought* (University of Chicago Press, 1953), p. 5.

5. Mencius envisioned this right as operating within an aristocratic, "feudal" society, in which the king, being *primus inter pares,* was subject to displacement when he failed to fulfill or violated the obligations of his position. The import of this dictum, which permits rebellion against the king in order to save the kingship, is conservative—it is a provision for the preservation of the status quo.

6. Ho Ping-ti, "Salient Aspects of China's Heritage," Ho Ping-ti and Tang Tsou (eds.), *China in Crisis* (University of Chicago Press, 1968), Vol: I, Book One, p. 1.

7. Ho Ping-ti, "Salient Aspects," p. 16.

8. William Appleman Williams, *The Tragedy of American Diplo-*

macy (New York, Dell, 1962), especially Chapter 1, "Imperial Anticolonialism."

9. Louis Fischer, *This is our World*, p. 140. Cited in Myrdal, *Asian Drama*, Vol. I, pp. 123–24.

10. John Gittings, "China and the Cold War," *Survey*, Special Issue, No. 58 (January, 1966), pp. 196–208.

11. The extent to which *Chinese* Communism has become the enemy is revealed by the absence of any disclaimer in Hyman Kublin's unit on Russia. Only in the China unit is the reader treated with a prophylatic essay: Adlai Stevenson's shade is called up to testify on "The democratic point of view with respect to Communist China. . . ." (Kublin, II, p. v.).

12. Mao Tse-tung, "Problems of War and Strategy," *Selected Works of Mao Tse-tung* (Peking, Foreign Language Press, 1965), Vol. II, pp. 219–232.

13. Cited in Richard Barnet, *Intervention and Revolution: The United States in the Third World* (New York, World Publishing Company, 1968), p. 25.

14. Prepared remarks by Ithiel de Sola Pool in Richard M. Pfeffer, *No More Vietnams?* (New York, Harper, 1968), pp. 207–208, 207, and 203 respectively.

15. Wright, "Introduction," *Studies in Chinese Thought*, p. 17.

16. These five volumes are: *Studies in Chinese Thought*, edited by Arthur F. Wright (University of Chicago Press, 1953); *Chinese Thought and Institutions*, edited by John K. Fairbank (The University of Chicago Press, 1957); *Confucianism in Action*, edited by David S. Nivison and Arthur F. Wright (Stanford, Cal., Stanford University Press, 1959); *The Confucian Persuasion*, edited by Arthur F. Wright (Stanford University Press, 1960); and *Confucian Personalities*, edited by Arthur F. Wright and Denis Twitchett (Stanford University Press, 1962).

17. Robert Redfield and Milton Singer, Foreword to *Studies in Chinese Thought*, p. v.

18. The support is more than intellectual. Scholars prominent in the China field have acted as consultants or readers for a number of the high school units. Howard L. Boorman, C. Martin Wilbur, George B. Cressey, John K. Fairbank, and Paul Cohen have lent their names, and, incredibly, their brains to the publication of three of the high school units analyzed above.

   Another area in which the high school units' approach to China is corroborated by the academic world is the obsession with modernization. See Jim Peck's article in this volume.

19. Wright, "Introduction," *Studies in Chinese Thought*, p. 2.

20. Benjamin Schwartz, "The Intellectual History of China: Pre-

liminary Reflections," in *Chinese Thought and Institutions,*
pp. 24–26.

21. Merle Curti, "The Setting and the Problems," in Merle Curti
(ed.), *American Scholarship in the Twentieth Century* (Cambridge, Mass., Harvard University Press, 1953), p. 5.
22. Nivison, "Introduction," *Confucianism in Action,* p. 17.
23. Wright, "Introduction," *The Confucian Persuasion,* p. 8.
24. Nivison, "Introduction," *Confucianism in Action,* p. 18.
25. *Ibid.,* p. 12.
26. *Ibid.,* p. 24.
27. A "matched set of attitudes, beliefs, projected actions: a half-formulated moral perspective involving emotional commitment."
Marvin Meyers, *The Jacksonian Persuasion* (Stanford Cal., Stanford University Press, 1957), p. 6; quoted by Arthur F. Wright,
"Introduction," *The Confucian Persuasion,* p. 3.
28. Wright, "Introduction," *The Confucian Persuasion,* p. 4.
29. Nivison, "Introduction," *Confucianism in Action,* p. 4.
30. Benjamin Schwartz, "Some Polarities in Confucian Thought,"
Confucianism in Action, p. 52.
31. Arthur F. Wright, "Introduction," *Confucianism and Chinese
Civilization* (New York, Atheneum, 1964), p. ix; this book is a
selection of materials from the trilogy *Action, Persuasion* and *Personalities.*
32. For a detailed discussion of the elitest posture of pluralism and
its consequences, see Michael Paul Rogin, *The Intellectuals and
McCarthy* (Cambridge, Mass., M.I.T. Press, 1967).
33. Christopher Lasch, "The Cultural Cold War: A Short History
of the Congress for Cultural Freedom," in Barton J. Bernstein
(ed.), *Towards a New Past* (New York, Pantheon Books, 1968),
p. 338. Our analysis of American ideology derives in part from
the views of Lasch, Rogin, and Williams.
34. Edwin O. Reischauer and John K. Fairbank, *A History of East
Asian Civilization: East Asia: The Great Tradition* (Boston,
Houghton Mifflin, 1960), p. 311. The similarities are noted also
by Etienne Balazs, but he draws opposite conclusions. He fears
that world development is converging toward a system of bureaucratic technocratic states. "This new bureaucracy copies unaware,
or rather re-creates, many of the patterns of thought and organization belonging to the old Chinese scholar-officials." The political
goal of this convergence is a totalitarian state led by an educated
elite. See *Chinese Civilization and Bureaucracy. Variations on a
Theme* (New Haven, Conn., Yale University Press, 1964), Chapters
2 & 7; the quotation is on p. 25.

The first study of the effects of bureaucracy—namely the national security manager bureaucracy—on America is Richard Barnet's *Intervention and Revolution*. The topic is discussed more briefly in Richard M. Pfeffer's *No More Vietnams?*

35. Lucian W. Pye "Foreign Policy" in Fitzgerald (ed.), *The China Giant*, p. 144.

36. Benjamin Schwartz in his article "China and the West in the 'Thought of Mao Tse-tung,'" (Ping-ti & Tsou [eds.] *China in Crisis*, Vol. I, Book One, pp. 365–79) points out that the West has contradictory legacies—one "emphasizes technico-economic progress" (e.g., Turgot, Condorcet, and Saint-Simon); the other stresses the moral need to overcome injustice, social evils, etc. (e.g., Rousseau). It is Rousseau's view that is embodied in Mao's anti-technocratic revolution.

37. John K. Fairbank, "Still Mysterious," in *The New York Review of Books*, Vol. XII, No. 11 (June 5, 1969), p. 19.

38. Reischauer & Fairbank, *East Asia: The Great Tradition*, pp. 290–294.

39. The link between pluralism and Adam Smith is in fact the recognition by the pluralists of irrationality in Smith's equilibrium. This is accommodated by letting people interact in groups. The groups become the atoms of social interaction and the combination of their energies and frictions moderate both their positive and negative efforts *à la* Madison's design.

40. For a criticism of this view of Taiwan, see Richard C. Kagan, "Taiwan—Another Greece?" *Dissent*, Vol. XVI, No. 1 (January–February, 1969), pp. 64–68.

41. For a staid articulation of this view, see John K. Fairbank, "Perspective on Vietnam," *New Republic*, Vol. 158 (January 20, 1968), pp. 15–17.

42. Lucian W. Pye, "Foreign Policy," in Fitzgerald (ed.), *The China Giant*, pp. 139–140, 144.

43. Lines from the lyrics of the song on this subject in the post-World War II Rodgers and Hammerstein musical about the Pacific War, "South Pacific."

The Roots of Rhetoric: The Professional Ideology of America's China Watchers

❧ *James Peck*

At the heart of all our difficulties in the Far East lies a preposterous and almost incomprehensible fact. The great country of China, form-ing the heart of Asia, a country which for many years we befriended above all others and in defense of whose interests, in part, we fought the Pacific war, has fallen into the hands of a group of embittered fanatics; wedded to a dated and specious ideology but one which holds great attraction for masses of people throughout Asia; finding in this ideology a rationale for the most ruthless exertion of power over other people; associating this ideological prejudice with the most violent currents of traditional nationalism and xenophobia; linking their power to the arrogance and pretension traditional to governing groups in a country which long regarded itself as the center of the world; consumed with ambition to extend to further areas of Asia the dictatorial authority they now wield over the Chinese people them-selves; sponsoring for this reason every territorial claim of earlier Chi-nese governments for which history could show even the flimsiest evidence; and now absolutely permeated with hatred towards our-selves, not only because the ideology pictures us all as villains, but also because we, more than any other people, have had the strength and the temerity to stand in their path and to obstruct the expansion of their power.

George F. Kennan[1]

❧ THIS PORTRAYAL of China by one of the most respected intellectuals ever to have emerged from the shadowy laby-rinth of the American diplomatic establishment mirrors twenty years of concentrated work by American China scholars. Not every China expert would accept all of Ken-nan's assumptions or express them in such strident form. Yet over the last two decades the China profession has evolved a style of thought, a mode of asking questions, which has largely substantiated such views in both the public and scholarly worlds. Many China watchers, probably the majority, have pleaded for "tolerance" and "patience" toward the People's Republic as she gradually learns, aided by a flexible American containment policy, to "adjust" to the "international community of nations" and the "rationalizing" qualities implicit in the "modernization" process. While protesting against certain aspects of America's foreign policy toward China, however, their thought and work has reinforced, at times deepened, the ideological justifications that support America's role in Asia and her attitudes toward China.

This essay is concerned with the professional ideology exhibited in the writings and speeches of China experts, with the dominant perspectives and key concepts, the lenses through which they see and describe China.[2] It seeks to map out and then explore one particular aspect: the utilization of a theory of modernization to counter theories of American imperialism and to justify the role of the United States in post-World War II East Asia.

Underlying the various interpretations of China's confrontation with the "West" in American studies of China has been a basic, seemingly obvious, theoretical framework. Because of a unique constellation of pre-conditions, it is argued, the nation-states in the West succeeded in unleashing an almost Faustian power, an exaltation of energy symbolized by the enormous "rationalization" of man's economic and social machinery. The world-wide expansion of Western power which this entailed reflected a deep, traumatic conflict between the West and other cultures. By the end of the nineteenth century, the dominance of the West in Asia was a symbol of more basic processes to which China had to respond: modernization and the evolving world culture.

What is so frequently described as the "revolutionary

impact of the West" on Asia, this argument continues, "might be more accurately defined as the impact of the age of machine production on Asia."[3]

> We can perhaps better understand the nature of the age in which we live if we think not so much in terms of the influence of the West on the East as in terms of the successive impacts of the machine, first on the West and then on the East.[4]

Essentially, the "challenge to traditional ways of life, though greater in degree, is not different in kind from the challenge in the West."[5] All societies must respond and adapt to the new culture of science and the international system of technology.

In the West this process of adaptation was less violently disruptive; it has been for the most part an evolutionary process. In Asia the impact of scientific thought and the machine has naturally been more abrupt and harsh, "coming as it has from the outside and striking cultures that were not already in the process of creating a place for such developments."[6] Consequently, there has been little possibility for native institutions and the machine to adjust to each other by slow evolutionary steps.

> When the full-blown factory technique is forcibly inserted into a pre-industrial society, traditional social and political institutions often cannot meet the challenge, crumbling rather than adapting themselves to the new conditions.[7]

Here, then, lies the heart of the modern dilemma: if all traditional cultures are subject to the corrosive influences of this technological civilization, they do not all have the same capacity for resistance and above all the same capacity for absorption. Not all cultures can sustain and absorb the shock of modernity. Simply to begin the modernizing effort requires that each society jettison, or decisively reinterpret, the cultural heritage which has been its *raison d'être*. Even more, the "response" demands a spiritual and cultural vindication, some adequate ideological explanation for the failure of traditional ways and for the humiliation resulting from the Western impact. Rarely, though, is this new cultural self-identity compatible with the necessary adaptation required by the modern forms of technical, scientific, economic, and political rationality.

Cultural conflict within an evolving world society—such is the basic perspective adopted in the China profession for understanding China's confrontation with the West. Thus

> we discern two major factors that have shaped recent East Asian history—the forces of modernization originally introduced in large part from the West, and the native traditions.[8]

Since the external stimuli were so similar, the responses so different, the "more significant element in such situations of challenge-and-response was the way in which the local people reacted to foreign stimuli."[9] Since, indeed, "in both China and Japan the external sources were virtually identical,"[10] attention should be focused on the particular internal qualities of the native traditions; therein rests the key to understanding why some "responded" effectively and some did not.

Implicit in this concentration on internal factors is the obvious next question: Which traditional values support or hinder this process? And the obvious method: Compare a successful society (Japan) with an unsuccessful one (China). So, the argument continues, China saw itself as the very "center of the world" with its self-sustaining society and its isolated self-sufficient culture. However, in the nineteenth century, confronted with the enormous wealth and power of the European countries, China's traditional civilization "let her down. The old ways were indeed inadequate to modern times."[11] Bluntly put, the "requirements of modernization ran counter to the requirements of Confucian stability."[12] Just to assert that

> China was victimized by the foreign powers . . . leaves unanswered the basic and prior question—why did China not

respond to foreign encroachment earlier and more vigorously?[13]

Naturally this concern with the failure of traditional Chinese society is

> not intended to deny the evil effects of imperialist expansion, of which Western peoples, not having been on the receiving end, have been too often unaware.[14]

Yet the basic pattern of this confrontation is clear to the experts: not Western imperialism per se, but "circumstances made China the worst accident case in history."[15] Among the great civilized areas of the world, China was uniquely unprepared to handle and cope with the spread of European power. It was the very perfection, the "overall cohesion and structural stability of Chinese civilization that basically inhibited its rapid response to the Western menace."[16] To conclude from this inevitable cultural clash that one society victimized another would be to overlook the more profound nature of the conflict.

> Where I part company with them [the Chinese Communists] is, I don't think they were victimized by us or even by the British. I think they were victimized by circumstances of history; namely, that the world civilization which is spreading around, beginning in and expanding from Europe and now expanding with us and others, found China to be the last remaining, separate, distinct, isolated country which had its own culture and hasn't joined up. And this is the background, therefore, of real 'cultural conflict.'[17]

Not surprisingly, such a description is "emotionally unsatisfying" to Chinese patriots.

> It is like asking a man run over by a truck to blame it on a congested traffic pattern. He will say, No, it was a truck.[18]

Thus they seized upon the idea of Western imperialism (the truck) as an understandable response to modernization (the traffic pattern). Communism and the concept of imperialism appealed to the "racked" Chinese intellectuals. It "sank into minds that struggle to explain, and to cure the ills of the country; and it sank into hearts that rejected the West and yet desired its methods."[19] As Joseph Levenson noted:

> The very Western origin of the communist call to revolt, instead of putting a psychological hurdle in the way of Chinese acceptance, smoothed the path, for it guaranteed that the pre-Communist West, the West which had impinged on China, was as firmly rejected by its own critics as by the most hidebound Chinese traditionalist.[20]

History, clothed in Marxist garb, provided the Chinese with a partial psychological answer, China experts conclude, to the failure and disintegration of China's traditional culture.[21] Instead of understanding why circumstances made China history's worst accident case,

> Marxism-Leninism offers a devil-theory to explain it: how 'capitalist imperialism' combined with 'feudal reaction' to attack, betray, and exploit the Chinese people and distort their otherwise normal development toward 'capitalism' and 'socialism.' Thus a great Communist myth of 'imperialist' victimization becomes the new national myth.[22]

When the Chinese refer to "Western imperialism," they are in fact referring to the "modern world's dynamic expansion." For "this Western invasion is what Mao Tse-tung really means by imperialism"; behind "all the dated Leninist theorizing about economic exploitation lies the great fact of the modern world's development and expansion."[23] It is precisely this "grievance against modern history . . . which underlies the current vogue of seeing imperialism as the cause of modern China's difficulties"[24] and which requires "the need for an explanation of history in terms of evil and injustice."[25]

To be sure, the support of Western nations for the old regime in the nineteenth century made us appear as foreign oppressors, but

> sober historical fact and analysis suggest the opposite: that the old regime collapsed less from its oppressiveness than from

mere inanition, and the Westerners did far more to tear it all down than they ever did to prop it up. Never mind: revolutionary fanaticism and foreign guilt feelings propagate the myth, thereby meeting a need in Maoist cosmology.[26]

So today the United States finds itself the object of Chinese psychological projections, a convenient object through which to explain away China's modern predicament.

We find ourselves 'American imperialists,' caught in a role which has been partly thrust upon us and which we do not want: that of the outside oppressor, last target of Mao's revolution, tied in with the evils of China's past, cause of her inadequacies and obstacle to her rise.[27]

However psychologically satisfying the theory of imperialism may be for the Chinese, however understandable its adoption and the casting of America in the villain's role, it nonetheless is (numerous China watchers have decided) an image of the world "at variance with the general trend of modern historical understanding in the international world."[28] More dispassionate analysis, so it seems, would allow us to "perceive the growth of a modern order moving through a series of phases, for each of which we can point to certain signposts."[29]

Most emphatically, such an approach is not viewed by America's China experts as denying the brutality of the Western impact on China or the agonies of the Chinese as they attempted to adapt to the modern world. They do insist though that we recognize that

the spread of imperialism and colonialism and the resurgence of nationalism stand out as phases of broad cultural contact and conflict in the world-wide process of modernization.[30]

Such an approach reassuringly suggests as well that the age of imperialism, the stage of the most negative and seemingly destructive aspects of the encounter, was largely limited to the nineteenth century. In the twentieth century, particularly after 1945 when America became the dominant

Pacific power, it is replaced by an age of nationalism in which

> national independence offers more freedom to select and syn-
> thesize modern ways with the underlying tradition of the local
> society and culture. Modernization is now world-wide; it is
> not Westernization.[31]

Unfortunately, while nations in post-World War II Asia at last have the possibility for greater national independence and selectivity in their response, they are beset by the "violent sociological forces engendered and released by modernization in each of these countries."[32]

> The ancient-modern societies, states or nations of Asia are
> going through a *cycle of political and social metabolism* in
> their struggle for development and modernization. There is a
> constant interaction of *build up and break down* in the po-
> litical-social-psychological sphere at the local level of the
> countryside and the city level of urban aggregation.[33]

The crucial, indeed central, factor is that these nations be allowed to follow their independent ways under American protection without "aggression by seepage,"[34] for such subversion "greatly aggravates the tensions and rivalries, ambitions and harassments," and profoundly alters the course of development.[35] Left to work out their own fortunes, these nations will gradually realize the complexities of the modern world and turn from the tempting but over-simplified and emotional explanations of imperialism offered by fanatical ideologues. Rather encouraging in the estimation of various China watchers, then, is a growing "maturity" on the part of the nations of East Asia. "Even the psychological pressures built up by colonialism are beginning to sink slowly into history in some parts of Asia."[36] In spite of a metabolic cycle of political and social changes, "bit by bit efforts at change are becoming more constructive and realistic."[37]

By another of those strokes of fortune which characterize America's heritage, this development of independent nation-states in an increasingly interdependent world coincided with our growing "responsibilities" as the major power in the Pacific. After all, we are a nation which most ardently believes that "contact, open society, pluralism, the international trading world" are the most fruitful way to modernize.[38] A bit quixotic, perhaps, in our efforts to fashion the world in our own image, often naïve in believing that the new liberal world order can be built so quickly, frequently reluctant to understand the nature of our unique role and awesome responsibilities, the United States nonetheless finds itself leading the "new world oriented culture of technology and cosmopolitanism."[39]

> There is developing an ever more closely linked network of relationships around the world integrated by modern technology and communications, the common language of English, and the cosmopolitan customs of the younger generation in every urban center of the world—even in China. These are the new world forces—a post-Marxian and post-capitalist—twenty-first century, not nineteenth.[40]

It is, then, within this international world framework that America is described by China watchers as assuming its responsibilities: the promotion of independent nation-states each with the right to establish its own goals and objectives and to realize them internally through the means they decide are appropriate. In this role, as Herbert Feis argued in 1950, America is "the chief advocate of a cluster of principles that ban imperialist action of all sorts."[41] Imperialism meant the "exertion of forcible control over the territory or life of another. It meant unwilling subordination, loss of power . . . to act independently."[42] So clearly, Feis concluded, the partnership among nations that America is creating "is not imperialist in design, in fact, or in temper."[43]

> The lonely soldier in Korea is not on an imperialist errand; nor his brother in Iceland; nor his cousin patrolling the Formosan Straits, nor the Five-star General and his staff in

France, striving to organize and equip a combined force; nor the Admiral bargaining for bases in Spain. The oil geologist in Saudi Arabia and the public health doctor in Iran are where work called them, not imperialist purpose. . . . So too are the heavyweights of American influence—the directors of large corporations, bankers (public and private), cabinet officers, senators on their varied business. Assertive they may be, but not imperialist, and no more assertive than at home. All are where they are by consent, not force.[44]

It is precisely against this modern, cosmopolitan world that China seems to react. Though American China experts hoped that China's incorporation into the world order could be resolved through the process of her " 'moderation' and 'assimilation,' " and a "gradual accommodation between the Chinese state and the international community," the Chinese regrettably retain their sense of cultural superiority, national humiliation, and "messianic zeal"[45] which combine to prevent this necessary adaptation.

The point of this is psychological: Peking is, to say the least, maladjusted, rebellious against the whole outer world . . .[46]

Such "hostility toward the world," moreover, constitutes a continuous threat to America's effort to build a secure and viable world order. Unlike the Chinese vision of ruthless revolutionary struggle throughout the world, the United States projects the

vision of a region of independent states cooperating to achieve stability and prosperity with the help of American and other non-Communist aid and protected by the United States from Communist threats.[47]

By relying on American support and power, East Asian nations can develop their national unity and strength. To allow the creation of a "Communist dominated region under Chinese suzerainty" would so alter the "fundamental pattern of the nation-state system" that it would deal a

devastating blow to the hope of creating a global order of

sovereign states able to coexist and harmonize their policies despite competing political systems.[48]

Thus the United States must make it clear that it is

determined to do all it can to help all of the non-Communist states in the area, whether aligned with the West or non-aligned, to build strong, viable states.[49]

Whatever the differences between the United States and the non-Communist nations of East Asia, proper American policy would reveal a community of values entitling us to be their guardians and guides. Simply put, America's emergence as a Pacific power ensures an Asian community in which the struggling nation-states can develop with the assistance of a non-imperial power—"an extraordinarily minimal objective for a super-power."[50]

This, then, is the conception of America in the work of China watchers: the non-imperial guardian of the independence of Asian nations against Communism, the benevolent, well-intentioned supporter of their efforts to modernize their societies through non-violent methods. Such a view of America is rooted in the belief that the obstacles to independent development in Asia are not related to either American actions or the international system the United States promotes. Rather they are largely the result of the enormous difficulties involved in adapting the traditional societies of Asia to a world culture founded upon science and technology, modern modes of organization, and rational standards of efficient government procedure.

Not only is this conception of modernization used to justify America's presence and continued expansion into Asia, but it also provides the ideological alternative to theories of American imperialism and a critique of the revolutionary Marxist worldview.[51] For though American China watchers have sought to explain how and why the theories of American imperialism and revolutionary Marxism were so emotionally satisfying to the Chinese, it is our theory of modernization which could be understood as a "psychologically" comforting rationalization of America's imperial role and its consequences.

Assuredly, few American China watchers viewed themselves as instruments of the American government or as its official ideologues. But if few were involved in the actual decision-making process within the government—if, indeed, many were criticized and persecuted during the McCarthy period—they nonetheless proved influential in justifying America's policies. This was not because many approved of the actual course of American policy toward China after 1949, but because by the work they did not do they upheld significant portions of the official definition of reality and, by the work they did, even elaborated upon it.

Ever since the mid-1940's, leading figures in the China field have sought an alternative to Communist theory in order to provide the United States with the ideological weapons to fight the cultural cold war. As they saw it, during the "transitional" stage between the traditional society and the emergence of a modern social system, Communism is particularly attractive to the members of the intelligentsia. The crucial battle of the cold war, therefore, would be fought over the influential intellectual and professional groups in Asia. Whoever could appeal to them most effectively would emerge victorious. For it is the "historical theories in men's minds more than any other factor under human control," concluded Edwin Reischauer, "that gives direction to the tremendous transformation of Asia now under way." Thus America must offer to the "potential leadership groups a theory of history that will explain and justify their present travail and will clarify the way ahead of them,"[52] some picture of the

modern world and its history more meaningful than Marxism-Leninism. The non-Communist explanation of the social process—of imperialism, colonialism, nationalism, economic growth, social order—must make more sense to Asians than the Communist explanation.[53]

This conscious effort to formulate a theoretical alternative to Communism and its arsenal of ideological weapons, however, meant far more in practice than a critique of revolutionary Marxism. Their intense effort to discredit "Communist perspectives" rested upon an idealized image of America's international role and her capacity to promote non-violent forms of change. This allowed little tolerance for revolutionary solutions to Asia's problems. The following comparisons between a few of the assumptions of the two styles of thought—revolutionary Marxism and the China watcher's theory of modernization—do not seek to justify revolutionary Marxism, but only to suggest the kinds of questions and the wealth of formulative notions left unasked by China watchers. Such comparisons indicate that what was rejected was not primarily revolutionary Marxism, but any fundamental criticism of America's role in Asia and any form of really sympathetic understanding of revolutionary movements.

While American China watchers have viewed the primary obstacles to development in the internal structures of a country, the revolutionary Marxist stresses the barriers in the nature of world-wide capitalism and the influence of imperialism from without on non-Western societies. But, replies the China expert, "Japan's success in modernizing under rather similar handicaps in the same period is simply brushed aside."[54] In Japan, it is bluntly argued,

> the process of modernization began . . . because Japanese feudal society was receptive to innovations based on Western ideas and institutions, [while] China, on the other hand, resisted change . . . and consequently fell prey to foreign imperialism.[55]

Thus

> the rapidity and effectiveness of the Japanese reaction must be explained primarily by the traditional civilization rather than by accidents of geography or variations in the challenge from the West.[56]

This stress by American China watchers on the internal factors which prevented a successful Chinese response,[57] moreover, results in an evaluation of the Western powers as agents, in Schumpeter's phrase, of "creative destruction," merely the instruments of a painful but unavoidable step in the developmental process. Thus China, unlike Japan, lacked the necessary cultural background and consequently bore the full brunt of Western imperialism—not China bore the full impact of the Western powers and therefore could not respond.

Precisely this assumption that Japan and China labored under similar handicaps imposed by the West indicates a strong ideological element which has guided reflection on the dynamics of the impact of Western nations. For if it is true that Japan's remoteness spared her "from the full force of Western imperialism after 1800"; that "the political and territorial thrust of Western imperialism had largely spent itself by the time it reached Japan and was further weakened by its own inner rivalries"; that in a "different environmental setting, Japan's feudal heritage could well have exerted a more stifling influence on social change in modern times"[58]; that, finally, the world system of multilateral trade patterns at this particular time was exceptionally favorable to Japanese exports[59]—if, in short, the particular external context in which Japan "reacted" is to be examined, not assumed, then a far different style of questioning the relationship between internal and external factors and a consequent shift in the evaluation of their interaction is possible.

If, for example, one begins with the premise that Japan's escape from imperial domination depended partly upon a unique configuration of external circumstances, and if her avoidance of colonial or dependency status proved to be unrepeatable almost everywhere else, this suggests that an "underdeveloped" country, once penetrated, finds the Japanese road of conscious imitation of Western capitalism closed to itself.[60] Such a type of analysis brings into question the China watcher's belief that internal factors were the primary reason for China's prolonged domination by Western powers. For from this perspective it is plausible to argue that before 1949 the Chinese

> revolution never was completed for the simple reason that foreign imperialism was entirely too strong to permit the Chinese people to take control over their own destinies. The Second World War which brought about the defeat of Japan, most dangerous and most powerful of the imperialist countries in the Far East, plus the weakening of Western European imperialism, was what made the Chinese revolution possible and also what changed it in a new direction.[61]

In addition to this emphasis upon internal factors, the explaining-away of imperialism is also evident in the China watcher's picture of the evolving modern world order. Whereas he has focused on the development over several centuries of a commercial and scientific-industrial complex in the West and then its spread throughout the rest of the world, the revolutionary Marxist usually stresses that

> the unlimited industrial advance of the Western world has been possible only at the expense of the so-called underdeveloped world, which has been doomed to stagnation and regression.[62]

Though both theoretical perspectives emphasize the penetration of Western economic power into China, the modernization approach, by concentrating on the "creative destruction" resulting from Western investments and the world trading system, can maintain that the "economic tragedy" of the once colonial and semi-colonial lands of Asia today is not so

> much that they formerly suffered from 'economic imperialism' as that they did not have enough of it in the form of solid investments by the West.[63]

Theories of imperialism, on the contrary, not only insist that the exportation of capital and the control of foreign markets have been traditional instruments of foreign control and domination, but that even trade by itself, far from leading to development, "tends to have backwash effects and to strengthen the forces maintaining stagnation or repression."[64] The international economic system, therefore, is less an environment in which the non-Western areas can "modernize," than a place where

> the 'natural' play of the forces in the markets will be working all the time to increase internal and international inequalities as long as their general level of development is low.[65]

Consequently, a study of imperialism requires an exploration into precisely those questions glossed over by the modernization approach: the power of the metropolitan countries to block the formation of vital domestic industries in the dependent countries competitive with their own operations; the domination of mercantile over industrial capital; and the subordination of the economic life of a dependent nation to the severe fluctuations of the primary commodities market.

Instead, therefore, of seeing an evolving world order of independent self-determining states under the benevolent protection of America, the revolutionary Marxist sees the social system of capitalism as necessarily generating conditions that develop one part of the world system at the expense of another. Thus bourgeois nations face proletarian ones, and revolutionary socialism is rooted in the semi-peasant, semi-proletarian masses of the Third World rather than in the developed metropolitan capitalist societies.

Here, too, is another contrast between the two theories. While American China watchers concentrate upon the role of elites, whether it be the gentry's efforts in China to understand the West during the nineteenth century or the growth of the modern bourgeoisie, the revolutionary Marxist points to the condition of the peasantry and the urban proletariat which sparks their revolutionary movements. Where China specialists had favored close Amer-

ican ties with the educated elite in China during the pre-
1949 period and urged reforms from the top down as the
only means to avoid a peasant revolution "exploited" by
the Communists, the latter mobilized the population, particularly the rural dwellers, bringing them into the political
process from the bottom up, so to speak. And while China
watchers warn repeatedly of the risks of revolution from
below, the revolutionary Marxist argues that the needed
strength to withstand Western power comes out of a revolutionary transformation that rejects dependency-generating
ties with the West.

Underlying these different characterizations of the role
of elites are sharply contrasting conceptions of "violence"
and "order." China watchers generally argue that

> social change must be gradual and cautious, that it can only
> succeed if it builds slowly upon the basic 'felt needs' of a
> majority of the ordinary people, and that the programs must
> be formulated in such a way as to avoid, whenever possible,
> head-on clashes with the obvious obstacles to change strongly
> entrenched in all traditional societies.[66]

The kind of world they want, in short, is "a world in which
there is change, but within a context of stability."[67] For
American interests are not compatible with violent upheavals; as they see it, we live in a world where "violence
is too dangerous."[68]

> The Russians say: 'Even though we are in favor of revolution,
> in the kind of world we live in violence is too dangerous.' I
> share that view.[69]

Violence, though, is narrowly defined by the China watcher
as a quality of those individuals or groups who challenge
existing arrangements. The revolutionary Marxist, on the
other hand, concentrates on institutional violence, the
human costs of stability, and the violent powers of the
ruling elites. And while the former stress the immediately
observable kinds of social violence, the latter insist that
order, like violence, is politically defined and that the con-

ceptions of orderly and nonviolent change only reflect the interests of those powerful enough to enforce their definitions upon the population.

Both perspectives, moreover, whether insisting upon the need for reform by Westernized elites or revolutionary action by the masses from below, agree upon the weakness of the bourgeoisie. For the revolutionary Marxist the lack of an independent indigenous industrial sector reduces the role of the nascent bourgeoisie, while the revolutionary consciousness among the masses makes the middle class too fearful of mass uprisings to risk a major reform movement that would strongly challenge the reactionary elements. The Chinese merchant-industrial class, some of them argue, not only failed to cut the cords which bound them to the landlords, but fashioned new chains tying them firmly to foreign capital. Having divorced themselves from the workers in the cities and particularly from the peasant masses in the countryside, the Chinese bourgeoisie did not possess the capacity for the "progressive" political role their counterparts in Europe had played. Instead, these bourgeoisie found themselves linked in an uneasy alliance with Chiang Kai-shek. Thus revolutionary transformation of Chinese society from the bottom up was the only plausible course for true national independence.

Set against this analysis of the weakness of the middle class is a suggested style of action theorized about in the late 1940's and later promoted by China watchers as part of the ideological underpinning of the containment policy —an approach later labeled "nation building." American China experts have by and large been most receptive to and have helped formulate the belief that development is far more than a matter of economic growth within a given social structure. The very modernization of that structure is a process of social, economic, ideational, and political change that requires the remaking of society. When they speak of the revolutionary nature of economic development, it is this kind of penetrative change that is meant—changes in the inherited pattern of life, the family structure, the notions of authority, class, and privilege. And "we owe it to the Asians as well as to ourselves not to abandon the revolution halfway but to help carry [it] through as vigorously as possible towards its full realization."[70]

What group, however, could make such changes? To many of those in the China field, particularly those instrumental in formulating an ideological alternative to Communism, American government's failure in China was symbolized by an inflexible commitment to Chiang Kai-shek's regime which prevented assistance to the one group which could reform China while facing West: the modern professionals and the liberal strata, the bourgeoisie. Indeed, the very

> key to our position in China has been China's modern liberal class, the professional men trained in this country, the students in the Christian colleges in China, the Shanghai businessmen who believe in free enterprise under the protection of law.[71]

America's failure in China, in short, resulted from a fundamental misunderstanding of the manner in which such groups could be effectively aided in their efforts to reform China. American military and economic assistance to Chiang's reactionary regime after 1945 had only provided fodder for the Chinese Communist propaganda mill to promote the "myth" of American imperialism, while so strengthening the position of the extreme right wing within the Kuomintang that all hopes for meaningful reform measures were ended. America simply failed to support those in China who shared our values and conceptions of non-violent development.

> Why did not our policy support more vigorously those elements in Chinese society which really represented our principles? What did we do for modern Chinese private banking establishments like the Shanghai Commercial and Savings Bank? What did we do, with our millions of American aid, for private Chinese educational institutions like Nanking Uni-

versity in Tientsin? What did we do to support the efforts of genuine democrats in the early Democratic League. . . . The answer is not one to be proud of.[72]

Part of the lesson of the Chinese revolution for various American China watchers, therefore, was clear. If the United States was not to become wedded to corrupt and reactionary regimes like Chiang's in other parts of Asia, if our involvement in the politics of another country was not to be biased on the side of the status quo, it was imperative that American influence reach farther than "the top layers of demoralized and sticky-fingered officials of the old regime."[73] The "missionary zeal," the American sense of "righteousness and benevolent intervention," meant in practice a complete penetration and modernization of an "underdeveloped" area through an influx of teachers, investors, advisers, modern businessmen, military officials. Simply to provide aid and support for a political regime was totally inadequate, for the development of any Asian area, while undoubtedly a native process, "cannot be conducted only by the native governments concerned."[74] The Western educated, reform-oriented bourgeoisie elements would be the instruments through which reforms essential to prevent revolutionary upheaval were carried out. Such a conception of America's role in social reform, reinforced by our experience in China in the 1940's, appears a striking forerunner to the nation-building policies later attempted in such places as Vietnam.[75]

These contrasts between the China watcher's theory of modernization and revolutionary Marxism only begin to indicate the ideological perspective underlying contemporary Chinese studies and its consequences for understanding China and revolutionary change in Asia. And if in our questions frequently lie our principles of analysis, our evaluations and values, then it is hardly surprising why so little sympathy exists for revolutionary movements among China specialists. For having cut themselves off from modes of questioning which could treat revolutionary situations with genuine understanding and perhaps even appreciation, they find it difficult to describe and evaluate the Chinese revolution from any but hostile perspectives. At best, they can offer "psychologically" understandable explanations for Chinese reactions to the West or American power.

To examine the reasons for this hostility to revolutionary movements, however, requires a demystification of America's actual role in Asia and the modernization theory which has served to justify our involvement in the domestic affairs of numerous Asian nations. For the idealized image of America is intricately interwoven with a staunch faith in our ability to promote non-violent forms of social change. That is why the lack of introspection about America set the stage for the view of China and revolution which is today so dominant. And that, too, is why it will only be through such introspection and the questioning it requires, that a more accurate, less biased and more sympathetic view of China and revolution can emerge.

Notes

1. George Kennan, "A Fresh Look at Our China Policy," *New York Times Magazine* (November 22, 1964), p. 27.
2. While drawing upon the writings of almost all the leaders of the China field, particular stress is placed on the work of John K. Fairbank and Edwin O. Reischauer. Both men were instrumental in formulating many of the major tenets and assumptions which have guided thought about contemporary China throughout the 1950's and 1960's. Professor Fairbank's enormous influence in shaping the field of Chinese studies through his position at Harvard University, moreover, is paralleled by Professor Reischauer's public stature as one of the leading popularizers and articulate spokesmen about Chinese and Japanese relations with the United States. Together they have written the major textbooks in the field: *East Asia: The Great Tradition* (Boston, Houghton Mifflin, 1960) and (with Albert Craig) *East Asia: The Modern Transformation* (Boston, Houghton Mifflin, 1965).

3. Edwin O. Reischauer, *Wanted: An Asian Policy* (New York, Knopf, 1955), p. 70.

4. *Ibid.*, p. 72.

5. *Ibid.*, p. 71.

6. *Ibid.*, p. 71.

7. *Ibid.*, p. 71.

8. Fairbank, Reischauer, Craig, *East Asia*, p. 10.

9. *Ibid.* "For example, the challenge of foreign warships led some East Asians to try to exclude the foreigner and others to learn from him in self-defense; the stimuli (warships) were similar; the responses were various." p. 5.

10. Marion Levy, "Contrasting Factors in the Modernization of China and Japan," in *Economic Development and Cultural Change,* p. 163.

11. John K. Fairbank, "The Great Wall," in *New York Review of Books* (March 28, 1968), p. 28.

12. Mary Wright, *The Last Stand of Chinese Conservatism* (New York, Atheneum, 1966), p. 9.

13. Fairbank, Reischauer, Craig, *East Asia,* p. 404.

14. *Ibid.*, p. 407.

15. John K. Fairbank, *United States Policy With Respect to Mainland China,* Hearings before the Committee on Foreign Relations, Senate, March, 1966 (Washington, D.C., U.S. Government Printing Office, 1966), p. 102.

16. Fairbank, Reischauer, Craig, *East Asia,* p. 407.

17. Fairbank, *United States Policy With Respect to Mainland China,* p. 109.

18. John K. Fairbank, "New Thinking About China," in *China: The People's Middle Kingdom and the U.S.A.* (Cambridge, Mass., Harvard Univ. Press, 1967), p. 95.

19. Conrad Brandt, *Stalin's Failure in China* (Cambridge, Mass., Harvard Univ. Press, 1958), p. vii.

20. Joseph Levenson, *Modern China and its Confucian Past* (New York, Doubleday, 1964), p. 176.

21. Albert Feuerwerker is an exceptionally good example of this mode of analyzing China. See, for example, his article, "China's History in Marxian Dress," *American Historical Review,* Vol. LXVI, No. 2 (January 1961), p. 323.

22. Fairbank, *United States Policy With Respect to Mainland China,* p. 102.

23. Fairbank, "Why Peking Casts Us as the Villain," in *China: The People's Middle Kingdom,* p. 107.

24. Fairbank, "An American View of China's Modernization," *Ibid.,* p. 23. Again, the Chinese are depicted as formulating a theory of

imperialism in order to explain the difficult confrontation with science and technology. "How indignant we could feel if only we could blame urbanization, traffic, jet noise, and even drug abuses and the wildness of youth, all on foreign invaders." John K. Fairbank, "Still Mysterious," *New York Review of Books* (June 5, 1969), p. 19.

25. Fairbank, "Why Peking Casts Us as the Villain," in *China: The People's Middle Kingdom*, p. 107.
26. Fairbank, "The Great Wall," p. 29.
27. *Ibid.*, p. 30.
28. Fairbank, "An American View of China's Modernization," in *China: The People's Middle Kingdom*, p. 17.
29. *Ibid.*, p. 23.
30. Fairbank, Reischauer, Craig, *East Asia*, p. 414.
31. *Ibid.*, p. 802.
32. Kenneth Young, "Asia's Disequilibrium and American Strategies," in W. W. Lockwood (ed.), *The United States and Communist China* (Princeton, N.J., Haskins Press, 1965), p. 45.
33. *Ibid.*, p. 45.
34. "Peking has developed a dual strategy of sanctuary warfare by political proxies in Asia which I call 'aggression by seepage.' It consists of two interdependent parts: first, the methodical planned establishment of privileged sanctuaries within Chinese control, and, second, the careful organization of proxy parties outside Chinese frontiers adjacent to or near the sanctuaries." Young, "Asia's Disequilibrium," pp. 46–47.
35. *Ibid.*, p. 45.
36. Edwin O. Reischauer, *Beyond Vietnam: The United States and Asia* (New York, Vintage, 1967), p. 77.
37. *Ibid.*, p. 77.
38. Fairbank, *United States Policy With Respect to Mainland China*, p. 124.
39. Kenneth Young, *Diplomacy and Power in Washington-Peking Dealings: 1953-1967* (Chicago, Univ. of Chicago Press, 1967), p. 28.
40. Young, "Asia's Disequilibrium," p. 51. This rather sanitary view of technology and technological progress is strikingly apparent in Edwin Reischauer's description of this "great change in human civilization": "It may be very much pleasanter during the period of transition to be in the society where the innovation comes through gradual evolutionary steps rather than in a society where it comes through foreign conquest, but in the long run it may make little difference where the change comes first. . . . The significant thing is the technological advance, not the identity of

those who first achieved it." Reischauer, *Wanted: An Asian Policy*, pp. 72–3.

41. Herbert Feis, "Is the United States Imperialist?" *Yale Review*, September, 1951, p. 17. Although Feis is not usually classified as a China watcher, he has contributed some of the basic books in the field: *The China Triangle: The American Effort From Pearl Harbor to the Marshall Mission* (New York, Atheneum, 1966) and *The Road to Pearl Harbor* (New York, Atheneum, 1966).

42. *Ibid.,* p. 13.

43. *Ibid.,* p. 17.

44. *Ibid.,* p. 13. Fortunately, adds Feis in a comment highly indicative of the underlying assumptions of America's China watchers, our economic policies, no less than our political concerns, are barriers to imperialism. "Our full impact on other nations is not to be understood without taking account of influences we generate merely by being what we are. . . . We are the main source of capital; whether we provide little or much at any time makes a great difference in the rate of economic activity everywhere. We conduct a substantial part of all world trade, and the part grows greater. The state of economic activity in the United States affects decisively the price movements of all internationally traded raw materials. . . . Our bids shape markets and create surpluses and scarcities. For these reasons the economic condition of many other countries is vitally connected with ours. This, then, in rough outline is the image of American pressure in the world; or rather, a rough outline of its main elements. It is not the image of imperialism, but that of a forerunner in the creation of a system in which imperialism would fade. . . . The path which we seek to travel is towards commonwealth, a cooperative society of independent nations." *Ibid.*, p. 24.

45. James C. Thomson, Jr., Testimony, *On the Nature of Revolution*, Hearings before the Committee on Foreign Relations, Senate (Washington, D.C., U.S. Government Printing Office, 1968), p. 67.

46. Fairbank, "How to Deal with the Chinese Revolution," in *China: The People's Middle Kingdom*, p. 129.

47. Robert Blum, *The United States and China in World Affairs* (New York, McGraw-Hill, 1966), p. 51. Indeed, as Edwin Reischauer argued in a similar vein, "We have in fact staked our whole future as a nation on a free association of equal allies and beyond that, on a world order in which democratic procedures of discussion and voting, rather than force, will be used to settle international disputes." *Wanted: An Asian Policy*, p. 250.

48. Fred Greene, *United States Policy and the Security of Asia* (New York, McGraw-Hill, 1968), p. 41.

49. A. Doak Barnett, *Communist China and Asia* (New York, Vintage, 1961), p. 475.

50. "Our basic interests are quite minimal," argues Robert Scalapino. "They lie in the development of independent political entities in this region. They lie in giving these independent political entities the type of international support for nation building and economic development that will render the region a stable one. Our primary interest in southeast Asia, in short, is that it achieve true independence and sufficient political and economic development to keep it separate from Communist bloc power. This is an extraordinarily minimal objective for a superpower, and it should be made clear to the peoples of the world." Testimony, *Sino-Soviet Conflict*, Hearings before the Subcommittee on the Far East and the Pacific of the Committee of Foreign Affairs, House (Washington, D.C., U.S. Government Printing Office, 1965), p. 241.

51. In analyzing the conflict between the China watcher's theory of modernization and "revolutionary Marxism," we shall be talking about each as if it represented an ideal type. For the purposes of this paper, references to revolutionary Marxism are only meant to convey a general style of questioning and evaluation. Since numerous China experts were interested in refuting "Communist perspectives," they tended to lump all the different perspectives in the Marxist tradition together. Consequently, in order to indicate some of the types of questioning which have been rejected, it has been necessary to draw on perspectives that at times might be more accurately labeled "Leninist," "Marxist," "Maoist," etc. The use of the term "revolutionary Marxist" is purposefully designed not to be equivalent to any particular "branch" of the Marxist tradition. At times, too, individuals who could in no way be considered Marxist (like Gunnar Myrdal) are used to exemplify the broad range of questioning neglected by American China watchers.

52. Edwin O. Reischauer, "Our Asian Frontiers of Knowledge," *University of Arizona Bulletin* (Tucson, September 1958), p. 11.

53. Fairbank, "Communist China and Taiwan in U.S. Foreign Policy," in *China: The People's Middle Kingdom*, p. 57.

54. Fairbank, "The Great Wall," p. 28.

55. George M. Beckmann, *The Modernization of China and Japan* (New York, Harper & Row, 1962), preface.

56. Reischauer, *Wanted: An Asian Policy*, p. 52.

57. Success and failure are used here in the traditional sense. It seems plausible to argue, though, that the costs of Japan's response were as great as China's. As Barrington Moore argues, the Japanese "price for avoiding a revolutionary entrance" into the twentieth

century "has been a very high one." *Social Origins of Dictatorship and Democracy* (Boston, Beacon, 1966), p. 313.

58. William W. Lockwood, "Japan's Response to the West: the Contrast with China," *World Politics,* October 1956, pp. 51–54.

59. William W. Lockwood, *The Economic Development of Japan* (Princeton, N.J., Princeton Univ. Press, 1954), p. 403. "It was Japan's good fortune that the foundations of her modern development were laid in an era when the world economy as a whole was expanding, and still organized on liberal principles for the most part." (p. 311) "Far more important, however, was the relative freedom and efficiency of the world system of multilateral trade. Within wide limits, it enabled her to buy and sell wherever her advantage lay, offsetting the resulting exchange balances with little or no regard to their pattern of distribution. Only with the weakening and breakdown of the system . . . did it become apparent how basic this was to the economic opportunity of the Japanese. Despite their meager physical resources, it enabled them through their industry and enterprise to advance and prosper economically." (p. 403)

60. "It is hard to deny that the lack of foreign domination was the decisive factor making possible the industrialization of Japan, encouraged by all the resources of the State." Ernest Mandel, *Marxist Economic Theory* (New York, Monthly Review Press, 1969), p. 476. Also, see David Horowitz, *Empire and Revolution: A Radical Interpretation of Contemporary History* (New York, Random House, 1969), p. 114.

61. Jack Belden, *China Shakes the World* (New York, Harper & Brothers, 1949), p. 3.

62. Mandel, *Marxist Economic Theory,* p. 441. As Andre Gunder Frank notes, "the economic and political expansion of Europe since the fifteenth century has come to incorporate the now underdeveloped countries into a single stream of world history, which has given rise simultaneously to the present development of some countries and the present underdevelopment of others." "Sociology of Development and Underdevelopment of Sociology" in *Catalyst,* Summer, 1967 (Buffalo, N.Y., State University of N.Y. Sociology Club). The difference between the modernization approach of the China watcher and revolutionary Marxism partly rests in the different evaluations of this phenomenon of "underdevelopment." The former stresses that once certain internal variables become conducive to modernization, a non-Western area will not find its way blocked by the international system, while the latter continually points to the opposition of the Western

nations to independent development on the part of the "under-developed" world. Moreover, those Western critics of theories of imperialism who point out that the imperial country may have lost far more in financial terms than it gained, overlook the interests of particular groups or classes who profited.

63. Reischauer, *Wanted: An Asian Policy*, pp. 101–102.

64. Gunnar Myrdal, "International Inequalities," in Richard S. Weckstein (ed.), *Expansion of World Trade and the Growth of National Economies* (New York, Harper, 1968), p. 63.

65. *Ibid.*, p. 73.

66. A. Doak Barnett, *Communist China in Perspective* (New York, Praeger, 1962), p. 41.

67. Barnett, *United States Policy With Respect to Mainland China*, p. 80.

68. *Ibid.*, p. 79.

69. *Ibid.* This leads, as Senator Fulbright pointed out, to the conclusion that Doak Barnett would have opposed the American Revolution.

"Barnett: To the extent that we can effectively use our influence for desirable revolutions by nonviolent means, I think that our government should be in favor of some kind of revolution, but should try to avoid violent revolutions.

Chairman Fulbright: Would you consider our own revolution a violent one or a nonviolent one?

Barnett: Well, yes; it was a violent one.

Chairman Fulbright: And having had our origin in the formation of the country from a violent revolution, isn't it a little odd that we should be allergic to anyone else having a violent revolution?" (*Ibid.*, p. 79)

70. Reischauer, *Wanted: An Asian Policy*, p. 208.

71. John K. Fairbank, "Can We Compete in China?" *Far Eastern Survey* (May 19, 1948), p. 114.

72. John K. Fairbank, "Toward A Dynamic Far Eastern Policy," *Far Eastern Survey* (September 7, 1949), p. 210.

73. Fairbank, "Toward A Dynamic Far Eastern Policy," p. 210.

74. *Ibid.*, p. 210.

75. It also appears a striking forerunner to Samuel Huntington's ardent belief that "the more extensive the American involvement in the politics of another country, the more progressive or reform-oriented is its impact on that country." *No More Vietnams?* Richard Pfeffer (ed.), (New York, Harper & Row, 1968), p. 223.

Asian Scholars and Government: The Chrysanthemum on the Sword

❦ Judith Coburn

❦ ON MAY 3, 1946, a policy paper signed by Dwight D. Eisenhower was forwarded to former Secretary of War Henry L. Stimson. The paper argued that civilian resources mobilized during the war must be available to the Army in peacetime. It said in part:

> A premium must be placed on professional attainments in the natural and social sciences as well as other branches of the military. . . . It is our duty to support broad research programs in educational institutions, in industry, and in whatever field might be of importance to the Army. . . . The association of military and civilians in educational institutions and industry will level barriers, engender understanding, and lead to the cultivation of friendships valuable for future cooperation.[1]

Bringing scholars and industrialists into the process of government was not a novel idea; a few economists and political scientists had joined the migration of lawyers to Washington during the New Deal. But the notion of organizing the academic community and linking it institutionally to government—and specifically to the military— was an idea born of World War II mobilization and the development of intelligence operations. For the first time, large numbers of scholars had served as government analysts and contributors to war-time policy. After the war, the consensus among government planners was that the degree of cooperation with science and industry achieved during the recent war should by no means be considered the ultimate. There appears little reason for duplicating within the Army an outside organization which by its experience is better qualified than we are to carry out some of our tasks.[2]

Science and scholarship were to become the cornerstones upon which the superstructure of the national security state would be built.

Equally important was the conviction among policy-makers that the United States had emerged from World War II with vast new global responsibilities in a world about which they knew precious little. Britain and France had been brought to their knees; their vast liberated empires required a new Protectress. Although American power had brought about the defeat of the Axis powers, the world hardly seemed stable or secure. American leaders were faced with a number of major challenges in the post-war era: the left in Europe and nationalism in the Third World, the threat of the Soviet Union and her possible alliance with this left, and the decline of the Western European bulwarks against Communism. It was clearly a post-war world in which continued mobilization and vigilance was necessary.

As the American involvement in Asia increased, the Asian scholar was a vital resource to the American government. Ruth Benedict, whose massive study of Japanese culture was influential in American policy toward Japan during the late years of the war and the Occupation, describes the problem:

Crises were facing us in quick succession. What would the Japanese do? Was capitulation possible without invasion? Should we bomb the Emperor's palace? . . . When peace came were the Japanese a people who would require martial law to keep them in order? Would there have to be a revolution in Japan after the order of the French or the Russian revolution before international peace was possible?[3]

Her role exemplifies the new function of social scientists:

> The question was how the Japanese would behave, not how
> we would behave if we were in their place. . . . I had to look
> at the way they conducted the war itself and see it not for the
> moment as a military problem but as a cultural problem. In
> warfare as well as peace, the Japanese acted in character.
> Their leaders' way of whipping up war spirit, of reassuring
> the bewildered, of utilizing their soldiers in the field—all
> these things showed what they themselves regarded as the
> strengths on which they could capitalize.[4]

One of the few beneficial effects of the war in Vietnam
has been to force intellectuals to take a hard look at their
relationship to government. In one view, social scientists
emerged from their ivory towers during World War II,
sold out to Cold War mongers for high cash rewards and
ended as willing handmaidens of military planners.[5] Other
critics focus on documentary "war research" conducted by
social scientists like Ithiel Pool, policy advising by professors like Milton Sacks and Robert Scalapino, and weapon
technologists like Edward Teller.[6] Another less critical
view traces the links between government and scholars to
the patriotic impulses of World War II and the continued
ideals of public service among academicians in the Cold
War era.[7]

At the same time, it is fashionable, especially among lib-
eral Asian scholars, to decry the lack of influence by the
Academy or career experts on government policy in general
and Asian policy in particular. Thus, Edmund Clubb of
Columbia University lamented at a recent meeting of the
Association for Asian Studies that

> The China policy of today, the Asia policy of today, are not
> by any stretch of the imagination to be viewed as the handi-
> work of career Asian experts. Our China and Asian policies
> are the creation of men at the top of government alone.[8]

According to this argument, China specialists for a decade,
and especially since 1961, have argued that the United

States should step up contacts with China, not build walls of isolation; it is the reluctance of policy-makers to heed the experts that has warped our policy. A different version of the view that Asia scholars are isolated from policy-makers blames the McCarthy era. Because of the traumas of the McCarthy era, scholars have been excessively timid in getting involved in the more controversial, political questions of policy, especially in the early stages of the Vietnam war.[9]

Policy-makers are the first to agree that scholars have limited influence. One well known National Security Council staffer in the Nixon Administration said recently that most academic work is not entirely relevant to what the government is debating. For instance, advocates of trade with Red China fail to take into consideration domestic political factors or the reaction of Asian allies and effects on the power balance in the area. Students of the policy process often agree; M.I.T.'s Lincoln Bloomfield, for example, writes:

. . . in foreign policy and diplomacy generally, my unresearched impression is that unless they are extraordinarily timely, new scholarly syntheses are not usually welcomed, grasped or read (by policy makers).[10]

Few in government or the Academy, however, will dispute that there is a highly developed relationship between academia and the government; the critics of this phenomenon are, of course, primarily confined to the university. The problem with many of the conspiracy or ineffectuality theories, however, is that they fail to relate the contributions of social science to America's international posture and its supporting ideology. Much of the apparent contradiction between the increasing integration of the university into government and scholarly feelings of powerlessness can be resolved by an analysis of the role of knowledge in a post-industrial society. One of the most significant accounts of the role of the scholar in the new technocracy is by John Kenneth Galbraith, himself a prime example of the new breed of scholar-technocrat. In *The New Industrial State,* Galbraith writes:

> With the rise of the technostructure, relations between those associated with economic enterprise and the educational and scientific estate undergo a radical transformation. There is no longer an abrupt conflict in motivation. Like the educational and scientific estate, the technostructure is no longer exclusively, or perhaps even primarily, responsive to pecuniary motivation. Both see themselves as identified with social goals, or with organizations serving social purposes. And both, it may be assumed, seek to adapt social goals to their own. If there is a difference it is not in the motivational system but in the goals.[11]

Galbraith correctly describes the convergence of interests between these sometime enemies, the industrialist and the educator. I believe that not only are their motivations the same, but their goals also are similar; differentiation occurs only at the functional level.

The new role of social scientists in the post-World War II technocracy is directly related to institutional changes in the universities and the behavioral revolution. The development of the research center, and social scientists' interest in government policy has its roots in several early twentieth-century trends in American social science: the traditionally pragmatic bent of social science in the United States, the emergence before World War I of research as a significant function of the university, and the trend toward interdisciplinary research. These trends were reinforced in the 1920's by another American phenomenon, the private foundations, which provided university research centers with the funds needed for rapid growth. In 1939, Robert S. Lynd in his lecture series, "Knowledge for What," called for the application of all available knowledge to solve the social problems of the time. Lynd's ideas were the foundation for the group of social scientists, led by Harold Lasswell, who later popularized pragmatic and empirical orientations in the social sciences under the term "the policy sciences."[12]

A 1927 report by the Social Science Research Council outlined the challenge to social scientists to prove their relevance:

> Out of the ferment of the post-war era we already can see new forces arising, which, if they mature, will modify the entire relationship of civilized nations. These elements of historic process cannot be studied adequately by the means, and through the instruments at our disposal at present. They cannot be referred to the casual or incidental interest of those who make this field an academic avocation.[13]

But while American social scientists were preparing themselves intellectually for policy-relevant work, their relationship to government policy-making awaited institutional definition. World War II shook the provincialism of the American university, its social scientists, and its institutional framework.

During World War II, many social scientists served as analysts and operatives for the Office of Strategic Services (the precursor of the CIA) and the Office of War Information. The result of this experience was a redefinition of the intellectual interests of social scientists and the reorganization of the university. The war produced a generation of area experts: either young men trained in Army Asian language programs at large universities like Michigan, or sociologists and lawyers who worked on the Eastern Europe or Russian desks at OSS, the new breed of Kremlinologists. Political scientist Robert Dahl has written of this period:

> The confrontation of theory and reality provoked in most of the men who performed in Washington or elsewhere, a strong sense of the inadequacies of the conventional approach of political science for describing reality, much less for predicting in any given situation what was likely to happen.[14]

Another account stresses the collective impact of this experience:

Many hundreds of researchers in politics, economics, psychology and sociology, driven by . . . war demands, discovered in various degrees the value of interdisciplinary teamwork, the unbelievable expansion of United States interests into novel geographic and functional areas, and the potential for applying what used to be called academic techniques to meeting the most practical demands.[15]

Out of these experiences, area studies was born. As the array of scholarly talent which had served the government during the war divided itself between the universities, foundations, and newly reorganized government offices, policy-makers and scholars feared a gap between intellectual resources and their application to government needs. But the seeds of cooperation between the institutions of the technocracy were also forged by this dispersal of talent. Men like John Gardner, Clyde Kluckhohn, William Langer, and John Fairbank who had served together in war-time intelligence had a community of interests which shortly received institutional buttressing. The government defined the policy research, the foundations donated the resources, the scholars provided the expertise, and the university administered.

The University community had, of course, traditionally seen its role as serving society; it had always produced an elite whose ideas and influence shaped policy. But never had the links and the needs been defined so directly. L. Gray Cowan, the historian of the Columbia Area Studies Institute wrote of the need to continue war-time training programs in the social sciences:

It was strongly impressed upon the minds, not only of the officials of government, but also of the university faculties, that a reservoir of trained personnel must be created by continuing and expanding these programs leading toward professional work in the field of international relations in the post-war era, so that never again would the United States be caught critically short of the personnel necessary for the expanded operations of government agencies. Not only the needs

of the war period, but also the immensely expanding responsibilities of American foreign policy as foreseen even during
the war called forth continued requirements for this type of
personnel.[16]

The result was a proliferation of area studies research institutes; Harvard's Russian Research Center, for example,
was staffed by top OSS scholars on the Russian desk who had
returned to Harvard after the war and was funded in part by
the Carnegie Corporation, and in part by a massive Air
Force contract to interview Russian refugees. The usefulness of these centers was well recalled by the then Secretary
of the Navy Paul Nitze in a 1966 address at the University
of Edinburgh:

> How did these centers respond to the Government's needs?
> First of all they attracted men of scholarly qualities who were
> interested in learning about, and working with, national
> security problems. These men were free from direct govern-
> ment responsibility, lived in an atmosphere of academic free-
> dom, and had sufficient time to study and reflect on the very
> serious challenge at hand.[17]

These were not, of course, merely government research
factories. The scholars' own intellectual work and teaching was inspired by the same motives and values that encouraged the establishment of the research institutes.
Harold Lasswell, whose book *The Policy Sciences,* published
in 1951, heralded the new interest in government policy
problems, wrote:

> The point is that all the resources of our expanding social
> sciences need to be directed toward the basic conflicts in our
> civilization which are so vividly disclosed by the application of
> the scientific method to the study of personality and culture.[18]

Lawrence Chamberlin, the former Vice President of Columbia University wrote of the necessary structural changes
in the university:

> The need for applying a blend of disciplines and skills to the
> problems of little known areas—for purposes of warfare, gov-

ernmental administration, and diplomacy—precipitated the establishment of new research and instructional patterns because the conventional departmental structures were simply not adequate to meet the demands of the job.[19]

Besides the methodological and organizational questions, the war and the immediate aftermath produced a broad consensus on many foreign policy issues, the most important of which, of course, was the Soviet Union and its role in international politics. Donald Blackmer acknowledges:

> I do believe that the terms in which the conflict [the Cold War] was explained, by scholars as well as government spokesmen, had the effect of creating a partially distorted image of the Soviet Union, an image which—correct or not—suited the national needs of the early post war years but did not prepare us adequately to meet the circumstances of the sixties.[20]

American Cold Warriors likewise shared the conviction that America had inherited from her dominant role in World War II the responsibility for managing the shape of the post-war international economy and political world order. This meant simultaneously blocking the expansion of Russian (i.e., Communist) hegemony over China and easing Third World countries into independence under the benign tutelage of the United States. As we have seen, this was a job for scholars as well as policy-makers. Asian scholars who had worked for the government during the war were presented with the operational problem of American policy toward the occupied areas in Asia. Many OSS and OWI researchers followed the OSS Office of Research and Analysis when it was transferred to the State Department in 1946. At this time, in contrast to the issue of confrontation with the Soviet Union, many Asian issues, particularly China and Vietnam, remained open, allowing for divergent interpretations of events. In the late forties, Asian scholars like Cora Dubois and Milton Sacks thought that American involvement or support of the French in Indochina, would, as Dr. Dubois wrote in memos at the time, "embroil us in a twenty year war in Indochina." But, with "the loss of China" the political climate of the fifties tolerated no dissent on Cold War issues. The right wing and its friends in Congress believed "liberals" in the State Department had "lost" China, and were planning to desert Chiang Kai-shek. In early 1949, security investigators began visiting heads of divisions in the State Department's intelligence branches, inquiring which researchers had written passages of memos critical of United States policy toward China and Indochina. The Chinese intervention in the Korean war added fuel to the China Lobby's crusade against China hands in the State Department. In a short time, all but the most dedicated of the scholars-turned-bureaucrats had retreated to the protective climate of the Academy.

But the loyalty purges of the late Truman years gave way to McCarthy era vendettas against "wrong thinkers" in government and the education establishment. The investigations, which took their toll in the academic community, were focused, however, on the liberal hands in the foreign service. Besides the foreign service officers, the attacks singled out Owen Lattimore, a professor at Johns Hopkins University, who had advised the government of Chiang Kai-shek. He was branded a traitor because of his disillusionment with the Kuomintang. The Lattimore case and particularly his connection to the primary scholarly organization of the Asian field, the Institute for Pacific Relations, drew the attention of investigators to the scholarly community. In his book on the effects of the China Lobby on American foreign policy, Ross Koen wrote:

The most immediate and direct effects of the acceptance of the China Lobby propaganda were unquestionably felt by the organization most intimately concerned with the Far East, the Institute for Pacific Relations. Ultimately, however, these effects were also felt by other organizations (such as the Foreign Policy Association and the Council on Foreign Relations) and by foundations (such as Ford, Carnegie and Rockefeller) which provided much of the money to finance the undertakings of the scholarly organizations.[21]

One of the results of the McCarthy investigations was that the IPR lost its tax exempt status: the prelude to its total demise. Koen points out that foundation support for IPR, which was $100,000 a year in 1951, primarily from the Carnegie and Rockefeller Foundations, had dropped to $15,000 in 1952. More important, the IPR never recovered from the attacks on its loyalty, even in the eyes of the scholarly community. Support for IPR, primarily from John D. Rockefeller, III, was shifted to the newly founded Asia Society. The Asia Society refused to merge with the dying IPR in 1957, stressing "the Society was only interested in social and cultural activities."

There is considerable debate about the effects of these years on the scholarly community. Many scholars who lived through the horrors of the McCarthy years think there has been no permanent imprint, in spite of the shattering impact of the investigations on free speech at the time. It is widely believed, however, among liberal members of the field that the McCarthy investigations, particularly the Lattimore case, reinforced the general disillusionment felt by Asian scholars in the late forties with the process of government advising and policy-making by scholars. More recently, critical scholars have argued that the fears of controversy engendered by the McCarthy era prevented an entire generation of scholars from critically analyzing United States policy in Vietnam.[22] A look at the roster of early scholarly critics and teach-in activity against the Vietnam war confirms this theory; with the exception of a few experts on American foreign policy, nearly all of the early Vietnam critics were not Asian scholars or social scientists, but self-made experts. The Association for Asian Studies did not take up the question of the Vietnam war until 1968, when the issue was forced on them at their annual meeting by the insurgent Committee of Concerned Asian Scholars. Whether this early reluctance to speak out on the war came directly from the personal traumas of the McCarthy era or from the ideological consensus on American foreign policy produced by those years is perhaps a question better left to psychiatrists. Suffice it to say that the consensus existed, as other essays in this book show, and as the record of the profession on the war demonstrates.

Asian scholars frequently contrast their field and Russian studies to stress their independence from government. The fact that Russian experts did not suffer from McCarthy era attacks suggests to them that the Russian field was more closely aligned with government views than the Chinese field. It is true that the backgrounds of the majority of the scholars in these two fields have produced significant differences.

Experts on the Soviet Union were few before World War II. The immediate post-war boom in Russian studies was largely a product of government and foundation interest in the Soviet Union as "the Enemy." Many scholars in the field were trained in social science and later persuaded to turn their skills to "the Russian problem." Pre-World War II Chinese studies, on the other hand, were dominated by historians and students of Chinese culture and history. In the immediate post-war period, the pattern of Chinese studies differed considerably from Russian studies. Because Russian studies developed initially in a Cold War context, the field was dominated by professional anti-Communists, military strategists, and Russian or Eastern European émigrés. China experts, on the other hand, typically came from a sinological tradition and were less intellectually involved in the study of Chinese military strategy and politics.[23]

During the fifties, China scholars were less directly involved with government than their Soviet counterparts. Because of the nuclear arms race and the Cold War confrontations in Europe, the overriding policy interest of the American government was the Soviet threat. Although the Korean War sparked the Army to fund a number of studies of war prisoners, government research interest in Asia remained at a low level. The China Lobby kept up its attempts to prove Mainland China was the enemy of mankind, but the fact that China presented no nuclear threat meant that the China experts were not blessed with the kind of Defense Department largesse Russian experts were. The State Department, which was interested in the China question for diplomatic reasons, had learned its lesson from the McCarthy era; to this day it requests only a mere $100,000 a year for university social science research in contrast to the over $138 million spent by the military.

But the fact that Asian scholars received little money from the government is not the only test of the interaction between government and the scholar. Professor Blackmer, in his paper on Soviet Studies, asks the rhetorical question of whether Russian scholars' analysis was affected by their relationship with the government. His answer, as relevant to Chinese as to Soviet studies, is:

> How could it have been otherwise? Specialists on the Soviet Union were citizens as well as scholars, no more immune than anyone else to the postwar climate of fear and frustration . . . they had good reason to be profoundly convinced that there was a vital job to be done of educating the American public and raising a new generation of scholars to an appreciation of the Communist threat and of how it could be countered.[24]

Asian scholars were on the front lines of the great cultural war against Communism. Unlike the Russian scholar, who was not schooled in Russian culture, China scholars had a heavy stake in defeating the Communist threat to Chinese cultural traditions. While government coffers remained closed from the late forties the major foundations began to build up Chinese studies centers at major universities. The conclusions of a 1949 report on plans for the best use of the foundation's resources were symbolic of the Ford Foundation's commitment to the role university social scientists could play in foreign policy. In the words of President H. Rowan Gaither, Jr., the Foundation's trustees "decided in

September, 1950, that initially the Foundation would devote its resources to efforts to advance world peace, democracy, economic well-being, education, and the knowledge of the behavior of man." Between 1951 and 1966, the Ford Foundation was to spend $270 million on international affairs; $155 million went to the development of area centers and international studies at American universities. The Rockefeller and the Carnegie Foundations agreed on the importance of these centers, following Ford with their more limited resources.

This holy crusade, like all crusades, had its dark side. Asian experts who had migrated from the State Department to the anonymous safety of the CIA and a few "enlightened" policy-makers realized it was important that Asian scholars get government financing for research and travel. Since no money was forthcoming from a conservative Congress and policy-makers thought it best that these scholars appear "independent" of government, the CIA set up a network of foundations and "research" organizations. Academics with proper anti-Communist credentials were rewarded with trips to Asia and grants by the Asia Foundation, the Congress for Cultural Freedom, and other CIA front groups.

The Asia Foundation was (and is) a major weapon in the American government's attempt to build up anti-Communist elites in Asia, though its effectiveness has been reduced by its exposure as a CIA front in 1966.[25] American and Asian scholars were its pawns (or occasionally, vice versa), sometimes unwittingly, sometimes not. The major part of the Foundation's resources went to supporting Asian magazines and cultural organizations in cooperation with the Congress for Cultural Freedom. One such project in 1955, sponsored by the Congress for Cultural Freedom in conjunction with the International Rescue Committee (another CIA aided group), provided books in French and English for the students and faculty of the new university in exile in Saigon; the school had become the nucleus for the refugees from North Vietnam. Another such project is the annual grant by the Asia Foundation to a variety of professional associations such as the American Political Science Association and the American Sociological Association, to bring the Foundation's carefully screened Asian scholars to annual professional meetings.[26]

The availability of these resources, although primarily to support Asians, meant that American scholars were exposed to a carefully chosen and groomed intelligentsia who gained their professional visibility at home and abroad through the mediation of the CIA. Although the Asia Foundation did not spend a great deal of money directly on American scholars and their research, it sent many young scholars overseas for language and cultural training and to teach in Asia Foundation-supported schools. During these years, American scholars, as American citizens, saw Asia through the prism of American Cold War interests; as scholars they saw Asia and her intellectual elite reflected in a CIA looking-glass.

In the early sixties, as the balance of nuclear terror supposedly stabilized, and independence movements swept the Third World, American preoccupations shifted from nuclear holocaust to counter-insurgency. In its most sophisticated form, this approach included the use of non-military weapons like aid programs, political infiltration, and education to assure non-Communist development. The new style was clearly articulated by Defense Secretary Robert McNamara in his Montreal speech, taking to task advocates of reliance on conventional military power to maintain America's global supremacy:

> There is still among us an almost irradicable tendency to think of our security problem as being exclusively a military problem. We know that our military mission to be most effective requires understanding of the political, social and economic setting in which we fulfill our responsibilities.[27]

This sophisticated approach to defense planning in the computer era has been aptly named "The McNamara

Revolution." The accompanying changes in foreign policy and the intellectual work behind it might be better called "the Rostow Revolution." Walt Whitman Rostow, head of the State Department's Policy Planning Council under Kennedy, and an architect of Johnson's early Vietnam strategy, had, through his work in development economics at M.I.T., developed a special view of the Third World and the Communist threat. In his book, *View From the Seventh Floor,* Rostow wrote of the Communists:

> They are the scavengers of the modernization process. They believe that the techniques of political centralization under dictatorial control—and the projected image of Soviet and Chinese Communist economic progress—will persuade hesitant men, faced by great transitional problems, that the communist model should be adopted for modernization, even at the cost of surrendering human liberty. They believe that they can exploit effectively the resentments built up in many of these areas against colonial rule and that they can associate themselves effectively with the desire of the emerging nations for independence, for status on the world scene, and for material progress.[28]

The problem, according to Rostow and his colleagues in other universities, was to get there first with American plans and M.I.T. economists.

This new strategy was the ticket for social scientists. For Asian scholars the growing American preoccupation with the Third World in general and counter-insurgency in particular meant new money and the possibility of rehabilitation in the eyes of government policy-makers. Policy-makers and the military had affirmed their interest not only in the Chinese threat, but all Asian nations with instability problems. The major enemy was no longer the Soviet Union or even China as hostile nuclear powers, but Communist-inspired change in the Third World.

As the nuclear bomb spawned a generation of nuclear strategists in the universities, the new counter-insurgency strategy midwifed a generation of development strategists.

If the SAC bomber was the symbol of the fifties, the Special Forces man was the embodiment of the Kennedy era. Development was another weapon of the Cold War, and military strategists were still in command. A report by the Defense Science Board (the group of top university advisers to the Defense Department) summarized the military's interest in social science:

> The DOD mission now embraces problems and responsibilities which have previously not been assigned to the military establishment. Pacification, assistance and the battle of ideas are major segments of the DOD responsibility. Hardware alone will not win modern wars without the effective use of manpower in foreign environments, an understanding of the dynamics of social change, and a perception of the varying needs, attitudes, and ethics of other peoples.[29]

For the universities, this development was to be far more revolutionary than the advent of nuclear strategy. The military's interest in development and insurgency was much more far ranging in its effect on the social sciences than its interest in nuclear strategy or Communist ideology in the fifties. Counter-insurgency strategists needed to know the possible political, social, and economic factors in a country's development to do their work. One Army Lieutenant General summed up the scope of the problem:

> . . . if those people [the military] go in there, we think they will do a better job if they understand some of the output of behavioral science research which tells them, for example, that in this country there is a strong division between this group and that group, to be careful of certain superstitions or observe these social boundary lines concerning women, if you will, or about any one of a number of the potential areas of individual or group conflict. If our people go in ignorant, without any guidance, we don't think they will do the same effective job.[30]

The result was the dominance of the Pentagon over all other government agencies in funding overseas research by social scientists; by the mid-sixties, the Pentagon was spending $45 million for overseas research by social scientists on such varying topics as witchcraft in the Congo, the tribes of Northeast Thailand, and "troop-community relations" in Korea. Hundreds of millions more were being spent on psychological training to equip soldiers to serve in foreign countries.

But perhaps more important for the long-range effect on the scholarly community than the military's interest in social science was the Kennedy administration's rejuvenation of the liberal ideal of public service. Although the institutional reorganization of the university to serve government research needs had been developing with foundation help since World War II, the Kennedy administration accomplished the integration into government of the most "enlightened" and heretofore most critical members of the Academy. Previously, social scientists had been involved with government either as military strategists or as experts on Communism. Most of these scholars were conservatives, identified with militant Cold War anti-Communism. The Kennedy strategists' development of counter-insurgency theory sparked liberal interests in the problems of the Third World. If serving the government no longer meant mouthing Cold War rhetoric, but instead supporting independence movements and designing economic development plans to promote stability, university social scientists could gladly join the government team. These new interests brought under the government wing hundreds of social scientists and development economists who had been drawn into area studies by the liberal causes of anti-colonialism and economic development, but who had remained critical of the Dulles diplomacy.

The roles that American social scientists play in relation to government can be grouped in three general categories: public relations, intelligence gathering, and pacification. Asian scholars play these roles much as other social scientists. Agreement with the specifics of government policy in one's field of expertise is not necessary; many Asian scholars like

John Fairbank and John Lewis are still called as government consultants in spite of their opposition to present policy on China or Vietnam. However, social scientists who work for the government, or define their work as policy-relevant, do share certain common views. These views might be summed up as an interest in implementing rather than substantially changing the operation of the American political system. Professor Galbraith describes this consensus in an updated version of Daniel Bell's "End of Ideology" thesis:

> Social innovation no longer has overtones of revolution and the academic, like the large, intellectual community no longer engages in disquieting conversations on revolution. The revolution as delineated by Marx, assumed the progressive immiseration of the working class. Instead of the expected impoverishment, there has been increasing affluence. . . . Everything on which the revolution seemed to depend, and even the revolution itself, has disintegrated. Not even academic disputation can easily survive such an erosion.[31]

Noam Chomsky, who might agree with Professor Galbraith's formulation of this consensus, disagress sharply with its *raison d'être:*

> A good case can be made for the conclusion that there is indeed something of a consensus among intellectuals who have already achieved power and affluence, or who sense that they can achieve them by "accepting society as it is" and promoting the values that are "being honored" in this society.[32]

An examination of the roles Asian scholars play in regard to two policy problems—China and Thailand—reveals the superficial variety in function and the basically similar ideology and effect of these intellectuals.

In a 1967 article in *Atlantic Monthly,* Harvard's James C. Thomson discusses the issues facing policy-makers and China experts in the early days of the Sino-Soviet split. Almost in passing, he casts interesting light on the function China scholars play in formulating policy. He describes a series of policy-planning meetings in the State Department in 1962 which were faced with such questions as: "How to deal with bipolar adversaries? How to approach fractured Communist parties in third countries? Should we try to manipulate the split or lie low? And of central importance, what to do about mainland China?"[33]

This approach is hardly surprising to anyone familiar with State Department views on China: it is a typical statement of the American belief that our adversaries—China and Russia—threaten the political stability of the world and must be kept in check. What is much more interesting, however, is how the bureaucracy and "the intellectuals" in the Department and the White House, like Roger Hilsman, Arthur Schlesinger, Thomson and others, finally agreed to deal with the touchiest problem: What to do about China? According to Thomson, Secretary of State Dean Rusk had his own view of how to meet the problem: "Why not encourage," the Secretary of State mused, "a series of studies of the China problem in all its ramifications, to be undertaken on the outside? By something *solid* like the Council on Foreign Relations, perhaps under foundation grant." The result was an eleven-volume study on "The United States and China in World Affairs," edited by Robert Blum, the now deceased former president of the Asia Foundation, and written by top China experts, including A. Doak Barnett, A. M. Halpern, Lucien Pye, and Alexander Eckstein.[34]

This example is of interest for several reasons. The volumes produced represent a distillation of the views of top American China experts on many facets of the "China problem" and of Sino-American relations. More important, the idea and execution of the study suggest how scholars are mobilized and resources made available for government policy studies. The example defines the role of the area expert (as distinguished from the social scientist-pacifier) and his function as a public relations man for policy-makers.

It was natural, of course, for Secretary Rusk to suggest that the Council on Foreign Relations sponsor the study. He is one of its charter members. The Council has been one of the major go-betweens for government, industry, and the academy, and its off-the-record seminars provide the ideal place to float new policy ideas. Started in 1921, CFR allocated itself the continuing task of educating policy-makers and businessmen, by bringing them into contact with well-known scholars from the Eastern establishment. One of these scholars was Henry Kissinger, now head of President Nixon's National Security Council staff, whose books on nuclear strategy were published by the Council and shaped American defense strategy in the fifties. Kissinger's book, *Nuclear Weapons and Foreign Policy,* a carefully drawn critique of Eisenhower's nuclear policy, stressed the need for a flexible use of nuclear weapons as opposed to the Dulles doctrine of massive retaliation. It was one intellectual foundation on which Kennedy strategists later rebuilt American strategic policy. In spite of CFR's "conservative" orientation, projected by its major publication, *Foreign Affairs,* the Council transcends partisan political issues. Although most of its corporate members and contributors are Republicans, Theodore White reports in his *Making of a President, 1964,* that of the eighty-two names on a list prepared for President Kennedy to staff his new State Department, sixty-three were CFR members.[35] In this sense, the most important function of CFR is producing a consensus among scholars, foundation officials, businessmen, and policy-makers on American foreign policy.[36]

At the time of Rusk's proposal, the Sino-Soviet split and the imminent development of a Chinese nuclear bomb were fostering government interest in the resources of the scholarly community. Foundations like Carnegie, Rockefeller, and Ford had supported East Asian centers in universities during the fifties, but had primarily provided support to the established centers like Harvard, staffed primarily with experts in language, art and history. The sixties, with the growing threat of a Chinese nuclear presence, and American belief that the Chinese were responsible for insurgent movements throughout Southeast Asia and elsewhere, sparked new foundation and government interest in Chinese studies. Research on the kind of policy questions that concerned the State Department was particularly stressed. The Sino-Soviet split meant to liberal policy-makers that China could no longer be dealt with merely as an Asian adjunct of Soviet Communism. China specialists who had been working in Chinese history or thought were encouraged to "apply" their familiarity with the country to the strategic problems Communist China presented for the United States. This new strategic interest in China of the early sixties also coincided with a general liberalizing of American attitudes toward China. As a result, younger policy-makers from CIA and State, many of them on sabbaticals at universities, began to pick the brains of the scholars who had a more benign view of the Chinese than State Department China hands.

But the most important role of the scholar-public relations man is not to furnish policy-makers with new ideas. In the CFR study, as elsewhere, their task was to hush the clamors for liberalization of our China policy by the younger China hands inside and outside the State Department. The result of the weighty eleven-volume study of course, was that the Rusk containment policy received the academic seal of approval.

That the study affirmed old views is hardly surprising; many of the scholars who participated in the series had been spinning out the same analysis since the late fifties. In any event it is inconceivable that any group of scholars, whatever their views, could have a mitigating effect on the inflexible Mr. Rusk. Nevertheless, the job of "teacher of princes" is a well established and respected role for social scientists and China experts. Ithiel Pool in a recent paper has described this role for social scientists:

> They see themselves as taming the violence of man's untutored nature by instilling the quality of reason and the humane

heritage of the arts. It is the policy scientist, who by the practice of intelligence, tames the exercise of naked force in the practices of government and preserves respect for the humanity of man.[37]

As modern-day Machiavellis, liberal China specialists are engaged in a constant struggle to fend off the forces of irrationality, especially the right-wing China Lobby with its nuclear designs on China. To try to achieve this, China scholars keep up a constant traffic to Washington. This relationship was institutionalized in 1966 by the appointment of State Department advisory groups on the Far East and Southeast Asia.

It is not entirely clear who advises whom in these meetings. Most scholars agree that, as far as they are concerned, few new ideas come from these sessions. One Harvard participant says, "The panels are useful to give the State Department a forum to defend its policies. Left to themselves, they would not have to do that." One China hand in the State Department has a slightly different view, however. "The main purpose of these sessions is not to exchange policy advice," he says, "but to acquaint the scholars with the complexities of our policy process." Once convinced of the validity of those complications to rapid change in policy, the argument goes, the scholar-diplomat is more appreciative of State Department policies.

The other function of the scholar-diplomat is to venture where government fears to tread. Scholars from the Center for International Affairs at Harvard, for instance, were recently involved in a three-year series of talks with Japanese leaders on security problems presented by the Sino-Soviet split, Chinese nuclear development, and the cultural revolution. Professor Henry Kissinger, while still at Harvard, helped set off a round of Vietnam peace-feelers by traveling to Paris with messages to be transmitted to Ho Chi Minh by some French professors. After the detonation of the Chinese bomb, some Asian scholars were indirectly involved in a Defense Department project to assess Chinese nuclear policy and capabilities. The Pentagon feared a panic among American allies in Asia and an astronomical demand for further build-up of forces. American planners judged such a further build-up unnecessary, and dispatched embassy people as well as a few scholars to reassure Asian bureaucrats that the Chinese hadn't perfected their delivery capability yet.

The main public relations role for area specialists is to rationalize government policy. In this sense, scholars can also be important mediators between society's values and the government's interests. Granted, most liberal China experts believe that the conservative views of the American public on China and the top policy-makers who share these views, are responsible for our unenlightened China policy. As one scholar who worked for the National Security Council put it, "The problem with our China policy is Peking, Dean Rusk, and domestic politics, in that order." Yet if experts in the field are the major source of information for policy-makers and the public, perhaps the problem with our China policy may lie closer to the doorstep of the Academy than China experts admit. The fact that China experts see Peking as the major reason for America's unenlightened China policy is a value judgment shared by their pupils among the public and the policy-makers. If China scholars have any real influence in their relationship with the government, it is in these basic attitudes, transmitted through scholarly writings and lectures on China.

What are these values? Professor Thomson describes American attitudes toward China in his *Atlantic* article:

> No other nation in Asia has been on the receiving end of so much American goodwill, good works, and philanthropy. . . . An open door to China came to mean . . . 400 million potential Christians—our special receptacle for the outflow of our altruism, and our special protectorate against the obvious greed of the European and Japanese predators. We admired Chinese culture, liked the Chinese people, delighted in Chinese food and deplored China's patent incapacity for effective

self-government. China made us feel good: it fed our sense of benevolence and moral superiority.[38]

The only problem with this view (a curiously benign description of current American attitudes toward our Asian enemy), according to Professor Thomson, is that "our emotional investment [in China] was uniquely high, far out of line with our strategic or economic interests." Thomson does not state his view of American strategic interests, implying that there is sufficient agreement among China experts on this point that it need not be explored. In a sense, what American strategic interests are, in Thomson's description, or the eyes of the scholarly community, is less important than their belief that Asia is "our special receptacle against the obvious greed of European and Japanese predators." Although Thompson admittedly describes these views as those of the American public, they are shared by the majority of American Asian scholars.

Most scholars, agreeing with Thomson's description of the benevolent role the United States played toward China prior to World War II, see the American role toward China now as a problem of "taming the Chinese dragon." As Dwight Perkins and Morton Halperin put it:

Whatever United States intentions toward the Communists' continued existence in China were, American policy was clearly directed at checking any further Communist expansion. Therefore, setting aside Mao's ideological predilections, he had to reckon with American opposition any time he desired to extend Chinese power.[39]

This view of the policy motivations behind American policy in the Far East has been effectively challenged by David Horowitz, Gabriel Kolko, and John Gittings writing on the formation of the American Empire. Gittings, for example, concludes:

The Open Door was the diplomatic prerequisite for dollar diplomacy, according to Taft's definition of American policy as including active intervention to secure for our merchandise and our capitalists opportunity for profitable investment.[40]

In the post-war period, American hegemony in Asia was predicated on the independence of Asian colonies from their British, French, and Dutch masters, and the encirclement of the Chinese Communists after the "loss" of China.

Viewed from the perspective of perpetual American military interventions in Asia and the encirclement of China by American military bases, it is hard to believe that China's attitude toward the United States could be anything but hostile. But Mr. Gittings' perception of China is not shared by American policy advisers or must China experts. The major issue of United States-China relations, as Thomson expresses it,

> is not to isolate it [China] or make it go away, but how to ease it into some sort of rational and mutually acceptable relationship with the other three quarters of mankind.[41]

This sentiment was echoed in the December 20, 1967, statement on China by the Freedom Affairs Institute.[42] The group, which included senior academic China advisers such as A. Doak Barnett, Robert Scalapino, and Lucien Pye, designated themselves as "moderate scholars." The goal of American policy in the Far East, as they see it, is "to avoid a major war in the Asia-Pacific region." To do this, "it is essential that the U.S. continue to deter, restrain, and counterbalance Chinese policy." The obstacle, of course, to waging peace in Asia is "the isolationist fanaticism" of the Chinese. Thus, the "humanizing" function Professor Pool prescribes for scholars is directed not toward United States policy-makers, but toward the Chinese. This view dovetails nicely with tougher anti-Communist views of government policy-makers on China, and impedes China scholars from taking too critical a swipe at the fundamentals of United States Asian policy.

Once the parameters of policy are set, the China scholars are useful in another role: that of intelligence-gatherer. Having accepted the Cold War consensus, the scholar begins to gather data that directly or indirectly support it. Once consensus is reached, critical questioning is unnecessary. Ithiel Pool writes of this data gathering:

> The intelligence function is the bringing to the consciousness of the decision maker knowledge of the conditions and consequences of his action. It includes the devices of interviewing, experimentation, espionage, participant observation, analysis, model building, introspection, computation, the census—everything that if done with rigor and objectivity deserves to be called broadly scientific.[48]

Admittedly, for China experts who are shut off from contact with the culture which they are trying to study, all study of China takes on the coloration of the gathering of intelligence. But if Professor Pool's view is accepted, all social science research is of use to a policy-maker as intelligence.

Most government sponsored university research on China fits this category, accepting the framework of official categories and responding to current policy issues as defined by the government. This process was reinforced by a major development of the sixties—the sponsorship of most research on China by the Defense Department and the Arms Control and Disarmament Agency. This research is focused almost exclusively on the economic and political factors which affect Chinese military capability. For example, scholarly research sponsored by the government on Chinese economic development is largely confined to in-depth studies of individual sectors of the economy that will help government strategists predict the resources China can commit to building nuclear and conventional military capabilities. The CIA in recent years has zeroed in on the question of agricultural productivity as a measure of which resources China can divert to defense; scholars and Chinese research assistants in American universities like the University of California at Berkeley have received CIA contracts to make these estimates.

By far the most compelling recent issue for China watchers both inside the government and in the university has been the cultural revolution. The CIA, in particular, took an interest in this question, and sent teams of its own China experts touring the country, interviewing scholars and offering money to support their research; this CIA-scholarly relationship is judged crucial by some scholars working on contemporary political and military problems since the CIA is a prime source of inside information.

Interest in China is not new in the Agency; some of the more liberal government China experts fled there during the McCarthy era to do their work in peace, away from the judging eyes of Congress and the right wing. Interest in China in the Agency, however, has reached a new high. The CIA has stepped up efforts to recruit graduate students in Chinese studies into the Agency, and has begun, in recent years, sending CIA analysts on sabbaticals to top university China centers. Researchers at Harvard, for example, were in 1967, 1968 and 1969 working on a massive translation project of Red Guard newspapers. Financed, according to Harvard, by the East Asian Research Center, the project was directed by a top CIA China expert who recently returned to the Agency from a year at Harvard.

A significant part of the China watching goes on from Santa Monica, California, the headquarters of the RAND Corporation. Most RAND researchers are preoccupied with the strategic questions of China's nuclear capability. The effect of the cultural revolution, of course, bears on this problem. In a recent RAND document, Alice Langsley Hsieh writes:

> As a result of the latter ("the so-called Great Proletarian Cultural Revolution"), students of Chinese Communist affairs have been forced to revise radically, if not reverse, many of their earlier assessments of the political cohesion and stability of the Communist Chinese regime. However, to date I have

seen little evidence that the "Cultural Revolution" has affected China's nuclear-missile progress. Nor have I seen any evidence that the "Cultural Revolution" has changed the basic premise underlying China's military strategy.[44]

Most of the RAND writing and government contracts reflect this exclusive interest in the cultural revolution—its effects on China's military strength and foreign policy intentions.

The other major policy preoccupation of China experts has been the strategic question of whether a massive Chinese ground intervention in Indochina is possible. This question was the source of consultations between scholars and policy-makers at countless State Department panels, luncheon conferences, and private telephone calls in recent years. It has also precipitated a plethora of Defense Department-sponsored studies of Chinese foreign policy objectives; a particular preoccupation is the factors that went into the Chinese decision to cross the Yalu River and intervene in the Korean War, and whether this intervention is analogous to the Vietnam situation. The question caught a number of liberal university Chinese experts in a political dilemma. For many years they had been arguing in State Department meetings that Chinese statements about sparking anti-imperialist revolts were primarily rhetorical since Chinese foreign policy was non-interventionist in practice. Although this view had no apparent impact on State Department China policy, one scholar recalls that Secretary Rusk took up the argument when the same liberal scholars argued that China might intervene in Vietnam if the United States continued bombing the North.

Such politicking is not within the normal purview of intelligence-gatherers or technocrats, however. This apparent conflict of views on whether China is an aggressive power has not been discussed in any literature so far, and China strategists confine themselves to reporting "the facts" rather than focusing on "political" questions of United States policy. Thus a RAND Corporation report steps delicately around the point:

. . . in fact, in the course of 1965, after the initiation by the U.S. of the bombing of North Vietnam, the Chinese were genuinely concerned about the possible spill-over of the bombing from North Vietnam to the mainland—a concern that was revived to some degree in August of this year when the United States initiated attacks within ten miles of the Chinese border; that the Chinese are not likely to go out of their way to intervene in Vietnam and thus face the possibility of a direct confrontation with the United States. . . .[45]

The purpose of the intelligence-gatherer's job is not to question the wisdom of an American bombing policy which might bring China into the war, or of the United States war policy in general. Noam Chomsky writes of the scholarly views on whether the United States should intervene in Vietnam:

The spectrum of "responsible" opinion extends from those who proclaim openly that we have the right to those who formulate our goals in a way that presupposes it.[46]

But if intelligence-gatherers and scholarly public relations men operate within the confines of United States policy objectives, it is the social scientist-pacifier who helps define these goals and prepares the way for the substitution of American values into foreign countries. The social scientist-pacifier is not an expert on a country or region like the area specialist, but a theorist who studies the structure and function of society and its various elements. In the international context, such a social scientist is a theorist of social change and development, of conflict and conflict resolution, and of revolution. Ithiel Pool writes of his function that

it is the social sciences that give us the most reliable information about where riots breed, how criminals can be controlled, whether insurgents will maintain rule of a university or village, and how nuclear war can be avoided.[47]

More important, it is the social scientist, the vanguard of American modernization force, who uses his tools to substitute democratic values for those of the indigenous culture.

Harold Lasswell recognized this function as early as 1942, when he wrote:

> The developing science of democracy is an arsenal of implements for the achievement of democratic ideals. We know enough to know that democracies do not know how to live: they perish through ignorance . . . without knowledge democracy will surely fail.[48]

The objectification of this kind of social science, and its application to government policy reached new heights in the Kennedy era. In this post-nuclear age, social science sought to become to counter-insurgency what physics had been to the nuclear age. Roger Hilsman wrote of this period:

> By 1961, the great debate on nuclear strategy and on the implications of the limited, conventional war in Korea had clarified the requirements for deterring both. In the meantime, however, the Chinese Communists had become the advocates of a more subtle use of force, a way under and around our defenses. . . .
>
> "Revolutionary warfare equals guerrilla tactics plus political action" ran one slogan. It was a way of using military force, not across national boundaries but inside them—a new kind of "internal war."[49]

The new strategy, developed by scholar-diplomats like Rostow and Hilsman had to be sold to policy-makers, especially the military. Robert Kennedy and other liberals turned, appropriately enough, to the universities who had developed the idea to provide this education. After much hurrying to and from Cambridge to Washington and back, a group of scholars from M.I.T., including Max Millikan, Lucien Pye, and Donald Blackmer, put together a seminar for high level "students" from State, DOD, AID, and the CIA. Throughout the early months of the Kennedy administration the seminar met, and visiting scholars discussed theories about social change, instability, and Communist exploitation of the modernization process. Later many of those scholars shifted their attention to the military's war colleges, where they continue to teach occasional courses on counter-insurgency.

Indochina was the testing ground for these theories. Social scientists at Michigan State, of course, had been conducting their own laboratory on police security, terrorism, and political stability in Vietnam since the mid-fifties. But at the time, Vietnam was not defined by the Eisenhower administration as a "military" problem, and American intervention in the internal affairs of that country was still limited to CIA activity.[50] By the time the new Kennedy counter-insurgency strategy was developed, Vietnam had become enough of a military problem so that social science experimentation independent of direct military application was impossible.

In the 1960's, Vietnam became the social scientists' Manhattan Project. Hundreds of social scientists have trooped off to 'Nam for the summer to perform evaluations of popular support of the South Vietnamese government and the effectiveness of Vietnamese forces for the Defense Department, and make studies of land tenure patterns and economic plans for AID. During a war-time situation, of course, scholarship is tightly controlled. Most research is carried out by military contractors like the Stanford Research Institute and RAND. University researchers are hired by these groups as consultants or researchers. Although some social scientists maintain they are learning valuable lessons about "urbanization" and "political socialization," they are deeply involved in studying such military problems as NLF defectors, and the lack of popular support for South Vietnamese regional and popular forces. United States troops, if they were withdrawn on United States terms, would be replaced with droves of American development economists, financed by the Ford Foundation and AID, to put Vietnam on its feet, and attempt to reconstruct a high producing capitalist economy.

More instructive for the future of United States policy in Asia than the role of social scientists in Vietnam at present, however, is the lessons these scholars have drawn from

Vietnam. Their primary conclusion is that the biggest problem in Vietnam was the ill-timed and clumsy use of large-scale United States military force, a mistake which should not be repeated. Ithiel Pool thus concludes that

> To the American government the lesson is that it must find effective ways of responding to limited disruptions by means short of war. We have learned, for example, that divisions of troops are not very effective against undergrounds, and we have to learn how to use police and intelligence operations.[51]

Social scientists, if their role in Vietnam and their relation to government during the Kennedy era are any indication, will play the vanguard role in this pacification effort. In this light, the role of social science in Thailand is perhaps more informative and typical than the Vietnam example. One obvious reason is that without a war of the scale going in Vietnam, social scientists have greater freedom to move about to conduct their research in Thailand. Drawing on the bitter American experience in Vietnam, social scientists are seeking ways to defeat Thai insurgents by political and economic methods, and by the substitution of American values for indigenous ones.

The volume of research alone suggests this conclusion. The current list of projects on Thailand sponsored by the Pentagon is sixty-three pages long, and lists 508 reports already delivered. The reports reflect Professor Pool's advice; the research reflects a preoccupation with counterinsurgency and "village security" rather than large-scale conventional military intervention on the Vietnam model. In 1967, the Defense Department's Advanced Research Projects Agency (ARPA) project AGILE, the DOD's world-wide counter-insurgency R&D program, had 157 American anthropologists, engineers, ordinance specialists, and other technical experts in Thailand, at an annual cost of $10 million.[52] As one Army researcher puts it, "The strategy in Vietnam was to send ten Marines for every peasant. In Thailand it's ten anthropologists." Most of this research is being sponsored by ARPA or AID in conjunction with the Tribal

Research Centre in Chiengmai or American-funded Thai research groups in Bangkok.

What is it these researchers are worried about? In an article in the *Boston Globe* in 1966, former American Ambassador to Thailand and President of the Asia Society, Kenneth Young, writes:

> The main trouble Thailand faces in coping with actual Communist revolutionary warfare comes from the physical and psychological gap between the government and the people in remote, vulnerable borderlands.[53]

What frightens the American and Thai governments is the security of the northeast border, an area peopled by the Red Lahu tribe which extends into Burma. The area also touches Laos at a point where the Pathet Lao are strong, and is close to China's Yünnan Province. The major "cash" crop in this area is opium, the consumption of which—according to Western anthropologists working for the government—is the reason for the tribe's general disinterest in politics. The combination of this area's proximity to "Communist dominated" areas of China and Laos, and the peasants' apathy, makes them ripe for Communist insurgency, according to Thai and United States officials.

Much of the social science research in Thailand has been anthropological work in the northeast region on the prevention of opium consumption and the loyalty of particular tribes to the Thai government; its ideological framework is the same cultural imperialism that has helped suppress the populations of Latin American and African countries. The Thai government has programs supported by AID "to stabilize tribal communities" by relocating them in settlement areas like the early Vietnamese strategic hamlets and the pacification program. American and Thai economists are at work on agricultural demonstration projects or "rural development" programs, which are a part of these stabilization programs. Border Security is the special responsibility of the Border Patrol Police (BPP) which is financed and staffed, according to social scientists doing evaluations on its work, by Americans.

ARPA social science research is aimed at defining village political structure in the remote regions of the country. Based on these studies of the structure and customs of the villages, the government sends out teams of "self-help" experts including sanitary engineers and information officers "newly armed with understanding of these tribes." According to one military magazine, "information of this type is vital to the Thai military in attempting to counter insidious forms of subversion."[54] Other research examines the village security systems.

American social scientists working for ARPA are dedicated to stopping a potential Thai Liberation Front; ARPA is engaged in developing counter-insurgency technology, like infra-red detection devices, to find insurgents under jungle cover. Many other social scientists are at work in Thailand for AID on economic development missions, studying the modernization process. As yet few have come to the conclusion reached by one disillusioned scholar who had worked extensively for AID. He describes his work this way in an interview:

> The original idea, we were told, was to test a theory of decentralized, democratic economic development by evaluating the Thai transportation system. The idea behind the program was to encourage the Thai government to be more responsive to the peasant population by giving the peasants construction materials and letting them build their own roads.

The point of this program, however, he soon realized, was:

> to evaluate the local road building program and its effect on government mobility around the country for military purposes. The hope had been for the peasants to build the roads in order to free up the bureaucracy for other strategic tasks.

Equally important to the Thai Government have been the social scientists working in a number of institutional building programs in the country. One of the largest projects, a training Institute in Public Administration, parallels work being done in other Third World countries by American universities, and is similar to the work done by Michigan State University in Vietnam in the mid-fifties. Some of this involves American police officials, who are training Thai border security patrols. Other duties of a less military nature are being performed by a joint Thai-Indiana University project, started in 1955 by AID's predecessor, the International Economic Administration. The project trains Thai bureaucrats in modern methods of administration.

The role of the Americans involved in this training is typical of the role social scientists play overseas in promoting political stability through the teaching of American values and systems to indigenous peoples. Although designed to be courses in democratic administration, American advisers, like the Diem advisers from Michigan State, have a rather lax view of Thai democracy, which is known for its despotic character. Writes one American professor:

> It is also true that Thailand's democracy differs from the Western form. There have been cases of violence against persons opposing the state, yet these have been rare rather than common events and are insignificant beside the violence of some of Thailand's neighbors.[55]

A recurrent note throughout the writings of these advisers is the obstacle native culture provides to the modernization process. Thus one professor writes:

> A recurrent note through all the chapters of this book has been the conflict between an ancient culture and newer ideas, techniques and values which for a hundred years have been intruding from the West. This conflict has been apparent in the efforts to introduce Western administrative institutions and practices in Thailand.[56]

All this goes on, of course, with the willing cooperation of the Thai officials, who, like Diem and Thieu, more closely resemble their world-traveling American advisers than their own people.

Rarely is the application of Western ideas to Asian political forms, or the performance of the Western models themselves, considered. A recent study by the Indiana group concludes:

> Opinions of Americans who have been engaged in these programs range from extreme optimism to extreme pessimism about the impact of Western ideas. The optimists' view is that the superiority of Western ideas and values is so demonstrable that they are bound to prevail. They believe that the processes of economic growth are inevitable and that, reinforced by popular education and the desire for higher material standards of living, Western ideas and values sooner or later break down the old traditions which have obstructed them. . . . The pessimists see the forces of tradition and religion effectively blocking the acceptance of Western ideas or misapplying them in strange ways. They admit that Western machines, techniques, material goods, sports and amusements, have an appeal to people everywhere, but they think these cannot be accepted and used without affecting old spiritual and cultural values.[57]

What defines a pessimist in this world is merely that America's cultural take-over of Asia may not work.

Within this framework, and the objectives of American foreign policy, there is little difference between military sponsored research and economic development work, or between a Special Forces man, a pacification expert, or a social scientist. The identity of values and shared ideology between American social scientists and the government is so extensive that it is no longer a simple question of how the government influences scholars or how scholars influence government. Nor is the integration of the university into national and international planning merely a matter of institutional ties which can be severed. To the cultures affected by American interventions and scholarly treatises, the Asian scholar is the chrysanthemum on the sword.

Notes

1. This memo is from the Yale University collection of Stimson papers; I am indebted to Gabriel Kolko for bringing it to my attention.
2. *Ibid.*
3. Ruth Benedict, *Chrysanthemum and the Sword: Patterns of Japanese Culture* (New York, Meridian, 1946), p. 3.
4. *Ibid.*, p. 5.
5. This view is typified by Marshall Windmiller's essay, "International Relations: The New American Mandarins," in Theodore Roszak (ed.), *The Dissenting Academy* (New York, Pantheon Books, 1968).
6. The best such muckraking on university and military ties is Mike Klare's pamphlet. "The University Military Complex" (1969), available from the North American Congress on Latin America, P. O. Box 57, Cathedral Park Station, New York, New York.
7. See, for example, William Polk's essay, "The Problems of Government Utilization of Scholarly Research in Foreign Affairs," in Irving Horowitz's volume, *The Rise and Fall of Project Camelot* (Cambridge, Mass., M.I.T. Press, 1967).
8. See O. Edmund Clubb's essay, "McCarthyism and our Asian Policy," in *Bulletin of Concerned Asian Scholars,* No. 4 (May, 1969), pp. 23–26.
9. See Richard Kagan, "McCarran's Legacy: The Association for Asian Studies," in *Bulletin of Concerned Asian Scholars,* No. 4 (May, 1969), pp. 18–22.
10. Lincoln Bloomfield, "The Political Scientist and Foreign Policy," paper published by the Center for International Studies, M.I.T., 1967. Irving Horowitz in his well-known critique of the Army's *Project Camelot,* the multi-million dollar study of instability in Latin America, seems also to agree. In *The Rise and Fall of Project Camelot* (Cambridge, Mass., M.I.T. Press, 1967), he writes, "To be a servant of power is distinct from being a wielder of power." Horowitz seems more troubled by social scientists' willingness to conform to Army dictates on the project than by their naïve enthusiasm for the study of counterinsurgency.
11. John Kenneth Galbraith, *The New Industrial State* (Boston, Houghton Mifflin, 1967), p. 288.
12. *Selective Directory of University Centers of Foreign Research,*

U.S. Department of State, Office of External Research Publication No. 8378 (Washington, D.C., April 1968), p. v.

13. *Ibid.*, p. vi.
14. *Ibid.*, p. vii.
15. *Ibid.*
16. L. Gray Cowan, *A History of the School of International Affairs and Associated Area Institutes* (New York, Columbia Univ. Press, 1954), p. 6.
17. *Directory of University Centers*, p. viii.
18. Harold D. Lasswell, "The Policy Orientation," in David Lerner and Harold D. Lasswell (eds.), *The Policy Sciences: Recent Developments in Scope and Method* (Stanford, Cal., Stanford Univ. Press, 1951), p. 8.
19. *Columbia Envoy* (New York, Columbia Univ. School of International Affairs, 1965), Vol. II, No. 1, p. 3.
20. Donald Blackmer, "Scholars and Policy Makers: Perceptions of Soviet Policy." Paper presented at 1968 meeting of American Political Science Association.
21. Mr. Koen himself was a victim of the China Lobby; his book, originally accepted by the MacMillan Company in 1958 for publication, was revised, tinkered with, and worried over by Macmillan editors because of its critical view of the China Lobby; it was finally printed in a 1960 edition, but, because of "unidentified" problems, never published. A number of copies did get into libraries and to reviewers, and are collectors' items among China scholars. For those who might want to search local libraries, it is: Ross Koen, *The China Lobby in American Politics* (New York, MacMillan, 1960). Mr. Koen has only recently gained legal rights to his manuscript, and is in the process of revising it, hopefully for publication. The quotation is from p. 153 of a review copy of the original MacMillan version.
22. Kagan, "McCarran's Legacy."
23. Donald Blackmer uses this distinction in his paper to argue that Russian specialists are *less likely* rather than more likely to see "mutual interests," especially strategic ones, between the Russians and the United States; he implies, therefore, that military strategists are more "realistic" and less wedded to ideology. In Chinese studies the distinction is important, but goes the other way. Area specialists tend to be more benign toward China because of their previous admiration for Chinese culture; in this sense, they are like anthropologists.
24. Blackmer, "Scholars and Policy Makers."
25. In 1962, Asia Foundation representatives were refused admission to Burma on grounds they were CIA agents. In 1966, the Indian

Government ordered all Asia Foundation activities to cease in India because of CIA connections. At this point it was widely accepted by Asian and American scholars that the Asia Foundation was a CIA front. It was not until 1968 that the Foundation admitted it had ever gotten money from CIA. Since that time, the Foundation has gotten $3 million from the State Department.

26. The Asia Foundation, unlike other foundations which make public their financial records (as required by law), does not. Annual reports describe the program in general, but not individual recipients or sums involved.

27. *New York Times,* May 19, 1966.

28. Walt W. Rostow, *View from the Seventh Floor* (New York, Harper & Row, 1964). p. 114.

29. *Report of the Panel on Behavioral Sciences* (Washington, D.C., Defense Science Board, 1968).

30. Testimony, "Behavioral Sciences and the National Security," hearings before the Committee on Foreign Affairs, Report No. 4, House (Washington, D.C., U.S. Government Printing Office, 1966).

31. Galbraith, *The New Industrial State,* p. 290.

32. Noam Chomsky, *American Power and the New Mandarins* (New York, Pantheon Books, 1967), p. 348.

33. James C. Thomson, Jr. "Dragon Under Glass: Time for a New China Policy," *Atlantic Monthly,* Vol. CCXX, No. 4 (October, 1967), p. 55.

34. *Ibid.,* pp. 55–56. Thomson says later in the article that he regretted this evasive response to the China problem; his enlightened views are also indicated by his use of the descriptive term "Mainland China" for a country whose capitol is still Peiping to top State Department officials.

35. David Horowitz, "The Foundations: Charity begins at Home", *Ramparts,* Vol. VII, No. 11 (April, 1969).

36. Another super-Establishment foreign policy organization which contributes to this process is the Foreign Policy Association; while CFR concentrates on producing the consensus among top Establishment figures, FPA concentrates on disseminating these views to the public through a nationwide network of local chapters which hold seminars, conferences and meetings.

37. Ithiel de Sola Pool, "Content Analysis and the Intelligence Function," unpublished paper submitted to the National Academy of Sciences panel on the Behavioral Sciences.

Ithiel Pool is one of the most important Defense Department contractors for work in Vietnam.

38. Thomson, "Dragon Under Glass," p. 56.

39. Morton Halperin and Dwight Perkins, *Communist China and Arms Control* (New York, Praeger, 1965), p. 3.
40. John Gittings, "The Origins of China's Foreign Policy," in David Horowitz (ed.), *Containment and Revolution,* (Boston, Beacon, 1967), p. 186.
41. Thomson, "Dragon Under Glass," p. 56.
42. *New York Times,* December 20, 1967.
43. Pool, "Content Analysis and the Intelligence Function."
44. Alice Langley Hsieh, "Communist China's Military Policies and Nuclear Strategy," paper (RAND Corporation, November, 1967).
45. *Ibid.*
46. Chomsky, *American Power and New Mandarins,* p. 247.
47. Pool, "Content Analysis and the Intelligence Function.
48. Cited in *ibid.*
49. Roger Hilsman, *To Move a Nation* (New York, Doubleday, 1967), p. 413.
50. Stanley Sheinbaum, "Introduction" to Warren Hinckle's article, "MSU: The University on the Make," *Ramparts,* Vol. IV, No. 12, (April, 1966).
51. Richard Pfeffer, (ed.), *No More Vietnams?* (New York, Harper & Row, 1968), p. 206.
52. *Aviation Week and Space Technology,* Vol. 85, No. 25 (December 19, 1966).
53. Kenneth Young in *Boston Globe,* August 29, 1966.
54. *Aviation Week and Space Technology.*
55. Joseph Sutton, "Political and Administrative Leadership," in Joseph Sutton (ed.), *Problems of Politics and Administration in Thailand,* (Bloomington, Indiana University, 1962), p. 16.
56. Joseph B. Kingsbury, "Improving Public Administration in Thailand," in Sutton (ed.), *Problems of Politics,* p. 203.
57. *Ibid.,* p. 202.

The Great Asian Conspiracy

✪ *John Gittings*

. . . Stalin, working through the Cominform, launched an offensive in the East, which can roughly be dated from Zhdanov's speech of September, 1947. It involved guerrilla warfare in Indochina, Burma, Malaya, Indonesia, and the Philippines. And after the Chinese Communists came to power in . . . 1949, the offensive in Asia reached its climax in the invasion of South Korea.[1]

✪ THE THEORY OF the great Soviet conspiracy in Asia after World War II, expounded here by W. W. Rostow, formerly Special Assistant to President Johnson, is not always stated quite so baldly, but its essential ingredients can still be encountered in many standard works on the history of the Cold War. It has received special attention in recent years, on account of its apparent relevance to the present Vietnam war, in connection with which it offers a tempting analogy: The Viet Cong is to Hanoi what the Viet Minh was to international Communism—a subversive movement manipulated from outside, conspiratorial rather than revolutionary in character. More generally the analogy can be applied to the relationship between, for example, the South American liberation movements and Cuba, or between the Pathet Lao and Hanoi, or between the Thai Patriotic Front and Peking.

In a larger sense this explanation of Soviet post-war Asian policy typifies the crude, mechanistic approach adopted by many writers towards the role of the "Communist Side" in the Cold War. The Free World muddles along, stemming the tide of Communist expansionism by instinct and good luck rather than by premeditated design (and certainly not by any "conspiracy" of its own). The Truman Doctrine filled the anti-subversive breach in Greece; the Marshall Plan saved Western Europe from the fate already suffered by Eastern Europe. Both were inspired but improvised moves, taken at the last moment in the face of dire necessity. Then came the Berlin Airlift, another triumph of the Western genius for improvisation, followed by the establishment of NATO. Thwarted in the West, Stalin looked East, once again taking the Free World temporarily by surprise. By 1948, a rash of subversion had spread over Southeast Asia as a result of Stalin's attention. The Chinese Communists came to power in Peking, thus spurring the Viet Minh in Indochina to greater efforts and binding them indissolubly to the "Communist bloc." Soon the Korean War forced the United States to take the threat in the East as seriously as it had the threat in the West. And so the plot thickens, leading us in the last decade or so to the crises in the Middle East, Cuba, and again Vietnam.

Underlying this sequence of events lies a widespread assumption, which is shared by many writers who would not necessarily accept the conspiracy theory in its crudest form. The assumption is this: by and large it is the Communists who have set the pace, and the West has been forced to respond. And while it is usually conceded that the concept of a monolithic Communist conspiracy no longer holds good in these days of poly-centric diversity, many of the more Machiavellian attributes of the Soviet Union have been inherited by "revolutionary" People's China.

In this paper I intend to discuss the conspiracy theory as it relates to the first post-war decade of Asian revolution and particularly to Vietnam, and the arguments in its favor which are advanced by the "conspirationists" (to coin a word). The dominant theme is therefore that of the Soviet conspiracy; but a variant version, that of the Chinese conspiracy, must also be taken into account.

I shall show that these theories of Moscow-or-Peking-inspired "subversion" in Southeast Asia are not supported

even by the evidence—such as it is—which the conspirationists adduce. These same theories are also based upon a
complete misunderstanding both of Soviet and Chinese policies and of Sino-Soviet relations during this early period. A
more fundamental objection to the conspiratorial approach,
however, is that it is simply irrelevant to any serious inquiry
into the underlying causes of Asian revolution. The colonial
powers' stubborn attempt to recapture territories which
they had ignominiously lost to the Japanese, the new mood
of militant nationalism which they encountered, the sharp-
ening of familiar economic and social grievances, the
equivocal role of the urban elites, the arrival of American
power on the scene—all these features of post-war Asia
are downplayed or even denied by the conspirationists.
Instead they sleuth around like amateur detectives in the
corridors of Communist "front" meetings, or like cryptog-
raphers in the pages of the *People's Daily* and *Pravda,*
piecing together a sinister (but essentially boring, because
so familiar) tale of Red intrigue. The corridors of the State
Department or the Pentagon, however, they leave severely
alone.

Some may regard the subject which I have chosen in this
paper as a futile exercise in tilting at windmills. The best
known advocates of the conspiracy theory have admittedly
fallen into liberal academic disfavor, and many are excluded
from the orthodox conference circuit. Yet the conspiratorial
view of early post-war international relations is by no means
confined to the wild men of the far Right. Conceived at the
height of the East/West confrontation in the early 1950's,
and developed by cold war scholarship of the time, it has
become standard currency in many more recent "liberal"
studies of the period. There is little to choose for instance
between the views of Professor Frank Trager and those of
Professor Doak Barnett on this subject, as the reader can
readily establish from the passages by both authors cited
below in this essay.[2] In some instances the conspiracy thesis
is clearly adopted by a writer out of sheer intellectual lazi-

ness—he has not bothered to go back and read the relevant documents for himself, and relies on a second-rate interpretation (sometimes of dubious sponsorship); in other cases it is equally clear that the writer believes in the theory, although he would be quick to deride those who openly profess their faith in the "Communist conspiracy."

I · SOVIET POLICY: THE COMINFORM MEETING

In 1947 the growing strength of Communist groups in post war Asia and the highly fluid situation in many Asian countries led the Soviet Union to call for a militant policy of insurrection by Asian Communist parties, a shift which coincided with a new intransigence in Soviet actions elsewhere. This policy was publicly heralded by Andrei Zhdanov at the foundation meeting of the Cominform in September and October 1947, which was called to revive the coordination of action among Communist parties everywhere.[3]

THE ESTABLISHMENT OF the Cominform at the end of September, 1947, signified, so we are told, a calculated "shift to the Left" by Stalin, precipitating the division of the world into two blocs. It was also the occasion for a "shift to the East" in Soviet policy, since Stalin, checkmated in his attempts to subvert Western Europe, saw more fertile ground for his militant strategies in the anti-colonial battlefields of the East, (although the Western Communist parties were also encouraged to take a more "intransigent" line). The new policy was communicated to the Cominform conference by the Soviet delegate and theoretician Andrei Zhdanov.

The global implications of this version of the events of 1947 lie outside the scope of this essay, but it does illustrate a general weakness inherent in the conspiratorial view of the origins of the Cold War. Certainly Zhdanov's speech, and the whole proceedings of the Cominform conference, took a rigid and pessimistic view of the world situation. But it does not follow that this situation was *created* by Zhdanov, the Cominform, or Stalin. The Cominform's Manifesto acknowledged that the world was divided into two rival camps, but it did not engineer that division. Historians may differ on how to apportion responsibility for the post-war breakdown of cooperation between the Allies, but wherever the blame lies, it is not in a solitary speech or manifesto. The issues at stake are too broad to be discussed further here. To mention only two: Was the Marshall Plan a genuine offer of cooperation between Western and Eastern Europe, spurned by Stalin in favor of his more "militant" strategy, or did its terms effectively discourage Soviet participation? Did the Cominform conference lead to a withdrawal by the Western Communist parties from the governments of their countries, or had they already (as in France and Italy) been excluded?

We are concerned, however, with the argument that the foundation of the Cominform marked a watershed in Soviet foreign policy between two alternative and chronologically consecutive policies, "a drive into Western Europe" being superseded by "Soviet sponsorship of revolutions in the East."[4] We shall consider later whether such a shift took place at all either in 1947 or 1948, and whether the various anti-colonial movements in the East ever enjoyed Soviet "sponsorship" in any effective sense of the word. But as far as the Cominform itself is concerned, there is no evidence in its proceedings of a marked increase of interest in Asian affairs, far less of a call to arms in the anti-colonial struggle.

Nor does the evidence support Barnett's assertion (quoted above) that the Cominform was convened in order to revive the coordination of Communist parties throughout the world. The scope of the Conference was in fact severely limited, as was the attendance. "So little did Stalin think of turning the Cominform into any genuine instrument of international revolution," Isaac Deutscher has observed, "that he did not ask the Chinese and other Asian parties to adhere to the new organization.[5] Indeed there were no delegates or even observers from Communist parties outside those of nine European countries. The Cominform's Manifesto was almost entirely devoted to a critique of American imperialism in a European context: the Marshall Plan, its allies in Britain and France, and the right-wing European socialists. In its sole specific reference to United States policy outside Europe, the Manifesto referred briefly to United States plans "for the enslavement of China, Indonesia, and the South American countries," and to the use of Japan as "a weapon of US imperialist policy . . . in Asia." But there was no endorsement or even any mention of the Communist-led revolutions in China, Indochina, or anywhere else. On the contrary, the Manifesto stated that Communist parties must collaborate closely in "the official policy of [their] nations," a formula which had no relevance to those parties which were in armed opposition to the established government. Nor did the Manifesto refer to, or far less explicitly approve of, the tactic of armed struggle.[6]

Similarly the key speech delivered by Andrei Zhdanov to the Cominform conference, of which so much has since been made, was almost entirely concerned with the supposed contradictions of the capitalist world and with America's plans for "enslaving Europe." It was only within this West-oriented context that Zhdanov referred to "the crisis of the colonial system," which had given rise to "a powerful movement for national liberation in the colonies and dependencies." Attempts to crush these movements by military force, Zhdanov went on to say, "increasingly encounter armed resistance on the part of the colonial peoples and lead to protracted colonial wars."

This was hardly a "directive" on Zhdanov's part, but rather a statement of fact. It would have been altogether remarkable if he had omitted to refer with approval to the anti-colonial struggles which were already under way. Yet he did not do so at any great length; even Trager admits that "the speech had little to say about the colonies, [although] it did insist that 'the ruling classes of the metropolitan countries can no longer govern the colonies on the old lines.' "[7] (Zhdanov was hardly the only person after the war to "insist" upon this statement of the obvious.) The fact is that Zhdanov completely failed to provide an explicit "line" to the Communist Parties of the colonial world. For a start, while describing the division of the world into two blocs, he did not make the membership of the anti-imperialist bloc sufficiently clear for the purposes of most colonial parties. The bloc was, of course, led by the Soviet Union and it included the people's democracies of Eastern Europe. As for the rest of the world, he said vaguely, Indonesia and Vietnam were "joining" the anti-imperialist camp, while India, Egypt and Syria were "in sympathy" with it. It was also "supported" by the fighters for national liberation in the various colonies and dependencies. Yet the most successful liberation movement to date—in China—was not mentioned by name, a further example of the lukewarm Soviet attitude toward the Chinese Communists. Moreover, while Zhdanov's speech conveyed a general impression of militancy, which could reasonably convince any Communist reader (if he still needed to be convinced) that the age of the common front against fascism was over and that to this extent the new line was "left" rather than "right," it was fatally ambiguous on two vital questions of tactics. First, did Zhdanov regard those independence movements under the control of the "national bourgeoisie" as part of the imperialist or of the anti-imperialist camps? His approving reference to Indonesia and India (i.e., to movements led respectively by the "bourgeois" Sukarno and Nehru) would suggest the latter, yet subsequent Soviet pronouncements on this question leant towards the former definition. Second, did Zhdanov advocate strikes, parliamentary and legal opposition or armed struggle as the main tactic in those countries where the choice was still open? The simple answer is that he failed to do either, and clearly was not concerned with such problems, since he only devoted one "brief paragraph out of over two closely printed newspaper pages . . . to the colonial areas."[8] An article by the prominent Soviet orientalist, Zhukov, published in December, 1947, went rather further, acknowledging the success of armed struggle in China and Vietnam, yet "nowhere did he imply that Communists elsewhere in the East should arise in arms against either foreign imperialism or a local bourgeois regime."[9]

The obvious moral has been drawn by Kautsky, one of the few writers to critically study the text of Zhdanov's speech (and the other documents frequently quoted by the conspirationists) before leaping to conclusions:

> The composition of the Cominform, the reports made at its establishment . . . and the contents of its newspaper are clear evidence of the lack of attention devoted to Asian affairs by Moscow, an attitude of which disbelief in total Communist victory in China must have been a part.[10]

THE CALCUTTA CONFERENCE

In February 1948 two important Communist gatherings, attended by representatives of Communist parties throughout South and Southeast Asia, were held at Calcutta; the Southeast Asia Youth Conference, and the Second Congress of the Indian Communist party. Apparently the new Cominform "line" was pressed home at these meetings, for almost immediately thereafter the Communist parties of South and Southeast Asia either adopted or intensified the strategy of militant insurrection.[11]

WE COME NOW to the next link in the conspiratorial chain: the Calcutta Conference of Feburary, 1948 (properly known as the Southeast Asian Youth Conference). At Calcutta, according to many authorities, a Soviet "directive" in the spirit of the Cominform's "new line" was transmitted to the Asian Communist parties, thus triggering off a wave of revolutionary violence throughout South and Southeast Asia. The Cominform's "turn to the left," so Frank Trager among others has written, "had crucial significance for Southeast Asia, as the February 1948 Calcutta Conference was to indicate." And while Trager concedes that no documentary evidence exists of the "directives," he is "inclined to be satisfied with conclusions of high probability based on inference from strong circumstantial evidence."[12] So, presumably, to judge from the quotation above, is Barnett.

Before examining the "evidence," it should be made clear that the whole question of the Calcutta Conference is a red herring. It is illogical for so much importance to be attached to this event, simply because it carries a specific title and date, thus providing a spurious element of 'hard fact' to bolster the argument. For if the Soviet "line" had already been publicized at the Cominform conference, to be followed by an internal "directive" within the international Communist movement, and if Moscow was sufficiently in touch with the Asian anti-colonial movements to "sponsor" their revolutionary efforts in 1948, then the precise mechanics whereby such a "directive" was transmitted should only be of secondary importance. The Calcutta Conference as such should only merit a passing reference, since everyone concedes that there is not a shred of direct evidence that the "directive" was transmitted during its proceedings. Even if it were, one would assume that Moscow had other opportunities for making its desires felt apart from this one occasion. Yet in most accounts of the conspiratorial theory, Calcutta occupies a pivotal position in the supposed "transmission belt" between Moscow and Asia.

The facts are these: The Conference, co-sponsored by the World Federation of Democratic Youth and the International Union of Students, was attended by some nine hundred Asian delegates, the majority of whom were non-Communist. It had been planned for since March, 1947, and was postponed from the original target date of November. It was not a hard-core Communist conference, although it could be unsympathetically described as a "front." The only delegates from the Soviet Union were Central Asians who played a minor role in the proceedings, and the Conference was ignored by the Soviet press. Only one recognized Asian Communist leader (Than Tun of Burma) attended; no one was present who could reasonably be regarded as the bearer of a Soviet "directive."[13]

It is interesting to note how even these simple and verifiable facts have been distorted in the writings of some conspirationists. First, the membership of the conference: According to Trager, "Soviet, Yugoslav and Australian delegates were also present, as were guests from elsewhere in the Communist world."[14] Malcolm Kennedy writes of "representatives from the Soviet Union and European satellite states."[15] While both statements are technically true, the Soviet delegates were from the Central Asian Republics, and only Yugoslavia and Czechoslovakia from the "satellite states" sent observers. Second, the vast size and motley composition of the Conference, which hardly provided ideal conditions for the transmission of directives so secret that their existence has never been verified to this day, is ignored in most accounts, as is the significant lack of Soviet press coverage.

In the third place, attention is rarely drawn to the obvious ambiguities in the Conference's final report (just as similar ambiguities are overlooked in most discussions of Zhdanov's Cominform speech). Six months after the Cominform meeting and Stalin's supposed "turn to the East," the "line" was still remarkably shaky. Zhdanov's failure to define precisely the role of the "national bourgeoisie" is repeated in the Conference report. While stating that "the national bourgeoisie . . . has compromised with imperialism," the report also called for unity with "all democratic and progressive forces." The Conference also failed to give its explicit support to the tactic of "armed struggle,"

although it lavished praise upon the independence movements of China, Indochina, and Indonesia.

THE ASIAN PARTIES

---

*In 1948, when the rash of Communist-led insurrections broke out in
Southeast Asia . . .*[16]

THE THEORY OF the Soviet "directive" is based in the last
resort upon the chronological sequence of Communist-led
Asian revolution after the Calcutta Conference. Vietnam
can be explained as an exception to the rule (McLane
writes of an "early start in Indochina," as if Ho Chi Minh
had perversely jumped the Soviet gun). So, at a pinch, can
Thailand, where there was no resort to arms, and which
exchanged ambassadors with the Soviet Union in May,
1948. This leaves the Philippines, Burma, Malaya, and
Indonesia, where it can be argued that armed revolt in all
cases broke out *after* the Calcutta Conference. On closer
examination, the argument becomes untenable. A state of
sporadic civil war, marked by periodic attempts at negotiations, had existed in the Philippines since the elections
of April, 1946, when the United States-backed Liberal
Party led by President Roxas denied the Hukbalahap
leaders the seats which they had legally won.[17] In March
1948, Roxas outlawed the Hukbalahaps, but his successor
Quirino re-opened negotiations. In May (after the Calcutta
Conference, it should be noted) the Central Committee of
the Philippines Communist Party rejected an open resort
to armed struggle. In spite of the break-down of the new
negotiations, the party leadership still avoided outright
rebellion, and supported the Nacionalista candidate in
opposition to Quirino in the presidential elections of November, 1949. It was only after the rabidly anti-Communist

Quirino had engineered his victory by rigging the elections that the Huks called for total mobilization, and full-scale armed resistance broke out.

The cases of Burma, Malaya, and Indonesia, each with its own specific characteristics, also underline the danger of argument by analogy. The steady deterioration in Burma of the war-time Anti-Fascist People's Freedom League finally led to armed resistance by the Burmese Communist Party beginning in March, 1948. But the BCP (often known as the "White Flags") were only one of many organizations which took to arms around this time. A dissident Communist group—the Communist Party of Burma or "Red Flags"—had been fighting since mid-1946. The Malayan insurgency began in June, 1948, also conveniently close to the Calcutta Conference. But it must be seen in the context of growing British repression of the trade union movement, the declining influence of the Malayan Communist Party, and internal friction within its ranks.[18] Indonesia only qualifies for inclusion on the basis of the abortive Madiun uprising of September 1948. This disastrously adventurist attempt, which inflicted a severe setback on the Indonesian Communist Party, was launched by "a group of second-echelon Communist leaders in Madiun,"[19] taking the official leadership entirely by surprise. (There is an interesting parallel here with the equally abortive and probably unauthorized coup of September 30, 1965.) It can hardly be interpreted as evidence of the Soviet master plan in action.

The most striking feature of the Soviet attitude toward Asian revolution is rarely commented upon by the conspirationists, and never satisfactorily explained. For in fact the Soviet press and leaders in their public writings and speeches showed very little interest in these far-off anti-colonial struggles. Even the Chinese civil war was sparsely reported until April, 1949, when the People's Liberation Army was on the last lap toward victory. In this case Moscow's silence almost certainly indicated a degree of disapproval, and the evidence suggests that Stalin had no desire to encourage the birth of a united, albeit Communist, China. He had sought to dissuade Mao and his colleagues from taking up arms against Chiang Kai-shek in 1946, and he appears to have hoped for a compromise end to the war which would leave China divided—and weak.

China may perhaps be regarded as a special case, in view of its uneasy geo-political relationship with the Soviet Union and of Mao Tse-tung's assertion of doctrinal independence from Moscow. But the Indochinese war was also poorly served by the Soviet press. When the anti-French war broke out, Soviet coverage was "appropriately sympathetic to the Vietminh cause but noncommittal concerning any specific assistance the Vietnamese might expect."[20] It was also very sparse; only one item on Vietnam was published in the Soviet press in the six months following the Cominform meeting—and that was a book review.[21] Coverage gradually increased as the Viet Minh themselves scored more victories, and as the Chinese revolution brought that part of the world into greater prominence. But Vietnam was not really on the Soviet map until after Moscow had recognized the Democratic Republic of Vietnam at the end of January, 1950.

The behavior of the French Communist Party, which continued to support official French policy in Indochina for several months after the war broke out in December, 1946, may throw some light upon Soviet policy. It is unlikely that the Soviet Union ever expected the French CP to win power, but at the least it might remain within the Ramadier coalition and help to influence the French government in a favorable direction. No doubt the French Party leaders themselves were more concerned for the political future of France than for the fate of the Viet Minh. One can even detect a straightforward streak of Churchillian chauvinism in some of their statements.[22] One report claims that in September, 1945, the French Communist group in Saigon warned the Viet Minh not to endanger Soviet plans— which "might well include France as a firm ally of the

U.S.S.R. in Europe"—by any premature adventures.[23] If this was Soviet policy, as transmitted through the French CP, it only matched Soviet policy at the same time in China, where the future of Soviet relations with the Nationalist Government was not to be disturbed by ill-advised action on the part of the Chinese Communists.[24]

In spite of Soviet recognition of the Democratic Republic of Vietnam (DRV) on January 30, 1950 (eleven days after China had done so), there is no evidence that the Viet Minh derived any immediate benefit from it. It is generally agreed that Soviet military aid to the DRV (as distinct from the Chinese supply of ex-Soviet weapons) was not forthcoming until toward the end of 1953.[25] As late as spring of 1953 the Soviet Union promptly denied a Western report of an aid agreement between itself, China, and the DRV. There was no mention of diplomatic or cultural exchanges until after the Geneva Conference.[26] In 1951, according to Ho Chi Minh, Vietnamese delegations visited China and North Korea, thus strengthening "the age-old friendship between our three countries." As for the Soviet Union, he merely remarked that "those of the delegates who had the chance of visiting the Soviet Union, [on their way to and from international conferences in Berlin, Warsaw and Vienna] are overjoyed because they can tell us of the great triumph of socialism and the evergrowing happiness enjoyed by the Soviet people."[27] Other Vietnamese comments on the Soviet Union were equally laudatory but vague. If the Soviet Union was actively helping and encouraging the DRV, it did not beat any drums about it, nor did the Vietnamese. One assumes that the Soviet attitude was sympathetic, but there is no firm indication of a specific Soviet policy until the summer of 1953. It was then that both the Soviet Union and China began to urge that the war should be ended by negotiations. The provision of direct Soviet aid at around this time may be closely connected with the pressure for negotiations. It would both help the Viet Minh to improve their military position before the conference table was reached, and serve as an inducement to persuade them to come to the table in the first place.

The low level of Soviet attention to developments in Indochina also applied *a fortiori* to the less successful revolutionary movements elsewhere in Southeast Asia. As one writer has observed:

> Soviet pronouncements on Southeast Asia were usually even vaguer than those on other parts of the world. . . . The Soviet news items not only demonstrated the usual tendency to exaggerate the strength and successes of the Communists but, in some instances, showed such ignorance of the actual situation as to raise questions about the sources of the information available to the Russians.

The same writer also notes that there is no evidence of any wartime liaison between Moscow and the resistance movements of Southeast Asia; after the war a few Russian-trained leaders held key positions in Indonesia, Indochina and the Philippines, but apparently none in Burma or Thailand (nor, one might add, in Malaya or, for that matter, China).[28] Even supposing that Moscow sought to wield its baton after 1947, one is still left in doubt as to who were the members of the orchestra.

I have deliberately deferred to this stage any discussion of the Indian Communist Party (CPI), which features prominently in several versions of the conspiracy theory. The CPI was probably more responsive to Moscow than most of the home-grown and battle-tested movements in Southeast Asia. Documentation of its shifts in policy and leadership is also easier to obtain and has been fully analyzed by Kautsky. If its experience is any guide, its leaders showed less skill in interpreting the Soviet "line" than any of the latter-day commentators, and it brought them nothing but trouble.

In brief, the CPI was already faction-ridden by the time of the Cominform conference. While successive leaders of the Party used Moscow's pronouncements during 1947–50 to buttress their position, they invariably remained out of step with the Soviet position (which was admittedly always hard to define). In 1947, the CPI was already dominated by the "left" tendency. Zhdanov's speech may have assisted the "left" leader Ranadive to replace the more moderate Joshi as General Secretary. But Ranadive promptly adopted a much more extreme position of opposition to the "national bourgeoisie" than was ever endorsed by Moscow. Another aspect of his "ultra-left" approach was a strong emphasis upon urban as opposed to rural insurrection. This brought him into conflict with the Andhra Party Committee (which had led rural fighting in Hyderabad since 1946, a full year-and-a-half before the Calcutta Conference) and ultimately to overt criticism of Mao Tse-tung. Ranadive was eventually replaced in 1950 by the Andhra leadership, after a definite hint from Moscow that he would go. But the new leaders in turn stepped out of line, failing to heed warnings from both Moscow and Peking that India was not considered ripe for revolutionary violence. In 1951 the Andhra faction lost much of its influence, and the CPI at last fell in step with the general Soviet view.[29]

By now it will come as no surprise to learn that according to W. W. Rostow, the Hyderabad fighting (which actually began in 1946) only commenced in March, 1948 after the Second CPI Congress.[30] Nor to learn from another source that the CPI's adventurist line simply stemmed from the Zhdanov speech which had "set the seal of international approval on insurrectionary tactics."[31]

A more plausible view is taken by Kautsky (significantly the only author out of all those quoted here who has researched the relevant documents first-hand). He writes:

> Moscow's indecisiveness displayed in its failure to formulate a clear policy line for the Indian Communists between 1945 and 1949 can be explained most easily by Soviet preoccupation with the West during this period . . . it was apparently not sufficiently interested in India to bother to formulate [a party line] even at a time when the CPI would have greatly welcomed guidance from abroad.[32]

II · THE CHINESE ALTERNATIVE

China openly encouraged revolutionary actions by the Communist movements in South and Southeast Asia, in line with the strategy of armed revolt in this part of Asia which had been called for by the Cominform in 1947.[33]

THE CHINESE COMMUNISTS do not feature very prominently *before* 1949 in most of the conspiratorial versions of events in Asia, perhaps partly because of the embarrassing lack of attention paid by the Russians themselves to the Chinese revolution. But this omission is a big mistake for any conspirationist worth his salt. A much better case could in fact be made out for Peking rather than Moscow as the source of Asian revolution even before 1949. (That they have failed to do so may stem as much from their unfamiliarity with the earlier Chinese sources as with their belief in a Soviet-dominated monolith.)

The fragmentary and inchoate views of the Soviet Union on the anti-colonial question assume an even more hesitant character when compared with the forceful pronouncements of the Chinese Communists on the same subject. Thus in an editorial of October 7, 1947 (two days after the publication of the Cominform Manifesto), the New China News Agency, while praising the "united front for peace and democracy" which was being established in Europe, also emphasized what the Manifesto had neglected, namely "the just wars for national liberation waged by the peoples of the East, and first of all by our own people of China."[34] Directly commenting on the Cominform Conference, a writer in an authoritative Hong Kong Communist journal emphasized the point: The main question was whether the people dared to resist United States imperialism "if necessary by armed resistance." Some parts of the world were further ahead in the anti-imperialist struggle than others; some people had established a base from which to oppose imperialism—as in Greece. Others had "not only established and strengthened a base but have gloriously advanced—like China." (The same writer, incidentally, also emphasized for his readers that the Cominform was *not* a new Comintern).[35] In an important speech at the end of December, 1947, Mao Tse-tung claimed that "a great national liberation movement" had arisen throughout Asia, and he described—perhaps with deliberate exaggeration—the Cominform Manifesto as a "call to battle" which inspired the oppressed people of the world.[36]

Similarly in a message of congratulations sent to the Calcutta Conference, the Chinese Communist Party praised the growth of "armed struggle" (a term which, as has been noted, was not used in the Conference's own report), and claimed that "in this respect the people of China have set forth extremely valuable experience for the peoples of the Asian countries."[37] The unofficial Hong Kong Communist press was again more outspoken: The Chinese revolutionary movement played "a leading role" in the anti-colonial popular struggle; the Chinese student movement should "shoulder the vanguard and model role in the international, and especially in the Southeast Asian, student movement."[38]

Should we then conclude that it was not the Russians after all but the Chinese under Mao Tse-tung who transmitted directives at the Calcutta Conference? For if revolutionary propaganda is evidence of incitement to revolt, then the New China News Agency's broadcasts from the loess hills of North Shensi are much more culpable than Zhdanov with his perfunctory remarks at the opening of the Cominform. This conclusion comes close to being drawn by Harold Hinton, (writing *after* the Sino-Soviet dispute had emerged into the open and in so doing shaken the previous belief in a monolithic nature of the alliance between Moscow and Peking). The Chinese Communists' revolutionary exhortations, writes Hinton, and its own example, "probably helped to precipitate armed risings in Burma, Malaya, Indonesia, and the Philippines in 1948."[39]

This, interestingly enough, has also been the Soviet view in recent years. Obviously unconvinced by the conspiracy theory as it applies to them, they now have no hesitation in applying it to the Chinese. It is not only in recent years, they explain, that "China's neighbors are subjected to subversive activities by the Mao group." In order to gain leadership of national liberation movements in Asia, the Chinese have always been willing "to sacrifice the interests of the progressive forces." Just as Peking's hand lay behind the adventurist and disastrous coup in Indonesia of October, 1965, so the Chinese provoked ultra-revolutionary tactics twenty years ago all over Asia.

> In 1948, the Mao Tse-tung group, in a bid for the hegemony of Asia, incited the Burmese, Malayan and Philippine Parties to armed struggle although the conditions for success were lacking. The Communist Parties in these countries were thereby weakened, many thousands of seasoned revolutionaries exterminated and the Parties isolated from the people.[40]

Mao Tse-tung, so the Soviet press concludes, has resorted to "the Great-Power chauvinism that took shape at the time of the Tang dynasty in the Middle Ages."[41]

China's revolutionary role before 1949 may still be a mystery to most people except the Soviet propagandists. But *after* the establishment of the People's Republic, Peking comes on the revolutionary scene in a big way, with a functional division of labor between Moscow and Mao which makes the latter, in effect, Stalin's Chief of Staff. As Barnett describes it, Peking became "a regional center for Asian Communism," and Moscow was willing "to delegate special responsibilities to the Chinese Communists."[42] Thus one more untested hypothesis is added to the foundations of the conspiracy theory; it has already been taken for granted that Moscow wants to stir up Asian revolution, and that the Asian revolutionaries will dance to the Soviet tune. Now it is further assumed that the chain of command runs from

Stalin through Mao to the grass-roots, and hence that the policies of all three are broadly in harmony.

When China joins the conspiracy club as a junior partner in 1949, she does so with respectable credentials. Most accounts of this development provide the same kind of circumstantial detail with which the Soviet "shift to the East" of two years before was treated. A wealth of identifiable names, organizations, and dates is attached to bolster up the theory. Liu Shao-ch'i is the Zhdanov of China; his famous speech at the November, 1949, Conference of Asian and Australasian Trade Unions in Peking is the equivalent of Zhdanov's address to the opening session of the Cominform. It was at this meeting, says Barnett, that Liu "proclaimed China's new mission" of inspiring Communist insurrection in many Asian countries. The Conference itself served the same function as the Calcutta Youth Conference, enabling the Chinese to communicate their "line" to the revolutionary movements over whom Peking now claimed leadership, just as Moscow's agents had propagated the Zhdanov line in Calcutta. As Tang Tsou writes, Liu in his address to the Peking Conference "claimed for Communist China the leadership of national revolutionary movements in all other countries of Asia on the basis of the success of the political-military program worked out by Mao Tse-tung." Finally, the permanent Liaison Bureau which was established by the Trade Unions Conference in Peking is described by several writers as the equivalent of "a Far Eastern Cominform," to be used by Peking as an organizational conduit for propagating its line.[43]

Liu Shao-ch'i's speech—or at least one sentence of it—is perhaps the most widely known and quoted document from the Chinese People's Republic in its first year. What does Liu actually say and what does it amount to? First, he expresses pride in the achievements of the Chinese revolution, and in the fact that the World Federation of Trade Unions is holding the first Asian and Australasian Trade Unions Meeting in Peking. Second, he praises the successes of Asian national liberation movements, especially in China and Vietnam. Third, he argues that conventional trade union goals—"improvement of workers' living standards and labor conditions" and so on—can be solved only *after* the colonial powers have been driven out. Fourth, he says that the road taken in China is the right one for most colonial or semi-colonial peoples to follow (this is the famous and often misquoted sentence).[44] Fifth, he describes the precise features of the Chinese road—or "the way of Mao Tse-tung"—laying special stress upon the formation of a broad "united front," led by the proletariat and based on a worker-peasant alliance, but including most of the petty bourgeoisie and part of the national bourgeoisie.

The effect of this speech would depend on who was listening to it; a revolutionary fighter from Vietnam or Malaya would hardly need to hear it in order to be convinced of the value of "armed struggle" in which he had been engaged for several years. He would be much more interested in the Chinese formulation of "united front" tactics; if he was an ultra-leftist by inclination, he might even suspect Liu Shao-ch'i of advocating too soft a policy on the question of cooperation with the national bourgeoisie.

For people in the revolutionary business, in fact, Liu's speech clearly advised a level-headed approach to their trade, avoiding the kind of adventurist policies which were still being advocated by the Ranadive leadership in India. The "way of Mao Tse-tung" was the right road—but only in countries "where similar situations prevail" to those in China.

Yet Liu was not arguing primarily with revolutionaries in the field, but with trade union leaders from most of Asia who belonged to the Moscow-backed and mainly Europe-oriented World Federation of Trade Unions. Three years earlier, the Chinese Communist delegate to the WFTU executive meeting in Moscow (June, 1946) had urged it to "pay more attention to Far Eastern affairs."[45] Early in 1949, with the Chinese victory in sight, the WFTU had finally agreed to sponsor the conference which Liu was now addressing. It was a prestigious occasion for the Chinese—the first international conference to be held in Peking since they had won power—and they intended to make the most of it. In the struggle against colonialism, so Liu's message to the conference ran, you must put first things first: do what we did in China, get rid of imperialism before you try to improve working conditions, and take up arms (in the right circumstances) to do so.

In addition to the provisos which Liu himself included, a more elaborate and cautious interpretation of the "way of Mao Tse-tung" formula was provided by another Chinese speaker, Li Li-san, four days later. Li explained that the Chinese victory had been possible because of the use of a wide variety of tactics—armed and peaceful, legal and illegal, urban and rural. It stemmed from the following factors (in this order): (1) support of the masses, (2) successful practice of armed revolution, (3) the practice where necessary of legal urban struggle (at this point Li criticized himself for his left-deviation, back in 1930, of promoting urban risings), (4) Party leadership, and (5) a favorable international climate.[46] Li's self-criticism was probably also aimed indirectly at ultra-leftist critics, and his speech made explicit what has always been implicit in the Chinese approach: that you should use your head when making revolution. Given a political climate in 1949 when revolution was in the air or in the making in many parts of Asia, this was the main theme of the Chinese "line," not some dogmatic and all-inclusive call to arms.

The subsequent ramifications of the alleged Chinese Conspiracy may be dealt with very briefly. There is, needless to say, no evidence that the WFTU Liaison Bureau set up in Peking after the Conference of November, 1949, ever assumed the task of "coordination of the Communist movements in Southeast Asia."[47] It was indeed, according to one account, "virtually moribund for its first few years of existence."[48] After 1949 (and before) the Chinese Communists displayed much more interest in the various Asian revolutionary movements than had the Soviet Union, but they clearly did not succeed—nor did they make any attempt which has been detected—in sparking off a new wave of insurrection in Southeast Asia. No evidence has yet been provided of substantive Chinese aid to the Malayan guerrillas, and China's only contribution to the Indian revolutionary scene was to hint, in the *People's Daily* of June 26, 1950, that the situation was not ripe for violence.[49] There remains the case of Vietnam.[50]

Obviously the Chinese were going to support the Viet Minh, even if the United States had not already decided (as we shall see) to move toward underwriting the French. Clearly Chinese military aid helped the Viet Minh to advance the date of their (partial) victory achieved at Dienbienphu, although opinion varies on the extent of such aid. (It has been described by one writer as "valuable and perhaps indispensable," by others as "never wholehearted."[51]) It is also evident that for security reasons alone, the maintenance of at least the northern part of Vietnam out of Western hands was a vital Chinese interest, although the South—as Chou En-lai demonstrated at the Geneva Conference in 1954—was expendable. In actual fact the volume of Chinese military aid was limited until late in 1953,[52] perhaps partly because the Korean front enjoyed a much higher priority, and the aid agreements reached between China and the Democratic Republic of Vietnam were not very far-reaching.[53] It is not necessary however to conclude that the Chinese were reluctant to support the Viet Minh beyond a certain point; for as events showed there was no need to do so. By 1949 the DRV was already the only effective and popular political alternative to a succession of French-sponsored puppet governments. As Robert Guillain has observed, all that China needed to do was to ensure that the DRV did not lose the advantage which it had already gained. "Thus when France began using Vietnamese troops and receiving more American aid following the Korean War, the Chinese in turn stepped up their own aid program just enough to restore *l'équilibre*. When French fortunes rose [as a result of American aid], so did Chinese aid."[54]

The view that the Chinese Communists somehow instigated the Viet Minh to resist the French, and thereafter saved them from defeat, is only tenable if it is assumed that Vietnam—unique in the post-war world—was the one colony where the nationalist uprising would be permanently defeated by the reigning colonial power. Even the arch-conspirationists do not attempt to defend this assumption; they rely rather upon the insinuation—often conveyed parenthetically—that the Chinese somehow warped and deformed the nationalist struggle into an element of the international Communist conspiracy. In much the same way, some defenders of recent United States policy in Vietnam, while compelled to admit that Hanoi is not simply a Chinese puppet, seek to imply that Peking's influence is as substantial and noxious as it is indefinable.

Thus, in the first chapter of a recent study of the anti-French war in Vietnam, the armed struggle of 1947–49 is virtually written off as a period of waiting for a "more favorable" moment: the victory of Mao on the Chinese mainland. The author's sketchy three-page background description of the origins of the Viet Minh is largely confined to previous Chinese influence upon it.[55] The same writer goes on to attach a sinister significance to China's diplomatic relations with the DRV, which, on the face of it, indicated a lack of Chinese interest rather than an excess of it. Peking recognized the DRV on January 18, 1950, but the first Vietnamese representative did not present credentials until April, 1951, and then not at ambassadorial level. The Chinese did not send their own envoy to Vietnam until September, 1954. Peking, concludes the author darkly, "clearly intended that high-level diplomatic dealings be kept under wraps."[56]

Other writers have suggested that the Chinese used the DRV "for expansionist purposes," or "to fulfill both traditional Chinese imperialist ambitions and its modern ideological convictions," or simply that Mao's victory "internationalized" the Vietnam war.[57] Without a rigorous analysis of traditional and modern Chinese policy interests in the Indochinese area, such language is as meaningless as it is dangerously emotive. It does however prompt this writer to speculate for a moment about the "purposes" and "ambitions" of another great power which "internationalized" the Vietnam war.

III · THE UNITED STATES INTERVENES

IN JANUARY, 1950, the Democratic Republic of Vietnam issued an appeal for diplomatic recognition, which was swiftly granted by China and the Soviet Union, followed by the East European countries. In February, 1950, recognition of the French-sponsored states of Vietnam, Laos, and Cambodia was accorded by the United States and Great Britain, also followed by a number of Western countries. This happy chronological sequence provides apparent backing for one of the most popular myths in Cold War historiography, namely that Ho Chi Minh, by aligning himself with the Communist bloc, compelled the United States, hitherto reluctant to support a French colonial war, to intervene in Vietnam. As a corollary to this argument, it is sometimes asserted that American aid to the French in Vietnam did not begin in earnest until the outbreak of the Korean war and the Chinese intervention. Thus in Vietnam as elsewhere, American commitment was said to be a response to, rather than the cause of—or even coincident with—the commitment of the Communist powers.

P. J. Honey, the well-known Vietnamese linguist, writes that "until late in 1949 Vietnamese resistance continued as a coalition of these groups [nationalists and Communists]." But the revolution in China emboldened the Communists to impose their own control on the movement. Chinese and

Soviet recognition of the DRV provided "confirmation of the political shift." Honey concludes that

> the consequence of Ho's decision was involvement of both the United States and Communist China in the Indochinese war, thereby increasing the scale and significance of the conflict and causing more bloodshed, suffering and damage to the Vietnamese people . . . the decision evinced a callous disregard for the sufferings of his own people.[58]

The fatal flaw in this argument lies in the very chronological sequence on which it is supposedly based. For it was already clear in mid-1949, before the Vietnamese Communists had allegedly imposed their control on the resistance and long before Chinese and Soviet recognition, that the United States was reconsidering its policy of non-involvement. The prospect of imminent Communist victory in China, though its consequences were still unclear, led Washington to change its mind.

On June 21, 1949, the Department of State officially welcomed the forthcoming formation of Bao Dai's "new unified State of Vietnam" which had been envisaged in the Elysée Agreement.[59] In July, Secretary of State Acheson turned his attention to "the general problems which were confronting the United States in Asia," and authorized Ambassador-at-Large Philip Jessup to examine the question. Jessup's post was one of great importance. It entitled him to represent the President and Secretary of State at international meetings, and its purpose was to enable the Secretary of State to remain in Washington as principal foreign affairs adviser to the President.[60] Jessup's mission was based on the assumption that "it is a fundamental decision of American policy that the United States does not intend to permit further extension of Communist domination on the continent of Asia or in the Southeast Asia area," and he was asked to draw up "possible programs of action" to this effect.[61] The adoption of such an all-inclusive policy of containment of China by Acheson in July, 1949, led logically and inevitably to American support for the French. Thus America's instinctive mistrust of Communist-led national liberation, until now roughly counterbalanced by its dislike of old-fashioned colonialism, began to get the upper hand. As Frederick Nolting, former United States ambassador to Saigon, observes:

> In 1946–47 . . . the United States urged France to support a non-Communist nationalist counterforce to the Vietminh. By 1949 . . . another and more compelling reason was added for U.S. support of the anti-communist forces in Indo-China— Mao Tse-tung's stunning victory in China. The United States decided to send military aid for France and its Vietnamese allies, beginning with the very modest sum of fifteen million dollars for military aid and 25 million for economic assistance.[62]

Both the recognition of the states of Indochina and the granting of military aid, however, were necessarily conditional upon the ratification by the French Assembly of the Elysée Agreement. For reasons of French internal politics, this was considerably delayed. Meanwhile in November, 1949, Malcolm Macdonald, the British High Commissioner in Southeast Asia, paid a short visit to Vietnam, and delivered a personal goodwill message to Bao Dai from Foreign Secretary Ernest Bevin.[63] After this visit "it began to appear that Britain might be considering recognition."[64] On January 27, 1950, the Elysée Agreement was finally ratified. On the same day, Jessup arrived in Vietnam, with a message to Bao Dai from Acheson, which promised the "constant attention" of the United States government. The Department of State, which, we are told by one authority, "had been awaiting the news of the ratification with much impatience,"[65] announced recognition of the Indochinese States on February 7 as "independent states within the French Union." Britain on the same day announced recognition of them, in rather more cautious wording, as "Associate States within the French Union." Later in the same month, the United States asked to be informed of French requirements regarding stores and equipment.[66]

The United States, clinging to its old dislike of colonialism, apparently still hoped to grant aid directly to the Associate States and perhaps to pressure France into giving them full independence, but its reservations were not maintained for long (although even after aid was granted, American attempts to by-pass the French authorities continued to cause friction). On May 8, 1950, after meeting with the French Minister in Paris, and also with Ambassador Jessup who was there, Acheson issued a statement promising "economic aid and military equipment," on the grounds that "neither national independence nor democratic evolution exist in any area dominated by Soviet imperialism."[67] At the end of May Robert Blum was appointed head of the United States aid mission to Vietnam with an initial budget of $23,500,000.

It is sometimes suggested that the occasion and cause of America's intervention in Vietnam was the outbreak of the Korean War. It is true that President Truman, in his statement of June 27, not only announced the intervention of the Seventh Fleet between Taiwan and China, but also stated that he had "directed acceleration in the furnishing of military assistance to the forces of France and the associated States in Indochina, and the dispatch of a military mission to provide close working relations with those forces." "Acceleration" is the key word here. The Korean War certainly increased the sense of urgency with which the United States sought to underpin the French in Indochina. But this underpinning operation was entirely consonant with the policy of commitment already embarked upon before the critical day of June 25. The Korean War did not change American policy in Vietnam because no change was needed.

Dean Rusk underlined the point in his testimony to the Senate Foreign Relations Committee in January, 1966. The "first involvement" of the United States in Vietnam, he explained, began "in 1949–50." The process had already begun, according to Rusk, before the spring of 1950 when he became Assistant Secretary of State for Far Eastern Affairs. ". . . the question of aid to France came up in the spring of 1950, but the policy involvement and the discussions with the French Government over it preceded it by some period." And Rusk also explained that

> After the Communists took over authority in Peiping [Peking], we and the British and the French were consulted on this situation and pretty well agreed that the security of southeast Asia was of vital interest to the free world. The joint effort therefore to find an agreement with the nationalists on the one side and to prevent a Communist takeover on the other was a common thread of policy throughout that period.[68]

CONCLUSION

It would be foolish to deny that, at various times in the history of the international Communist movement, the Soviet Union has, through the intermediary of the Comintern (before its dissolution in 1943) or of its own Party, attempted to and often succeeded in issuing "directives" to the Parties of other nations. It is also true that on many aspects of foreign as of domestic policy, there is a definable Soviet "line." But the evidence suggests that, as far as postwar Southeast Asia was concerned, the Soviet Union (1) did not attach sufficient priority to the area to formulate an easily definable "line," and (2) did not enjoy the kind of unquestioning obedience in the various Southeast Asia revolutionary movements which would insure that such a "line," even if it were crystal clear, would be followed. In the first place, the Soviet Union was preoccupied (as was also the United States) with European affairs to a degree which precluded any major initiative in Southeast Asia. Secondly, the indigenous revolutionary movements (which were by no means limited to Communist Party membership), were not accustomed to defer to Moscow with the same docility that had been shown by the pre-war European Parties. It is also arguable, at least in China and possibly in Vietnam, that the Soviet Union under Stalin's leadership was not anxious to encourage the emergence of independent, Communist-led nations which could not be easily controlled by the Soviet Party.

Both in output and intensity, the Chinese "line" on Asian revolution was far less equivocal than that of the Soviet Union. As we have seen, the advocate of a Chinese rather than of a Soviet "conspiracy" in the area would enjoy a much richer array of source material—if he did his home-work in the Chinese press of the period. Liu Shao-ch'i's praise in November, 1949, for the revolutionary "way of Mao Tse-tung" is only the best-known of many similar statements during the years 1946–51, while China's abusive condemnation of such Asian leaders as Sukarno and U Nu —"the feeble-minded bourgeoisie of the East"—can be judged by those who look for conspiracies to be equally damning.

Yet to regard China's revolutionary statements as evidence of some pan-Asian plan for subversion is to miss the point. Of course the Chinese were in favor of people who made revolution—as long as they did so intelligently and without adopting counter-productive tactics. And of course the Chinese Communist victory must have helped to inspire revolutionaries elsewhere to greater efforts. The fact remains that all of the insurgent movements in Asia had begun to operate well before the Chinese Communists came to power (and several had already passed their peak of activity). China "intervened" with aid or troops only in Vietnam and Korea. Both were areas where a change in the balance of power involving an increase in Western influence or control would constitute a threat to Chinese security.

Elsewhere the Chinese intervened with advice, and in this sense it may be true that Peking regarded itself as the source and fount of Asian revolution. The Chinese Communists are proud of their achievements to the point of chauvinism, and have never been backward in self-praise. Nor is this simply a human foible; by asserting the unique value of the Chinese revolution and of Mao's theories, the new government of the People's Republic was in effect declaring its doctrinal independence from the Soviet Union and Stalin.[69] Even at this early stage, it is quite possible that China hoped to establish its own "constituency" among the Asian Communist parties, and to insure that Asian revolutionaries turned for advice to Peking rather than to Moscow. Nevertheless the Chinese "line"—and this has been a consistent feature from Liu Shao-ch'i's speech of November, 1949, right until and including Lin Piao's essay (September, 1965) on People's War—stresses the need for self-reliance and a pragmatic approach to revolutionary tactics. In theory this was designed to avoid the kind of counter-productive deference to foreign advice and aid which had been a feature of the Chinese Communist Party in the late 1920's; in practice it meant that China did not need to get involved anywhere that her own national security did not dictate.

Should one conclude this article by turning the tables upon the advocates of a Soviet or Chinese conspiracy in Southeast Asia in the early post-war period, by showing that the real conspiratorial thrust came from the United States? Certainly the degree of conscious American involvement in this area, and the relatively early date at which it began, has been played down as consistently as the involvement of the Communist powers has been played up. How deep, how conscious and how early in date was America's imperialist thrust into Asia? These are vital questions which should concern anyone who seeks to explain Soviet and Chinese policies of the same period. In this as in other areas of the world and phases of the Cold War, the policies of the great powers are inter-dependent, acting and reacting upon one another: they cannot be viewed in isolation.

Yet in the last analysis the conspirationists' approach is

not merely harmful because it distracts our attention from taking a cold look at United States imperialism in Asia. More important is the way in which it encourages us to ignore what the Asians themselves are doing in Asia. After World War II the whole region was involved in a vast social and political upheaval—a "revolution" or turning upside-down of society in the full sense of the word (and one that had begun long before and is still in progress). Which is more important: this colossal, turbulent, and exciting process of national liberation, or some alleged secret directive from Moscow or Peking? And which had more influence on events in Asia?

Those who believe in the supreme power of "directives" and in the infinite cunning of Communists will always see the revolutionary process as the product of conspiracies. Their view is admirably put in the following quotation from a textbook on United States policy in Southeast Asia:

> Subversion can be understood as an insidious assault from within upon the institutions of a nation, culminating on occasion in armed revolt or insurgency. If Communist inspired, subversion or insurgency is supported by international communism acting with many different weapons—psychological, economic, diplomatic, and military—as the situation dictates.[70]

Certainly both the Soviet Union and China have at different times in their histories given some aid and support to insurgent movements elsewhere—although probably never as much as the revolutionaries themselves would have liked. But this does not help to explain why some of these movements have succeeded while others have been halted, far less why they began at all. A second opinion, diametrically opposed to the one quoted above, goes to the heart of the question:

> The conditions leading to revolutionary warfare are not created by conspiracy. They are inherent in the dislocations and demands produced by rapid social change, and are predicated on the failure of ruling élites to respond to the challenge of modernization.[71]

Notes

1. W. W. Rostow, Speech at University of Leeds, February 23, 1967, in *Viet Report,* Vol. III, No. 3 (June-July 1967), p. 31.
2. This is not meant to be an *ad hominem* argument. But the broad similarity of views between two so apparently dissimilar scholars is impressive. The relevant passages are: A. Doak Barnett, *Communist China and Asia* (New York, Vintage Books, 1961), pp. 151–57; Frank N. Trager, "The Impact of Marxism," in Trager (ed.), *Marxism in Southern Asia* (Stanford, Cal., Stanford Univ. Press, 1959), pp. 263–273.
3. Barnett, *Communist China and Asia,* pp. 151–52.
4. Charles B. McLane, *Soviet Strategies in Southeast Asia, an exploration of Eastern policy under Lenin and Stalin* (Princeton, N.J., Princeton Univ. Press, 1966), pp. 349–50. I have used McLane's analysis extensively; he refutes in great detail the more facile attempts to explain Asian revolution as the sole consequence of shifts in Soviet policy. He still believes however that at the Cominform meeting Moscow again "faced East," and henceforth sought to "project" its new doctrine into the strategies of the colonial Communist parties.
5. Isaac Deutscher, *Stalin* (London, Penguin Books, 1966), p. 570.
6. The Manifesto was published on October 5, 1947.
7. Trager, "Impact of Marxism," p. 265.
8. John H. Kautsky, *Moscow and the Communist Party of India* (New York, John Wiley and Sons, 1956), p. 28.
9. McLane, *Soviet Strategies,* p. 356.
10. Kautsky, *Moscow and the CPI,* p. 27.
11. Barnett, *Communist China and Asia,* p. 152.
12. Trager, "Impact of Marxism," pp. 263–64.
13. McLane, *Soviet Strategies,* pp. 359–60.
14. Trager, "Impact of Marxism," p. 266.
15. Capt. Malcolm Kennedy, *A Short History of Communism in Asia* (London, Weidenfeld and Nicolson, 1957), p. 359.
16. Barnett, *Communist China and Asia,* p. 152.
17. Roxas's policy towards the Hukbalahaps has been described as one of "forcible suppression, with however, ultimately an attempt at conciliation marked by some double-dealing by both sides," H. M. Vinacke, *A History of the Far East in Modern Times* (London, Allen and Unwin, 1960), p. 810. One writer states baldly

that the Huks "began a civil war in 1946," Alvin H. Scaff, *The Philippine Answer to Communism* (Stanford, Cal., Stanford Univ. Press, 1955), p. 3.

18. See further Anthony Short, "Communism and the Emergency," in Wang Gungwu (ed.), *Malaysia, A survey* (London, Pall Mall Press, 1964), pp. 151–53.

19. Herbert Feith, "Indonesia," in George McTurnan Kahin (ed.), *Governments and Politics of Southeast Asia* (Ithaca, N.Y., Cornell Univ. Press, 1964), p. 202.

20. McLane, *Soviet Strategies*, p. 274.

21. *Ibid.*, p. 432. Bernard Fall provides some interesting statistics on the paucity of post-war Soviet writings on Indochina, in *Le Viet-Minh* (Paris, Librairie Armand Colin, 1960), p. 118.

22. Thorez was reported to have said that he "ardently wished to see the French flag fly over all the corners of the French Union," quoted in Bernard Fall, *Viet-Nam Witness, 1953–66* (New York, Praeger, 1966), p. 23.

23. For further discussion of Soviet policy during the Chinese civil war, see John Gittings, *Survey of the Sino-Soviet Dispute* (London, Oxford University Press, 1968), pp. 11–14.

24. *Ibid.*, p. 24.

25. Fall, *Le Viet-Minh*, p. 119; P. J. Honey, *Communism in North Vietnam* (London, Ampersand Books, 1965), pp. 53–54.

26. McLane, *Soviet Strategies*, p. 440.

27. Ho Chi Minh, "The imperialist aggressors can never enslave the heroic Vietnamese people," January, 1952, in *Selected Works*, Vol. III (Hanoi, Foreign Languages Publishing House, 1961), p. 318. This is the sole reference to the Soviet Union (although the "brilliant example" of China was praised) in an article which was published in the official Cominform journal (April 4, 1952).

28. Joseph Frankel, "Soviet Policy in South East Asia," in Max Beloff (ed.), *Soviet Policy in the Far East 1944–51* (London, Oxford University Press, 1953), pp. 208, 212.

29. This discussion of the CPI is based upon Kautsky, *Moscow and the CPI*.

30. W. W. Rostow, *The Prospects for Communist China* (Cambridge, Mass., M.I.T., 1954), p. 202.

31. Ralph Retzlaff, "Revisionism and Dogmatism in the Communist Party of India," in Robert A. Scalapino (ed.), *The Communist Revolution in Asia* (Englewood Cliffs, N.J., Prentice-Hall, 1965), p. 312.

32. Kautsky, *Moscow and the CPI*, p. 27.

33. Gavin P. Boyd, *Communist China's Foreign Policy* (London, Pall Mall, 1962), p. 7.

34. New China News Agency (North Shensi) editorial on "The European Situation" October 7, 1947, trans. in NCNA *Weekly Bulletin No. 21*, London, October 28, 1947.

35. Ch'iao Mu (pen name for Ch'iao Kuan-hua, later a Deputy Foreign Minister of the CPR), "Shih-chieh jen-min ta-fan-kung" ("Great Counter-offensive of the people of the world"), *Cheng Pao,* Hong Kong (October 25, 1947), pp. 7–12.

36. Mao Tse-tung, "The present situation and our tasks," December 25, 1947, *Selected Works,* Vol. IV (Peking, 1961), p. 173.

37. NCNA (North Shensi), "Congratulations on the opening of the Southeast Asia Youth Conference," February 16, 1948, quoted in Hinton, *Communist China in World Politics* (Boston, Houghton Mifflin, 1966), p. 69.

38. Hu Tang, "Tung-ya-nan ch'ing-nian ta-hui sheng-li k'ai-mu" ("Victorious opening of Southeast Asia Youth Conference"), *Cheng Pao,* Hong Kong, March 30, 1948, p. 16.

39. Harold C. Hinton, *Communist China in World Politics* (Boston, Houghton Mifflin, 1966, p. 25.

40. See broadcasts by Moscow Radio and Radio Peace and Progress on July 12, 13, 24, 1967 & August 6, 30, 1967; translated in *BBC Summary of World Broadcasts, Part 1, the USSR,* Nos. 2517, 2521, 2533, 2544, 2557 (Caversham, 1967).

41. Given the hysterical nature of Soviet anti-Chinese propaganda, which now matches that of Taiwan, these charges of Chinese complicity in provoking "subversion" have no substantive merit. But it does seem unlikely that the Russians would seek to blame Mao for a policy which—if the Zhdanov-Calcutta theory were correct—they had taken the lead in promoting. The historical record can only be bent so far; enough Asian Communists are still around who would recall what really happened. If the Soviet charges have the slightest evidential value, it can only be that they may dimly reflect Soviet disapproval or disinterest at the time for the Asian revolutionary movements of the late 1940's.

42. Barnett, *Communist China and Asia,* p. 152.

43. Frankel, "Soviet Policy," pp. 210–11; Trager, "Impact of Marxism," p. 272; Werner Levi, *Modern China's Foreign Policy* (Minneapolis, Minnesota, Minnesota Univ. Press, 1953), pp. 326–27; Oliver E. Clubb, Jr., *The United States & the Sino-Soviet Bloc in Southeast Asia,* (Washington, D.C., Brookings Institution, n.d.), pp. 14–15; Hinton, *Communist China in World Politics,* pp. 25–26; Melvin Gurtov, *The First Vietnam Crisis, 1953–1954* (New York, Columbia Univ. Press, 1967), p. 7. Tang Tsou, *America's Failure in China, 1941–1950* (Chicago, Chicago Univ. Press, 1963), p. 563.

44. The vital sentence reads thus. "The path taken by the Chinese people in defeating imperialism and its lackeys and in founding the CPR is the path that should be taken by the peoples of *many (hsu-to)* colonial and semicolonial countries in their fight for national independence and people's democracy." The official NCNA translation rendered *hsu-to* as "the various," implying that Liu was talking about *all* colonial and semi-colonial countries. This seems to have been a mistake. Further on in the same speech, Liu says, according to NCNA, that "armed struggle can and must be the main form taken by the people's liberation struggles in *many* colonial and semi-colonial countries." Here the same phrase *hsu-to* has been translated correctly as "many." (My italics throughout.)

   All the usual authorities quote the first phrase ("The path taken by the Chinese people . . .") from the NCNA version, as Barnett, *Communist China and Asia*, p. 153. They can hardly be blamed for doing so, but the point illustrates an inherent danger in relying upon translations—even those of official origin.

45. Interview with Liu Ning-yi, in *Ch'un Chung* (Hong Kong), Vol. XII, No. 2, August 3, 1946.

46. *Hsin-hua Yueh-pao,* Vol. I, No. 2, December 1949.

47. Frankel, "Soviet Policy," p. 210.

48. Kennedy, *Short History*, pp. 365–67.

49. *People's China*, July 1, 1950; Kautsky, *Moscow and the CPI*, p. 127.

50. I shall ignore the view, expressed as far as I know only by Hinton, that the Chinese Communists inspired the Korean war. He argues that Mao, during his visit to Moscow in winter 1949–50, persuaded Stalin to give consent and logistical support to a three-pronged offensive, in Vietnam, against Taiwan, and invasion of South Korea. This theory flies in the face both of common sense and of available evidence. Hinton, *Communist China*, pp. 26, 208, 230.

51. Hinton, *Communist China*, p. 237; George McTurnan Kahin & John W. Lewis, *The United States in Vietnam* (New York, Dial Press, 1967), p. 271.

52. Chinese aid to the DRV seems to have amounted to the following: (1) mainly light arms until late 1953, including United States arms captured in Korea; (2) the training of Viet Minh troops in military camps in Southwest China; (3) some Chinese advisers attached to the Viet Minh forces; (4) some Chinese non-combatant troops, such as engineers and communications experts.

53. There is no official record of agreements between China and the DRV. Even those alleged by French sources are limited in extent. It was apparently agreed that Chinese forces "should

only intervene to prevent the annihilation of the Vietminh's forces; Chinese assistance, except in this emergency, would be confined to training, supply and advice." Joint measures were also agreed upon for "bandit clearance," i.e., the elimination of Chinese Nationalist units and French commandos on the Sino-Vietnamese border. R.I.I.A., *Survey of International Affairs, 1952* (London, Oxford Univ. Press, 1953), p. 420; Fall, *Le Viet-Minh,* p. 119.

54. Quoted in Gurtov, *The First Vietnam Crisis,* p. 14.

55. *Ibid.,* pp. 1–6.

56. *Ibid.,* pp. 9–10.

57. Levi, *Modern China's Foreign Policy,* p. 345; Clubb, *The United States and the Sino-Soviet Bloc,* p. 15.

58. Honey, *Communism in North Vietnam,* pp. 51–3. Honey's surprise at Ho's "decision" to seek Chinese and Soviet backing is slightly disingenuous, since he argues elsewhere that it was Chinese aid which "More than any other single factor ended French rule in Vietnam." *(Ibid.,* p. 12) There is no evidence for this assertion but it answers the questions in terms of his own argument.

59. *Department of State Bulletin,* (Washington, D.C., July 18, 1949).

60. Jessup had been appointed Ambassador-at-Large in February 1949, Keesings Contemporary Archives, p. 9820.

61. Acheson's top-secret memorandum of July 18, 1949 to Jessup is reproduced in *Nomination of Philip C. Jessup; Hearings before a Subcommittee of the Committee on Foreign Relations* (Washington, D.C., U.S. Government Printing Office, 1951), p. 603.

62. Frederick Nolting, in *Foreign Service Journal* (July, 1968), p. 19.

63. Keesings, p. 10493.

64. *Annual Register,* 1949, p. 431

65. Donald Lancaster, *The Emancipation of French Indochina* (London, Oxford University Press for R.I.I.A., 1960), p. 204.

66. *Ibid.,* p. 205.

67. R.I.I.A., *Documents on International Affairs, 1949–50,* p. 609.

68. *Hearings on Supplemental Foreign Assistance, Fiscal Year 1966—Vietnam,* Foreign Relations Committee, Senate (Jan. 28, 1966), Part 1, pp. 6–7.

69. There is considerable evidence of divergences between China and the Soviet Union on important points of doctrine. Professor Benjamin Schwartz has discussed these fully in his *Ideology in Flux* (Cambridge, Mass., Harvard Univ. Press, 1968). The Russians, as he points out, "made no concessions to Chinese claims that Mao had made original theoretical contributions to the storehouse of Marxism-Leninism." Conversely the Chinese took pains to emphasize that the Chinese Revolution was for the East

(or colonial world) what the Russian Revolution had been for the West (or imperial world). Mao's view of the "united front" strategy as including part of the national bourgeoisie seems to have been unpopular in Moscow before 1949. After 1949, there was an important discrepancy (also discussed very fully by Schwartz) between the Soviet and Chinese views on the nature of proletarian leadership in the transitional stage from capitalism to socialism. It is hardly too much to say that at no time from 1949 onwards did the Chinese and Russian brands of Marxist-Leninist theory genuinely coincide—except for the occasional verbal compromise.

70. R. H. Fifield, *Southeast Asia in United States Policy* (New York, Harper & Row, 1958, p. 160.

71. Eqbal Ahmad, in Marvin Gettleman (ed.), *Vietnam* (London, Penguin Books, 1966), p. 373.

Occupied Japan and the American Lake, 1945-1950

✺ John W. Dower

✺ FROM SEPTEMBER, 1945 to April, 1952, Japan was isolated from normal international contact as the United States conducted an unprecedented experiment in what is often described as "demilitarization and democratization." It was an undertaking of great energy and impressive scope, and to many Americans its results represent the single rose in an area which more and more has become America's crown of thorns. To them, Japan is proof of American wisdom, idealism, and benevolence; proof of the exportability of the American way of life; proof of American understanding of Asian problems and Asian personality; and a solid anchor to the deterrence cordon that stretches down to the Philippines and then hooks around Asia to Europe.

America's war-time allies played no appreciable role in the Allied Occupation of Japan. The civilian sector of the United States government was similarly excluded from the tasks of civil reform. The Japanese government, unlike its vanquished German ally, retained administrative functions, but it had no ultimate legal authority whatsoever. As Supreme Commander of the Allied Powers, General Douglas MacArthur took his orders directly from the American Joint Chiefs of Staff. "Your authority is supreme," the Joint Chiefs informed him in one of their earliest instructions,[1] and on a later and more rueful occasion MacArthur himself told a congressional committee, "I had not only the normal executive authorities such as our own President has in this country, but I had legislative authority. I could by

fiat issue directives."[2] One commentator has observed that
the power granted MacArthur in Japan was even greater
than that possessed by American theater commanders in the
war just past,[3] but this was more than just an exceptional
role in an exceptional situation. To a considerable extent
the authority exercised by MacArthur and his staff in Japan
reflected the greatly augmented decision-making power
which remained in the hands of the United States military
establishment on a global scale even after the war.[4] In Japan,
however, the sense of paradox was perhaps closer to the
surface. Japan was to be demilitarized by the military, decentralized by a hierarchy, democratized from above. It was
to undergo a revolution from without, bloodless and without revolutionaries.

Despite these contradictions, democratization did become
a major task of the Occupation, and in the early months in
particular a broad spectrum of notable reforms was initiated. For good reasons, most studies have focused on these
internal developments, but one result of this has been to
convey an impression of Occupied Japan as a country *in
vacuo*—neither greatly affected by nor greatly influencing
developments on a larger international stage. And this in
turn has helped gild the image of American benevolence.
The fact remains, however, that the reforms in Japan were
introduced with a primary concern for American security,
and while initially this meant eliminating the possibility of
Japan as a future aggressor, very shortly it came to mean
strengthening and utilizing Japan to play a positive role in
United States strategic policy against assumed threats from
recent war-time allies—first the Soviet Union, then China.
The United States military began to use and in some cases
rehabilitate Japanese air and naval bases as soon as the war
ended,[5] and American control of Japan not only locked into
a larger sphere of dominion in the Pacific, but also bore
particular relation to developments in China, Eastern
Europe, and Occupied West Germany. Well before the
Korean War, Occupation policy had been unilaterally re-

vised by the United States to build Japan into an anti-Communist workshop and base.

Prior to 1950 only one important State Department official even visited Japan.[6] That was George Kennan, and his visit offered no solace to those who opposed the Occupation's "reverse course" away from reform toward economic rehabilitation. Policy decisions involving such volatile issues as curtailment of reparations and removal of restrictions on industrial production were investigated and executed predominantly under the military aegis, and rarely did they receive the support of other countries. To virtually all of America's Cold War allies in the Pacific, to say nothing of Russia and China, American activity in Japan after 1947 was ominous and provocative, and it was widely acknowledged that these later policies frequently constituted a unilateral revision of some of the basic premises of the Occupation. The distance between General MacArthur's image of Japan as the "Switzerland of the East" and John Foster Dulles's vision of Japan as the linchpin in an iron noose of American containment in Asia was clearly immense in scope and very short in time. Inevitably, this gives the American Occupation of Japan a schizophrenic cast.

I · CONTROL OF JAPAN

STALIN HAD VOICED the fear of "capitalist encirclement" repeatedly from the 1920's, and throughout the war-time conferences he made clear his concern that Japan and Germany be held down once they had been defeated. His position was no more severe than that of the other Allies in the war-time and immediate post-war period. In late May of 1945, three months after the Soviet promise at Yalta to enter the war against Japan, Harry Hopkins cabled from Moscow that "the Marshal expects that Russia will share in the actual occupation of Japan and wants an agreement with the British and us as to occupation zones."[7] No such agreement was made with either country, for at Potsdam Truman decided that the United States would control Japan unilaterally. He reached this decision, he later recorded in his *Memoirs,* because "our experience with them in Germany and in Bulgaria, Rumania, Hungary, and Poland was such that I decided to take no chances in a joint setup with the Russians. . . . The Russians were planning world conquest."[8] By a ricochet effect, one is left to conclude, Great Britain and China would also have to be excluded from any share of control in Japan.

In the several weeks following the Hiroshima bomb, various exchanges took place between the United States and Russia concerning the Occupation of Japan. Some commentators have found in these incidents an early indication of hostile Soviet intentions toward Japan, but this does not seem warranted. Stalin did request that the landlocked Soviet Army be allowed to accept a token surrender in the northern part of the northern island of Hokkaido, but he accepted Truman's refusal with little more than a ritual protest.[9] Foreign Minister Molotov proposed that there be two Supreme Commanders—MacArthur and Marshal Vasilevsky—but he accepted Ambassador Averell Harriman's point-blank rejection of this suggestion, and the Soviet Union did not oppose MacArthur's nomination as sole commander.[10] On August 19, the Red Army proposed modifications of the Instrument of Surrender of Japan which would have compromised MacArthur's authority, but on August 27, the Red Army also stated that "if these corrections may create any sort of difficulty for General MacArthur, then the General Staff of the Red Army will not insist on these corrections."[11]

The Soviet Union also immediately announced its acceptance of an American proposal of August 21 calling for the establishment of an obviously powerless Far Eastern Advisory Commission which was to have its headquarters in Washington. Great Britain and the Commonwealth nations, on the other hand, raised strenuous objections to the lack of influence they would wield through such a body, and withheld consent to this proposal until October 1. A few days after the formal Japanese surrender on September 2, Russia stated that it believed a four-power control council (the United States, Soviet Union, Great Britain, and China) was also desirable for Occupied Japan.[12] Since the issue of a control council subsequently was to become a bone of contention between Russia and the United States and is frequently cited as yet another example of Soviet obstructionism, it is worth noting that Foreign Secretary Ernest Bevin stated at this time that the British cabinet endorsed this Soviet proposal.[13] This could hardly have come as a surprise to the United States, since prior to the Japanese capitulation Great Britain, like Russia and China, had indicated that it anticipated participating in the Occupation of Japan. Stalin also personally declined the opportunity to place a contingent of Soviet troops in Japan with the dry comment that any forces other than American might restrict the rights of General MacArthur, and although the matter of Soviet troops was raised subsequently, it was never a significant issue.[14]

It may be argued that the Russians had little room for maneuver in these matters, but if that is so, then there is no point, either, in interpreting such exchanges as significant examples of hostile Soviet behavior toward Japan. A better indication of Soviet intentions in the Far East came in Korea, where the Soviet forces accepted the Japanese surrender down to the thirty-eighth parallel as agreed upon and did not proceed further, even though the nearest American troops were 600 and 2,000 miles away (in Okinawa and the Philippines), and the Red Army was militarily capable of occupying the entire peninsula. Truman acknowledged that "even the 38th parallel was too far for any American troops to reach if the Russians had chosen to disagree."[15]

On August 29, two days after the Soviet General Staff had submitted its message withdrawing suggestions which "may create any sort of difficulty for General MacArthur," the

United States sent its "Initial Post-Surrender Policy for Japan" to the Supreme Commander without consulting or even informing any of the Allies about the contents of this lengthy directive. This fundamental document, which dealt not only with American conduct in Japan but also with the role of the Allies in the Occupation, remained secret until public statements by MacArthur forced Acting Secretary of State Dean Acheson to release the text on September 22, while Secretary of State James Byrnes was attending the London Conference of Foreign Ministers. Almost immediately after he saw the directive for the first time, Molotov injected the issue of control in Occupied Japan into the conference, although Japan had not even been listed on the original agenda, and the London conference subsequently broke down in large part over this unforeseen issue.[10]

American statements on this problem hardly cleared the air. President Truman told a press conference that the "Japanese Government" had been approved by all the Allied powers, and that he couldn't remember if the Soviet Union had previously suggested a control council. If the Allies wished to express their opinions about the Occupation, they could do so through the "Joint Chiefs of Staff." Assuming he meant the Combined Chiefs of Staff, the President was then asked how the Soviet Union could do that since it was not represented on the Combined Chiefs of Staff. Then, Truman answered, the Russians could express their views through the White House or to General MacArthur through their representatives in Japan (the following month Stalin temporarily withdrew General Derevyanko from Japan because MacArthur was treating him like "a piece of furniture"). Acheson was more suave. He stated that he believed the policy statement had been presented to the Allies before being sent to General MacArthur, which was false, and also that the United States had no intention of excluding anyone from the Occupation, which was also false.[17]

Several days later (October 1), one of the first Soviet warnings about the Occupation was raised by a Russian journalist in an article entitled "Eliminating Seats of Aggression or Preserving Them?" He quoted statements in the American press about preserving Japan as an armed buffer against the Soviet Union, and warned in particular that elimination of the potential for aggression in both Germany and Japan demanded thoroughgoing reform of the economic structures of both countries.[18] These tandem fears concerning Japan and Germany were to be fed by numerous developments in the course of the next several years.

The discord over Japan which took place at the London conference marked the first really serious and open expression of Soviet-American confrontation concerning Allied participation in the Occupation, and over the next several months considerable energy was devoted to attempting to reconcile the opposing positions. It became increasingly apparent that the Russians' main concern was Eastern Europe and they were attempting to draw a parallel between Soviet control in this area and American control in Japan and the Pacific. On numerous occasions both Stalin and Molotov specifically described the "control council" they envisioned for Japan as being along the lines, not of the German arrangement, but of the councils already existing in Rumania, Hungary, and Bulgaria.[19] Reference to the control arrangements in these key areas of Soviet-American tension carried a double edge. On the one hand it would tend to formalize American control in Japan and the Pacific as a *quid pro quo* for Soviet control in the three former Nazi satellites; on the other hand, it served as an unhappy reminder to the Americans that the controversial control councils in the three countries had been modeled on the Anglo-American occupation regime established in Italy in 1943.[20] The Italian precedent is, in fact, illuminating when placed in conjunction with later American attitudes toward Japan. Italian troops had fought on the Russian front, while Japan was undeniably the historic enemy of Russia. Although the

East - West ↔ USSR

direct Soviet war effort against each country had been minimal, Russia's indirect contributions to Allied victory over both Italy and Japan were not to be lightly dismissed. The Anglo-American campaign against Italy had been possible because Russia was simultaneously bearing the brunt of the land war against Germany. Similarly, without in any way denigrating the overwhelming burden carried by the American forces in the Pacific theater, Japan's capitulation was still partly determined not only by the psychological and military effects of the Soviet declaration of war, but also by developments on the Western front. In the words of Theodore Ropp, "Midway was the decisive battle of the Pacific war, unless the Battles of Britain, Moscow, and Stalingrad can be said to have doomed the entire Japanese enterprise."[21] By rejecting Soviet requests for an effective role in the Italian Occupation and establishing instead a precedent of occupation-by-actual-conquest, the United States and Great Britain severely prejudiced their case concerning control over the East European satellites. When Truman subsequently justified unilateral American control of Japan by pointing to Soviet intransigence in these other countries, he left himself vulnerable to accusations that he was playing a complex double game.

By December, when the foreign ministers met again at Moscow, it appeared that the United States had accepted the basic premises of the Soviet position. In essence the relevant agreements negotiated by Byrnes and Molotov at this time exchanged American recognition of the controversial regimes in Rumania and Bulgaria for Soviet acquiescence in the dismissal of its demands for a really meaningful role in the control of the Japanese Occupation. As agreed upon at Moscow, Allied participation in the Occupation of Japan was to be channeled through an eleven-power Far Eastern Commission meeting in Washington and a four-power Allied Council meeting in Tokyo. In theory these organs provided a forum for discussion of basic policy concerning the future development of Japan, but as was widely recognized, they were in fact structured to ensure ultimate American control. At the Moscow conference, Molotov and Byrnes also came to an understanding that the former Japanese mandated islands would be disposed of in accordance with American wishes, in return for which it was understood that the United States would support Soviet claims to the Kuriles and South Sakhalin, as had been agreed upon at Yalta.[22] The Russians had clearly settled for token participation in the Occupation of Japan and for American control of an area of strategic concern to the Soviet Union, but they did so with the understanding that the United States would similarly acknowledge Soviet interests in the Balkans.

They were wrong. A portion of the American press applauded the agreements reached at Moscow as realistic, and Byrnes was supported in his decision by such prominent diplomats as Averell Harriman and Charles Bohlen. But others attacked Byrnes for appeasement.[23] Leading Republicans such as John Foster Dulles, Senator Arthur Vandenberg, and Claire Booth Luce seized the opportunity to launch their campaign for a hard line against Russia; Sumner Welles denounced the agreements as a betrayal of the Balkan peoples; and in a memorandum of January 5, 1946, to Byrnes, Truman dressed-down his Secretary of State in these terms:

> I do not think we should play compromise any longer. We should refuse to recognize Rumania and Bulgaria until they comply with our requirements; we should let our position on Iran be known in no uncertain terms and we should continue to insist on the internationalization of the Kiel Canal, the Rhine-Danube waterway, and the Black Sea Straits, and we should maintain complete control of Japan and the Pacific. We should rehabilitate China and create a strong central government there. We should do the same for Korea.
>
> Then we should insist on the return of our ships from Russia and force a settlement of the Lend-Lease debt of Russia.
>
> I'm tired of babying the Soviets.[24]

The United States, in short, expected both "complete control of Japan and the Pacific" and compliance with its requirements in Central and Eastern Europe and the Middle East. This was over a year before the Truman Doctrine and several years before it is generally acknowledged that the decision was reached to secure Japan as a permanent fixture in what Bevin glumly referred to as the "Monroe sphere" of the Pacific.[25] But the die was clearly cast at an early date, and mutual suspicions and recriminations about Japan developed subsequently with an inevitability that kept pace with and intermeshed with the bitter tensions that were developing on the larger stage outside Japan. Just as the United States found it difficult to accept the explanation that the Soviet Union was acting in accordance with basic security concerns in expanding its frontiers of influence, particularly in Eastern Europe, so the Communists (including the Chinese as well as the Russians) became more and more unable to believe that American-controlled "democratization" of Japan was not primarily remilitarization and capitalist exploitation in new guise, or that American "defense posts" in the Pacific were not in fact advance bases for the launching of an American attack against the Asian continent.

II · THE AMERICAN LAKE

UNILATERAL CONTROL over Japan was part of a vaster pattern of expanding American power, for with the elimination of the Japanese navy and air force, the United States also assumed unprecedented control of the Pacific north of the equator. As early as 1943, it was generally taken for granted that the United States would retain pre-eminent influence in this area after the war.[26] From 1944 on, responsible military officers, cabinet officials, and congressmen publicly maintained that the United States would hold on to whatever Pacific bases it deemed necessary to its security, particularly among the three archipelagos (the Carolines, Marshalls, and Marianas, collectively known as Micronesia) which Japan had held since 1920 under a mandate from the League of Nations.[27] By early 1945 the position that the United States should preserve its "national security interests" by indefinitely controlling key islands in the Pacific had received unanimous endorsement within the highest circles of the American government.[28] Secretary of War Henry Stimson recorded in his diary for March 18, 1945, that President Roosevelt himself was

> just as keen as anybody else to take the full power of arming them and using them to protect the peace and ourselves during any war that may come, and for that reason his people at San Francisco will be trying to form a definition of trusteeships or mandates which will permit that to be done.[29]

As Stimson's comments indicate, the United States delegation to the founding conference of the United Nations was concerned with drafting a trusteeship provision which would protect the national interests of the United States in the Pacific. To this end, a special category of trust territory known as "strategic areas" was created, and this was tailored to ensure American control over the disposition of the conquered Pacific islands. At the time of the San Francisco conference, congressmen led by Senators Harry Byrd and Charles W. Tobey demanded assurance that the veto provision in the United Nations would not jeopardize American control over the former Japanese mandates and they received such assurance from Secretary of State Edward Stettinius, United States representative to the United Nations, Harold Stassen, and Senate representatives to the conference, Tom Connally and Arthur Vandenberg.[30] Exactly how this was to be managed was made somewhat clearer by the Senate Foreign Affairs Committee which, on the basis of letters from the Secretaries of War and Navy, reported on July 16, 1945, that "no island in the Pacific occupied by the United States could be placed under trusteeship without this government's consent, and therefore only on terms agreeable to the United States."[31] Underlying this hard-headed approach was a controversy over tactics within the United States government, for despite general agreement upon the necessity of de facto United States control, the State Department and the War and Navy departments disagreed upon how this should be effected: the State Department argued for at least nominal United Nations legitimization, while the military establishment tended to favor outright annexation of the desired islands.[32] Between January and April of 1945, Stimson and Navy Secretary James Forrestal had unsuccessfully proposed several quasi-legal formulations by which they hoped to exclude the islands from United Nations supervision,[33] and in May, 1945, at the very time of the San Francisco conference, a subcommittee of the Senate Naval Affairs Committee was adding its voice to the call for annexation.[34] This debate continued until 1947, when the islands were formally placed under sole United States control as strategic area trusteeships, but it was essentially an academic debate. As many commentators later pointed out, the issue was between outright annexation or stopping one step short of that.[35]

Well before the capitulation of Japan, the Pacific islands had thus become one touchstone of American intentions concerning the post-war period. Policy-makers were confronted with the problem of reconciling their determination to control the islands with the pledges against territorial aggrandizement and territorial expansion originally expressed in the Atlantic Charter and the Cairo Declaration.[36] Much of the verbal juggling which ensued was directed at evading this dilemma. American spokesmen took refuge in the fact that the United States had been blessed with flanks that opened upon vast seas and sparsely peopled islands, and not upon populous land masses: thus "imperialism," "colonialism," "exploitation," were not involved. Even if one accepted this argument, however, the basic question still remained whether the United States would resort to unilateral or international control in an area where it believed its own national interests to be particularly involved. If a nationalistic pose were adopted—what critics called "security imperialism"—it was clear that the Allies would be able to use this to justify imposing similar control over their own respective areas of particular interest. American actions in the Pacific, in short, were related to Soviet interests in Eastern Europe and British, French, and Dutch desires to reassert control in Southeast Asia. Foreign Secretary Anthony Eden clearly had this in mind in 1943 when he urged the United States to assert outright ownership over the mandated islands,[37] and Churchill laid the issue on the line early in 1945 when he wrote to Eden:

> If the Americans want to take the Japanese islands which they have conquered, let them do so with our blessing and any form of words that may be agreeable to them. But "Hands Off the British Empire" is our maxim.[38]

Stimson, who insisted that the United States must have "absolute power to rule and fortify" the Pacific islands, recognized a relationship between United States interests in the Pacific and Soviet interests in the "buffer states" of Eastern Europe.[39] Truman did not, and made this clear at an early date. Near the beginning of his speech from Potsdam on August 9, the President observed that

> though the United States wants no territory or profit or selfish advantage out of this war, we are going to maintain the military bases necessary for the complete protection of our interests and of world peace. Bases which our military experts deem to be essential for our protection, and which are not now in our possession, we will acquire.[40]

He went on to note that these bases would be acquired "by arrangements consistent with the United Nations Charter"—but as indicated above, the relevant articles of that Charter had been drafted to conform to these particular United States intentions. Then, further on in his address, Truman declared that

> Rumania, Bulgaria and Hungary . . . are not to be spheres of influence of any one power.

Within the next several weeks and months it became apparent that the bases which the United States deemed necessary to its security were many indeed, and by no means restricted to the former Japanese mandates. Nevertheless, the President consistently refused to acknowledge the existence of an American sphere in the Pacific, and equally consistently continued to denounce Soviet attempts to unilaterally organize the area east of the Elbe. Other Americans were more sensitive to the contradiction. Both Walter Lippmann and James Reston devoted columns to it, and Lippmann suggested that the United States was "incurring the grave suspicion of using morality as an instrument of our own power politics."[41]

At the San Francisco conference, no mention had been made of specific areas that might fall under the trusteeship provisions. As a result, public knowledge of which bases the United States intended to maintain emerged piecemeal in the course of the ensuing months. The first official indication came approximately ten days after Truman's Potsdam address in a widely publicized report by the Subcommittee on Pacific Bases of the House Committee on Naval Affairs. This report stated that the United States "must retain" all of Micronesia (including even the British mandated islands of the Gilberts), plus the conquered outlying Japanese islands (specifically the Ryukyus, Izus, and Bonins), plus the major island bases on territories of other Allied powers (especially Manus, Nouméa, Espiritu Santo, and Guadalcanal), plus "all land-plane bases now under the control of the Allies in the Pacific," plus the pre-war American islands (such as Guam). The subcommittee also expressed the opinion that it was difficult to see how anyone could challenge American "retention of authority" over the Kuriles after the war. The press described this report as a plan "to make an American lake out of the Pacific Ocean."[42]

On September 5, three days after the formal surrender of Japan, the Navy recommended retention of nine major bases in the Pacific and six in the Atlantic. The Pacific ring, necessary to "keep an aggressor far from United States shores," was made up of Kodiak; Adak, in the Aleutians; Hawaii; Balboa, near the Panama Canal zone; the Guam-Saipan-Tinian complex; Iwo Jima; Okinawa; Manus, in the Australian-controlled Admiralties; and the Philippines. Assistant Secretary of the Navy H. Struve Hensel made clear the Navy's view that other islands also should be kept to keep them out of the hands of any other nation, and both he and Forrestal stressed the fact that additional recommendations would be forthcoming from the Army Air Forces and others. Questioned in particular on the inclusion of Okinawa, Mr. Hensel replied that the Navy would "rather keep Okinawa as one of our own."[43] In an editorial on September 7, the *Washington Post* quoted Admiral Raymond A. Spruance, commander of the Fifth Fleet, to the effect that both Okinawa and Iwo Jima provided bases that "would hem in China more effectively than Japan," and thus, along with Manus, ought to be placed under international control.

Hensel's announcement was by no means the last word, or even the Navy's last word, on the question of the Pacific bases. On September 19, Fleet Admiral Ernest J. King, Commander-in-Chief of the Fleet, testified that he personally preferred American sovereignty rather than international trusteeship over the conquered islands. On October 1, following a thirty-nine-day inspection tour of American bases, a War Department Subcommittee of the House Appropriations Committee reported to the President that "we should keep former Japanese islands in the Pacific, and negotiate for bases on Allied islands which American forces occupied during the war."[44] The President himself seemed to be thinking along similar lines. He was asked about United States policy concerning the former mandated islands at a press conference on January 15, 1946, and, as described in a *Department of State Bulletin:*

The President declared that those we do not need will be placed under UNO trusteeship, and those we need we will keep. Asked how long we intended to keep these islands, Mr. Truman said, as long as we needed them.[45]

Exactly what "those we need" were, however, was still indefinite, and it soon became apparent that the Navy had more expansive plans in mind than had been suggested the previous September. On February 14, 1946, Vice Admiral Forrest P. Sherman, Deputy Chief of Naval Operations, testified before the Senate Naval Affairs Committee that it was the official Navy position that United States foreign policy in the Pacific should be: "Maintain strategic control of the Pacific Ocean Area." To accomplish this end, Admiral Sherman proposed maintenance of a total of thirty-three naval bases and airfields in twenty-two separate localities. The bases were as follows:

1 Main Naval Base: Hawaii

1 Major Operating Base: Guam-Saipan

1 Major Operating Base, Caretaker Status: Manus

2 Secondary Operating & Repair Bases: Adak, Philippines

6 Secondary Operating Bases, Small: Kodiak, Dutch Harbor, Attu, Midway, Samoa, Ryukyus

7 Air Bases: Johnston Island, Palmyra, Canton Island, Majuro, Wake, Marcus, Iwo Jima

4 Combined Air Bases and Fleet Anchorages: Kwajalein, Eniwetok, Truk, Palau

11 Air Fields: Hawaii, Kodiak, Dutch Harbor, Adak, Attu, Midway, Samoa, Manus, Guam-Saipan, Philippines, Ryukyus[46]

Between March and May, hearings held on congressional appropriations for the fiscal year beginning July 1, 1946, indicated that Admiral Sherman's list of bases was being adhered to very closely, with funds also being allotted for the upkeep of bases on Subic, Leyte, Samar, Puerto Princesa, Christmas Island, New Caledonia, and Espiritu Santo—as well as in "Japan, Korea, China."[47] On May 30, Fleet Admiral Chester W. Nimitz, Chief of Naval Operations, revealed in testimony before a Senate subcommittee that

> the Pacific Fleet will have in active status an amphibious force adequate to lift 1 reinforced marine division, 7 carriers, 6 escort carriers, 2 battleships, 17 cruisers (8 heavy and 9 light), 72 destroyers, 39 submarines, 16 destroyer escorts.[48]

This was considerably larger than the Atlantic Fleet. On July 7, before the issue of the Pacific islands had even been submitted to the United Nations, the United States dramatically revealed that it had particular plans for yet another atoll in Micronesia. On that day, ninety-eight obsolete warships were bombed at Bikini in the Marshall Islands in the first atomic test since Nagasaki.[49]

American imposition of unilateral control over a Pacific "security zone" did not go unchallenged in the United States. Admiral Spruance had singled out the location of the Ryukyus vis-à-vis China as early as August, 1945, and made the simple and rare observation that "it would be a sore point with us if a foreign power held a string of islands blockading our coast."[50] Other commentators sharpened the edge of the debate—first, by pointing out that as of August 9, 1945, it was necessary to think in terms of nuclear technology; and second, by asking what enemy the United States was really directing its bases against. In the November, 1945, issue of *Harper's,* for example, Colonel Frederick Palmer, the well-known war correspondent, explicitly asked whether the Pacific bases were being maintained against China or Russia. He focused on the problem of the Ryukyus, and observed that "if we insist on holding Okinawa, from which we could readily reach Port Arthur and Vladivostok with supersonic, pilotless, jet-propelled planes bearing atomic bombs, we may well excite deep Russian suspicions."[51] Colonel Palmer's prediction was correct, although the Soviet Union appears to have muted its criticism of American activity in the Pacific for a surprisingly long time. The December, 1945, issue of the official Soviet publication *New Times* observed rather dryly that since many of the United States bases were located "from 9–10,000 kilometers from the American continent . . . the arguments usually advanced that the United States needs the given bases to guarantee the security of her own territory are not always convincing."[52] By September, 1946, Soviet commentaries had more bite. "If this can be called 'defense,'" asked a Soviet admiral writing in *Pravda,* then "what is 'attack'?" The admiral placed the Pacific bases in the context of a world-wide expansion of American naval power—specifically seeing Okinawa as a strategic Pacific counterpart of Iceland and Greenland—and noted that "under the projected plan of American control over the former Japanese mandated islands, United Nations control must not be extended to them: thus, the United States is attempting to maintain 'secret bases.'"[53]

Two months later, the United States did submit its trustee-ship proposals for Micronesia to the United Nations, but in essence this did not invalidate the Soviet comment about "secret bases." In accordance with the "strategic area" category first defined at San Francisco, the American draft proposal designated the United States as sole administrator for the former mandates, with authority to declare any part of the area under its jurisdiction "closed for security reasons"; under this type of unique closed-door trusteeship, even the United Nations itself would be prohibited from inspecting the territories placed in trust under its own auspices.[54] Confronted with criticism that this distorted the principle of collective security, John Foster Dulles, United States representative to the Trusteeship Committee of the General Assembly, served notice that if the United Nations did not accept the American proposals, the United States would simply ignore the international body and continue its *de facto* occupation of the Pacific islands.[55] In a sense this proved a successful trial run for the style Dulles was later to bring to the creation of a separate peace with Japan and a more formal containment policy for the Pacific. The United States proposal was approved by the United Nations Security Council essentially as submitted in April,

1947, and by Congress the following July. It covered only the former Japanese mandates, leaving open the problem of Okinawa and the other outlying Japanese islands, and the arrangement could not be altered, amended, or terminated without the consent of the United States. The United States military thus had met its alleged requirements in Micronesia, while the State Department had attained a paper victory. Just as unilateral American control of Japan had been covered over by the fiction of an Allied occupation, now American control of the Pacific was deemed adequately disguised by a posture of collective responsibility under the United Nations.

* * *

In 1949 and 1950, considerable debate ensued as to whether South Korea was or was not a part of the American "defense perimeter" in Asia. The general contours of this perimeter, however, were clearly drawn; it extended from Alaska and the Aleutians through the four main islands of Japan, the outlying Japanese island chains of the Ryukyus, Bonins, and Volcanos, and the three sprawling archipelagos of Micronesia, to the Philippines. South of the equator, American defenses meshed with those of Australia and New Zealand, with the restored colonial regimes in Southeast Asia, and in particular with Great Britain's newly created defense system extending from the Indian Ocean "through the heartland of Africa to the Atlantic bulge of West Africa pointing toward America."[56] This was the bedrock of America's military containment policy toward Asia, and it was taken for granted before John Foster Dulles, before the Korean War, before the victory of Communism in China, and even before the capitulation of Japan. During the war and in the immediate post-war years, China also was considered to be a part of the American sphere in Asia.

Firm and far-sighted plans for post-war military use of the Philippines were set forth in a joint resolution by both houses of Congress on June 29, 1944. By this resolution, the United States reserved the right to obtain air and naval bases in the Philippines after the Islands became independent on July 4, 1946. This resolution was approved by the Philippine assembly in July, 1945, and formalized in the Military Bases Agreement of March 1946, whereby the United States obtained 99-year leases upon the use of more than twenty bases in the Philippines.[57] The potential military significance of this agreement was revealed at a news conference held by General H. H. Arnold in mid-August, 1945, at which the commander of the final, *post*-surrender air raid on Japan announced that America would soon have a new super-bomber capable of carrying improved atomic bombs anywhere on the globe within a few hours. To illustrate this, General Arnold displayed a map of the world with five ellipses drawn on it, each representing a perfect circle ten thousand miles in diameter (the projected total cruising range of the new bomber). Together the five circles encompassed the entire earth except for small parts of the Arctic and Antarctic; and the base chosen to illustrate potential American control of China and the Western Pacific, as well as all of Russia except its westernmost regions, was near Manila.[58] Nor was American interest in the Philippines purely strategic. By the United States-Philippine Trade Act of 1946, the United States was granted preferential rights which virtually assured that it would continue to dominate the Philippine economy as it had in the colonial period.[59]

In the immediate post-war years it was also possible to regard China as a potential part of the American security zone, for there the United States stood closest to Chiang Kai-shek at a time when few, including Stalin, foresaw how imminent and inevitable was the demise of the Kuomintang regime. Already in 1944, John Service was discussing China in terms of its anticipated role as "a possible counter-weight to Russia," and this view represented a natural response to the removal of Japan as an anti-Communist buffer in Asia. American material support of the Kuomintang regime was directed toward this end, and contrasted markedly with the Soviet policy of non-involvement in the Chinese civil war. The famous Wedemeyer Report of September, 1947, enunciated both prickly sides of this military concern very clearly:

> Any further spread of Soviet influence and power would be inimical to United States strategic interests. In time of war the existence of an unfriendly China would result in denying us important air bases for use as staging areas for bombing attacks as well as important naval bases along the Asiatic coast. Its control by the Soviet Union or a regime friendly to the Soviet Union would make available for hostile use a number of warm water ports and air bases. Our own air and naval bases in Japan, Ryukyus and the Philippines would be subject to relatively short range neutralizing air attacks. Furthermore, industrial and military development of Siberia east of Lake Baikal would probably make the Manchurian area more or less self-sufficient.
>
> On the other hand, a unified China friendly or allied to the United States would not only provide important air and naval bases, but also from the standpoint of its size and manpower, be an important ally to the United States even though her poor communications and lack of modern industrial development would make her contribution less effective than would otherwise be the case.[60]

At approximately the same time (on September 1, 1947), the *New York Times* summed up some of the "concrete factors entering any estimate of China's importance in the Pacific pattern of power" as follows, in an article entitled "US Bases in China Held to Be Vital: Our Sphere of Influence Now Goes as Far as Sinkiang, Adjoining Soviet Asia":

> First, Manchuria presents the possibility, under complete Communist domination, of becoming another Outer Mongolia, employable in time as an economically rich base for penetration into northern China on a big scale. Together with northern Korea, Siberia, Sakhalin and the Kuriles, it flanks an American-occupied Japan, standing at the end of a long sea supply line.
>
> Second, from a military standpoint China is important to

long-range aerial warfare. Manchuria and Sinkiang constitute possible fighter-plane bases on an aerial route leading from Okinawa through west China to the important Lake Baikal industrial region of the Soviet Union.

Third, the concentration of population in China provides a tremendous reservoir of manpower within a large area that has exerted a strong influence on the rest of the Far East.

Fourth, aside from the resources of Manchuria, China contains basic strategic materials, including tungsten, antimony, tin and perhaps uranium. There has been a preliminary investigation of reported uranium deposits.

Fifth, largely undeveloped, China also offers considerable potentialities as a market. This, however, is not considered as important as the security factors.

However important it may have been in the overall picture, the economic side of China's projected role in the new American empire, as in the case of the Philippines, was certainly not neglected. Twentieth-century American bureaucrats revived nineteenth-century dreams to envision a future China which would provide—in the words of the OSS in 1945—"a large scale market for American goods and capital." To this end, Washington's policy-makers placed a priority upon the restoration of "open door" economic opportunities in a shattered China, and attempted to ensure that private American firms would not meet competition by nationalized Chinese enterprises.[61]

By the time of the Wedemeyer Report, however, the Kuomintang debacle was underway and American planners had already begun to resurrect Japan as the inevitable pivot of power in their strategic planning for Asia. By this transformation, Japan did not merely replace China, but began to emerge as the logical bastion *against* China, as well as against the Soviet Union. The strategic significance of Japan as an "unsinkable aircraft carrier" athwart the Asian land mass is apparent, for the islands extend some fifteen hundred miles from near the Kuriles in the north to below Korea in the south. In the period before the detonation of the first Soviet nuclear device (August, 1949) and before the development of the vast SAC-ICBM-Polaris complex, it was obvious that control of Japan provided the United States with potential bases from which to attack the Soviet Far East and particularly Vladivostok, Russia's strategic eastern harbor and the target of Japan's surprise assault four decades earlier.[62]

General MacArthur had described Japan as the "western outpost of our defenses" as early as July, 1946,[63] and unofficial reports from Tokyo suggested that this strategic dimension of the Cold War was close to the surface in Japan from the very beginning of the Occupation. As early as December, 1945, it was reported that MacArthur headquarters was split into "two warring camps" coalescing around Major General Charles Willoughby, Chief of Military Intelligence, and Brigadier General Courtney Whitney, Chief of Government Section, with the former opposing extensive purges and reforms on the grounds that a conservative Japan was a necessary ally for the United States in "the coming war with Russia."[64] Harold Isaacs reported from Japan in 1946 that "every correspondent in Tokyo heard officers of general rank describe Japan as 'the staging area for the next operation.' "[65] Mark Gayn recorded in his *Japan Diary* for May 27 of the same year:

> Here, today, one lives in an atmosphere of frontline trenches. Increasingly a correspondent's critical news report of this or that activity in Headquarters is greeted with the angry comment:
> "We're at war with the Russkys. Whose side are you on?"
> With war on Russia supposedly imminent, it becomes imperative to modify reform.[66]

Darrell Berrigan reported on flights of B-29's over Japan and Korea in August, 1946, and expressed a similar view that the American military staff in Japan gave the impression that they were really there to prepare for the "inevitable" war with Russia, and that this had become a greater concern to them than reforming *zaibatsu*.[67] This sense of crisis, moreover, appears to have made a strong and immediate impression even upon the average Japanese citizen. Three months after Hiroshima, the writer Jun Takami made this cryptic entry in his diary:

> *November 7.* In the streets, rumor of an American-Russian war. If Japan becomes the battleground, this time it can't be saved. Everywhere, gloomy faces.[68]

As the Cold War intensified and attempts to create a control system for nuclear development faltered, more elaborate justifications for Japanese gloom became available. The *Bulletin of Atomic Scientists* of July, 1947, for example, described United States Navy Department thinking as follows:

> What is necessary to reach the target is a launching base relatively near the target—to put it literally, within five hundred miles. . . . Under the conditions of war in which atomic bombs are available to a possible enemy, the importance of depriving the enemy of bases near one's own shore and preferably of acquiring and maintaining bases close to his territory remains as great as before. The logic supporting this proposition derives from the characteristics of atomic bomb carriers presently known or conceivable. . . . The outlying base, if properly placed, is also a tremendous advantage to the defense as a further measure of protection against long-range bombing aircraft. For such bases provide means of advance protection and interception which greatly augments the obstacles to penetration of vital territories by attacking bombers. These bases may themselves be vulnerable to atomic bomb attack, but so long as they are there, they are not likely to be by-passed. In this respect the advanced base may be likened to the pawns in front of the king on a chess-board; meager though their power may be individually, so long as they exist and the king stays severely behind them, he is safe.[69]

An increasing number of Japanese became aware of this general logic and disenchanted with the possibility of having to protect the king in this manner. The belief that Japan might become an American pawn in any major conflict between the super-powers underlay much of the opposition to the peace treaty and security pact with which the Occupation was terminated.

* * *

The metaphor of the Pacific as an American Lake was not anti-American propaganda, but an image imbedded in the American tradition. Sympathetic journalists used the expression as a matter of course, and in 1949 General MacArthur himself announced that

> Now the Pacific has become an Anglo-Saxon lake and our line of defense runs through the chain of islands fringing the coast of Asia. It starts from the Philippines and continues through the Ryukyu archipelago which includes its broad main bastion, Okinawa. Then it bends back through Japan and the Aleutian Island chain to Alaska.[70]

In giving the image a more explicitly racial cast, MacArthur was tapping a strain of thought that ran deeper than nationalism and recalled the racism and Social Darwinism which had accompanied America's first great thrust into the Pacific at the close of the nineteenth century. That earlier exercise in "insular imperialism" had resulted in the country's initial territorial acquisitions in the Pacific—Hawaii, Wake, Midway, Guam, Samoa, and the Philippines—and much of the rhetoric of the expansionists of the 1890's was picked up and carried forward by the expansionists of the 1940's. In a sense, America's post-war position represented the fulfillment of Theodore Roosevelt's wish of 1900 "to see the United States the dominant power on the Pacific Ocean," and Senator Albert Beveridge's assertion in the same year that "the Pacific is our ocean."[71]

The new American Lake, moreover, was fed by more than just the rhetoric of the expansionism of the past. It also drew upon some of the basic strategic, commercial, and psychological assumptions of the earlier period. As early as 1898, Whitelaw Reid and his fellow expansionists on the peace commission for the Philippines had expressed the hope that by adding the Philippines to Hawaii, "it would be possible for American energy to . . . ultimately convert the Pacific Ocean into an American Lake." Reid even urged President McKinley to assert American control over Micronesia.[72] This more commercially oriented view, best typified by Brooks Adams's vision of Asia as the new Far West, was reiterated at the Republican convention of 1904 when Chauncey Depew described the world as an American marketplace and "the Pacific as an American lake . . . because the world is ours, and we have conquered it by Republican principles."[73] Providing an over-arching framework to such concerns were the more rigorous geopolitical theories expounded in Alfred Mahan's disquisitions on the role of naval power—and on the necessity of countering the northern menace of expanding Russian power in Asia. Visions of China being absorbed by Russia to form "the most powerful Empire ever known among men" flicker through the rhetoric of these early expansionists with a kind of uncanny contemporaneity—two decades before the establishment of the Soviet Union, five decades before the creation of the People's Republic of China.[74] Similarly, fear of an industrialized China did not originate with American perceptions of Mao's success, but rather forms a familiar theme in American writings at the turn of the century. The desire to forestall such development, to perpetuate dominance over the Orient, is expressed there as well.[75]

More ambiguous psychic drives also appear among the lines of continuity. To a certain degree, for example, the sense of mission which motivated both religious and political evangelists of an earlier era re-emerged in the post-war American assertion of a global role as guardian at the gates—no matter how many or how far away the gates might be. Where the resonance was perhaps most striking of all, however, was in the underlying and unquestioned assumption of American righteousness and fair play. In a sense the policy-makers of the mid-twentieth century consciously drew upon

the past for the ultimate defense of America's right to unilaterally organize the Pacific, and found their justification
in the open-door myth that, as Stimson phrased it, "we had
always stood for freedom and peace in the Pacific."[76]

The continuities are illuminating, but the creation of a
post-war American power ring in the Pacific was defended on
its own terms.[77] It was justified as due recompense for the
blood and treasure lost in the Pacific War: almost 250
thousand dead, and huge sums expended to establish and
equip several hundred bases in the Pacific theater alone.[78]
It was described as necessary for the prevention of future
aggression in the Pacific: the islands of Micronesia had been
stepping stones in the Japanese advance on Southeast Asia,
and the attack on Pearl Harbor had been launched in part
from Kwajalein in the Marshalls. The primary "mission"
of the power ring, however, was asserted to be nothing less
than the defense of the Western hemisphere and the continental United States itself: "to occupy, maintain and
defend such bases in the Pacific area as are required to insure
our superiority on the sea, on the land, and in the air in
order to protect the United States and its possessions against
any probable enemy."[79]

At the same time, however, it is clear that what was
more significant to America than the debt of blood and
treasure, in the final analysis, was the unprecedented productive power which the country possessed when the guns were
finally stilled.[80] And it was recognized that no country, including the now shattered Japan, had ever intended to
threaten the national existence of the United States, or been
remotely capable of doing so.[81] Nonetheless, the highest
officials in the United States government took for granted
a pre-eminent concern for national security in the post-war
world and unanimously agreed upon the necessity for un-
hampered control over virtually the entire Pacific. It does
not seem entirely inappropriate to speculate what their response would have been if instead of 250 thousand persons,
between 15 and 25 million had been killed;[82] if instead of

a quadrupling of industrial production, the entire country east of Chicago had been destroyed;[83] if instead of mild rationing, five thousand citizens a day had starved to death in a three-year siege of one of America's great cities;[84] if instead of an ocean buffer thousands of miles wide, the western flank had bordered upon populous nations, some of them invaders of the recent war, and natural land corridors through which the country had been attacked and devastated three times since Napoleon.[85] This was the experience of the Soviet Union, and a part of the background of the issue in Eastern Europe. It underlay the question of spheres of influence and the problem of double standards of international behavior.

III · THE WORKSHOP IN THE LAKE

THE IMAGE OF JAPAN as a buffer and "springboard" appeared with increasing frequency as the Cold War intensified. Of even greater importance in the international context, however, was the decision by American policy-makers to encourage Japan's re-emergence as the "workshop" of Asia. This entailed what is commonly known as the "reverse course," and was a matter of intense controversy. The controversy focused on the issue of priorities, for in shifting its emphasis away from reform and toward economic development, the Occupation administrators deemed it necessary to oppose the labor movement, curtail the reparations program, remove agreed-upon production controls on war-related industries, and reinstate purged businessmen and officials. The necessity of the reverse course generally is explained in terms of internal Japanese problems and the continuing burden this placed upon American taxpayers called upon to support the Occupation. It is pointed out that for the first several years of the Occupation Japan experienced severe inflation and a very serious food crisis, and that reparations, industrial ceilings, labor agitation, and the like impeded recovery from the widespread devastation of the war. This focus on the internal context reinforces the image of the Occupation as a kind of detached experimental station and tends to obscure the question of for whom the workshop was to work. It was hardly mere happenstance that the determination to revitalize Japan coincided with the decline of the Chiang Kai-shek regime, and that the reverse course in Occupied Japan followed very closely upon a similar reversal of policy in occupied West Germany. Japan was slated to become the anti-Communist workshop of Asia, and it was to a considerable extent for this reason that its internal problems were particularly important.

After Mao's victory in 1949, John Foster Dulles asserted that if Japan's industrial plant and technical skills were to fall into Communist hands, it would shift the world balance of power.[86] This was dominoes on a global scale— Japan: Asia: World—and has been a basic premise of most official and academic thinking about Japan ever since. From May, 1950, to September, 1951, Dulles devoted himself to designing a peace treaty and series of security pacts which were to ensure that this would not happen, and the result was ironic and possibly tragic. For if Dulles feared the specter of a rearmed, renascent Japan aligned with Russia and China, these latter countries had no less a fear of the same Japan aligned against them. As in much of the Cold War, move bred counter-move and prophecies fulfilled themselves. At the very moment Dulles was in Tokyo for his first round of negotiations, attempting to persuade Prime Minister Yoshida to rearm Japan, war erupted in Korea. Four months later (October 26, 1950), Dulles transmitted to Jacob Malik a memo concerning the draft peace treaty with Japan, together with a formal acknowledgment of America's intention to maintain post-treaty bases in Japan proper, while continuing to administer the Ryukyu and Bonin islands. On that very same day, Chinese forces attacked South Korean troops at the Yalu and at points within North Korea.[87] Where did it all begin?

On September 2, 1946, the first anniversary of the formal Japanese surrender, General MacArthur revealed to an unsuspecting world that the "revolution of the spirit among the Japanese people . . . represents an unparalleled convulsion in the social history of the world."[88] This observation in itself represented a not insignificant convulsion in American rhetoric about Asia, and the refurbishing of the Japanese image can be noted from this time on. On December 21, 1946, and again on February 3, 1947, MacArthur sent communiqués to the War Department urging that the problematic reparations program for Japan should be terminated with completion of the interim reparations schedule,[89] and the restoration of the Japanese workshop can be said to have commenced with this highly volatile proposal. Beginning with the publication of a report by the Special Committee on Japanese Reparations on February 24, a procession of special committees produced a series of increasingly less restrictive economic guidelines for Japan. In February, 1948, the United States gave clear indication that it was re-evaluating its entire economic policy toward Japan by beginning a prolonged abstention from discussion of economic issues in the Far Eastern Commission. On December 11, the FEC was abruptly informed that an interim directive had been issued to MacArthur by the American government requiring the Japanese government to execute a program of economic stabilization. And in a major policy pronouncement on May 12, 1949, the United States announced that it had unilaterally decided to terminate all reparations payments for the duration of the Occupation and to permit Japan "to develop its peaceful industries without limitation." By "peaceful industries" the United States was referring to what had been described in previous documents as "Japanese Industrial War Potential." What the May 12 announcement meant was that previously designated production levels were to be removed in the seven following war-related industries: iron and steel, light metals, metal-working machinery, ship-building, oil refining and storage, synthetic oil, and synthetic rubber.[90] In the meantime, Occupation authorities had allowed the *zaibatsu*-dissolution program to lapse by mid-1948, after only thirty organizations out of a scheduled total of 325 had been investigated.[91]

Simultaneous with the abandonment of the anti-trust program, Occupation authorities began to impose curbs on labor union activity. This reached a high point in July of 1948 when MacArthur, faced with a general walk-out by the railway and communications unions, ordered the Japanese government to revise the National Public Service Law to prohibit government employees to strike. By this act some 2,800,000 public employees—whose wage scale was among the lowest in the country—were deprived of the legal right to join labor unions or utilize dispute tactics. This decision not only contributed greatly to polarization of the political situation within Japan but also caused dissension within the Occupation bureaucracy itself, and led to the resignation of the chief of Labor Section. In December, the Supreme Commander unofficially warned Japanese seamen, private railway personnel, and workers in the electric, coal, and fiber industries that strikes would be regarded unfavorably.[92]

The implications of the reverse course were spelled out in many ways. One of the earliest public descriptions of Japan as a workshop, for example, occurred in Dean Acheson's famous speech at Cleveland, Mississippi, on May 8, 1947.[93] There the Assistant Secretary of State characterized Japan and Germany as "two of the greatest workshops of Europe and Asia," and went on to state that "the United States is prepared to take up the reconstruction of Japan and Germany independently, without waiting for an agreement of the four Great Powers." The timing of the address was significant. It occurred two months after the Truman Doctrine, at a moment when the government was deeply involved in the formulation of the Marshall Plan. It also came at a time when a basic re-evaluation of America's China policy was underway, and thus represented one of the early open indications of the reversal of roles of China and Japan in American strategic thinking. Previously Acheson himself had informed the House Foreign Relations Committee that the Truman Doctrine would not apply to China, and two months after the Cleveland speech it was again Acheson who confidentially initiated discussions of a containment policy toward China.[94] In threatening to go-it-alone in the economic sphere, Acheson was in effect preparing the ground for a vocabulary of unilateral action in the peacemaking as well, and talk of a Japanese peace treaty without Russian participation actually did become current in the United States at around this time.[95] By advocating the economic rehabilitation of Japan while that country was still under American domination, Acheson also caused widespread concern that the United States was attempting to bind Japan to the dollar bloc, and that together the two countries would proceed to gain control of virtually the entire Asian market.[96] Moreover, in explicitly coupling Japanese and German recovery, Acheson immediately and predictably evoked the old Soviet fear of encirclement. The Russians felt the old Axis pincers tightening,[97] and they were not alone in their apprehension. The war was barely two years past, and only America, West Germany, and Japan seemed willing to forget it and to view with keen anticipation the resurrection of the former Axis workshops.

A lucid description of some of the dilemmas involved in reviving a former enemy as an ally was provided by Secretary of the Army Kenneth Royall in January, 1948. In a widely quoted speech, Royall observed that

> . . . The destruction of synthetic rubber or shipbuilding or chemical or non-ferrous metal plants will certainly destroy the war potential of Japan, but such destruction may also adversely affect the peace potential.

The dissolution of the *zaibatsu* may present in itself no serious economic problem, but at some stage extreme deconcentration of industry, while further impairing the ability to make war, may at the same time impair manufacturing efficiency of Japanese industry—may, therefore, postpone the day when Japan can become self-supporting.

. . . Another borderline situation between demilitarization and economic recovery is presented in the case of personnel. The men who were the most active in building up and running Japan's war machine—militarily and industrially— were often the ablest and most successful business leaders of that country, and their services would in many instances contribute to the economic recovery of Japan.[98]

What is to be done, Royall asked, but it was a rhetorical question and did not imply that the matter was open to discussion. The following month the United States began its fifteen-month abstention from discussion of economic problems in the FEC, and it became more and more apparent that the United States had unilaterally decided to eliminate controls and ally with those able and successful business leaders of Japan "who were the most active in building up and running Japan's war machine—militarily and industrially."

At the very beginning of March, George Kennan became the first important State Department official to visit occupied Japan. His "Mr. X" article had appeared eight months previously to crystallize the conception of a containment policy in Europe, and prior to turning his attention to the East he had been intensively involved in the drafting of the Marshall Plan. In his *Memoirs,* Kennan records that he considered

my part in bringing about this change [in Occupation policy] to have been, after the Marshall Plan, the most significant constructive contribution I was ever able to make in government. On no other occasion, with that one exception, did I ever make recommendations of such scope and import; and on no other occasion did my recommendations meet with such wide, indeed almost complete, acceptance.[99]

Those recommendations, which were approved with little modification by the State Department, the services, the National Security Council, and the President, he summarized as follows:

> The regime of control by SCAP over the Japanese government should . . . be relaxed. The Japanese should be encouraged to develop independent responsibility. No further reform legislation should be pressed. The emphasis should shift from reform to economic recovery. The purges should be tempered, tapered off, and terminated at an early date.
>
> An effort should be made to reduce occupation costs. Reparations should be generally halted, the opposition of the other Far Eastern Commission powers notwithstanding. The settlement of property claims should be expedited.
>
> Meanwhile, we should not press for a peace treaty. Precedence should be given, for the time being, to the task of bringing the Japanese into a position where they would be better able to shoulder the burdens of independence. When the time came for its negotiation the treaty should be brief, general, and nonpunitive. (This last was in contrast to the lengthy, legalistic, and largely punitive drafts that had previously been circulating in the State Department.) Pending conclusion of a treaty, we should retain tactical forces in Japan; but their numbers, their cost to the Japanese, and their adverse impact on Japanese life and economy should be reduced to a minimum. Whether we should plan to retain armed forces, bases, and other military facilities in Japan in the post-treaty period should be left for future decision. We should, however, make up our minds that we will be in Okinawa for a long time to come, and should accordingly assume full responsibility for restoring economic stability and normal political conditions for the native population of the island. (We had heretofore refrained from doing this on the grounds that we did not know how long we were going to be there.) The Japanese police establishment, meanwhile, should be reinforced and re-equipped, and there should be added to it a strong, efficient coast guard and maritime police force.

Kennan regarded the initial directives pertaining to Japan as having been based on "unreal hopes for great-power collaboration in the postwar period"; the land reform program in early 1948 as in "a situation of great confusion and instability"; the basic concept of *zaibatsu* deconcentration as bearing "so close a resemblance to Soviet views about the evils of 'capitalist monopolies' that the measures themselves could only have been eminently agreeable to anyone interested in the future communization of Japan"; the categorical purge as "sickeningly similar to totalitarian practices"; the reparations program as harming Japan and "doing very little to strengthen anybody else's economy"; and the weakening and decentralization of the Japanese police as insane:

> It was difficult to imagine a setup more favorable and inviting from the standpoint of the prospects of a Communist takeover. The Japanese Communists at the same time were being given a free field for political activity and were increasing their strength rapidly.

Like Acheson, Kennan had come to believe that Germany and Japan were "two of our most important pawns on the chessboard of world politics." In a long and cordial conversation with MacArthur he assured the Supreme Commander that there would be no need for him to be concerned about the reaction of the Allies or to feel himself obliged to consult with the FEC or "bound by views it [the United States] had expressed at earlier dates with a view to implementing the terms of the surrender." In a fundamental sense, these conclusions were based upon views which Kennan and his Policy Planning Staff were advancing by mid-1947 concerning the relative positions of China and Japan on the chessboard:

> If, then, the deterioration of the situation in China did not seem to constitute in itself any intolerable threat to our security, what it did do was to heighten greatly the impor-

tance of what might now happen in Japan. Japan, as we saw it, was more important than China as a potential factor in world-political developments. It was . . . the sole great potential military-industrial arsenal of the Far East. Americans, laboring under that strange fascination that China has seemed to exert at all times on American opinion, tended to exaggerate China's real importance and to underrate that of Japan. I considered then, and hold to the opinion today, that if at any time in the postwar period the Soviet leaders had been confronted with a choice between control over China and control over Japan, they would unhesitatingly have chosen the latter. We Americans could feel fairly secure in the presence of a truly friendly Japan and a nominally hostile China—nothing very bad could happen to us from this combination; but the dangers to our security of a nominally friendly China and a truly hostile Japan had already been demonstrated in the Pacific war. Worse still would be a hostile China *and* a hostile Japan. Yet the triumph of communism in most of China would be bound to enhance Communist pressures on Japan; and should these pressures triumph, as Moscow obviously hoped they would, then the Japan we would have before us would obviously be a hostile one.

One of the most significant aspects of the Kennan analysis was that he explicitly minimized the possibility of an overt Chinese or Soviet threat to Japan, emphasizing instead the greater possibility of internal upheaval. Thus he stressed the importance of strengthening Japan's economy and police, but advocated a settlement which if at all possible did not entail the post-treaty maintenance of American military forces in Japan proper. It was obvious, of course, that any proposed peace treaty with military appendages would be unacceptable to the Soviet Union—that is to say, once the United States committed itself to a settlement with Japan entailing continued American military presence there, it was itself deciding upon a separate peace, and invitations to Soviet participation were largely meaningless. At the same time, Kennan's own analysis implied that any settlement which aligned "the sole great potential military-industrial arsenal of the Far East" against China would represent not merely a balance of power in Asia but a balance of hostility heavily weighted against China. Kennan did not stress this side of the coin, nor did he dwell upon the response that might be expected simply by permitting the re-emergence of a powerful anti-Communist Japan, but he did at least attempt to avoid overbalancing the equation further by adding the indefinite perpetuation of the American military component. On this crucial qualification Kennan's views were ignored—and, in his own opinion, with tragic consequences.

The procession of consultants and advisers to Japan accelerated in 1949 and 1950, each visiting individual or committee announcing an increasingly conservative prospective for Japan. It is worth noting again that with very few exceptions these groups were sponsored by the military, and in no case were non-American advisers seriously consulted. As analyzed by critical Japanese commentators, this shaping of Japan as an anti-Communist workshop and base meant counter-revolution both at home and abroad. Japan was to be developed not only as a military base against China and the Soviet Union, but also as an industrial base supporting the counter-revolutionary cause in Southeast Asia. This latter prospect was discussed in a series of conferences held during the first half of 1950. Domestically, this necessitated suppression of leftist agitation and encouragement of the emerging Yoshida "tripod" of party-bureaucracy-finance.[100] It was hardly surprising that the era of loyalty investigations and McCarthyism in America had its counterpart in Japan. Within the Occupation bureaucracy, American advisers critical of the shift of priorities were investigated by General Willoughby's G-2, identified as "leftists and fellow travelers," and dismissed. On the Japanese scene itself, "Red purges" took place in government, business, and educational circles—a phenomenon accentuated by the return to public life of previously purged Japanese politicians and businessmen, as both Kennan and Royall had proposed.[101]

IV · THE OCCUPATION IN WORLD OPINION

CONTRARY TO THE IMPRESSION given in many accounts, international opinion concerning the Occupation did not polarize along strict Cold War lines. In fact, examination of the response of other countries to American policy in Japan reveals several striking facts. First, on most major issues the United States rather than the Soviet Union found itself in the minority and subject to criticism and charges of violating basic principles. Second, the most bitter opposition to American initiatives in Japan on the part of America's "free world" allies came *after* such landmark events of the Cold War as the Truman Doctrine, the Czechoslovakian coup, the Berlin blockade, the "loss of China," and the outbreak of the Korean War—clearly revealing that American evaluations of and responses to developments in Asia were not widely shared even among the anti-Communist allies of the United States. And third, the almost unanimous opposition among other nations to the reverse course in Japan was multi-faceted, reflecting not only vivid recollections of the Japanese as marauders, but also deep apprehension of a workshop Japan as once again an exploiter of Asian raw materials and markets—and even as exploiter-by-proxy for the United States. The official United States government publication describing the activities of the eleven-nation Far Eastern Commission dates this period of general opposition to American Occupation policy from the very beginning of 1948 and traces its roots to the fact that

> the U.S. Government had basically changed its position in regard to the underlying principles for the settlement of the most important issues then remaining before the Commis-

sion. It concluded that Japan should pay no reparations and should be subject to no level for its industry. The United States announced as a policy that, with the delay in convening a peace conference, Japan should step-by-step be granted by the Commission, in large measure, the rights, both in domestic and foreign matters, which it would normally obtain only by a treaty of peace. The new position taken by the U.S. Government on these issues was opposed by nearly all of the other members of the Far Eastern Commission. Compromise was practically impossible between a policy, held by most of the members of the Commission, that Japan should pay reparations and be subject to an upper level for its industry and a policy, held by the United States, that there should be no reparations and no level of industry.[102]

To judge from even the official record, it appears that the United States met general opposition on virtually every major issue. Thus the same publication notes that all nations resented American domination of the Occupation and complained that

Since the occupation was admittedly an Allied responsibility, it seemed only reasonable and appropriate that official missions in Japan, whose recommendations might strongly influence the character of policy decisions to be passed by the Commission, should not be composed solely of U.S. members. . . . The missions nevertheless remained exclusively American.[103]

Concerning the date set by Occupation authorities for Japan's first post-war Diet election (April 10, 1946), the FEC sent a communication to MacArthur stating that

the members of the Commission are not without the apprehension that the holding of the election at such an early date may well give a decisive advantage to the reactionary parties.[104]

American initiative in drafting a new constitution for Japan, of dubious legality in any circumstances, provoked particular concern within the FEC:

The members of the Commission doubted that the pending draft Constitution expressed the free will of the Japanese people. . . . they were apprehensive that it would be pushed through the Diet without adequate time for consideration.[105]

The problem of Japanese fishing and whaling rights "led probably to more hard feelings on the part of some of the FEC countries than any other issue," and provoked a general consensus among most delegations that

General MacArthur has issued his authorizations [for Japanese fishing rights] without adequate consultation with states which had a direct concern in the matter and without proper respect for their views and their interests.[106]

From 1947 the United States attempted to persuade FEC members to sanction a gradual resumption of international contacts by the Japanese through attendance at international conferences, commercial contacts abroad, etc., but even as late as mid-1949, with the exception of the United States delegation

There was no acceptance of the principle that the progressive resumption by Japan of its international responsibilities should be facilitated.[107]

Although MacArthur and the Japanese conservatives defended the imposition of curbs on the trade union movement on the grounds that Communist instigation underlay much of the labor unrest in Japan, some members of the FEC agreed with the delegate from Australia that, on the contrary, General MacArthur's own "unwise handling of the labor problem in Japan" had in fact contributed to the appeal of the Communists. Here as on other issues, the United States found itself essentially isolated:

The general subject of trade unions and labor policy was before the Commission and its committees for several months. This issue led to vigorous criticism, as well as defense, of General MacArthur and finally aligned practically all other countries on the Far Eastern Commission against the United States.[108]

With regard to the pivotal decision to revise the National Public Service Law in mid-1948:

> However persuasive and strong the U.S. position may have seemed to the American delegation, it received no support from any other country. In regard to the rights of government employees in Japan, the United States stood isolated and alone.[109]

From around May, 1948, the Soviet Union began to use the FEC to accuse the United States of planning the re-militarization of Japan. Such claims had been advanced earlier through other forums, and took such forms as the charge that the purge of militaristic elements was not being pursued in a thoroughgoing manner, inquiries into alleged construction on Japanese bases, etc. This was denounced as propaganda at the time, but the United States government's own publication states that beginning in 1948 the United States began to consider rearming Japan, and

> By 1950, as the apprehension of an attack by the Soviet Union increased, the original policy of the United States in regard to the continued demilitarization of Japan was almost completely reversed. The U.S. Government came to favor a reasonable measure of armament by Japan as a partial protection against the Soviets. Some of the other Allies also tended to follow the United States in this change of policy. The Soviet Union, however, and some of the countries which had suffered most severely from the Japanese during the war, especially the Philippines and China, were opposed to any measure which seemed to indicate an increase in Japanese military strength.[110]

The heart of the remilitarization issue, however, was more complex than simply bases and soldiers. It was implicit in the whole problem of economic reconstruction, and became explicit in the key United States policy announcement of May 12, 1949, calling for the abandonment of reparations and elimination of all production controls on war-related industries. In citing this as a violation of basic policy,

critics had reference among other sources to Article 11 of
the Potsdam Declaration, which stated that "Japan shall
be permitted to maintain such industries as will sustain
her economy and permit the exaction of just reparations
in kind, but not those which would enable her to re-arm
for war." They also referred to the basic principles of demilitarization set forth in such documents as the "United
States Initial Post-Surrender Policy for Japan" (August
1945); the "Draft Treaty on the Disarmament and Demilitarization of Japan" proposed by Secretary of State Byrnes
in June, 1946; the renunciation of war and of the right to
maintain war potential in the new Japanese Constitution,
promulgated in November 1946; the "Basic Post-Surrender
Policy for Japan" passed by the FEC in June 1947; and the
"Prohibition of Military Activity in Japan and Disposition
of Japanese Military Equipment" passed by the FEC as
late as February 1948.[111] A series of votes on the May 12
statement taken within the FEC revealed that

> No other delegation was willing to align itself with the
> United States on this issue. . . . In taking this position, the
> United States found itself at odds with all the other govern-
> ments represented on the Far Eastern Commission.[112]

A closer sense of the bitterness created by the American decision to pursue an all-out reverse course in Japan was expressed by the Philippine representative to the chairman of
the FEC:

> With all due respect for the opinion of these American ex-
> perts, I would like to say that so long as vital and far-reaching
> policies affecting not America alone but other countries as
> well were to be based on the findings and recommendations
> of these investigators, it would have been a wise thing to
> have sent mixed multi-national missions to Japan and thus
> ensure a certain degree of controls and counter-checks on
> their findings. . . .
>
> The Commission does not need, I am sure, to be told with
> what jubilation the news of the new United States policy
> was received in Japan. . . .

Nor need I tell you, Mr. Chairman, that in Manila the same news was received with dismay. Even with bitterness. . . .

I can recall, Sir, only one instance in recent years of a news report which created jubilation in Tokyo and consternation in Manila, and that was the news of the Japanese sneak attack on Pearl Harbor. . . .

If I speak with some bitterness, I would beg you, Mr. Chairman, to understand that I but reflect in moderation the sentiments of the Filipino people. . . .[113]

But if the Philippines and Great Britain and Australia and New Zealand and America's other Cold War allies were alarmed by the rapid and fairly extreme revision of America's position vis-à-vis Japan, they were at least spared the fear that this revision was deliberately and predominantly being directed against themselves. Neither the Soviet Union nor China could enjoy this modicum of reassurance. Prior to the Second World War, both Russia and China had relied for protection in the Far East upon a confrontation between Japan and the United States. Now, with the two countries allied, the scales appeared to be ominously tipped. Their fear, moreover, was not born just of the Cold War. Russia could trace war and the threat of war with Japan from 1904 through the Siberian intervention and the undeclared border wars of the 1930's to the very eve of Pearl Harbor; it is often forgotten that until almost the last moment Japan had been expected to advance north against the Soviet Union. And China's scars, of course, were deepest of all.

Four years prior to the decision to encourage Japan "to develop its peaceful industries without limitation," those industries had been provisioning Japanese armies pursuing a policy of "kill all, burn all, destroy all" in China.[114] Directly or indirectly, the Japanese had killed an estimated eleven to fifteen million persons in China, left sixty million homeless, and caused damage estimated at $60 billion.[115] The Chinese were neither moved by the physical plight of the Japanese nor impressed by their spiritual convulsions, and their popular indignation over American Occupation policy was vented in a spate of public protests and demonstrations as early as 1947. They recognized at an early date that the reverse course was double-barrelled—internally, a reverse from concentration on reform; externally, a reverse from support of China—and the outcry within China spanned all political complexions and extended even into the Legislative Yuan of the Kuomintang. Following a visit to Japan by Chinese journalists in the spring of 1947, virtually every Chinese newspaper carried reports that Japan "was tending to become less democratic, liberal, and peaceful than the Chinese people had hoped."[116] In October of the same year the *Ta Kung Pao* accused the United States of turning Japan into a fortress, and "realizing the dream of a New Order in Asia which the Japanese had been forced to abandon." Even the Kuomintang organ *Chung Yang Jih Pao* charged that the United States was dragging the Japanese people into another tragic war.[117] By May and June, 1948, "Anti-American-Aid-to-Japan" organizations had become the focal points for mass protests and even boycotts against the reappearance of Japanese goods on the Chinese market. In a manner compared by some to the Anti-Japanese People's Front of 1935–37, the movement spread to many cities and gathered support from a wide spectrum of students, professors, literary figures, politicians, merchants, industrialists, and workers.[118] On June 1, 1948, 334 professors in Shanghai signed a statement expressing fear of the revival of both a commercial and military threat from Japan. Seventy civic leaders in Hong Kong followed this with a similar protest the following day. On June 4, 282 public figures published a statement in *Ta Kung Pao* asserting, among other things, that "the so-called 'restoration of the Japanese economy' is actually the restoration of war industry—that is, in preparation for war by the United States in cooperation with Japan." Meetings and strikes occurred in Nanking, Shanghai, Peking, Tientsin, Hangchow, Foochow, and other cities, and United States

Ambassador to China John Leighton Stuart was bitterly denounced by over four hundred professors in Peking for raising the Red flag and charging that protesters were being "misled" by "sinister propaganda." The student councils of eleven colleges and universities in Peking and Tientsin joined in this personal protest to the American ambassador.[119]

If the Chinese fear of a revived military threat from Japan was to be dismissed as paranoic, what then was to be said about the same fear in Australia, New Zealand, and the Philippines? Even after the Communist victory in China and after the Korean War, the security treaties which John Foster Dulles negotiated with those countries were designed to reassure them of United States protection, not primarily against China, but against *Japan*.[120] And if charges that the United States was attempting to revive a dollar-oriented greater co-prosperity sphere in Asia were to be dismissed as Communist propaganda, did this apply also to similar reports in the American press? Following an interview of visiting American newsmen with MacArthur, for example, the Editor-in-Chief of the *Baltimore Sun* favorably compared MacArthur's plans for Japan with the Marshall Plan for Europe and told his readers that this would create an American-dominated "co-prosperity sphere for Asia." "In that co-prosperity sphere," he wrote in August 1947, "the Japanese factories will play the essential role of fabricating much of the raw materials produced by the other countries —Korea, Manchuria, China, Indochina, Siam, Burma, the Philippines, and even the Indies."[121] The prospect pleased Great Britain and the Commonwealth countries as little as it did anyone else, and their opposition to American Occupation policy is a story in itself, running from August, 1945, through the Canberra conferences of 1947 and 1949 into the post-Occupation period. It was widely assumed that control of the American Lake was not unrelated to the interest of American business in lakefront investments.

In the light of general opposition, the stereotype of the

Soviet Union intent solely upon obstruction and the fomenting of disorder in Japan bears reconsideration. In addressing the implications of the reverse course, Russian spokesmen also focused their criticism on the double fear of Japan as a revived arsenal and as a potential exploiter of Asian markets and raw materials. On September 23, 1948, the Soviet representative to the FEC submitted a moderately-worded statement to that body outlining his government's position on the issue of Japanese economic recovery; the gist of this was presented to the Commission as a motion on the following day:

> 1. No limitations should be imposed upon the restoration and development of peaceful Japanese industry which seeks to satisfy the needs of the Japanese population, nor upon the development of export in accordance with the needs of Japan's peaceful economy.
> 2. The revival and creation of Japanese war industry should be prohibited and there should be established, for a period of several years, a control over the fulfillment of this decision, to be exercised by those Powers most interested in preventing a new Japanese aggression.

After more than two months of nearly constant deliberation, the motion was defeated by a vote of one (Soviet Union) to ten. In explaining their final opposition, most of the FEC nations agreed with Russia's general principles but criticized both the wording of the first paragraph and the Soviet representative's explanation of it as being too imprecise to be of use in attempting to set a production ceiling for war-related industries. Concerning the second paragraph, it was felt that insofar as this applied to post-treaty relations with Japan it fell outside the jurisdiction of the FEC.[122] As this debate in the FEC was drawing to a close, the Soviets reiterated their alleged economic position vis-à-vis Japan on another forum, this time a conference of the United Nations Economic Commission for Asia and the Far East held in Australia from November 29 to December 9, 1948. Here, according to Max Beloff:

The Soviet delegate objected to the working-party report on the ground that it wished to see Asian development directed primarily along agricultural lines; whereas in the Soviet view, the Asian countries should be encouraged to develop their industries with the aid of tariffs so as to avoid being crushed by imports from the Western countries. With regard to Japan in particular, the Soviet delegation urged that the country's civilian industry should be permitted unrestricted development, coupled with a total prohibition on armament production.[123]

In 1949, as the United States stepped up its stabilization program, the Russians accordingly stepped up their attacks. Again, they reiterated their concern that controls were not being maintained to prevent the rebuilding of Japan's war-making capacity, but they also directed a major part of their criticism at the fact that the stabilization was being executed primarily at the expense of labor—through lay-offs, wage freezes, restrictions on union activity, etc.—and furthermore that it was being manipulated in such a way as to subjugate Japan to the American economy. They pointed, for example, to the fact that under American Occupation Japan had become far more dependent upon imports from the United States than had been the case in the pre-war period.[124] The United Kingdom and the Commonwealth countries voiced similar concerns.[125]

V · THE OTHER SIDE OF THE LAKE

IF ONE WERE TO BELIEVE all that American spokesmen said about Japan, then only MacArthur's unprecedented spiritual convulsion could indeed explain the great trust now reposed in Japan's future peaceful intent. For the Japan of the Potsdam Declaration of July, 1945, had been engaged in "conspiracy to conquer the world." The Japan known to the *New York Times* in 1945 was engaged in a " 'Holy

War' to make the Japanese Emperor the Emperor of the World;" and this hunger for world conquest characterized a nation "united for the single purpose of world conquest based on more than a thousand years of conflict." (United States Army). This was a land of "violence and greed" (Cairo Declaration), corrupted by a social and economic system "which makes for a will to war" (Dean Acheson), and as of September 22, 1945, "her punishment for her sins, which [was] just beginning," was to be "long and bitter" (Mac-Arthur).[126] This was of course the rhetoric of war, but it was also the rhetoric upon which the actions of war had been based. The total evil of Japan had permitted the waging of total war against it, pulverization of the cities and their citizens, exoneration from the need to probe outside of Japan for possible explanation of the causes of that war. Now twenty to thirty months later another evil had appeared which demanded a similarly totalistic response, and complete trust in the intent of the former enemy.

From 1948 on, the development of Japan as an anti-Communist bastion became increasingly obvious. The essence of Kennan's proposals were confirmed in a secret decision by the National Security Council in November 1948, calling for a strong and friendly Japan with a 150 thousand-man national police force and no post-Occupation controls over the various reform programs which had been initiated.[127] By the fall of 1949, the State Department had agreed to the necessity of maintaining an American military presence in Japan indefinitely,[128] and Congress had responded to the creation of the People's Republic of China by appropriating $58 million for military construction in Okinawa.[129] At the same time, Secretary of State Acheson reluctantly bowed to international pressure and announced that the United States would turn its attention to a peace settlement with Japan,[130] but the military establishment successfully stymied any progress along these lines until after the outbreak of the Korean War. As described in one account:

the Joint Chiefs of Staff, with the backing of Defense Secretary Johnson and Army Undersecretary Voorhees, were most reluctant to give up the secure base in Japan assured by the American command position obtaining under the Occupation for the uncertainties involved in dealing with a once more sovereign Japan, no matter how friendly to the west.[131]

In April, 1950, John Foster Dulles was brought into the Truman administration as Foreign Policy Adviser to the Secretary of State in an attempt to preserve bi-partisan harmony in the face of the Republican outcry over the "loss of China." The following month he was assigned the task of arranging a settlement with Japan, and in a memorandum written several weeks after receiving this assignment, Dulles set down some of the basic principles which were to guide him in this venture. One of these, as described by Frederick Dunn, was to break down the racial barrier that might prevent Japan from joining a Western alliance by attempting

> to capitalize on the Japanese feeling of racial and social superiority to the Chinese, Koreans, and Russians, and to convince them that as part of the free world they would be in equal fellowship with a group which is superior to members of the Communist world.[132]

Policy-making in the realm of Manicheanism thus placed one of the "Loss of China" group's most effective workers in the curious position of acting as midwife to the resurrection of Japanese racism.

On the eve of the Korean War, the options for Japan appeared to be either indefinite American Occupation; a re-armed Japan in alliance with the Western powers against China and the Soviet Union; or a partially re-armed Japan in which the United States continued to maintain military bases. When war erupted in Korea on June 25, 1950, Truman immediately assigned the Seventh Fleet to the Formosan Straits, thus interrupting the final stages of the

Chinese civil war and saving the Kuomintang regime on Taiwan from probable annihilation. This act not only developed into a binding American commitment to Chiang Kai-shek, but also—since the Fleet operated out of Sasebo—openly established Japan as, in the phrase of one Japanese writer, "a forward military base for intervention in the Chinese Communist Revolution."[133] If this was the beginning of a new stage for Japan, however, it was also the culmination of trends long apparent.

The problem of Japan and the Korean War exemplifies a problem which has plagued the post-war world: where does response become provocation? American officials were aware from 1945 that Stalin feared a revived Japan, or a separate American settlement with Japan.[134] The fear in China had been great even under the Kuomintang. Both the Chinese and Soviet press for 1949 and the first half of 1950 were shot through with expressions of alarm concerning reconstruction and remilitarization of Japan, and it has been observed that United States-Japanese relations were probably the most critical factor in Sino-Soviet policy in the period between Mao's victory and the outbreak of the Korean War.[135] The Treaty of Alliance which Mao and Stalin signed in February, 1950, would seem to confirm this; like the Sino-Soviet treaty of 1945 which Stalin had negotiated with Chiang, this called for mutual defense against "the revival of Japanese imperialism and the resumption of aggression on the part of Japan or any other state that may collaborate in any way with Japan in acts of aggression."[136] Dulles himself suggested on several occasions that the Korean War may have been a response to developments in Occupied Japan, and pointed out that the Russians had always attributed their defeat in the Russo-Japanese War of 1904–5 to Japanese control of Korea, which had enabled the Japanese to capture Port Arthur and attack Vladivostok. As might be expected, Dulles, described the war in Korea as Soviet aggression toward Japan: by controlling Korea in the south as well as Sakhalin in the north, "Japan would be between the upper and lower jaws of the Russian Bear."[137] No serious evidence, however, has ever been presented to indicate that either the Soviet Union or China contemplated aggressive action against Japan.[138] On the other hand, it was perfectly obvious before the Korean War that Occupied Japan was being denied the opportunity to play a future neutral role in Asia, but instead was destined to play a positive, anti-Communist role through an indefinite military partnership with the United States. Consequently, Korea's significance as a buffer between Japan and vital Russian and Chinese interests in the Maritime Province, Manchuria, and North China became correspondingly great.[139] Kennan had warned against such provocation in 1948. Looking back two decades later, he regretted, not the advice, but the fact that it had been ignored:

> . . . it is clear that among the various considerations which motivated Stalin in his decision to [authorize the attack in Korea] . . . were several that represented direct reactions to moves of our own . . . above all our recent decision to proceed at once with the negotiation of a separate peace treaty settlement with Japan, to which the Russians would not be a party, and to accompany that settlement with the indefinite retention of American garrisons and military facilities on Japanese soil. For some reason this connection—the idea that in doing things disagreeable to our interests the Russians might be reacting to features of our own behavior—was one to which the mind of official Washington would always be strangely resistant. Our adversaries, in the ingrained American way of looking at things, had always to be demonic, monstrous, incalculable, and inscrutable. It was unthinkable that we, by admitting that they sometimes reacted to what we did, should confess to a share in the responsibility for their behavior.[140]

In this light, the war was not an ideological thrust—not, as Truman claimed at the time, the first step in a general Communist plan of conquest. Rather, it reflected the view from the other side of the lake. Or, perhaps closer, the other side of the fear.

Notes

1. Harry S. Truman, *Memoirs: 1945, Year of Decisions* (New York, Signet, 1965), p. 504. The orders were formulated by the State-War-Navy Coordinating Committee (SWNCC).

2. Walter La Feber, *America, Russia, and the Cold War, 1945–1966* (New York, Wiley, 1967), p. 120.

3. Robert Ward, "Reflections on the Allied Occupation and Planned Political Change in Japan," in Robert Ward (ed.), *Political Development in Modern Japan* (Princeton, N.J., Princeton Univ. Press, 1968), pp. 489–90.

4. Compare Richard Barnet's presentation in Pfeffer (ed.), *No More Vietnams? The War and the Future of American Foreign Policy* (New York, Harper & Row, 1968), pp. 50ff.; Blair Bolles, "Influence of Armed Forces on U.S. Foreign Policy," *Foreign Policy Reports* XXII:14 (October 1, 1946), pp. 170ff; George F. Kennan, *Memoirs, 1925–1950* (Boston, Little, Brown, 1967), pp. 369–71.

5. Burton Sapin, "The Role of the Military in Formulating the Japanese Peace Treaty," Gordon B. Turner (ed.), *A History of Military Affairs in Western Society Since the Eighteenth Century* (New York, Harcourt, Brace, 1953), p. 760.

6. *Ibid.*, p. 753.

7. Robert E. Sherwood, *Roosevelt and Hopkins: An Intimate History* (New York, Harper & Row, 1950), p. 904.

8. Truman, *Memoirs*, pp. 455, 476. Actually the decision to control the Occupation had been reached by leading government officials prior to the Yalta Conference. See Gabriel Kolko, *The Politics of War: The World and United States Foreign Policy, 1943–1945* (New York, Random House, 1968), p. 547.

9. Truman, *Memoirs*, p. 485ff. Herbert Feis, *Contest Over Japan* (New York, W. W. Norton, 1967), p. 20.

10. Truman, *Memoirs*, pp. 475, 478. Feis, *Contest*, pp. 16–17. Kolko, *The Politics of War*, pp. 598–99. Charles Sulzberger, *A Long Row of Candles* (New York, Macmillan, 1969).

11. Truman, *Memoirs*, pp. 489–90.

12. *The Far Eastern Commission: A Study in International Coopera-*

tion, 1945–1952. (Washington, D.C., U.S. Department of State, Publication 5138, Far Eastern Series 60, 1953), p. 5.
Max Beloff, *Soviet Policy in the Far East, 1944–1951* (New York and London, Oxford Univ. Press 1953), p. 108ff. Max Beloff, "Soviet Far Eastern Policy Since Yalta," *Secretariat Paper No. 2* (New York, Institute of Pacific Relations, 1950), pp. 10–11. Gar Alperovitz, *Atomic Diplomacy: Hiroshima and Potsdam* (New York, Simon & Schuster, 1965), p. 192. William H. McNeill, *America, Britain & Russia: Their Co-operation and Conflict, 1941–1946* (Survey of International Affairs, 1939–1946) (London, Royal Institute of International Affairs, 1953), pp. 640–41. Feis, *Contest,* pp. 28, 37, 45.

13. Feis, *Contest,* p. 45.

14. *Ibid.,* pp. 61, 69, 129.

15. Truman, *Memoirs,* p. 490. Kolko, *The Politics of War,* pp. 602–3. The Red Army entered Korea August 12, while the first American troops did not arrive until September 8.

16. Feis, *Contest,* pp. 25–26, 30, 36. *Contemporary Japan* (Tokyo, January-April, 1946), p. 132. *Department of State Bulletin* XIII:327 (Washington, D.C., September 30, 1945), pp. 479–80. Raymond Dennett and Joseph E. Johnson, *Negotiating with the Russians* (Boston, World Peace Foundation, 1951), p. 122.

17. Feis, *Contest,* pp. 42–43.

18. D. Petrov, "Eliminating Seats of Aggression or Preserving Them?" *New Times* IX:19 (October 1, 1945), pp. 28–30.

19. Feis, *Contest,* pp. 56, 60–62, 76, 84, 92, 104, 116–18.

20. Kolko, *The Politics of War,* chapter 3. Martin F. Hertz, *Beginnings of the Cold War* (New York, McGraw-Hill, 1969), pp. 114–16.

21. Theodore Ropp, *War in the Modern World* (New York, Collier, 1962), p. 369. P. M. S. Blackett, *Fear, War, and the Bomb: Military and Political Consequences of Atomic Energy* (New York, Whittlesey House, 1949), p. 136. Kolko, *The Politics of War,* pp. 596, 598. Alperovitz, *Atomic Diplomacy,* pp. 189, 238.

22. Feis, *Contest,* chapters 9–11. Beloff, *Soviet Policy in the Far East,* pp. 113–14.

23. Feis, *Contest,* chapter 12. Richard D. Burns, "James F. Byrnes," in Norman A. Graebner (ed.), *An Uncertain Tradition: American Secretaries of State in the Twentieth Century* (New York, McGraw-Hill, 1961), p. 233ff.

24. Truman, *Memoirs,* p. 606. Compare Norman A. Graebner, *Cold War Diplomacy, 1945–1960* (New York, Van Nostrand, 1962) p. 26ff., and especially his quotation from Walter Lippmann on this occasion: "We do indeed live in a marvelous age . . . having

succeeded not only in tapping the sources of atomic energy but the source of moral revelation as well."

25. Feis, *Contest*, p. 90.

26. Frederick S. Dunn, *Peace-Making and the Settlement with Japan* (Princeton, N.J., Princeton Univ. Press, 1963), pp. 24–25. Kolko, *The Politics of War*, pp. 465–67.

27. For example, Secretary of the Navy Frank Knox in March, 1944, quoted in *Foreign Affairs* (July 1944), p. 641; Secretary of War Henry Stimson in June 1944, quoted in Kolko, *The Politics of War*, p. 465; Andrew J. May, Chairman of the House Military Affairs Committee in July 1944, quoted in the *New York Times*, July 27, 1944; Admiral Ernest J. King, Commander-in-Chief of the United States Fleet, in April, 1945, quoted in the *New York Times*, April 5, 1945. For other references, see Raymond Dennett, "U.S. Navy and Dependent Areas," *Far Eastern Survey* (April 25, 1945), pp. 93–95. Also *U.S. News* (July 13, 1945), pp. 21–23.

28. *Postwar Foreign Policy Preparation, 1939–1945* (U.S. Department of State, Publication 3580, General Foreign Policy Series 15, 1950), pp. 428–34, especially p. 430.

29. Henry L. Stimson and McGeorge Bundy, *On Active Service in Peace and War.* (New York, Harper, 1948), p. 601.

30. *New York Times*, January 16, 1946.

31. Quoted in Hans W. Weigert, "U.S. Strategic Bases and Collective Security," *Foreign Affairs* XXV:2 (January 1947), p. 256.

32. *Postwar Foreign Policy Preparation, 1939–1945*, p. 430.

33. Dunn, *Peace-Making*, pp. 56–57. Kolko, *The Politics of War*, p. 466.

34. Weigert, "U.S. Strategic Bases," p. 256.

35. See, for example, Rupert Emerson, "American Policy Toward Pacific Dependencies," *Pacific Affairs* XX:3 (September 1947), p. 266.

36. Dennett, "U.S. Navy and Dependent Areas," p. 95. Kolko, *The Politics of War*, p. 467. Eleanor Lattimore, "Pacific Ocean or American Lake?" *Far Eastern Survey* XIV:22 (November 7, 1945), pp. 313–16. John M. Maki, "Strategic Area or U.N. Trusteeship," *Far Eastern Survey* X:15 (August 13, 1941), 175–78.

37. Sherwood, *Roosevelt and Hopkins*, p. 716.

38. Quoted in Kolko, *The Politics of War*, p. 465. See also p. 607.

39. Stimson, *On Active Service*, pp. 600, 604.

40. *New York Times*, August 10, 1945. Prior drafts of the Potsdam speech stated the American intention to retain the Pacific bases even more baldly, and were toned down so as not to set a bad precedent (Kolko, *The Politics of War*, p. 592).

41. *New York Times*, October 14, 1945. *Los Angeles Times*, October 19, 1945.

42. *U.S. News* (August 24, 1945), pp. 33–44.

43. *New York Times*, September 6, 1945.

44. Lattimore, "Pacific Ocean," pp. 313–14.

45. *Department of State Bulletin* XIV:343 (January 27, 1946), p. 113.

46. Charles C. Kirkpatrick, "American Bases and American Policy—Pacific Ocean Area," in Earl Swisher (ed.), *Pacific Islands* (Boulder, Colo., Univ. of Colorado Press, 1946), pp. 48–49.

47. "Military Establishment Appropriation Bill for 1947," *Hearings before the Subcommittee of the Committee on Appropriations, House of Representatives*, 79th Congress, 2nd Session, pp. 113, 748. "Navy Department Appropriation Bill for 1947," *Hearings before the Subcommittee of the Committee on Appropriations, House of Representatives*, 79th Congress, 2nd Session, pp. 884–87. See also Bolles, "Influence of Armed Forces," pp. 174ff.

48. "Navy Department Appropriation Bill for 1947," *Hearings before the Subcommittee of the Committee on Appropriations, United States Senate*, 79th Congress, 2nd Session, pp. 4–5. Admiral Nimitz gave similar testimony before the House Subcommittee on Appropriations, *op. cit.*, p. 34.

49. David Horowitz, *The Free World Colossus: A Critique of American Policy in the Cold War* (New York, Hill & Wang, 1965), p. 266. D. F. Fleming, *The Cold War and Its Origins* (New York, Doubleday, and London, Allen & Unwin, 1961), pp. 379–80.

50. *New York Times*, September 6, 1945.

51. Frederick Palmer, "Our Pacific Bases: Think Twice!" *Harper's Magazine* (November 1945), pp. 422–23. William C. Johnstone, "Future of the Japanese Mandated Islands," *Foreign Policy Reports* (September 15, 1945), p. 199. *U.S. News* (February 1, 1946), p. 23. Maki, "Strategic Area," p. 177. Emerson, "American Policy," p. 265.

52. Colonel M. Tolchenov, "The United States' Overseas Military Bases," *New Times* (December 15, 1945), p. 30.

53. Rear Admiral E. Shvede, "Naval Expansion of the U.S.A." *Pravda* (September 12, 1946), translated in *Soviet Press Translations* I (Seattle, University of Washington), pp. 4–7.

54. Maki, "Strategic Area," pp. 175ff. Emerson, "American Policy," p. 263ff.

55. *New York Times*, November 7 and 8, 1946.

56. Weigert, "U.S. Strategic Bases," p. 253.

57. Bolles, "Influence of Armed Forces," p. 171. Claude A. Buss, "The Philippines: Problems of Independence," Earl Swisher

(ed.), *Pacific Bases*, pp. 21–22. Sung Yong Kim, *U.S.-Philippine Relations* (Washington, D.C., Public Affairs Press, 1968)

58. *Washington Post*, August 19, 1945. This issue includes a map of the projected global control which the new bombers would make possible on page 7M. General Arnold's announcement coincided with release of the previously mentioned report of the House Subcommittee on Pacific Bases, which received front-page coverage in the same issue of the *Post*.

59. Buss, "The Philippines," pp. 22–25. Whitney T. Perkins, *Denial of Empire: The United States and Its Dependencies* (Leyden, A. W. Sythoff, 1962), pp. 253ff. Abraham Chapman, "American Policy in the Philippines," *Far Eastern Survey* (June 5, 1946), pp. 164–69. Noam Chomsky, "The Revolutionary Pacifism of A. J. Muste," *C.C.A.S. Newsletter* (March 1969), pp. 47–48. Kolko, *The Politics of War*, pp. 604–6.

60. *United States Relations with China, with Special Reference to the Period 1944–1949*, Department of State Publication 3573, Far Eastern Series 30 ("The China White Paper"), pp. 565, 809–10.

61. Kolko, *The Politics of War*, pp. 615–617; also pp. 556–57, 561–62, 611. See also Gaddis Smith's review of Kolko in *New York Times Book Review* (April 13, 1969): "Few American leaders really believed that China under Chiang Kai-shek was capable of being one of the Big Four powers, and American sponsorship of her in that role was in part a transparent effort to extend American influence."

62. Blackett, *Fear, War and The Bomb*, pp. 77–79.

63. Walter Millis & E. Duffield (eds.), *The Forrestal Diaries* (New York, Viking, 1951), pp. 177–78.

64. Mark Gayn, *Japan Diary* (New York, Sloane, 1948), pp. 42–43, 239.

65. Harold R. Issacs, *No Peace for Asia* (New York, Macmillan, 1947), p. 199.

66. Gayn, *Japan Diary*, p. 239.

67. Quoted in Fleming, *The Cold War*, p. 419.

68. Jun Takami, *Saisen nikki* (Tokyo, 1959), p. 373.

69. Quoted in Blackett, *Fear, War and the Bomb*, pp. 83–84.

70. *New York Times*, March 2, 1949, quoted in Allen S. Whiting, *China Crosses the Yalu: The Decision to Enter the Korean War* (Stanford, Cal., Stanford Univ. Press, 1968), p. 39.

71. Howard K. Beale, *Theodore Roosevelt and the Rise of America to World Power* (New York, Collier Books, 1962), pp. 50, 81. Marilyn Young, "American Expansion 1870–1900: The Far East," Barton J. Bernstein (ed.), *Towards a New Past: Dissenting Essays*

in American History (New York, Pantheon Books, 1968), p. 178.

72. Thomas McCormick, *China Market* (Chicago, Quadrangle, 1967), pp. 119ff.

73. Beale, *Theodore Roosevelt*, p. 80.

74. Marilyn Young, *The Rhetoric of Empire: American China Policy, 1895–1901* (Cambridge, Harvard Univ. Press, 1968), p. 219. Walter La Feber, *The New Empire: An Interpretation of American Expansion, 1860–1898* (Ithaca, N.Y., Cornell Univ. Press 1967), p. 306. Akira Iriye, *Across the Pacific: An Inner History of American-East Asian Relations* (New York, Harcourt Brace & World, 1967), p. 89.

75. Iriye, *Across the Pacific*, pp. 6off., 105ff., 117.

76. Stimson, *On Active Service*, p. 602.

77. See, for example, the previously mentioned report by the Subcommittee on Pacific Bases of the House Committee on Naval Affairs, *U.S. News* (August 24, 1945), pp. 33–44, especially 36.

78. Bases built by the United States during the Second World War numbered 256 in the Pacific theater and 228 in the Atlantic theater (*New York Times*, September 5, 1945).

79. *U.S. News* (August 24, 1945), p. 36.

80. This outcome was apparent from an early date. In the January, 1944, issue of *American Magazine*, for example, Harry Hopkins offered the reassurance that "We will emerge from this war the richest and most powerful people in the world. Make no mistake about it." (quoted in Helen Mears, *Mirror for Americans: Japan*, Boston, Houghton Mifflin, 1948, p. 101).

According to David Horowitz, at war's end "Three-quarters of the world's invested capital and two-thirds of its industrial capacity were concentrated inside one country, the United States; the rest was shared over the other 95 per cent of the earth's inhabited surface." (*Free World Colossus*, p. 69).

81. Ropp, *War in the Modern World*, pp. 364–65. U.S. Strategic Bombing Survey, *Summary Report (Pacific War)*, p. 2.

82. According to the *New York Times*, April 4, 1969, total American combat deaths in both theaters during the Second World War amounted to 292,191. The total number of combat deaths in the course of American history, from the Revolutionary War through the Korean War but not including Vietnam, was slightly over 600,000.

Estimates of Russian civilian and military deaths incurred during the Second World War vary greatly, but it is clear that approximately 10 per cent of the entire population of the country died. Early official Soviet figures placed the number of Soviet citizens killed at between 15 and 20 million (Horowitz, *Free*

World Colossus, pp. 51–52). Isaac Deutscher places the number at over 20 million and makes the staggering observation that "in the age groups that were older than 18 years at the end of the war, that is, in the whole adult population of the Soviet Union, there were only *31 million men compared with 53 million women*." ("Myths of the Cold War," in David Horowitz (ed.), *Containment and Revolution* [Boston, Beacon, 1968], p. 13). C. P. Snow places the "total Russian dead in the Hitler war" at "almost 25 million or more than 1 in 10 of the national population." (*New York Times Book Review*, January 26, 1969).

83. The analogy was made by President John F. Kennedy and quoted by D. H. Fleming in *The Nation* (January 8, 1968), p. 53. For more detailed statistics on physical destruction in the Soviet Union, see Horowitz, *Free World Colossus*, pp. 51–52.

84. C. P. Snow, reviewing Harrison E. Salisbury's *The 900 Days: The Siege of Leningrad*: "No one knows, or ever can know, the exact number of dead in the Leningrad siege—but it must be somewhere between 1,000,000 and 1,250,000. . . . The daily diet of Leningraders in November and December, 1941 . . . was a good deal less than the starvation ration in Nazi concentration camps . . . and deaths by starvation or promoted by starvation had risen to 5,000 a . day." (*New York Times Book Review*, January 26, 1969.)

85. Poland had been the corridor through which German armies invaded the Soviet Union twice in twenty-five years. During the Second World War, Hungarian troops had penetrated Russia to the Don, and twenty-six Rumanian divisions had ravaged the Ukraine and penetrated to the Volga.

86. Dunn, *Peace-Making*, p. 203.

87. Whiting, *China Crosses the Yalu*, pp. 116, 156, 200.

88. *Political Reorientation of Japan, September 1945 to September 1948*, Report of Government Section, Supreme Commander for the Allied Powers (Washington, D.C., n.d.), p. 756.

89. *The Far Eastern Commission*, p. 152. Chapter 9 of this publication provides a useful summary of the reparations issue (see Note 12).

90. *Ibid.*, p. 70.

91. *Political Reorientation of Japan*, p. 776.

92. Harold S. Quigley and John E. Turner, *The New Japan: Government and Politics* (Minneapolis, Minnesota Univ. Press, 1956), p. 225. Baron E. J. Lewe van Aduard, *Japan: From Surrender to Peace* (N.Y., Praeger, 1954), pp. 87–88.

93. Acheson's speech is reproduced in Joseph Marion Jones, *The Fifteen Weeks* (New York, Viking, 1955), pp. 274–281.

94. *Ibid.,* pp. 195–96. Tang Tsou, *America's Failure in China, 1941–1950* (Chicago, Chicago Univ. Press, 1963), p. 506. Tadashi Aruga, "Amerika no tainichi seisaku to sengo no kokusai seiji," Yasaka Takagi (ed.), *Nichi-bei kankei no kenkyu (jo)* (Tokyo, 1968), pp. 125–130.

95. Dunn, *Peace-Making,* p. 69; *New Times* (August 27, 1947), pp. 7–10.

96. Commonwealth concern was expressed in the Canberra Conference called by Australian Foreign Minister Evatt in mid-1947.

97. La Feber, *America, Russia, and the Cold War, 1945–1966,* p. 60.

98. Royall's speech is reproduced in V. P. Dutt (ed.), *Select Documents on Asian Affairs—East Asia: China, Korea, Japan—1947–1950* (London, Oxford Univ. Press, 1958), pp. 631–637.

99. This and the following comments by Kennan are taken from Chapter 16 of Kennan's *Memoirs: 1925–1950* (Boston, Little, Brown, 1967).

100. For critical views by Japanese scholars, see Seizaburo Shinobu, "The Korean War as an Epoch of Contemporary History, *"The Developing Economies* IV:4 (December 1966), pp. 20–36; Shigeki Toyama, et al., *Showa-shi* (Tokyo, 1955, pp. 245–294; Kiyoshi Inoue, *Nihon no rekishi,* Vol. 3 (Tokyo, 1966), pp. 212–40.

101. Charles A. Willoughby and John Chamberlain, *MacArthur, 1941–1951* (New York, McGraw-Hill, 1954), p. 323. The peak of the "Red purge" occurred in the five months immediately following the outbreak of the Korean War, although twenty-four members of the Central Committee of the Japanese Communist Party and fourteen editors of the Communist organ *Akahata* were purged on June 6 and 7, 1950. Dr. Walter C. Eells, occupation adviser on education, had publically urged the purge of Communist professors from Japanese universities on numerous occasions beginning in the fall of 1949. Individuals purged for their war-time roles began to return to public life around October, 1950. For factual details on the Red purge, see Rodger Swearingen and Paul Langer, *Red Flag in Japan: International Communism in Action 1919–1951* (Cambridge, Harvard Univ. Press, 1952), p. 242ff.

Toyama and others see the period of Red purges as having begun in 1949 and been "disguised" under the rubric of "economic retrenchment." Toyama points out that most of the several hundred thousand workers laid off at this time were associated with the Japanese Communist Party or activist unions. (*Showa-shi,* p. 274).

102. *The Far Eastern Commission,* p. 228. The original eleven members of the FEC were Australia, Canada, China, France, India,

Netherlands, New Zealand, Philippines, Soviet Union, United Kingdom, and United States. In November, 1949, Burma and Pakistan joined to bring the total to thirteen.

103. *Ibid.*, p. 222; also pp. 213, 219, 221.

104. *Ibid.*, p. 34.

105. *Ibid.*, p. 53. On the controversial American drafting of the Japanese constitution, see Courtney Whitney, *MacArthur: His Rendezvous with History* (New York, Knopf, 1956), pp. 246ff. Also Theodore McNelly, "The Japanese Constitution: Child of the Cold War," *Political Science Quarterly* LXXIV:2 (June 1959), pp. 176–95.

106. *The Far Eastern Commission*, pp. 105, 122.

107. *Ibid.*, p. 97.

108. *Ibid.*, pp. 173, 170.

109. *Ibid.*, p. 174.

110. *Ibid.*, p. 66.

111. *Ibid.*, p. 67.

112. *Ibid.*, pp. 72, 151.

113. *Ibid.*, pp. 166–67.

114. Chalmers A. Johnson, *Peasant Nationalism and Communist Power: The Emergence of Revolutionary China, 1937–1945* (Stanford, Cal., Stanford Univ. Press, 1962), pp. 55–56.

115. Chang Hsin-hai, "The Treaty with Japan: A Chinese View," *Foreign Affairs* XXVI:3 (April 1948), p. 506. See also the statement by the Chinese representative to the FEC in *The Far Eastern Commission*, p. 145.

116. James T. C. Liu, "Resurgent Japan: A Chinese View," *Far Eastern Survey* XVII:3 (December 8, 1948), p. 270.

117. Dorothy Borg, "America Loses Chinese Good Will," *Far Eastern Survey* XVIII:4 (February 23, 1949), p. 43.

118. Liu, "Resurgent Japan," p. 270.

119. "Protest of Representatives of Chinese Public Opinion Against American Policies in Japan," *Pravda* (June 12, 1948), translated in *Soviet Press Translations* III:15, pp. 453–55. Tang Tsou, *America's Failure*, p. 478, indicates that the U.S. Embassy in Peking interpreted the Chinese protests against U.S. policy in Japan as a disguised attack on American aid policy toward China. For other indications of the Chinese response to American policy in Japan see the letter from Wang Yun-sheng in *Pacific Affairs* XXI:2 (June 1948), pp. 195–99. Also John F. Melby. *The Mandate of Heaven* (Toronto, Univ. of Toronto Press, 1968), pp. 254, 268.

120. La Feber, *America, Russia, and the Cold War, 1945–1966*, p. 118.

Fred Greene, *U.S. Policy and the Security of Asia* (New York, McGraw-Hill, 1968), p. 16. John Foster Dulles, "Security in the Pacific," *Foreign Affairs* XXX:2 (January 1952), p. 182.

121. Quoted in *New Times* (October 29, 1947), p. 12.

122. The entire Soviet statement is reproduced in Dutt, *Select Documents,* p. 622ff. See also *The Far Eastern Commission,* p. 162.

123. Beloff, "Soviet Far Eastern Policy Since Yalta," p. 29.

124. Beloff, *Soviet Policy in the Far East,* pp. 134–35.

125. Dunn, *Peace-Making,* pp. 81–82. Lewe van Aduard, *Japan,* pp. 116ff., especially p. 120.

126. Quoted in Mears, *Mirror for Americans,* pp. 105, 122, 51, 111, 110. The Manichean dimension cut several ways. While permitting toleration of wartime slaughter, it also undoubtedly played a role in gaining widespread American support for the radical reform proposals of the immediate post-war period. Without this vision of evil, it is difficult to imagine a conservative like MacArthur initiating truly significant reforms of a socialist cast, such as the early Occupation programs for land reform, *zaibatsu* dissolution, and encouragement of labor organization.

127. Dunn, *Peace-Making,* p. 77.

128. Lewe van Aduard, *Japan,* pp. 112ff., 122ff. Dunn, *Peace-Making,* pp. 8off.

129. Shinobu, "The Korean War," p. 26.

130. Lewe van Aduard, *Japan,* p. 120.

131. Sapin, "The Role of the Military," p. 754.

132. Dunn, *Peace-Making,* p. 100.

133. Shinobu, "The Korean War," p. 33.

134. Beloff, *Soviet Policy in the Far East,* p. 112.

135. Whiting, *China Crosses the Yalu,* pp. 34ff.

136. For the text of the 1945 treaty, see Harriet L. Moore, *Soviet Far Eastern Policy, 1931–1945* (Princeton, N.J., Princeton Univ. Press, 1945), pp. 265–77. For the 1950 treaty see Appendix to Beloff, *Soviet Policy.*

137. *Department of State Bulletin* XXIII:575 (July 10, 1950), p. 50. *Department of State Bulletin* XXIII:579 (August 7, 1950), p. 208.

138. Kennan, *Memoirs: 1925–1950,* p. 393. Also "Japanese Security and American Policy," *Foreign Affairs* XLII (October 1964), especially pp. 16–17.

139. Whiting, *China Crosses the Yalu,* p. 38. Compare Beloff, "Soviet Far Eastern Policy Since Yalta," p. 12.

140. Kennan, *Memoirs: 1925–1950,* p. 498.

Problems in Dealing with an Irrational Power: America Declares War on China

❧ *Edward Friedman*

❧ LOOK AT ANY SERIOUS, detailed study of Chinese foreign policy. They virtually all begin the same way. They describe the Chinese psyche. They tell of the peculiar Chinese world view, of the impact of one hundred years of frustration and weakness, and of the consequences of Leninist categories. Although some conclude this catalogue of cultural, historical, and ideological idiosyncrasies with the notion that China is xenophobic and pugnacious, while others conclude that China is isolationist and defensive, all agree that China must be understood first and foremost as a peculiar entity: China. The more general notions of national security and foreign policy considerations are at best seen as secondary features of calculations in Peking.

It is the thesis of this essay, however, that a study of China's foreign policy specialists trying to understand the direction and dynamics of American foreign policy will show that the men in Peking are formally rational. That is, they primarily consider events as might men who are caught up in international power politics. Such a study also will show as much about the United States as about the allegedly peculiar psyche of the Chinese. After all, China's very existence depends on a correct reading of America's intentions toward her. It therefore should not be surprising that the Chinese may offer a more solid and subtle analysis of our policy process, potential, and priorities than the reports of American academic-observers-cum-high-level-advisers.

Let's look at China's entrance into the Korean War. It

was that event that first and most significantly lent credence to the notion of an irrational China. It was during
the Korean War that America officially intervened in the
Chinese civil war and became the protector of Chiang
Kai-shek's remnant on Formosa. The political entangle-
ments of these events and the emotional consequences of
GI's fighting and dying against allegedly aggressive Chinese
led to an official United Nations condemnation and has
ever since largely colored, complicated, and controlled
relations between Washington and Peking.

An attack on southern Korea was not expected in June,
1950. Communist puppets despised by their own people
would not dare take on an American trained, advised, and
equipped army. After America intervened en masse in
that civil conflict, it was not expected that China would
enter the war. After all, they were not suicidal; our superior
fire power would wipe them out. Consequently China's
entrance into that already internationalized struggle was
analyzed as either imposed by Moscow or proof that China
was irrational. Peking could not have entered the war to
protect power plants on the Yalu River separating China
and Korea or to protect the industrial heartland of Manchuria just north of the Yalu. President Truman had already promised to protect China's interests in those plants
and to limit the war to Korea. The natural conclusion
therefore was that even though the Chinese may have
believed they were acting defensively, even though they
may have been willing to take great risks on behalf of
what were perceived as vital and threatened interests, it
was China's ideological mistrust of so-called imperialist
nations which led to an unnecessary extension of a local
conflict. Such at least is the most generally accepted theory.

But, is China's alleged ideological misperception largely
a projection of real American misconceptions? My hypothesis is that a formal, idealized, and incorrect understanding of how the American system works leads us time
and again to ascribe ideological blinders to opponents

because we are blind to the institutional and ideological irrationalities of our own system. The result of these systemic faults is that American foreign policy is all too readily out of control and aggressive while it defines itself as responsible and defensive. The other side sees the reality and responds. Failing to recognize this reality, Americans see the responses of others as provocations. The result can be another major war with China—or worse.

I

IN 1946 MAO TSE-TUNG and his colleagues were engaged in a major war with a coalition headed by Chiang Kai-shek which relied on a hostile and militarily strong America armed with nuclear weapons. America was engaged in an increasingly self-conscious crusade against revolution in Asia. By 1948 it had moved from democratization toward a return of the old ruling groups in Japan and southern Korea. It spoke of Russian aggression in Manchuria in terms very similar to those Mao had heard used by Japanese militarists some twenty years earlier in establishing pretexts for intervention. The Republican candidate for President "made it seem that with a Republican victory . . . a [last great] attempt [to save Chiang Kai-shek] would be made."[1] American Pacific military headquarters quietly helped Chiang Kai-shek establish an anti-Communist launching pad on Formosa from which the China coast was blockaded and China's coastal industrial cities were bombed by B-24's in 1948, 1949, and 1950. Consequently there is nothing very surprising in China's choosing not to go it alone against these potentially aggressive and militarily stronger forces which "will be plotting for a comeback,"[2] choosing instead to join in friendship with the Soviet Union against extreme right-wing forces backed by the United States. Unless America changed its policy toward Japan, a weak China had no place else to turn.

People familiar with European sensitivity toward a re-armed and resurgent Germany should understand China's fear of Japan. Hitler's army occupied Europe for five years. Japan's army ran over China for fifteen years. By 1948 China's leaders saw General MacArthur turn away from prosecuting alleged Japanese war criminals, rescind the order to dismantle factories used for making war, push old-line Japanese militarists and monopolists together and move for a water police that would eventually become a navy. MacArthur saw Asia as the place that would decide the fate of civilization for centuries to come. He saw himself as the man who would lead the crusade to destroy the threat of Communism in China. Sensitive to MacArthur's power and policies, the Chinese noted MacArthur's declaration

> that 1000 American bombers and large quantities of surplus U.S. military equipment, if utilized efficiently, could destroy the basic military strength of the Chinese Communists.[3]

Mao Tse-tung's experience in the hinterlands of China taught him the danger of isolation when confronted by a better armed opponent. Isolated in Kiangsi in the early 1930's, the Red base areas were surrounded and the Red Army decimated. In the mountains of Yenan, Mao became a strong advocate of a united front of many classes and many nations. He knew perfectly well that a militarily weak China could not by itself defeat Japan.[4] And Mao, at least as much as liberal American internationalists, learned a lesson from Manchuria and Munich. He mocked those who "talk of 'realism' of the Chamberlain type which accommodates itself to *faits accomplis.*"[5] He warned that "those who think they can halt the Japanese advance by making compromises with Japan at the expense of more Chinese territory and sovereign rights are indulging in mere fantasy."[6] Mao believed that aggressors feed on aggression, that a Japan able to take Manchuria would continue to march through China into Southeast Asia and would eventually try to grab the Southwest Pacific. Only armed force could stop Japan. The choice was war or surrender. "Those who hope that the moderates among the Japanese bourgeoisie will come forward and stop the war are only harboring illusions."[7]

Mao believed that the aggressors would halt only if the anti-fascist peoples united and gave Japan's rulers a fatal blow. To be free and to enjoy peace "mankind will not be able to avoid the calamity of war." Sounding much like inheritors of the Wilsonian vision of collective security, international cooperation, and a war to end wars, Mao asked the Chinese people to accept hardship, ruthlessness, and martyrdom to escape the fate of Abyssinia. He asked the Chinese people to "fight for perpetual peace in China and the whole world," fight for a world where

> Neither armies nor warships, nor military aircraft, nor poison gas will . . . be needed. Thereafter and for all time, mankind will never again know war.[8]

The ideals of Woodrow Wilson had a great appeal to Chinese intellectuals. Wilsonianism seemed to promise at a minimum a return of German-occupied China to the Chinese after World War I. Instead, the Versailles treaty permitted Japan to occupy the territory. Leninist anti-imperialism then held out the hope of fulfilling the promise of Wilsonianism. Commitment to American ideals led to opposition to American practices. If Mao's policies during the Korean war seem unrelated to contemporary American values, perhaps it is because America has cut itself off from much that is good in its heritage.

II

IT IS A SERIOUS and open question whether there is something in the geopolitics of Japan as an industrial nation and in its oligarchical social structure which produces expansionist tendencies in an age of international trade and competition. Some scholars believe there is a causal link between the character of Japanese industrialization and Japanese imperialism. Certainly the American Occupation forces which set out in 1945 to defuse and democratize Japan's economy and society in order to prevent the rebirth of an expansionist Japan believed there was a link. Their view and their fear were apparently shared by the Australian government which on seeing America rebuild Japan insisted on a mutual defense treaty with the United States to ensure against a resurgent Japan at least as much as against China.[9] Similarly the government of the Philippines, on seeing America move toward a rearmed Japan, felt the need for a mutual defense pact "at least in part to protect its territorial security from Japan 'resurgent and rearmed.' "[10] Yet even an extraordinarily able American specialist on China could describe similar concerns of Chinese leaders as "the standard Marxist-tendency to associate Japanese industrial interests with military expansionism. . . ."[11] Wherever that notion of standard Marxist tendencies leaves the reasoning of the American Occupation, the Australians, and the Filipinos, it left Washington in 1948 and after incapable of comprehending the Chinese view that

> An armed Japan is a serious menace to China. Like the French people who refuse to tolerate a rearmed Germany, the Chinese people will not see their former enemy rearmed.[12]

What was surprising given the alleged inexperience of the Chinese leaders in international politics was not that they saw a need to play it safe and ally with the Soviet Union which purportedly would have the atomic weapons needed to restrain possible military efforts emanating from Japan,[13] but that the Chinese had a complex and differentiated view of American foreign policy which permitted them to respond to the United States not in relation to American capabilities but in relation to American probabilities.

The Chinese suspected that generals like MacArthur

wished to turn Formosa into a great anti-Communist air and sea base. Nonetheless they knew that the priorities of the Democratic administration of Truman, Acheson, and Marshall were in Europe. Mao and his colleagues had seen Democratic administrations act on that priority during World War II. They had seen Marshall state and Acheson agree:

> we cannot afford, economically or militarily, to take over the continued failures of the present Chinese Government [of Chiang Kai-shek] to the dissipation of our strength in more vital regions where we now have a reasonable opportunity of successfully meeting or thwarting the Communist threat, that is, in the vital industrial area of Western Europe with its tradition of free institutions.[14]

Reports coming into China insisted that Truman was antagonistic to the Chiang Kai-shek clique because it backed Republican Thomas Dewey in the November, 1948, elections. The defeat of the Republican Party ended the likelihood of more large-scale aid to the anti-Communist remnants in China since Truman and Marshall apparently feared that such aid would "involve the USA in military difficulties and would also . . . hurt the Western European Military Alliance."[15] Thus after Truman's election, Mao on November 14, 1948, announced that

> The military situation in China has reached a new turning point and a balance of forces between the two sides has undergone a fundamental change. The People's Liberation Army, long superior in quality, has now become superior in number as well.[16]

Mao, however, made no mention of Chiang Kai-shek's "master U.S. imperialism" as he had earlier. Rather, on December 30, 1948, Mao came to speak of Chiang's government as one that in the past "had received large-scale military and economic aid from U.S. imperialism." Now, "The U.S. government had changed its policy of simply backing the Kuomintang's counter-revolutionary war. . . ." The United

States was suddenly in favor of compromise, coalition, a middle road. "At present, U.S. officials have . . . become deeply interested in peace. . . ."[17] Indeed the Chinese concluded a deal with an American business firm and even found signs in the *New York Times* and *Business Week* that American businessmen would prefer to do business with the new China rather than have their government waste more money on the forces of the old order and end up leaving China economically dependent on the Soviet Union.[18]

Although aware of plots and proposals of "the crazy interventionist group"[19] of conservative Senators, right-wing militarists and Chiang Kai-shek lobbyists, China's leaders still confidently concluded that America would not intervene. America would permit China's civil war to be fought to an end, permit the liberation of Hainan Island and of Formosa. After all, American foreign policy was made by its elected chief executive and his appointed and responsible officials. And Truman's policies were clearly distinguished from the predilections of McCarran, Chennault, and MacArthur.

China's leaders saw the United States as mainly interested in stopping further gains for Chinese Communism and other revolutionary movements. America was interested in holding the line, in forming

> a first line defense on such places as South Korea and KMT-controlled Taiwan, and a second line stand on islands like the Philippines which surround the Asiatic mainland.[20]

The Chinese believed that America's vital back-up defense line excluded southern Korea as well as Formosa. Those areas were desirable but expendable. Already in September, 1947, the Joint Chiefs of Staff had concluded that from the standpoint of military security, the United States had little strategic interest in maintaining troops or bases in Korea. By mid-1949 major American troop deployments had left Korea. As MacArthur said, America chose not to fight a ground war on the Asian mainland.

To be sure, the continuing blockade aimed at strangling the economy of the new China, and the continuing military aid arriving on Formosa, were acts of war. Yet they seemed the acts of a defeated and retreating power trying to establish a cordon sanitaire. To be sure, Chiang on Formosa or "a rearmed militaristic, Fascist Japan" or MacArthur himself might wish at some time to attack China; but Truman's election, America's European priorities, and China's growing ties with the Soviet Union removed that threat for the immediate future. America's military build-up in Asia and the threat of war seemed to center not around direct American-China confrontation but around America's effort "to nip Asia's nationalistic, emancipation movements in the bud."[21]

III

THE CHINESE saw America intervene in Greece with money, economic aid, military equipment, training, and advisers accompanying combat-sized units, but not with American troops. The Chinese expected similar intervention elsewhere. They saw America applying the Greek solution in Asia. That is what America had tried in China. It failed in China. America did not try to make up the margin of error with United States troops in China. There was little reason to believe it would change the policy elsewhere on the Asian continent. After all there was no need for it to do so. Its vital interests were secured by an unbroachable Pacific island chain.

The Chinese could readily read that even pro-Chiang senators such as Smith, Taft, and Knowland insisted that the Navy could do the job. Who favored sending American soldiers to fight in Asia? Senator Knowland made clear "that he advocated . . . the same kind of assistance which the United States was rendering Greece."[22] The *New York Herald Tribune* editorialized for the "despatch of a large-scale military mission to Formosa with a limited supply of equipment. The amount of aid would be comparable to that given the Greek Government in its fight on guerrillas."[23] That aid did not include American ground forces. And it predictably would not. China's leaders shrewdly read American intentions.

People's Daily, the official Communist Party paper, responded editorially on March 18, 1950, to a talk by Secretary of State Acheson on United States policy in Asia. The editorial confidently claimed that America's efforts to stop the revolutionary, anti-imperialist forces fighting civil wars in Asia would fail.

> If the people 'withdrew their support' from Chiang Kaishek, how can you imagine that the even weaker allies of Chiang Kai-shek—Quirino, Syngman Rhee, Bao Dai and the like—can get the people's support?
>
> If 'help on a massive scale' to China from the United States government ended in fiasco and 'great disappointment,' who can imagine that its help on a smaller scale in Southeast Asia will be effective? . . . American imperialism faces an insoluble dilemma. If it directs its main strength to Europe, the Asian peoples will win even greater victories. If it divides its strength between Europe and Asia, both the European and Asian peoples will win. . . . The era of Imperialist rule over Asia is doomed. This is the truth about Asia . . .

Korea in 1949 was said to be in the throes of a war of national liberation fought by "guerrilla units organized by the people" to resist a brutal police terror "sponsored by American imperialism."[24] Direct American intervention against the revolutionary movement seemed unlikely. As Chinese news analysis had it:

> Though there were and are many revolts exploding in South Korea only the Yosu revolt which occurred last autumn became known to the outside world. The Americans never used their own troops in quelling the past revolts except in Taiku where the rebelling Korean troops were intercepted and disarmed by U.S. troops as the former were passing the U.S. garrison.

The guerrilla activities have spread so much by now that almost all the mountainous areas have been occupied by these guerrillas and already people's committees have been set up in a few regions.[25]

Liu Shao-ch'i announced, "The Chinese people express boundless sympathy with the Korean people in their heroic struggle for independence, democracy and unification of their motherland."[26] Moral sympathy is to be distinguished from military support. In that war for independence the Chinese found that "October marked a new phase of the armed struggle of the southern Korean people."[27] It is likely that China, which chose at this time to announce the establishment of formal diplomatic relations with the governments of Ho Chi Minh and Kim Il Sung, saw both movements progressing from guerrilla to mobile warfare in preparation for positional warfare.[28] That is, Korea and Vietnam may have been seen as in the same position as China just a few years earlier. A push for complete victory might be imminent.

A Korean representative to the Peking ceremonies inaugurating the People's Republic of China told of soldiers abandoning Syngman Rhee's forces, of guerrilla attacking "the puppet armies equipped with American weapons. . . ." He then made the analogy with China explicit:

> Just as the American imperialistic aggression has been repulsed by the heroic Chinese people after arduous struggle, I believe we shall also drive out all the American imperialistic aggressors in Korea before long.[29]

Although they may not have been as sanguine about a victory "before long," the Chinese did accept the analogy. Chou En-lai explained that as America "supported Chiang Kai-shek in waging large-scale civil war," so "The United States is using similar methods to support the puppets Bao Dai, Syngman Rhee, and Quirino in undermining the national independence movements of the Democratic Republics of Vietnam and of South Korea and the Philippines."[30] "Not since the colonial system arose," *People's China* contended on February 21, 1950, "have conditions been so favorable for the oppressed peoples to stand up and overthrow the bonds that have been strangling them." That is, in a civil war—as opposed to an international war—the revolutionary people on their own could win. Koreans no more needed help from China to overthrow Rhee than Chinese needed help from Russia to defeat Chiang. "The Korean people," according to the Chinese government, "must reject foreign intervention and settle the problems of peace and unification in their own country by their own efforts."[31] There is no evidence of significant Chinese aid to the Koreans at this time. Perhaps to highlight Peking's commitment to that war as a civil war, at three o'clock in the afternoon on June 24, eighteen days after Mao called for such a policy, the Chinese government announced it was "demobilizing part of the People's Liberation Army."[32] A few hours later north Korean troops went south. Perhaps China was so little a part of the Korean planning that it was a mere coincidence.

It is extremely hazardous to speculate on the origins of the new stage of the Korean conflict. Surely Koreans experienced it as a civil conflict and greatly desired to see the nation united. One need not doubt that the guerrillas in the south, who apparently did not do as well as expected early in 1950, invited aid from their comrades in the north. It is also clear that such aid would have been impossible without military assistance from the Soviet Union. Perhaps the success of the Chinese guerrillas after the Russians had helped undermine the Greek guerrilla effort made it more difficult for Moscow to say no to Korean desires to fight the war to an end. That, however, is largely speculation.

What is fact is that the Chinese, who provided some military assistance to the Vietnamese in their fight against a foreign army, mainly cheered from the sidelines of Korea.

In Vietnam, setbacks to efforts at mobile warfare in 1950 led to a return to guerrilla warfare in proper Maoist fashion; in Korea an even worse situation led to a push by the northern army which was supposed to make guerrilla success throughout the south more likely.[32a] That strategy, similar to reliance on the arms of the Red Army in Eastern Europe, was not Maoist in inspiration. Mao's notions of protracted war and popular mobilization infused the practice of the Vietnamese, not the Koreans. Korea should not have led to war between China and America.

IV

AS WE ALL KNOW, America did intervene in Korea and Formosa. China's estimate that America would keep its armies out of Asia's civil wars was wrong. In trying to understand where in this instance Chinese leaders erred, I am not claiming that they generally see the world as it is. Which of us does? Elements of natural pride, from throwing the imperialists out of China, and fragments of personal experience in fighting against Japan, help compose the glasses through which the men in Peking see. Also Chinese leaders probably underestimate both the strength of the American capitalist economy and the willingness of the American people to support their government in overseas adventures. Similarly, American leaders not only have taken great pride in their defeat of the Axis powers and great warnings from Munich but have overemphasized China's economic difficulties and have underestimated the will and ability of China's people to fight for their government. Of course it is not surprising that two alleged enemies, each confident in the supposed moral superiority of his way of life, should denigrate each other's domestic successes, each other's domestic support. But the issue at stake here is elite analysis of foreign-policy-making, of the forces determining foreign policy.

On January 12, 1950, Dean Acheson warned of the new

"thrust of Russian imperialism." The Secretary of State found "that the Soviet Union's taking the four northern provinces of China is the single most significant, most important fact, in the relation of any foreign power with Asia."[33] The Chinese played up and knocked down this part of Acheson's talk. Subsequently, more detailed charges leaked by American "diplomatic channels" contended that Mao Tse-tung had agreed to let Liaoning and Antung provinces become part of Korea, and permit the Russians to station troops in Manchuria and Sinkiang with a single commander-in-chief, a Russian, in charge of all Communist forces.

The Chinese government officially denied the charges. "The *NCNA* is authorized to state" that the charges were "fabrications which could only have been invented by a madman." The Chinese offered a motive for America's madness:

> Why is Acheson rabidly manufacturing en masse such base fabrications at present? . . . The United Press Washington despatch of the 25th has voluntarily confessed that 'Secretary of State Acheson eventually hopes to drive a wedge between Peking and Moscow . . .'[34]

The Chinese, of course, were right. They read the news from America quite carefully and did a first-rate job of playing White House-ology. Splitting Russia and China was Acheson's goal. But there was more, and the Chinese missed it.

Since the end of the nineteenth century Washington had taken a special interest in Manchuria and worked to see China's northeast preserved as an area open to American business. Japan's conquest of Manchuria in 1931 and the failure of the League of Nations to act decisively added deep moral feelings and balance of power considerations to already profound economic concerns. As the war ended in 1945, presidential advisers on Communism and Asia did not believe that Yalta and the subsequent agreements between Stalin and Chiang Kai-shek would preserve the territorial integrity of China. Rather, according to Averell Harriman, once Russia is in Manchuria, it in the end "will exercise control over whatever government may be established in Manchuria. . . ." Joseph Grew thought Manchuria would "gradually slip into Russia's orbit to be followed in due course by China. . . ."[35] In 1946 an American journalist echoed government concerns that Russian penetration of Manchuria opened up the possibility of conflict with America. China was "the passive element" as Russian armies opened the prospect "of a new Manchurian separatism under Russian-dominated Communist auspices which, whatever the legal fictions devised, would amount to another division of China and the creation of a Soviet-sponsored buffer state."[36] By early 1949 the State Department saw "Russians or their agents . . . taking control of much of the North. Moscow hoped to create puppet separatist areas eliminating the 'China salient' that separated the Siberian heartland from Vladivostok."[37]

The Chinese Communists, however, were nationalists to the core. They gloried in the independence they had just won for China in Manchuria and elsewhere. How could they credit American claims that the precise opposite had just happened? Acheson may have been playing games, but the games were peculiarly congenial to Americans who in 1950 tended toward an extreme paternalism with regard to non-white people who had thrown out imperial rulers. Americans tend to believe not only that allegedly immature new leaders won't be able to govern properly, but that in addition these irresponsible children will be seduced by Russian (or Communist) imperialism. American leaders put little stock in the ability of Chinese nationalists to defend China. Already in 1945, as America displaced the defeated enemy in Japan and Korea,[38] Secretary of War Stimson looked forward to the creation of a Japan "sympathetic . . . to the United States in case there should be any aggression by Russia in Manchuria."[39]

The Chinese incorrectly took America's power politics

motive, the desire to split the Sino-Soviet alliance, as the only rational one. The Chinese incorrectly dismissed the American concern about a Russian take-over. The Chinese leaders missed the irrational and ideological elements which so largely rationalize American foreign policy. An imperious and imperial America was making the most of its newly created global power.

By the spring of 1950, Vietnam and Korea increasingly seemed to Washington to be outposts in an international cold war against Russian Communist imperialism. The Russian Red Army had taken East Europe. A coup had toppled the government of Czechoslovakia. China had been lost by America's ally, Chiang Kai-shek. Russia had taken the key area of Manchuria and northern Korea. This endless aggression had to be stopped, and soon Senator Joseph McCarthy would insist that "Soviet Russia conquered China,"[40] and administration liberals no longer demurred. Chinese leaders might think of Formosa or southern Korea primarily as local problems of unfinished civil wars; but to Washington these places increasingly were points in a system of global responsibility which necessitated containing Communist imperialism. By now Peking perhaps has established centers to study the peculiar American experience and psyche which have so largely created America's view of its role in the world.

China's leaders did already have some political anxieties. They saw Americans from MacArthur's headquarters "directing and assisting the Nationalist Party remnants in Taiwan, Hainan Island, and other places, for stubborn resistance." They saw military aid secretly provided to the Nationalists from American bases in the Philippines. They were aware that MacArthur's ambitions for Taiwan and Japan went far beyond defense.[41] Reports from Reuters, United Press, USIS, and the *New York Times* were cited by the Chinese to show MacArthur's involvement in and direction of the defense of Taiwan. Therefore official "Peking circles" swiftly branded as lies Truman's and

Acheson's assertions of January 5, 1950, that America would not interfere with the situation in Taiwan.

Acheson only excluded Taiwan as a base "for the time being." He held open the possibility of taking "all measures" if American forces were attacked. The Chinese, knowing that America hoped to cordon China off with military bases and that American forces stood in the way of a united China, worried

> that the American imperialists have not entirely given up their scheme to invade Formosa. Whenever they think fit, a pretext of 'an armed attack on American forces' can be fabricated to carry out their invasion schemes.[42]

Then on June 27, upon being informed of the new stage in the Korean War, Truman took the situation as a pretext to intervene in the Formosa area and declare that the American military would prevent the Chinese from carrying the civil war to an end on that island. Chou En-lai immediately replied that this American "armed aggression" against China used Korea as a "pretext . . . Truman merely discloses his premeditated plan and puts it into practice." What Chou En-lai did not yet see was how little Truman could freely call the shots and make China policy.

V

PRESIDENT TRUMAN did not respond to the enlarged war in Korea by sending American troops immediately to Korea to resist aggression. Indeed up until this time most American officials, assuming that in Korea the south could readily resist the north, tried to keep large, offensive weapons from the Seoul forces so that they could not invade the north. Thus it reflected certain American predispositions as well when the Seoul Defense Minister announced that

> by tomorrow morning we shall have defeated them completely. Our only cause for dissatisfaction is that there has been no order to advance into the North.[43]

But once American officials interpreted the attack as a probe in international Russian aggression, it could quickly be feared that the natives could not stand against the totalitarians. The Director of the Office of North Asian Affairs and John Foster Dulles wired from MacArthur's Tokyo base for the despatch of United States troops since Communist success in Korea "would start a disastrous chain of events leading most probably to world war."[44] Truman, however, refused to be "alarmist." He, nonetheless, insisted on the need "to hit those fellows hard."[45]

But "those fellows" were not the men in the advancing army from the north. All the American advisers in Korea asked for was "a ten-day emergency supply of ammunition."[46] MacArthur was authorized to provide that and other necessary equipment to the Seoul army. Truman instead struck hard in the Formosa area. He intervened in the Chinese civil war with American armed forces, James Reston of the *New York Times* was told, in order to avoid an additional war against Communists and to disarm the conservatives in Congress who had been making such an issue of Formosa.[47] Truman did not consider Taiwan vital in itself to America's defense plans. He acted aggressively not because such action was in the national interest but because if he were thought soft on Communism his other policy and political interests would suffer. He believed that his strong action would silence Republicans in Congress with their cries of softness on Communism and help win approval for a $50 billion military budget that the military wanted and budget-minded conservatives would not approve.

Yet in one essential, China's basic view of America's response to internecine war in Asia was right. In American eyes, Korea was Greece. Truman found that "this is the Greece of the Far East. If we are tough enough now there won't be any next step."[48] A caucus of the Senate Republican Policy Committee made the same point:

that the United States should give maximum aid to the Republic of Korea in the form of weapons and other military supplies but should not let the fighting drag it into war.[49]

With no promise of United States troops, the Ambassador from Seoul in Washington had to declare, "We don't expect American soldiers to give their lives for us. We will do the fighting and the dying."[50]

The United States reacted to Korea in 1950 as to Greece and China in 1947 with military aid but no American ground troops. As Senator Robert A. Taft pointed out:

> If the United States was not prepared to use its troops and give military assistance to Nationalist China against Chinese Communists, why should it take its troops to defend Nationalist Korea against Korean Communists? That certainly must have seemed a fairly logical conclusion to those who have inaugurated this aggression.[51]

News soon began to reach Washington that the southern armies were crumbling. More American military power was needed. American air power was then sent into the fight to "throw back the invaders" and "raise the morale of the shocked defenders." Secretary of Defense Johnson still made clear "that he did not wish to see [American] ground troops sent to Korea."[52] And air power was to be used only south of the thirty-eighth parallel.

What Truman and Acheson did not see was that their decision to save the Rhee government in southern Korea took much of the power to control events out of their hands and put it in the hands of militarists like MacArthur and domino-theorists like Dulles. Although the White House did not plan to commit American ground troops to Korea, much would now depend on the reports from and actions of military men on the spot.[53] Also the stand of strong anti-Communism won strong public backing in the press and the stock market.[54] To back off would be to lose that public support, to invite a political disaster. When the air power of the United States in southern Korea could not stop northern armies, the choices open to the President would seem very narrow indeed. Truman would not be in control of American foreign policy.

VI

MACARTHUR on his own expanded the war to the north. On June 29, he flew to Korea and weighed out loud how he could

"takeout" the airfields from which North Korean Yak fighters were operating. "Where's the President's directive?" he asked his Intelligence Chief, Major General Charles Willoughby. "How can I bomb north of the 38th parallel without Washington hanging me?" Willoughby, it turned out, had left Truman's directive in Tokyo. A half-hour later MacArthur emerged from his private cabin and remarked almost casually: "I've decided to bomb north of the 38th parallel. The B-29's will be out tomorrow. The order has gone to Okinawa (where the B-29 Superfortresses were based)."[55]

MacArthur's aide Courtney Whitney explains that the General "concluded that his authority . . . was permissive." Consequently, "There was no timid delay while authorization was obtained from Washington."[56] The White House then quickly approved bombing military targets in the north.[57] As opposed to Truman who wished to limit the war, MacArthur acted throughout to extend it. Truman believed the source of aggression lay in Moscow. Therefore Europe had to be strengthened. MacArthur believed the source of aggression lay in Asia. Therefore China had to be weakened.

China at first focused on the United States response in Formosa. The Chinese knew that Chiang hoped to use America in a larger war to counterattack the mainland. Chiang's government accepted America's neutralization of the Formosa Straits because it probably believed, on the basis of assurances from MacArthur and his friends, that the ban on its military activities would soon be lifted.[58] Truman was in fact inclined to accept Chiang's offer of troops to help in Korea. Truman's advisers disagreed. The Chinese fear that Chiang would get the United States to participate in his war with the People's Republic of China came close to being a fact. MacArthur worked to have the ban on Chiang's military activities lifted, to turn Formosa into a "base from which we would be able to attack objectives in Asia. . . ."[59]

General MacArthur was surprised by the extent of President Truman's commitment to save Rhee's government,[60] as no doubt were the Chinese. Political forces in America more powerful than either man forced the President's hand and transferred power into the hands of the General. After his trip to Korea, MacArthur decided that only American ground troops could stop the forces from the north.[61] "Give me two American divisions and I can hold Korea," was the General's position.[62] The White House then authorized the use of American ground troops but only to keep supplies moving and to protect American lives. This was said to be merely a limited guard action to retain a port and an air base.[63] Next the President gave MacArthur one regimental combat team for a counterattack.[64] No one opposed the increasing escalation. MacArthur was given what he asked for. It was not until July 8 that he asked for major reinforcements.[65] The troops on hand apparently had held out because the northerners had not planned on a swift march to the south. Instead they seem to have expected popular uprisings and guerrilla efforts to ruin the enemy's rear.[65a] That support base did not exist and so American troops had time to get in and change the direction of the war.

At the end of July MacArthur, without the approval of the State Department, flew to Formosa, purportedly to discuss with Chiang Kai-shek problems of military coordination. When MacArthur returned to Tokyo, Acheson had the leading State Department official on the General's staff, William Sebald

> ask the General for further information on the Formosa visit. . . . When I relayed Secretary Acheson's request for information, MacArthur made it clear that he had no intention of providing details.[66]

MacArthur's public statement was informative enough. Chiang was praised as a man whose "determination parallels the common interests and purposes of Americans, that all people in the Pacific should be free—not slaves." Thus by early August leaders in Peking had to worry not only about Truman but also about MacArthur, and his political goals, allies, and military power. Although China's leaders had to begin preparing for the eventuality of war with America in early August, that war would not occur till the end of November. What happened in between is crucial to an understanding of that clash.

VII

THE AMERICAN LEADERS involved in provoking the Chinese counterattack of late November and their spokesmen are quite explicit as to why the Chinese did *not* join the battle. They did not join the battle because of anything America did in November. Dean Acheson told William Sebald in Japan that the Department of State "considers it important" that, when people suggest that MacArthur's all-out attack toward the Yalu of November was a "threat" which led to a Chinese military response:

> when you encounter such explanations, you make it clear it is wholly at variance with the facts. It is unanimous considered judgment Joint Chiefs of Staff, supported by information from field commanders, the present Chinese offensive planned and staged over considerable period of time and that what happened is that two offensives collided.[67]

Although no evidence existed that the Chinese counter-attack would have been launched had there been no attack by MacArthur, McGeorge Bundy faithfully expounded this imaginative explanation for Acheson in 1952. He wrote:

> the statements and tactics of General MacArthur were surely not the heart of the matter [of Chinese intervention]. A larger question is raised around the decision to cross the 38th parallel in October. Some senior officers of the State Department are reported to have opposed this on the ground that it would lead to Chinese intervention and even Winston Churchill later said that he would have stopped at the neck of the peninsula north of Pyongyang, keeping clear of the sensitive Yalu River region. . . . the Administration had considered, in late November, the desirability of establishing a buffer zone near the Yalu, but the proposal was still tentative when it became obsolete as a result of the great Chinese counteroffensive.[68]

But "surely" MacArthur's unmentioned offensive preceded the Chinese counteroffensive. Didn't that make the buffer zone proposal obsolete? The United States Air Force's historian agrees with Bundy and Acheson that talk of a stopping point and a buffer is naïve because "The Chinese were not seeking to defend a buffer zone along the border; their purpose was to outflank, attack, and defeat the United Nations forces."[69] David Rees agrees: "There was no possibility that MacArthur had provoked the Chinese counteroffensive."[70]

Everyone seems so certain of Peking's precise intentions one would think they sat with Mao at the decision-making table. Richard Neustadt, a former member of President Truman's White House staff, insists that

> Chinese concern was not confined to anything so simple as a buffer zone along the border; an entity called North Korea, not the border, was the stake . . .[71]

The protests that the buffer zone, as a Chinese foreign policy objective undermined by MacArthur's November assault, should not be considered, do read forcefully; perhaps the voice of protesting innocence is too loud? Richard Rovere and Arthur Schlesinger, Jr., sounded the note in 1951. They found that

> if we had cut off a strip of North Korea and given it to China, a solution widely recommended, the Communists could have turned out the lights all over Korea any time the fancy took them. Knowing Communists, the Department said, the fancy would take them often.[72]

Not very enlightening. "The real case against MacArthur in October and November," continued our two stout defenders of Acheson, "was not that he provoked Chinese aggression but that he failed to prepare for it." The Chinese attack was inevitable. Consequently there is no need to study American political moves. Apparently none of those involved want us to take serious note of the events of November, 1950. They seem more interested in defending Acheson and his friends than in investigating and describing developments in Sino-American relations. Is it usually that way with the memoirs of academic advisers and inside-dopesters?

Acheson explained the situation that supposedly made November developments beside the point:

> Obviously it is fantastic to suppose that offensive involving half million men could have been prepared impromptu. . . . Appearance on Korean front of Chinese Communist troops of Korean ancestry as individuals and units, began during initial Korean assault and long before return to 38th Parallel, indicating Peiping would in any case feel free to assert itself in Korea regardless military situation.[73]

It is true that Koreans who had fought with the Chinese Red Army did return home to Korea and did eventually take part in the civil strife there. It is difficult to see what this necessarily has to do with a half million Chinese troops later entering Korea to fight an American army.

Acheson continued:

Department now in receipt unpublished report by neutral Asian journalist in Communist China written before offensive, which discloses that Communist China had by third week in November completed preparations for mass advance against United Nations forces designed to drive them back length of the Peninsula regardless of the risk of general war and had secured pledges of Soviet assistance in event reverse suffered. Report contains eyewitness account of feverish movement of troops in readiness for invasion as early as second week in October and of preparations for air raid defense in major north China cities recalling Jap days. This report paralleled from many other sources.[74]

It is true that in the middle of October Chinese troops were quietly and hurriedly moved into northern Korea. Unpreparedness invites aggression. Students of the aggression of the 1930's all understood that. Ever since the Pusan beachhead in southern Korea had held, Peking entered into talks with Moscow about a possible American counter-attack. After the successful American landing at Inchon "for six weeks all they [Chinese] did was to hint that if UN troops crossed the 38th Parallel, they might enter the war."[75] China was trying to signal so that war with America could be avoided.

Words availed nothing. Chou En-lai had the Indian Ambassador at Peking convey to Washington China's view that "no country's need for peace was greater than that of China," but

there were times when peace could only be defended by determination to resist aggression. If the Americans crossed the 38th Parallel China would be forced to intervene. Otherwise he was most anxious for a peaceful settlement . . .

The Indian Ambassador then asked Chou En-lai "whether China intended to intervene if only the South Koreans crossed the parallel." Chou "was most emphatic: 'The South Koreans did not matter but American intrusion into North Korea would encounter Chinese resistance.'"[76] Acheson understood this to mean that "China would send troops to the Korean frontiers to defend North Korea;" that "this action would not be taken if only South Korean troops crossed the Parallel."[77] On October 4 an "urgent telegram" from Washington carried this warning to Tokyo. "The inference was that, in this event, Chinese troops would be sent into North Korea."[78] Washington understood Peking's signal, but in Tokyo MacArthur brushed off Washington's nervous nellies: "I regard all of Korea open for our military operations unless and until the enemy capitulates."[79]

As early as September 27, MacArthur had been ordered to use only Korean troops in the areas bordering China.[80] This may have been in reaction to information provided by the Indian Ambassador to China who on September 25 had been told by the Military Governor of Peking that the Chinese did not intend to sit back with folded hands and let the Americans come up to their borders.

> We know what we are in for, but at all costs American aggression has to be stopped. The Americans can bomb us, they can destroy our industries, but they cannot defeat us on land.
>
> They may even drop atom bombs on us. What then? They may kill a few million people. Without sacrifice a nation's independence cannot be upheld.
>
> After all, China lives on the farms. What can atom bombs do then? Yes, our economic development will be put back. We may have to wait for it.[81]

Subsequently, MacArthur ignored the order of the Joint Chiefs of Staff, abandoned any restraining line for American troops and pushed toward the border. The Chinese could read in the *New York Times* about Truman's expression of surprise at this development for it was the President's "understanding" that only Koreans would move further north.[82] MacArthur also brushed off as inadvisable a State Department request that he publicly declare that he would not interfere with the power plants along the Yalu River.[83] Indeed quite frequently the State Department had asked him to give public assurances to the Communists that the UN command had no designs on territory beyond the Yalu—assurances that he had declined to give for fear they might be misrepresented as reflecting weakness.[84]

Clearly the Chinese would have been stark raving mad not to be anxious about the intentions of MacArthur. They noted that MacArthur was out of control and that even America's British allies were frightened.[85]

Having failed to dissuade America through peaceful diplomacy, Peking signaled next by what American international communication specialists might call armed diplomacy. Thus: "on the night of 1 November, occurred the first big clash between Chinese and American troops."[86]

> Sunday, 5 November 1950 . . . the whole of the 24th US Division and the attached Commonwealth Brigade were back across the Taenyong River. The Commonwealth Brigade was halted, ready to fight a delaying action if the Chinese Reds followed up too closely.[87]

Instead the Chinese "faded away."[88] But their point had been made. The Eighth Army retreated. By the end of the first week of November:

> There was a realization that the war might "drag out for some considerable time." There was talk of a "winter campaign" and a demand for arctic clothing.[89]

Chinese soldiers have explained why they made this attack which lasted from October 24 to November 8: "We checked the advance of the enemy towards the Yalu River." They had put a stop to the American "dream of marching towards the Yalu River." And, "Had we been late by just one minute these thugs might have advanced to the bank of the Yalu River."[90] MacArthur had acknowledged this Chinese success in "checking the United Nations advance toward the Yalu late in October." But as MacArthur saw it, "Their ultimate objective was undoubtedly a decisive effort aimed at the complete destruction of United Nations forces in Korea."[91] Undoubtedly? The evidence of their action and their words both to intermediaries in Peking and to their own troops was that the Chinese were primarily interested in stopping the American Army heading toward their borders.

VIII

AFTER THE CHINESE forces broke contact with MacArthur's army, attempts were swiftly made to establish a buffer zone along the Yalu. America had another opportunity to respond diplomatically to the signal which peaceful communications could not get across. The new signal seems to have been put forth in a manner not so different from the approved and prescribed rules of the game:

> Military action should not confront the opponent with an urgent requirement to escalate the conflict immediately in order to avoid or to compensate for the military or political damage being inflicted upon him. A demonstrative use of force may be self-defeating if it pushes the opponent to the extent that it requires an immediate strong military reaction on his part.

> *Provide pauses in military operations* . . . Time must be provided at each point for the opponent to assess the actions taken, to receive and reflect on the signals and proposals addressed to him.[92]

MacArthur responded to the signal and to the pause by escalating the war. "The presence of substantial Chinese forces did not deter MacArthur."[93] On November 5 apparently for the first time there, napalm was air-dropped in northern Korea.[94] MacArthur decided to bomb the bridges into Manchuria. Truman vetoed the idea. Instead Washington ordered MacArthur to "postpone all bombing of targets within five miles of the Manchurian border until further orders."[95] A buffer would be established. Against such instructions, however, MacArthur lodged the "gravest protest" and once again Washington gave way. On November

8, Air Force planes using napalm destroyed 60 per cent of the city of Sinuiju but somehow missed the adjacent bridge. Navy carrier planes then had to do the job for them.[96] On November 13 Washington in response to MacArthur's demands put the idea of hot pursuit into Manchuria to "six countries with troops in Korea." According to Acheson, "everyone in our government had favored doing this [hot pursuit]. But the six countries whose views were solicited were opposed, so the idea was dropped."[97] America's allies may thus have saved America from war with Russia which stood in a second line of defense against the spreading American military effort. According to the Indian Ambassador in Peking "the Chinese were certain that if Manchuria were attacked the Soviets would intervene."[98] Similarly in 1954 during a crisis in Indochina the objections of America's allies may have made it easier for the President to avoid a huge escalation counseled by the Vice President, Secretary of State, Navy, and Air Force, which would have meant war with China.

Meanwhile on November 9 Truman's highest level advisers, worrying that China might enter the war full force, decided to contact China to discuss a buffer. General Bradley, according to Truman's *Memoirs,* apparently felt that "if the Chinese desired only to set up a buffer area . . . negotiations might be fruitful." From MacArthur's headquarters the reaction to "a 'buffer' area . . . as evidence of the United Nations' good intentions" was denounced as evidence of a "disastrous course."[99] Nonetheless, apparently at the instigation of the British, a motion to protect China's interests in a frontier zone was put before the United Nations on November 10.[100] A Chinese representative was also asked to come to the United Nations to partake in its discussions. MacArthur tried to stop this initiative. He wired Washington:

> The widely reported British desire to appease the Chinese Communists by giving them a strip of Northern Korea finds a most recent precedent in the action taken at Munich on

29 September 1938 . . . Within ten months . . . Germany had seized the resulting impotent Czechoslovakia.[101]

It is not yet clear that the British and Indian intermediaries ever were given authority by Truman or his advisers to define a "neutralized zone" as more than an area where "America should be free to unify Korea under the cover of UN action."[102] Much of the story still remains hidden. But it does seem apparent that the Administration would not commit itself until it knew it had MacArthur on its side. On November 22 Acheson publicly denied the buffer story. Nonetheless, according to the *New York Herald Tribune:*

> Well-informed sources . . . indicated that agreement on the plan [for a buffer zone] to be presented to the Communist Chinese delegation at the UN, is near and is *awaiting* primarily *approval* of its military details *by* General Douglas MacArthur.[103]

And the Joint Chiefs of Staff did in fact so inform MacArthur on November 24. They explained that

> some sentiments exist at the United Nations for establishing a demilitarized zone between your forces and the frontier in the hope of thereby reducing Chinese Communist fear of United Nations Military action against Manchuria. . . .

The Joint Chiefs therefore suggested that in the Northeast MacArthur should order a halt at Chengjin, which was well south of the border, and elsewhere stop on "the terrain dominating the approaches to the Yalu River."[104] But MacArthur seems to have had the final say on America's political strategy, and to MacArthur such a notion as a buffer was "appeasement of Communist aggression. . . ." As he saw it:

> To give up a portion of North Korea to the aggression of the Chinese Communists would be the greatest defeat of the free world in recent times. Indeed to yield to so immoral a proposition would bankrupt our leadership and influence in Asia and render untenable our position, both politically and militarily.

> . . . I recommend that we press on to complete victory which I believe can be achieved if our determination and indomitable will do not desert us.[105]

MacArthur therefore replied to Washington that it was "utterly impossible for us to stop upon terrain south of the river as suggested." The next day, the day the Chinese delegates arrived at the United Nations, the all-out assault north toward the Yalu border of China's Manchuria began. Up until then, a former China specialist in the Australian government comments,

> the Chinese were prepared to sacrifice the military advantages of surprise and early intervention in the hope of a compromise settlement which may even have left the North Koreans in control of little more than the territory they still occupied south of the Yalu.[106]

These developments occurred in November, 1950, yet November is almost a non-word for the American academics-cum-high-level-advisers who have written about Korea. As they present events, China enters the war in October. Then MacArthur, because he does not prepare for the inevitable, is subsequently caught off his guard. What is missing is the policy of the Truman administration in the intervening month. Acheson is protected by silence. Yet it must be said that Acheson and his colleagues would not try too hard to stop an aggressively successful anti-Communist general in the field. Indeed they even sounded out the possibility of attacking into Manchuria by air. They gave in to pressures because the pressures were not unwelcome. In short it may be more apt to describe MacArthur not as a general out of control but as one permitted a rather loose leash by his Commander-in-Chief.

Some people who have been associated with the State Department insist that war with China would not have occurred had we understood each other's intentions, that is, had China given a clear signal of its intentions. But within two weeks of the success at Inchon, the Chinese had already delivered an unambiguous warning. MacArthur was not checked. These former American officials then acknowledge that China could indeed see itself threatened by an out-of-control MacArthur but all would have gone well had China intervened earlier. These men, rather than arguing that China was an aggressor in Korea, contend that China should have intervened earlier so that the President and his advisers who did not want a wider war would, forewarned, have checked the General.[107] But this view ignores the events of November. China did intervene hurriedly and then give the United States a chance to respond. After a long pause, MacArthur's all-out offensive was the American response. Truman would not stop him. In fact Acheson and his associates claim to have wanted to attack into China. The truth that these gentlemen imply but will not confront directly is that Mao Tse-tung and the Chinese Red Army had to save the United States from an aggressive American madness that the President himself could not restrain.

IX

MACARTHUR's late November offensive was, even according to McGeorge Bundy, a "provocation," and "this MacArthur knew. . . ."[108] The General saw China as "aggressively imperialistic with a lust for expansion."[109] Therefore he wanted to bomb China's industry, blockade its ports and unleash Chiang Kai-shek's troops. Even "the Pentagon had been concerned at that time lest MacArthur might later disobey another order with more serious results."[110] MacArthur was informed that administration officials blamed him for the escalation which was inciting wider war, for

> everytime . . . stop point was suggested, you replied you would not accept responsibility for security of your troops if decision was made; that this faced authorities with the dilemma of taking risk and replacing you with elections coming on or letting you proceed against their political and

diplomatic judgment and against some high military judgments also.[111]

This charge against MacArthur tells only part of the story. It ignores the ideology he shared with Truman and Acheson and leaves only partially stated the nature of political power in America. The liberal administration as well as the conservative General believed that Communism (or totalitarianism) was limitless aggression. The reason for not liberating northern Korea or China and thus destroying the source from which aggression and trouble would surely come was a lack of resources, not a lack of will. If one had limited resources, one had to choose priorities. For the administration Europe came first. But MacArthur's success at Inchon made it seem that perhaps he did have the wherewithal to carry it off. As Neustadt puts it, "Appetites rose as the troops went forward,"[112] Or should we say, aggressors feed on aggression?

The American military in the field would expand as far as it could go. After MacArthur's success at Inchon, General Ridgeway reports, "we operate[d] in a mission vacuum . . . without specific political or military objectives."[113] In that vacuum MacArthur made policy. It raised the question, "Who is President?"[114] In the Pentagon

> There were those who felt that it was useless to try to check a man who might react to criticism by pursuing his own way with increased stubbornness and fervor.[115]

It is possible that if China had not checked and blunted MacArthur's offensive and turned him into a militarily defeated and therefore politically defeatable general that MacArthur—who thought putting loyalty to the President before loyalty to the country a "dangerous concept"[116]—could not have been stopped from carrying the war into China.

Similarly the CIA was increasingly out of control—or in control—after its coup in Guatemala in 1954, until defeats at the Bay of Pigs in 1961 and Nam Tha in Laos in

1962, permitted the President to reassert his supremacy. But as in Korea in 1950, the world vision of the liberal President was little different from the supposed right-wingers in the field. If they could win, they could take the initiative. If Truman said no to attacking the Chinese Communists in 1947 and 1950 it was in large part because he felt he lacked the needed resources. If Kennedy said no to intervention in Laos in 1961 it was for similar reasons. When the resources seemed available in 1965, the President committed American troops to Vietnam. Once success abroad or failure at home calls doubts into question, there is little to stop the MacArthurs from continuing, pushing, expanding into the alleged ultimate source of potential aggression.

X

THE CHINESE armed signal of late October was accompanied by a statement of Chinese policy that

> The war in Korea has now entered a new phase. . . . The aggressive war of American imperialism . . . gravely threatens the security of our fatherland. . . . With China and Korea separated by one river, with 1000 *li* of common frontier, we can under no circumstances allow American imperialism, already proved to be China's most fierce enemy, to occupy Korea . . . and threaten the security of China.[117]

Most Chinese foreign policy statements were couched in similar language of national security. That concern for security led Peking to see and point out that there were differences in the American government as to where the American military would halt.

Although we are trying here, two decades after the fact, to put together some of the story of the buffer zone that never was, the Chinese of course were aware of it from the beginning.

When the American invaders were pressing toward the 38th Parallel, the US Government started a rumor that the US troops would stop at the Parallel. Later, it was said that the US troops would stop at a point some distance from the borders of the Soviet Union and China.[118]

Assurances in word had become worthless. British or American talk of a buffer zone could not in itself be trusted. If the United States hoped to convince China that America would stop at the Yalu, a buffer would have to be established in fact. If MacArthur's words about carrying the fight into Manchuria were to be disbelieved, the actual deployment of American troops would have to give them the lie. The Chinese concluded one review of betrayed American promises as to a stopping point:

> The 40th Parallel was then crossed in spite of all assurances to the contrary. This was followed by the circulation of the rumor that, with a view to avoiding coming into conflict with China, a buffer zone of 150 kilometers (later said to be 150 miles) shall be created. A couple of days after that and the bandit troops of Syngman Rhee were ordered to advance to the Chinese border, to be followed by American, English, and Australian forces. Are you still prepared to put your faith in such lies as that Truman has resolutely told MacArthur to avoid coming into conflict with China?[119]

Truman would not restrain MacArthur. Acheson argues that from October 26 to November 17 Washington had and lost its opportunity to set up a restraining line.[120] After that only the Chinese army could drive

> back the mad army of aggression which was already advancing near the Yalu River. Only then was the original fantastic plan of the imperialists smashed and the sacred resolution of our people to safeguard the fruits of victory recognized. Therefore the Chinese People's Volunteers are in a life and death struggle concerning the fundamental interests of our nation. . . .[121]

Responsible American power was of little account. Where MacArthur's military maneuvers were concerned, Acheson reports, "no one would restrain them."[122] MacArthur pressed forward. The Chinese asked, "When American troops were advancing north toward the Yalu River, have not the American authorities said that the American troops would only advance to a point 40 miles south of the Yalu River?"[123] Even the initial Chinese armed signal failed. As soon as the American forces "regained their breath, they started their wild adventures again."[124] Chinese signals for negotiation and a peaceful solution met no serious response from Washington.

America and its Asian allies only respected force. So subsequently in July, 1953, when Syngman Rhee threatened to upset the negotiated peace in Korea and fight on alone, the Chinese singled out and attacked the elite Korean White Tiger regiment and battered it as proof of Rhee's inability to win, "in case that son-of-a-bitch Syngman Rhee again refuses to acknowledge defeat!"[125] In 1953 and 1954 China ignored Dulles's threats of atomic retaliation and kept on providing aid to the Vietnamese. In 1961 China made clear that it would respond with force if large American combat units were sent to fight in Laos. Chinese troops in northern Laos make the meaning of the words clearer. In 1965 China let Washington know that 50,000 Chinese soldiers were entering northern Vietnam to limit American escalation there. One Chinese lesson from Korea was that it had to confront America with a determined Chinese military stand. Nothing less would deter the United States. This obvious fact would not need stating except that some high-level politicians and advisers have drawn from these events the erroneous lesson that China will cave in before a nuclear threat. Boom!

XI

MACARTHUR could act boldly because his "political allies [were] powerful."[126] Truman had to give in or court electoral defeat. Similarly in 1968 the President and Secretary of Defense committed themselves to a multi-billion-dollar antiballistic missile system which they did not want and did not believe in. It was another crafty move (necessitated by pressure from the Joint Chiefs and conservative southern congressmen who chair key congressional committees and the constituent interests they represent) which would decrease, not increase, American security. (As with Korea and Vietnam, however, if the costs came to seem too high some conservatives might turn against it.) In 1961 the President after the defeat at the Bay of Pigs abandoned thoughts of improving relations with China because he felt he could not afford more charges of softness on Communism. Can we then understand American foreign policy if we singularly stress the power of the President in his legal, institutional role? To be sure there is great institutional power in the presidency, but what of the coincidence in viewpoint of liberals and conservatives about the nature of the enemy, the powerful and vested reactionary interests and the institutionalized anti-Communist ideology which leads liberals to act much as conservatives? What is gained but a Pilate-like washing of unclean hands when China specialists insist that American support for Chiang Kai-shek at the end of World War II was not, as Mao would have it, the policy "of a group of people in the U.S. government," but rather that it "Stemmed inevitably from the legal position of Chiang as head of the Republic of China . . . ?"[127] Even if American specialists on China won't, China's leaders must try to explain to themselves why the American government in 1944 seemed interested in cooperation with the Red Army, in a coalition government in China which would protect and institutionalize the Chinese Communist Party, when by 1946 that executive branch in Washington committed itself to Chiang Kai-shek.[128] Their answer seems to be not that Roosevelt in 1945 and Marshall subsequently in 1946 were insincere but rather that there were forces in American society which negated the intentions of these individuals. China's attempt to identify these powerful reactionary forces is too quickly dismissed as a "distorted view of the world."[129] If one notes that "congressional and public opinion in the United States" left "the Truman administration little choice but to withhold recognition from the People's Republic of China" in 1949 and 1950,[130] then perhaps it is not such a useless venture to inquire into these forces which tie a president's hands or sorely limit his range of options. Thus there is much justice to the Administration's complaint in 1950 that political realities left MacArthur in charge. Those realities are in some ways even more institutionalized and formidable today.

XII

YET THERE IS ALSO an international logic beyond domestic politics in MacArthur's arguments. His notion that Korea had to be put in safe hands, that at the very least China had to be made militarily impotent and that Formosa was to be an unsinkable American aircraft carrier had a definite strategic logic once the point of view of the strategy is made clear. Louis J. Halle who had been a member of the State Department Policy Planning Staff wrote, in a book with a laudatory preface by Dean Acheson, of "our new position [which] appeared to give us a new stake in Far Eastern matters," Halle matter-of-factly discussed

> our sudden advent upon the Far Eastern scene in a new capacity, as the successor power to Japan, heir to all the interests that had long been identified with Japan's military and economic security.[131]

It was such a notion of security which had led Japan into Formosa, Southeast Asia, Korea, and war with China. But the desire for secure areas around secure areas can turn into a quest for global imperium. MacArthur was a little ahead of the State Department in time perhaps because his prior interest in the Philippines made him super-sensitive to a Formosa in potentially hostile hands. "Anyone who had been in the Philippines in December, 1941, did not have to be reminded of how vulnerable the Philippines were to Japan's Formosa-based bombers."[132] Thus a Philippine study could conclude from its point of view that

> By geographical position, Formosa together with the Philippines, forms the first line of defense of the United States in the Western Pacific littoral. American defense of the independence and territorial integrity of Formosa is essential to the defense and security of the Philippines.[133]

MacArthur, in part because of his concern for the Philippines, may have been a step ahead of the administration. But once Washington—as Tokyo before it—confronted the imperial problem of maintaining order and stopping "Communism" in Asia, Acheson and MacArthur were virtually indistinguishable. America had replaced the expansionist enemy it had defeated. Members of the Administration have described this process of military expansion when "the limits on our objective had not been finally determined" and might have included "the unconditional surrender of the new Chinese regime."[134] But when Chinese leaders call attention to America "following in the footsteps of the Japanese predecessors who also began with aggression against Korea and then the Northeast [i.e., Manchuria] and the interior of China,"[135] they are chided by specialists on Chinese politics in the United States for having an "ideologically colored view."[136] Yet who but a China specialist writing for an ideologically blinded American audience could seriously say of the men in Peking:

> Their ideological perspective did not permit them to distinguish between Japan of yesterday as an expansionist nation and the United States of today as a status quo power.[137]

It takes an endlessly expansive and expensive effort to rebuild a crumbling status quo.

The most careful study of Peking in this period correctly notes that for Chinese looking at what America would do next, "Utterances by 'authoritative spokesmen' in Tokyo were given equal weight (if not greater) with statements from Secretary Acheson and President Truman." That is, as we have seen, the Chinese were good American-ologists. They saw the reality of MacArthur's power in Tokyo. Yet that same fine study in conclusion chided the Chinese leaders as men who "departed sharply from reality" when they ignored "the true locus of power in Washington."[138] In fact the Communist Chinese long ago saw clearly, where liberal Americans are still confused.

Because we cannot see that we are not acting defensively, we call the Chinese blind. We see China almost singularly as an object, composed of various elements, that acts on the world instead of as a subject that reacts to and interacts with the dynamic initiatives of super-powers and their allies. Liberal illusions permit liberal self-righteousness which feeds and fosters the plans and policies of expansionist and militarist international reaction. The Korean decision, however, forced Chinese policy-makers to shed illusions about the locus of American power in the White House. Until Americans shed those illusions, they will not understand how out of control, how much of a threat, America has become. Instead Americans may ascribe to the psyche of Chinese leaders an irrationality which is actually and institutionally American. And we may therefore mistakenly undertake military adventures which will produce a needless, murderous, and massively destructive war with China.

Notes

1. McGeorge Bundy, *The Pattern of Responsibility* (Boston, Houghton Mifflin, 1952), p. 179.
2. *China Digest* (hereafter: *CD*) (Hong Kong, November 2, 1949), p. 7. *China Digest* was replaced in January, 1950, by *People's China* which itself was subsequently supplanted by *Peking Review*. It was an official, English language propaganda voice.

It published official news stories and speeches as well as interviews and analyses of foreign policy. I have only used its most official despatches or foreign policy analyses which were often repeated.

3. *CD* (April 20, 1948), p. 6.
4. *Selected Military Writings of Mao Tse-tung* (hereafter: *Mao*) (Peking, Foreign Languages Press, 1966), pp. 159, 191, 200–204, 214, 218 and 221.
5. *Mao*, p. 213.
6. *Mao*, p. 192.
7. *Mao*, p. 258.
8. *Mao*, pp. 222–224.
9. Walter La Feber, *America, Russia and the Cold War, 1945–1966* (New York, Wiley, 1967), p. 118.
10. Yung-hwan Jo, "Regional Cooperation in Southeast Asia and Japan's Role," *The Journal of Politics*, 30 (August, 1968), p. 782.
11. Allen S. Whiting, *China Crosses the Yalu* (New York, Macmillan, 1960), p. 36.
12. *CD* (April 6, 1948), p. 10 & (April 20, 1948), pp. 6–7. This is not to suggest that Whiting was unaware of the potential danger to China.
13. *CD* (February 8, 1949), pp. 14–15.
14. *The China White Paper* (Department of State Publication 3573, Far Eastern Series 30, Stanford Univ. Press, reissue 1967), I, p. 383.
15. *CD* (February 22, 1949), p. 14.
16. *Mao*, p. 373.
17. *Mao*, pp. 357, 383, 385 & 386, consecutively.
18. *CD* (January 11, 1949), p. 9.
19. *CD* (May 31, 1949), pp. 4–5.
20. *CD* (August 10, 1949), p. 4.
21. *CD* (August 10, 1949), p. 5.
22. Tang Tsou, *America's Failure in China* (Chicago, Chicago Univ. Press, 1963), p. 534. A magnificently researched study.
23. Cited in *Current Backgrounds* (hereafter: *CB*) 36 (Hong Kong, American Consulate General), p. 8.
24. *CD* (August 10, 1949), p. 15.
25. *CD* (September 7, 1949), p. 15.
26. *New China News Agency* (hereafter *NCNA*), January, 1950, #268.
27. *CD* (November 2, 1949), p. 23.
28. *NCNA*, January 1950, #261.
29. *NCNA*, March 1950, #304.
30. *NCNA*, March 1950, #318.
31. *NCNA*, June 1950, #413.
32. *NCNA*, June 1950, #415.

32a. "The North Korean Labor Party's Factions," *Jiyu,* May, 1967, translated in *Selected Summaries of Japanese Magazines,* June 26, 1967-July 3, 1967, pp. 8–11.

33. *Department of State Bulletin* (Washington, D.C., January 23, 1950). In this speech Acheson outlined America's defense perimeter and excluded Korea. The Chinese paid no overt attention to that part of Acheson's speech. It wasn't news. It was long established policy. The Chinese had long been aware of it.

34. *NCNA,* January 1950, #273.

35. Cited in Gar Alperovitz, *Atomic Diplomacy* (New York, Vintage, 1965), pp. 95 and 96.

36. Harold Isaacs, *No Peace for Asia* (Cambridge, Mass., M.I.T. Press, 1967), pp. 41–42.

37. As related by C. L. Sulzberger in the *New York Times,* July 1968. Walter S. Robertson, who was to be America's Assistant Secretary of State for Far Eastern Affairs, reports that "the policy of containment was initiated by President Truman in 1947 following costly, disillusioning experiences with Soviet Russia's callous disregard of written agreements in Europe and Manchuria." From "Vietnam in Red China," in Anthony Bouscaren *The Case for Free China* (Arlington, Va., Crestwood Books, 1967), p. 111.

38. Louis J. Halle, *Civilization and Foreign Policy* (New York, Harper and Bros., 1955), p. 243.

39. Gabriel Kolko, *The Politics of War* (New York, Random House, 1968), p. 599.

40. Cited in Tsou, *America's Failure,* p. 544.

41. *NCNA,* January 1950, #244, 246 & 253.

42. *NCNA,* March 1950, #258.

43. Cited in Glenn Paige, *The Korean Decision* (hereafter: Paige (New York, Free Press, 1968), p. 105.

44. Paige, p. 112.

45. Paige, pp. 114 & 124.

46. Paige, p. 110.

47. Tsou, *America's Failure,* p. 561.

48. Paige, pp. 148 & 174.

49. Paige, p. 154.

50. Paige, p. 159.

51. Paige, p. 217.

52. Paige, p. 165.

53. Paige, pp. 191 & 193.

54. Paige, pp. 194–97.

55. Roy Macartney, "How War Came to Korea," in Norman Bartlett,

With the Australians in Korea (Canberra, Australian War Memorial, 1954), p. 171.

56. Courtney Whitney, *MacArthur, His Rendezvous With History* (New York, Knopf, 1966), p. 326.
57. Paige, pp. 246–7 & 230–31.
58. Paige, pp. 249 & 258–9.
59. Cited in Tsou, *America's Failure*, p. 566.
60. Paige, p. 181.
61. Paige, p. 236.
62. Paige, p. 238.
63. Paige, pp. 245–46 & 250–51.
64. Paige, p. 256.
65. Paige, p. 261.
65a. "The North Korean Labor Party's Factions," *loc. cit.* note 32a above. South Korean sources acknowledge that in one mountain area some 40,000 people rose at the outset of the war and that revolutionary strength in other areas was not broken till December, 1954—that is, a year and a half after the armistice had stopped the war. (Cited in Young Jeh Kim, "The Purposes of North Korea's Guerrilla Warfare and the Reactions of South Korea," *Issues and Studies,* Vol. VI [August, 1970], p. 18.) What happened in other areas, how land reform teams fared, and much else of the Korean War remains hidden.
66. William J. Sebald, with Russell Brines, *With MacArthur in Japan* (New York, Norton, 1965), p. 123.
67. Whitney, *MacArthur,* p. 447.
68. Bundy, *Pattern,* p. 266.
69. Robert Frank Futell, *The United States Air Force in Korea 1950–1953* (New York, Duell, Sloan and Pearce, 1961), p. 222.
70. David Rees, *Korea: The Limited War* (New York, St. Martin's Press, 1964), p. 151.
71. Richard Neustadt, *Presidential Power* (New York, Wiley, 1960), p. 140; this is also Whiting's view.
72. Richard Rovere and Arthur Schlesinger, Jr., *The MacArthur Controversy and American Foreign Policy* (New York, Farrar, Straus and Giroux, 1951), p. 153.
73. Whitney, *MacArthur,* pp. 487–488.
74. *Ibid.,* p. 488.
75. Charles A. Willoughby and John Chamberlain, *MacArthur 1941–1951* (New York, McGraw-Hill, 1954), p. 402.
76. K. M. Panikkar, *In Two Chinas* (London, Allen and Unwin, 1955), p. 110.
77. Rovere and Schlesinger, *MacArthur Controversy,* p. 148.

78. Sebald, *With MacArthur,* p. 200.
79. Whitney, *MacArthur,* p. 398.
80. Tsou, *America's Failure,* p. 580.
81. Panikkar, *In Two Chinas,* p. 108.
82. Tsou, *America's Failure,* p. 582.
83. Whitney, *MacArthur,* pp. 401–402.
84. *Ibid.,* p. 416.
85. *Survey of the China Mainland Press* (hereafter: *SCMP*) (Hong Kong, American Consulate General) #14, p. 7; *CB* 36, pp. 12–13; *SCMP* 7, p. 14.
86. Bartlett, *With the Australians in Korea,* p. 38.
87. Ronald Monson, "The Great Retreat," in *Ibid.,* p. 199.
88. *Ibid.,* p. 200.
89. Lt. Col. Herbert F. Wood, *Strange Battleground: The Operations in Korea and Their Effects on the Defense Policy of Canada* (Ottawa, Canada, Ministry of National Defense, 1966), p. 51.
90. *A Volunteer Soldier's Day: Recollections by Men of the Chinese People's Volunteers in the War to Resist U.S. Aggression and Aid Korea* (Peking, Foreign Languages Press, 1966), pp. 4, 7, and 8.
91. Whitney, *MacArthur,* p. 422.
92. Alexander George, *Presidential Control of Force: The Korean War and the Cuban Missile Crisis* (RAND P-3627, July 1967), pp. 22 and 23.
93. Wood, *Strange Battleground,* p. 51.
94. Futell, *U.S. Air Force,* p. 210.
95. Whitney, *MacArthur,* p. 406.
96. Futell, *U.S. Air Force,* p. 212.
97. Rovere and Schlesinger, *MacArthur Controversy,* p. 154.
98. Panikkar, *In Two Chinas,* p. 117.
99. Whitney, *MacArthur,* p. 411.
100. Rees, *Korea,* p. 133.
101. Whitney, *MacArthur,* p. 411.
102. Panikkar, *In Two Chinas,* p. 116.
103. I. F. Stone, *The Hidden History of the Korean War* (New York, Monthly Review Press, 1952), p. 197. Emphasis added.
104. Whitney, *MacArthur,* pp. 417 and 418.
105. *Ibid.,* p. 412.
106. Gregory Clark, *In Fear of China* (Melbourne, Lansdowne Press, 1967), p. 31.
107. Cf. Louis J. Halle, *The Cold War As History* (New York, Harper and Row, 1967), ch. 21.
108. Cited in David Horowitz, *The Free World Colossus* (New York, Hill and Wang, 1965), p. 133.

109. Whitney, *MacArthur*, p. 410.
110. Matthew B. Ridgway, *The Korean War* (New York, Doubleday, 1967), p. 71.
111. Whitney, *MacArthur*, p. 446. For more on the political considerations which made it difficult for the President to restrain Mac-Arthur, cf. Dean Acheson, *Present at the Creation* (New York, Norton, 1969), p. 468.
112. Neustadt, *Presidential Power*, pp. 127 and 137.
113. Ridgway, *Korean War*, p. 226.
114. Neustadt, *Presidential Power*, p. 41.
115. Ridgway, *Korean War*, p. 71.
116. *Ibid.*, p. 228.
117. *SCMP* (*Hsueh-hsi,* November 1, 1950), p. 7.
118. *SCMP* 5 (*Jen-min jih pao,* November 6, 1950, editorial), p. 3. Dean Acheson has confirmed this Chinese reading that Mac-Arthur in mid-October, ignoring an established "restraining line" sixty miles south of the Yalu, . . . without warning or notice to Washington, ordered his commanders to "drive forward with all speed and full utilization of their forces." Acheson, *Present at the Creation,* pp. 453, 461, 462.
119. *SCMP* 8 (article by editor-in-chief of Shanghai *Ta kung pao* in Hong Kong *Ta kung pao,* November 10–11, 1950), p. 20.
120. Acheson, *Present at the Creation,* p. 468.
121. *SCMP* 14 (*Jen-min jih pao,* November 20, 1950, editorial).
122. Acheson, *Present at the Creation,* p. 467.
123. *SCMP* 21 (*Jen-min jih pao,* November 30, 1950, editorial), p. 2.
124. *SCMP* 22 (*Jen-min Jih pao,* December 2, 1950, editorial), p. 2.
125. *A Volunteer Soldier's Day,* p. 384; cf. Wilfred Burchett, *Again Korea* (New York, International Publishers, 1968), pp. 132–35.
126. Neustadt, *Presidential Power*, p. 32.
127. Whiting, *China Crosses the Yalu,* pp. 10 and 11.
128. Cf. John Gittings, "The Origins of China's Foreign Policy," in David Horowitz (ed.), *Containment and Revolution* (Boston, Beacon Press, 1967), pp. 190–197.
129. Whiting, *China Crosses the Yalu,* p. 10.
130. *Ibid.*, p. 12. Whiting and Tsou blame the Chinese for arousing this opinion. Gittings answers their argument. (*loc. cit.*, pp. 197–200.)
131. Halle, *Civilization and Foreign Policy,* p. 243.
132. Whitney, *MacArthur*, p. 369.
133. Simon Perez Tabu, "A Historical Study of the American Foreign Policy in Nationalist China From 1945–1955: Its Implications to the Defense of the Philippines," *Graduate and Faculty Studies* (Centro Escolar University, Manila, VIII, 1957), p. 127. Cf.

Walter Judd, "Containment of Red China Is Vital to U.S.," in Anthony Bouscaren, *The Case for Free China*, p. 87.

134. Halle, *Civilization and Foreign Policy*, pp. 243–244.

135. Cited in Whiting, *China Crosses the Yalu*, p. 128.

136. Tsou, *America's Failure*, p. 577.

137. *Idem*.

138. Whiting, *China Crosses the Yalu*, p. 169. Whiting's great, pioneering work was the accepted basis for viewing Chinese intervention for most of the next decade. It was far superior to previous notions of an unprovoked and aggressive China or of a China taking orders from the Soviet Union and not acting in terms of its own interests. This notion of the distorting ideological element as crucial is still reflected in 1968, for example, in John Spanier's *American Foreign Policy Since World War II* (New York, Praeger, 1968). "The Administration did not believe that the Chinese Communist leaders would consider the United Nations advance as a threat to their security, because they were Chinese first and Communists second." "But American policy-makers miscalculated." (*Ibid.*, pp. 95–96.) That is: in Whiting's terms the Communist element, an ideological element, a misperception, and not a matter of rational national security was decisive. The overwhelming mass of evidence argues otherwise.

The United States in Laos, 1945-1962

🌀 *Jonathan Mirsky & Stephen E. Stonefield*

INTRODUCTION

🌀 ON JANUARY 4, 1969, White House adviser Walt Rostow, looking back on his eight years' service in Washington, reflected on the importance of Laos in American foreign policy:

> . . . President Eisenhower told President-elect Kennedy that Laos [in 1961] was in a state of military and political disintegration and it was quite possible if not probable that he would have to put some troops in to save Southeast Asia. . . . We waited, as typically we have waited throughout our history, for a major crisis to be upon us before we moved.[1]

Such melancholy reflections on American inertia and blindness to danger are often heard in this country. *Did* the United States wake up too late in Laos, when decisive early action might have prevented yet another "Loss"?

Laos presents an instance, in fact, of determined, continuous, and committed American intervention, from 1945 to 1962, the time span of this study. Indeed, from 1945, when OSS operatives first made contact with the anti-Japanese resistance movement, to 1968 when American planes destroyed every village in parts of Samneua province,[2] Laos has been on Washington's action list.

From 1946 to 1963 Laos received more American aid per capita than any country in Southeast Asia. By 1958 the

Royal Lao Army was the only foreign army in the world *wholly* supported by the taxpayers of the United States. Between 1958 and 1960 Washington twice overthrew legally constituted Lao governments, and struggled continuously to prevent a neutral coalition which Peking, Hanoi, and Moscow were prepared to accept. After a CIA-sponsored Lao leader provoked a clash during the 1962 Geneva "cease-fire," the Kennedy Administration seriously considered a nuclear attack on China, although its own military observer on the scene reported no foreign troops engaged, other than American Special Forces. Clearly, despite Mr. Rostow's regrets, America has not neglected what it regards as its interests in Laos. Although there exist several studies of modern Laos and quantities of documentary material, in the end most authorities shrink from the assignment of major responsibility for the Laos tangle to the United States.[3]

What follows is an analysis of the relationship between a nation with a predominantly rural population of less than 3,000,000, and a nation with the greatest military and industrial power on earth. United States intervention in Laos must be viewed not merely in the context of a response to Communism, but in the perspective of Washington's self-motivated and increasing involvement in Asia. Fear of Communist China alone cannot explain American efforts in Laos. Chinese influence has been slight. But United States ties with the elite in Thailand and its instruments in Laos, an elite with whom American policy-makers feel at ease, made it mandatory for Kennedy as well as Eisenhower to strangle the movement toward Laotian neutralism and independence which characterized the Vientiane governments of 1958 and 1960. The Chinese were willing to support an unaligned Laos. The United States was not. It agreed to a settlement in 1962 largely because its Rightist allies proved ineffective and unreliable. The Vietnam story was prefigured in Laos. The Laos story may continue even after the one in Vietnam is completed.

THE RESISTANCE MOVEMENT
BEFORE 1950

LIKE VIETNAM, Laos developed during the Second World War a resistance movement against the French. The movement, however, developed not from a long period of national awareness and cultural pride, but from the ambitions of a tiny elite of perhaps two dozen figures. These were the Lao with whom the Americans first came into contact following World War II.[4]

The movement toward independence received its impetus when on August 29, 1941, the Lao King, Sisavangvong, concluded a treaty with France consolidating all of northern Laos under the jurisdiction of the capital, Luang Prabang. Four years later, on March 9, 1945, when they suddenly seized local control from the French, the Japanese pressured the King into proclaiming independence from France.[5] By August 18, Prince Phetsarath, Premier in the new Government, formed the Lao Issara, or Free Lao, movement.

On September 1, 1945, Phetsarath proclaimed the complete rupture of Laotian ties with France; on September 14, after placing all remaining provinces under the administration of Luang Prabang, Phetsarath, his brother Souvanna Phouma, and half-brother Souphanouvong, appointed a provisional national assembly and began work on a new constitution.[6] King Sisavangvong, however, vetoed the plan on September 17, declaring that Laos remained under the French protectorate. French forces, indeed, had already returned in the south, aided by Prince Boun Oum of Champassak who had worked with the French against the Japanese.[7]

Although dismissed from his Premiership on October 10, Phetsarath and the Free Lao placed the King under house arrest. By April 23, 1946, Sisavangvong agreed to cooperate with the Free Lao, accepting the position of constitutional monarch, but upon the arrival of the French in Luang Prabang on May 13, the Free Lao fled to Bangkok; from across the Mekong it mounted occasional harrassing raids against the French under the leadership of its Defense Minister, Souphanouvong.

Near the end of the war, American agents of the Office of Strategic Services had already arrived in Indochina.[8] Shortly after the Japanese surrender, the OSS appeared in Laos, under the direction of Major James Thompson (the founder in later years of the modern Thai silk industry). Thompson's mission was to investigate reports that French troops were crossing the Thai border to attack the Lao Issara in their bases. The OSS agents admonished the French to "cease their aggression," while Souphanouvong appealed to the United States for support—as did the Viet Minh— repeating Roosevelt's anti-colonial statements.[9]

Souphanouvong, as early as 1945, had sought support for the Lao independence movement from the newly proclaimed Vietnamese Republic. In late 1945, General Gallagher of the OSS arranged to fly the Prince to Hanoi where he met with Ho Chi Minh, who provided the Lao leader with an armed guard and a small supply of weapons. Souphanouvong returned to the Lao border on November 1, 1945, but maintained his ties with Hanoi, returning to North Vietnam in July 1946, where he conferred with General Giap.[10] Journeying between Bangkok and Laos, he was the Lao leader who maintained military operations against the French from 1946 to 1949, and on March 11, 1951, he signed the Vietnam-Khmer-Lao alliance, thus strengthening his ties with the Viet Minh.[11] A year before, in August, 1950, Souphanouvong, together with other dissidents, several of them non-Lao hillsmen, had formed the Pathet Lao or Lao National Movement.[12]

AMERICAN INVOLVEMENT
BEFORE GENEVA

ALREADY DURING WORLD WAR II the United States sowed the seeds of decades of conflict by deciding that the people of the Indochinese peninsula would not take charge of their own destinies. Roosevelt's intention to exclude the French from Indochina and to establish a United Nations trusteeship (once he discovered Chiang Kai-shek could not be persuaded to take over the area) was supplanted after his death by the Truman administration's support of the French against the Viet Minh.[13] On February 7, 1950, the United States recognized the French-sponsored government of Boun Oum in Vientiane, together with the Bao Dai regime in Saigon.[14] The Indochinese war became a skirmish in the larger struggle between Communism and the "Free World." But Washington was not merely responding to a "Communist" threat; rather, it was rationalizing its increasing activities in Asia. With the Korean war in 1950 came President Truman's famous speech on Communist aggression proclaiming that the Chinese revolution spelled aggression throughout Asia and pledging more rapid military assistance to France and the French Union States.[15]

The links between the Laotian situation and Thailand became clearer when in April, 1953, Viet Minh forces, fighting the French over a wide area, first occupied the province of Samneua and then threatened the royal capital of Luang Prabang. A second Viet Minh-Pathet Lao drive at the end of 1953 to southern Laos saw the beginning of organizing work amongst the hill people. Thailand, already Washington's most important Southeast Asian associate, voiced continual concern for its safety. The United States responded to Thai pleas with words of assurance and actual support, although even John Foster Dulles admitted that the prospect for Viet Minh invasion of Thailand was negligible.[16]

General Henri Navarre, French Commander in Indochina, alarmed at the passage of guerrillas between Vietnam and Laos, elected to station his troops at various checkpoints, including the North Vietnamese valley of Dienbienphu. Giap broke off his operations in Laos, and after seizing a number of vital outposts in the north, laid siege to the French lodgement at Dienbienphu itself, which fell in the spring of 1954,[17] thus essentially ending French colonial administration in Indochina.

During the last two years of French rule, 1952–54, the Eisenhower administration increased its aid in Indochina. John Foster Dulles was determined to avoid at all costs any charge that another country had been allowed to slip into the Communist camp, a charge leveled by Senator Joseph McCarthy against the Democrats after the revolution in China. In a speech to the Overseas Press Club on March 24, 1954, Dulles stated:

> . . . The imposition on Southeast Asia of the political system of Communist Russia and its Chinese Communist ally by whatever means would be a grave threat to the whole free community. The United States feels that the possibility should not be passively accepted.[18]

Regardless of the rhetoric of Dulles and Nixon, the Eisenhower administration was not adopting a new over-all policy. Under Roosevelt plans were developing for an intrusive American role in Asia. The policy of actively supporting colonialism and suppressing revolutionary movements initiated by Truman differed from the Dulles line only tactically. Both assumed an offensive posture in Asia.

Washington's actions did not stem from a defensive counter to Soviet or Chinese initiatives in Southeast Asia. Soviet military aid to the North Vietnamese amounted to little until the end of 1953—in fact, Soviet policy seemed ambivalent to the rise of Southeast Asian anti-colonialism. John Gittings shows that Chinese military assistance to North Vietnam only became meaningful in 1952, *after* the Viet Minh, who had already scored the long-term political and psychological victory, were on the offensive. The full-scale American involvement in Korea, which Edward Friedman has shown Peking did not anticipate, made the Chinese aware of the dangerous potential of American activities in Southeast Asia. It does not appear unnatural for Peking to protect its borders against French and American encroachment.

United States support for the French reassertion of its colonial status began in 1945, as did its disaffection with Indochina nationalists whose sudden seizure of power at the end of the war upset Washington's plans for "international control." Washington's efforts, however, were the result not of "Communist pressure," but of last-ditch French and American efforts to preserve the *status quo*. If that could not be accomplished, the Truman-initiated policies of increased militarization fostering radically altered political alignments—so successful in Europe with its rearmed Germany and NATO, and in Latin America with the Rio Pact—could be adapted to meet the needs of United States policy in Asia.

Gabriel Kolko in *The Politics of War* and *The Roots of American Foreign Policy,* and Victor Bator in *Vietnam: A Diplomatic Tragedy,* are but two of the historians who have demonstrated two principal American preoccupations in Asia: The areas' potential for investment and trade, and the accompanying necessity to stem the tide of revolution and nationalism which would limit our commercial penetration. In the case of John Foster Dulles this policy took the form of an hysterical anti-Communism, ornamented with "rollback," "enslaved peoples," and "massive retaliation," epithets which now arouse sad head-shaking among American diplomatic historians—who cannot, however, shake themselves loose from the dream of an active and *leading* role for the United States in Asia. During the Dulles period (years in which Vice-President Richard Nixon referred to the Indochinese struggle as ". . . not a civil war [but] a war of aggression by the Communist conspiracy against all the free nations")[19] there developed the view that any slippage into the "Communist camp" would lead to further voluntary desertions from the "free world" of its weaker members. American hegemony in many parts of the underdeveloped world—with fancied collapse of prestige and actual economic loss—could not stand defection.

The foundation for United States policy was laid; construction was quickened, although not initiated, by the Korean War. By 1954, Washington realized that it would have to go it alone, assisted no longer by the ex-colonial power, but only by its Asian clients.

GENEVA 1954

THE COLLAPSE of the French and the convening of the Geneva Conference shifted the Indochinese struggle from the battlefield to diplomatic circles.

As Eden shows in his memoirs, months before Geneva, the Americans were pressing for a mechanism to guarantee against further Communist successes in Asia. Although the British were alarmed at some of Dulles' more violent proposals, which might well have led to direct clashes with China, the Foreign Office did not oppose the general proposition that the West must hold the line.[20] Dulles and Anthony Eden eventually drew up conditions for a successful settlement on June 25. Eden later said a settlement was desired that (quoted here in part):

> Preserves the integrity and independence of Laos and Cambodia and assures the withdrawal of Vietminh forces therefrom . . .
>
> Does not impose on Laos, Cambodia, or retained Vietnam any restrictions materially impairing their capacity to maintain stable non-Communist regimes; and especially restrictions impairing their right to maintain adequate forces for internal security, to import arms and to employ foreign advisers.
>
> Does not contain political provisions which would risk the loss of the retained area to Communist control. . . .[21]

The last point demands special attention, for it precluded United States support for the ultimate Geneva agreements. If taken literally, it would not permit elections and unification of Vietnam in 1956 as specified in the agreements, nor would it allow Pathet Lao participation in Lao politics. (This very interpretation was made by United States officials in 1958, after Washington had overthrown a coalition government in Laos.) Dulles made clear to Eden that the United States did not consider itself "a party to the Conference results," although in its Final Declaration, the United States agreed not to overthrow them by force.[22]

Apart from the provisions dealing with military personnel and aid, the most important section of the Accords dealing with Laos held that:

> Pending a political settlement, the fighting units of the 'Pathet Lao' concentrated in the provisional assembly areas, shall move into the provinces of Phong Saly and Sam Neua, except for any military personnel who wish to be demobilized where they are.[23]

Such wording clearly left undefined the role the Pathet Lao should play in the two provinces. It soon appeared that the Pathet Lao administration responded with arms to Royal Lao Government units attempting to establish Vientiane's control in the two provinces, although the day following the Geneva Conference, July 21, the Royal Lao Government stated it would allow representation for the Pathet Lao in Phong Saly and Samneua until elections were held; the December, 1955 elections, however, did not extend to these areas.[24]

COLLAPSE OF THE FIRST COALITION (1954)

A SERIOUS CRISIS in Lao politics occurred in September, 1954, with the assassination of Kou Voravong, Vientiane's Defense Minister, who had advocated reconciliation and integration with the Pathet Lao (Only Wilfred Burchett, in *The Furtive War*[25] makes clear the advantage to the United States of this murder, probably by a Thai gun-man. Later killings, in 1963, of Quinim Pholsena and Kanthy Siphantong, pro-Pathet Lao leaders, had similar shattering effects on a neutralist coalition.) Voravong's death precipitated such political disorder that Souvanna Phouma, who was committed to neutrality, was forced to resign. Discussions during August and September between Souvanna and Souphanouvong had appeared likely to end the dispute between the Royal Lao Government and the Pathet Lao.[26] Katay Sasorith—traditionally inclined toward closer ties with Thailand—who formed the succeeding government in November, viewed the Pathet Lao as part of a North Vietnamese threat.

UNITED STATES POST-GENEVA OPPOSITION TO NEUTRALITY (1954–1958) AND THE ROLE OF THAILAND

DULLES LOOKED APPROVINGLY on the new anti-coalition Vientiane government as Washington prepared to replace the French in Indochina.[27] His determination to intervene further in Southeast Asia had become apparent with his convening in September, 1954, of the SEATO powers in Manila. The resulting treaty contained a protocol including the protection of Laos against "aggression," an American circumvention of the central provisions of the Geneva articles.[28]

It is evident that a neutral Laos was a major intention of those who drafted the Geneva Accords. Unlike the United States, China pledged itself to respect the Geneva agreements. It was in Peking's interest to do so; the Geneva Accords could have prevented French and American military intervention at China's border.

Chinese diplomacy therefore, worked to establish a rapprochement between the Royal Lao Government and the Pathet Lao, but China's policy was thwarted by Washington's rejection of the 1954 Geneva Accords, its creation of SEATO, and its subversion of neutralism. SEATO, by providing an open door for American intervention in Southeast Asia, constituted a menace to China. Chou En-lai, in August, 1955, attempted to counter the SEATO military danger by proposing an association of Asian and Pacific nations—including the United States—committed to Nehru's idea of "collective peace."[29] Like other Chinese diplomatic proposals, this one did not make any impression on the United States–SEATO bloc.

If SEATO alarmed the Chinese, it reinforced Thailand as the keystone of America's Southeast Asian intervention. In the military hierarchy in Thailand (which has ruled the country since 1938 except for a brief period after World War II) there is a strong tradition of rigid anti-Communism, which takes its domestic form in repression of the opposition. By the early 1950's, Thailand was a close military ally of the United States, intensifying a relationship which grew out of long-standing trade contact. In 1949 trade figures had exceeded by twenty times the pre-war level, and fifty American firms were on the scene.[30] In 1950 Washington was administering a $10 million military aid program in Thailand, and that year Bangkok not only participated in the Korean War but also became the first Asian government to recognize the Bao Dai regime in South Vietnam. The next year saw the establishment of an American Military Assistance Advisory Group (MAAG). Closely following a greatly expanded military assistance program in 1954 (including training, shipments of jet fighters, heavy equipment and arms, and strategic road building projects), Thailand participated in the formation of SEATO, and proposed that the organization's "umbrella" cover Laos, Cambodia, and South Vietnam—a proposal which coincided with Dulles's plans.

The strong anti-Communist posture of the Thai military and civilian bureaucracy, coupled with general national stability and invitations for American corporate investment, made Thailand an important factor in America's plans for Asian development. Thailand also afforded Washington a secure foothold in an otherwise highly insecure area.

Thailand's ruling elite, moreover, has close ties to Southern Lao elite families. Parts of Laos were annexed by Thailand both in the nineteenth century and World War II, and the modern extension of the Thai policy of maintaining a loyal neighboring state found its expression in Bangkok's desire for Laos to act as a friendly state between Thailand and North Vietnam and China. SEATO provided the Thai military with further self-justification of its strength and power, and strengthened Washington's right arm in policing Laotian politics. By including Laos (as well as Cambodia and South Vietnam) under the SEATO umbrella, the signatories of the Manila Treaty endorsed the American and Thai policy of turning Laos into a Cold War arena of confrontation with Peking.

In 1955, following the Dulles visit to the Katay government in Vientiane, the United States Operations Mission (USOM) was introduced into Laos, accompanied by an economic supplement to the Pentalateral Agreement of 1950 through which the United States supplied aid to the French Union States and to France.[31] The American position on military aid in Laos evolved in what may have been a unique manner. Following the Geneva Conference in 1954, the Joint Chiefs of Staff (JCS) refused to recommend "force levels" for Laos (a term referring to a supportable army), suggesting that instead the Royal Lao Army be reduced to the status of a police force. The Joint Chiefs based their position on the Geneva prohibitions against military advisers which made installing a normal Military Assistance Advisory Group (MAAG) impossible. As Arthur Schlesinger pointed out for a later period, the "lessons" of limited war in Korea seemed to have made the Joint Chiefs remarkably prudent.[32] Although American-caused devastation in Korea was immense, it failed to break the will of the North Koreans and the Chinese. General MacArthur's dismissal demonstrated to his brother officers that the United States would not again make a total commitment of American soldiers to a ground war in the Pacific, a lesson General Westmoreland would learn again when, following the 1968 Tet offensive, he asked for another 200 thousand troops, a request which, according to Townsend Hoopes, led to the General's recall. In January, 1955, when asked to reconsider their evaluation, the Joint Chiefs of Staff reported to the Secretary of State that their views remained unchanged "from the military point of view" but they could agree to mutual security support of Laos "should political considerations be overriding."[33] One year later, in 1956, the Joint Chiefs of Staff acquiesced on the question of an increase in Laotian forces, remarking that the increase *could* be justified "from a psychological, political, and morale aspect."[34] As late as 1958, however, the Joint Chiefs of Staff continued to maintain that the Royal Lao Army did not fall within force objectives.[35]

Prevarication by government officials on the United States role in training the Royal Lao Army continued long after American activities were in full swing. During a Congressional Hearing in 1958, Charles Shuff, an Assistant Secretary in the Defense Department, first maintained: "Its own interpretation of the Geneva agreement has prevented the United States from assuming a direct role in the training program. . . ." He went on to mention that owing to the Royal Lao Army's "intense desire . . . to learn English," a language laboratory and "a few officers with the requisite English" had been dispatched to Laos. Later in his testimony, however, Mr. Shuff described how America, in attempting to keep Laos out of Communist hands, assisted in "organizing, training, and equipping their forces. . . . The United States has provided the means of maintaining the Lao National Army as a military and psychological safeguard for the Government of Laos." The standard American pattern established itself: advisers, who were to be followed by troops and subsequent Americanization of the conflict.[36]

By 1959 the Royal Lao Army was wholly supported by the United States taxpayer. Roger Hilsman spells out the prevailing official view:

> . . . the most important factor in the State Department's reasoning was probably the Cold War atmosphere of the time and Dulles's policy of creating military alliances around the perimeter of the Communist World. Pro-western, anti-Communist neutrality might be the most that could be expected from a country like Laos, but it was consistent with Dulles's way of thinking that Laos should also have a military "trip-wire" that could offer enough resistance to Communist aggression to dramatize it and permit outside intervention.[37]

In Vientiane, Souvanna Phouma, Minister of Defense in the Katay government, remained convinced that an accommodation could be reached with the Pathet Lao.[38] Washington, however, believed that the Royal Lao Army (Laos' only "national" organization) should be fashioned into a force for national unification. Instead of the usual military advisers, the United States inaugurated the Program Evaluations Office (PEO) described by Major General John Heintges, its director from 1958 to 1961, as "a civilian organization very similar to MAAG," in which personnel substituted civilian clothes for their army uniforms.[39] PEO, although attached to USOM, possessed sole jurisdiction in spending cash aid funds. Like the CIA, PEO controlled its own communications; from time to time this caused considerable conflict with the Ambassador, the supposed chief of the "country team" in Laos.[40]

The stated purpose of United States support to the Royal Lao Government was presented in 1958 by Charles Shuff for the Department of Defense:

> Our national objective is to prevent Laos from passing into the Communist bloc and to encourage greater cooperation and stronger affiliation with the free world. Militarily, this is accomplished by assisting the Lao government in organizing, equipping, and training their armed forces. The United States has provided the means of maintaining the Lao national Army

as a military and psychological safeguard for the Government of Laos.[41]

In the light of the official American explanations for the support of the Royal Lao Army, one should also note the evaluations of Roger Hilsman and Arthur Schlesinger, both of whom were deeply involved in policy-making during the Kennedy period:

> Inevitably such an army became more political than anything else—a focal point for graft, the principal lever for ambitious men plotting coups, and a symbol of government repression in the villages to which it did intermittently penetrate. And such an army was probably self-defeating in its larger purpose. Giving the Lao a military weapon to meet what was at bottom a political threat probably created an issue of American "imperialism" that made the military threat more tempting.[42]

> It was a misbegotten investment. Laos simply did not have the national or social structure to absorb the remorseless flood of American bounty. Instead of raising living standards or even producing military force, aid led to unimaginable bribery, graft, currency manipulation, and waste.[43]

The problem with such conclusions lies in their assumption that another way might have "worked—a better army, more liberal politicians, more knowledge of "the situation," more "awareness." The pragmatic preoccupation with *how* to tinker remains: neither Hilsman nor Schlesinger seems perturbed by the problem of whether one should tinker in the first place.

DIFFICULTIES OF THE SECOND COALITION (1956–1958)

POLITICAL INFIGHTING in Vientiane made it impossible for the Katay government to continue in office, and Souvanna Phouma returned to the Premiership in March, 1956. His return brought about a change in the relations between Laos and SEATO, with which Katay had maintained close contact.[44] Fears had already been expressed that such an involvement might bring Thai troops onto Lao soil, a development historically distasteful to patriotic Lao.[45] Souvanna's goal was national unity, which he understood involved the reintegration of the Pathet Lao into Lao politics. Neutrality, moreover, might gain the support of China which had advocated non-intervention in Lao affairs at the Bandung Conference[46] and adhered to that policy until at least 1962. Souvanna visited Peking, where he declared his opposition to further Lao involvement with SEATO. He pointed out that the Laos protocol was formulated without Lao participation, and that in any event to accept the SEATO "umbrella" would be to violate the 1954 Geneva Accords.[47] While in Peking, Souvanna received China's support for Laotian independence but did not offer Peking diplomatic recognition.[48]

Continuing the movement towards coalition, Souvanna and Souphanouvong agreed on neutrality and peace on December 28, 1956, proposing a coalition government and supplementary elections to include the Pathet Lao, which had been excluded from elections in 1955.[49] Katay, recently returned from the United States, remained determined to prevent left-wing participation in the government, a course of action supported by Ambassador Parsons who encouraged the anti-coalition forces. (This was part of Parson's sixteen-month "struggle" which is discussed below.) Plans for a coalition so alarmed the National Assembly that it voted against continuing negotiations with Souphanouvong, thus forcing the resignation of Souvanna Phouma on May 30, 1957.[50] When, however, Katay and Phoui Sananikone failed to receive an endorsement to form a new government, Souvanna returned to his post, announcing his intention to continue the integration of the Pathet Lao into the government. The *New York Times* of May 31 reported official United States sentiment on this development: "The United States view is that the Pathet Lao members should be granted amnesty and allowed to re-enter politics, not as a party but as individuals." (This fear of "organized Communism" shows up again in the 1969 United States opposition to NLF participation in South Vietnamese politics, although "individuals" are not disbarred.[51])

Nonetheless, on November 7, a series of political and military settlements between the Royal Lao Government and the Pathet Lao, the Vientiane Agreements, were signed: two Pathet Lao Leaders, Souphanouvong and Phoumi Vongvichit, received cabinet portfolios after an agreement placed Phong Saly and Samneua, the two Pathet Lao governed provinces, under Royal Lao Government control. This "control" has never been more than nominal.[52]

Irritation in Bangkok at the new coalition stemmed from the Thai desire for Laos to be not only a buffer but an ally. A truly neutral Laos would be less predictable and no longer subject to Thai influence as was the Katay regime[53] which had switched the locus of Laotion commerce from Saigon to Bangkok.[54] The State Department termed the coalition "a perilous course of action," one that would allow the Communists to penetrate the government and eventually to dominate it.[55]

The Vientiane Agreements centered on including two Pathet Lao members in the cabinet, integration of 1,500 Pathet Lao troops into the Royal Lao Army (while the remaining 4,500–6,500 were to be demobilized), merging the Pathet Lao civil service into the Royal Lao Government, and on holding elections. Souphanouvong, assuming his position as Minister of Planning, asserted that the Pathet Lao was not Communist, and affirmed his desire to cooperate with the United States.[56] Roger Hilsman points out that Souphanouvong was the only Lao leader possessing an intimate knowledge of his country, having walked its length and breadth. "I came away from our meeting (after an encounter with Souphanouvong) wondering how events might have differed if French attitudes had been more flexible in those early years."[57] "Americans" should now be substituted for "French" in Hilsman's statement.

Due to American subversion, the coalition of 1958 was to be short-lived. J. Graham Parsons admitted that during his term as Ambassador in Vientiane, he "struggled for sixteen months to prevent a coalition."[58]

THE 1958 ELECTIONS AND UNITED STATES INTERVENTION

THE COLLAPSE of the Souvanna government occurred after the 1958 elections, which were held to enlarge the assembly from 39 to 59 seats, owing to the enfranchisement of women and redistricting. At this time the political arm of the Pathet Lao, the Neo Lao Hak Xat (Lao Patriotic Front), waged a successful campaign attacking the domineering nature and corruption of the American aid program. The electoral success of the NLHX proved especially humiliating for Washington since Ambassador Parsons had assured a Congress already concerned about the conduct of American operations that with a NLHX defeat the United States would receive "value for money."[59] As it turned out, there was to be no value for money.

The NLHX concentrated among other targets on the three-fold inflation of the Lao *kip*. American excuses as voiced by Ambassador Parsons attributed the inflation to a national loss of confidence following the Royal Lao Government-Pathet Lao negotiations. However the Lao economy could not withstand the volume of United States aid (especially army payments), the nature of many of the imports, or the inefficient import commodities system.[60] It may be that *American* confidence cracked badly when it became known that as Minister of Planning, Souphanouvong would be responsible for administering United States aid. Parsons maintained that the Vientiane coalition agreement precluded further American aid to Lao villages. The NLHX, on the other hand, charged the United States aid program with merely accentuating the dichotomy between the well-off and the poor. Indeed, less that 1% of aid funds between 1955 and 1963 ($1.9 million out of $480.7 million) were spent on improving agriculture, the livelihood of 96 per cent of the population.[61] The funds remaining after military expenditures went to road construction and similar projects and commodity-import subsidization.[62]

The American public uproar over corruption in the aid (ICA) program is now almost forgotten. But Haynes Miller, an "end-use investigator" in Laos for ICA from 1956 to 1957, offered his evaluation in the November 13, 1958, *Reporter*. "A Bulwark Built On Sand" confirms the extensive misuse of United States funds and the consequent enrichment of a few Lao, Chinese, Thai, and American enterpreneurs. Miller's three principle observations were: (1) Our military aid has been squandered on the Royal Lao Army, "an army that is almost entirely unsuited to the sort of fighting it might be called upon to do;" (2) "We have flooded a primitive country with money and goods it could not possibly absorb;" and (3) "Far from building up Laos as a bulwark against Communism, our policy may actually have served to strengthen the Communist position there." (Miller's account of the commodity import program and the notorious road-building schemes in which a few Americans made considerable profits invites comparison with similar operations in South Vietnam and Thailand, where the sums involved are much larger.) The American aid program, by resurfacing colonial roads as major domestic projects, ignored the feelings of the rural dwellers and further alienated governmental officials from the countryside. It enhanced the status of military and police careers for young men, thereby disturbing *bonzes* and other strong Buddhists, to whom the Pathet Lao subsequently appealed.[63]

The successful Pathet Lao exploitation of these themes prior to the 1958 election prompted "Operation Booster Shot," an American crash program designed to give aid to the villages. The project was limited, was the exception rather than the rule, and came three years too late. As Representative Porter Hardy commented, "We put the village aid program on when it had a political purpose . . . to serve to keep in power the rulers whom we had chosen to support."[64]

Roger Hilsman makes a blunt evaluation of this program:

> For years the commodity import program was inadequately supervised and controlled; it provided endless opportunities for graft; and it came to corrupt not only some of the individual Lao and Americans associated with it, but Lao society as a whole.[65]

Nor did the crash program prevent nine of the thirteen NLHX candidates and four of Quinim Pholsena's neutralist Santiphab (Peace) Party candidates from winning seats in the National Assembly. Souphanouvong polled the greatest number of votes in the election and was voted chairman of the National Assembly. Rightest candidates were more numerous, but the fact that the Pathet Lao candidates won in diverse areas of the country revealed their wide appeal.

The coalition's fate was sealed, however, by United States opposition. The elections were held in May, and on June 30 the United States, on the pretext of ending corruption in the import program and of meeting the need for monetary reform, suspended payments to the Lao government's New York bank account. The aid program doubtless demanded reform and revision, but the time selected to suspend funds —just as Souvanna Phouma was attempting to form a "satisfactory" cabinet (he even excluded the NLHX) out of the competing political groups—was strategic. When the Committee for the Defense of the National Interest (CDNI), a group of young rightists, ostensibly reformers, formed with CIA support specifically to combat Communist influence,[66] exploited Souvanna's American-created financial crisis, he found himself unable to meet their demands, whereupon the National Assembly dominated by a conservative coalition, the Rassemblement du Peuple Lao (RPL), denied him a vote of confidence. The United States had destroyed Souvanna Phouma, and the coalition came to an end. While disguising its destruction of Lao neutralism, Washington also succeeded in maintaining control of the Vientiane elite.

PHOUI SANANIKONE AND UNITED STATES SUPPORT

ON AUGUST 18, Phoui Sananikone assumed leadership of government, choosing a cabinet which included four CDNI members; there were no NLHX delegates, although Souphanouvong was Assembly chairman.

Phoui observed a staunch anti-Communist line, and United States aid was quickly resumed. After raising the possibility of a law against Communism, Phoui pledged his efforts "to co-exist with the Free World only."[67]

At the end of 1958, Phoui Sananikone seized an opportunity to consolidate his power. On December 15, an RLA military patrol was fired upon at Huong Lap, a remote region on the North Vietnamese border. This area was so sensitive that a hostile reception to Lao troops should not have been surprising.[68] On December 27, and again on December 31, North Vietnam charged that Laos had violated its border at Huong Lap. Souphanouvong called for ICC reactivation, while Phoui claimed that the Pathet Lao was planning a rebellion. On January 14, 1959, Phoui secured emergency powers from the National Assembly. Thus, by an incident which now appears manufactured,[69] Phoui remodeled his government to coincide even more closely with the desires of Marshal Sarit in Bangkok and of the Americans in Vientiane.[70] The pattern of creating emergencies in order to strengthen the Right in Laos became a familiar one, culminating in the Nam Tha "crisis" of 1962, which also involved the Thais.

On January 27, Phoui included army officers in his cabinet for the first time. Notable among these was Colonel Phoumi Nosavan, a CDNI Rightist, and former Pathet Lao Commander, who became Defense Secretary. Phoumi, who enjoyed strong CIA backing,[71] was related to Thailand's Marshal Sarit Thanarat, and the new Laotian government thus assured itself of Thai support.[72]

Although Souvanna Phouma had affirmed the validity of the Geneva Accords in 1958 (when he requested ICC adjournment), his successor departed from the path of neutrality and international agreement. On January 24, ten truckloads of United States arms and ammunition arrived in Laos.[73] On February 11, Phoui presented a policy statement renouncing the Geneva Accords and asserted that the Royal Lao Government had fulfilled its obligations and could not be restricted by military aid limitations, pending a political settlement in Vietnam.[74] The establishment of a Nationalist Chinese Consulate in Vientiane and raising the status of the South Vietnamese Legation to that of Embassy likewise departed from Souvanna Phouma's policy and increased tensions.[75] It was a dangerous course, motivated by a distorted notion of American interests rather than any primary concern for the peace, progress or integrity of Laos.

DIRECT UNITED STATES SUPPORT FOR THE ROYAL LAO ARMY

ON FEBRUARY 12, the State Department announced its support of Phoui's pronouncement on the Geneva Accords, and United States officials put forth the view that Washington could now establish a military mission in Laos.[76] The United States brought eighty Filipino military technicians ("technical assistants") to Laos and established a training section in PEO.[77] The immediate American support for Phoui's statement reinforced the charge that such repudiation was inspired by Washington's advice.[78] The Soviet Union, China and North Vietnam raised strong protests against the Royal Lao Government's repudiation of the Geneva Accords. In response to this criticism and pressure

the Royal Lao Government denied repudiation and asserted that only foreign bases and troops provided for in the
Geneva Accords would be allowed.[79]

The Royal Lao Government had previously agreed to
accept 105 Pathet Lao officers as officers in the Laotian Army,
accompanied by the remainder of the two battalions (1,400
men). But integration did not proceed smoothly. Almost
half the Pathet Lao troops were non-Laos, with a large concentration of Meos and Khas, who were not enthusiastic
about integration into the all-Lao central government.[80]
Sisouk na Champassak, Secretary of State for Information
at the time, explained why the Royal Lao Government
agreed to include Pathet Lao officers:

> Once the agreement was reached, the weapons surrendered,
> and the two battalions scattered throughout the country, the
> commissions would be nullified by demanding, for example,
> that the new officers pass examinations appropriate to their
> rank.[81]

This would obviously eliminate most of the officers as they
were illiterate.

When the battalions refused integration on the Plain
of Jars on May 11, Souphanouvong and three other Pathet
Lao leaders were placed under house arrest. On May 17,
one battalion accepted integration; the other (including
their families, households, and livestock) slipped away from
their encampment.[82] Although the military integration
scheme was obviously rigged, the Pathet Lao's failure to enter
into it became a cornerstone of American rationalization for
further intervention.

In mid-1959 following publication of the previous year's
Congressional hearings on Laos,[83] United States policy
moved in the direction of further involvement. In the face
of the report's grim nature this development provides an
excellent example of the escalation of American activities
in Southeast Asia following an unpleasant public exposure.
On July 24 the Royal Lao Government announced and was
granted its request for United States military advisers to

help re-equip and reorganize the French-trained army, an arrangement made, it seems, to circumvent Article Six of the Geneva Accords.[84]

In August, in the midst of increased fighting, the Soviet Union charged that Laos had violated the Geneva Accords by "concluding a treaty legalizing the presence of United States military personnel and handing over the Laotian Army to their control."[85] This charge was in response to the July 24 agreement. In fact, toward the end of August the United States increased its military aid, and PEO, with one hundred additional military advisers (in civilian clothes), established training teams at military centers to begin (with the French) technical and weapons training for the whole of the 29,000-man army.[86]

The Royal Lao Government reported on July 29 that Pathet Lao troops, accompanied by North Vietnamese, attacked government posts in Samneua province. On August 4, Phoui's government issued a complaint to the United Nations. After increased fighting between government troops and the Pathet Lao, Vientiane requested on September 4 that the United Nations send troops to combat what the Royal Lao Government termed Viet Minh aggression. Small Pathet Lao groups were magnified in reports from far-reaching outposts into huge assault forces, and press reportage in the United States reached heights of undocumented sensationalism.[87] Western journalists appeared in Vientiane, far from the fighting.

> The single biggest impetus to the apparent urgency of the military situation was given by the groundless reports circulated by Lao Military officers, unwittingly or deliberately . . . on the basis of such reports Lao officers in Vientiane hypothesized North Vietnamese battalions marching through Laos.[88]

The Subcommittee of the United Nations Security Council investigating the Royal Lao Government's charges of North Vietnamese aggression issued its report in November.[89] It reported no evidence of North Vietnamese aggression or invasion of Lao territory.[90]

On the other hand, American actions, attempting to eliminate a legitimate Laotian political force, lent credence to the Pathet Lao charge of United States imperialism.[91]

PHOUMI NOSAVAN: FULL COMMITMENT TO THE UNITED STATES

AS THE CDNI PRESSED for intensification of pressure against the Pathet Lao, Phoui considered re-entering negotiations with the Pathet Lao, with an eye on the elections scheduled for 1960.[92] The political struggle in Vientiane led to the exclusion of CDNI members from the cabinet (a move confirmed by the National Assembly); but the death of Katay Sasorith further weakened Phoui's political strength.[93] This enabled Phoumi Nosavan to stage a coup d'état whereupon the king dismissed Phoui Sananikone on December 30. Thus, just as a more moderate policy promised to change the solidly pro-American regime, it fell. Both the CIA and the PEO helped Phoumi successfully enact his take-over.[94]

Although Washington engineered the downfall of Phoui Sananikone's government, the American Ambassador accompanied the British and French to Luang Prabang on January 4, 1960, calling on the king to express concern over the recent coup.[95] As the Assembly was not in session, the king appointed Kou Abhay, a Laotion elder statesman, to lead a provisional government until the April elections, a government dominated by the CIA's favorite, Phoumi Nosavan. Once a comrade-in-arms of Prince Souphanouvong, Phoumi realized early the ambitions of the United States in Laos. Hilsman claims: "He came to forget the interests of his country in blindly pursuing ends and ambitions that were purely personal."[96] Schlesinger comments that Phoumi recognized "Defense and CIA were committed to him."[97] As with other American favorites in Southeast Asia the United States found Phoumi to be a willing enough servant until its tactics changed. At that point, a parallel with Vietnamese leaders since 1968, manipulation proved more difficult.

In choosing Phoumi Nosavan as its man in Laos, the CIA played another repetition of its old theme: the army is the only organization capable of promoting national unity and leading the way toward "modern" development. Furthermore, Phoumi Nosavan was on "our side." Although the new American Ambassador Horace Smith did not regard Phoumi highly, his usefulness seemed obvious to Washington during 1960.[98]

THE 1960 ELECTIONS

THE ELECTIONS OF APRIL, 1960, were farcical, and the CIA played an important role. Candidates were required to deposit an exorbitant fee, voting districts were gerrymandered, and the election count was rigged, as the ludicrous returns indicated. A Foreign Service officer observed CIA agents distributing "bagfuls" of money to various village headmen at election time.[99]

The NLHX was excluded from the April elections. Sisouk na Champassak, who served as Phoumi's spokesman, asserted that the government did not depart from democratic procedures in its electoral revisions. Nonetheless, he stated that

> electoral districts were revised to break up Pathet Lao zones of influence and prevent the movement from forming highly compact groups . . . a minimal educational standard was required . . . This . . . contained a trick; more than half the Pathet Lao leaders and propagandists had no schooling and so were automatically excluded from the race.[100]

While Souphanouvong and other Pathet Lao leaders remained under arrest, the Royal Lao army decided to forcefully "suppress Communist propaganda in the provinces."[101] Polling places were reduced in number, allowing a large number of troops to be stationed at each, while a nine-battalion "raiding operation" took place in the insecure Boloven Plateau area "to prepare a favorable climate for the elections."[102]

The results of the elections were as expected: no NLHX or Santiphab candidates were elected. "In one area, for instance, a candidate who voted for himself together with a dozen members of his family still polled no votes."[103] The utilization of illegitimate elections in Southeast Asia is a popular policy in Washington: parallels between this Laotian election and those in South Vietnam in 1967 are obvious.[104] Many RPI candidates who were elected moved to General Phoumi's new party, while his nephew, Prince Somsanith, became Prime Minister. Souvanna Phouma was voted National Assembly Chairman.

On May 23, Souphanouvong and fifteen other Pathet Lao leaders escaped from captivity, taking their guards with them. There was no longer any Pathet Lao or leftist representation in Vientiane.

> The swing to the right now was complete. It had been overwhelmingly a swing to the south, to southern Laos from which came Phoumi and most of his friends, and to Siam . . . The Americans had moved from the outside to the inside of the Laotian problem.[105]

KONG LE'S COUP (1960)

IN THE MORNING of August 9, 1960, twenty-six-year-old Paratroop Captain Kong Le staged a nearly bloodless coup in Vientiane. Kong Le, of peasant Pou-Thai origins, had received American Ranger training in the Philippines and had risen rapidly in the army.[106] The reason for his move, often stated by him, was "Lao must stop killing Lao." He maintained that in the fighting against the Pathet Lao, his troops had never encountered a North Vietnamese or Chinese.[107] The call for an end to Laotian strife was the key to the coup and the source of its popular appeal.[108]

Kong Le drew attention by his coup to a central factor in the Laotian conflict: there existed, and exists, in Laos a genuine struggle between competing groups which in Western terms can only be called Right, Center, and Left. Souvanna Phouma, up to 1962, was recognized by all three sides as a linchpin holding the framework together.

Nor was the internal tension confined to the small Lao elite of historic importance. Antedating, of course, any politics in Vientiane are the links between the peoples of Laos and their neighbors. The "non-Lao" of the Northeast are traditionally close to similar groups in North Vietnam, while the Lao along the Mekong and down into "the panhandle" feel kinship with what in fact is a much larger group of Lao in northeast Thailand. The amorphous nature of the Lao-Thai frontier transcends any immediate political strains between the two countries, and explains a good deal of the Thai alarm whenever Laotian fighting approaches the Mekong. Interestingly enough, while the Meo under Vang Pao in the vicinity of the Plain of Jars have for several years been bought off by the Americans, their relatives across the Mekong in Thailand have been moved away from the border because Bangkok regards them as a security threat.[109]

These internal struggles, and the importance at least up to 1964 of Souvanna Phouma, were recognized by Peking. The United States, by deciding that Laos constituted an area vital to American security, and supporting the Right, raised the civil conflict onto a global plane.

Kong Le's aims, therefore, in addition to ending the civil war, were "resistance to foreign pressures, the removal of foreign troops from the country, and the suppression of those who were 'making their harvest off the backs of the people.' "[110]

At Kong Le's insistence, the Assembly passed a unanimous motion of no confidence in the Somsanith government. Somsanith, in Luang Prabang, resigned, and Souvanna Phouma once again became head of the Lao government, with Quinim Pholsena as his Minister of the Interior; Kong Le declared his coup at an end on August 17.

SOUVANNA, PHOUMI, AND WASHINGTON

PHOUMI SUBSEQUENTLY DECLARED a state of martial law, suspending governmental activity and preventing the king from investing the Souvanna Phouma government. He then moved his forces to his home base at Savannakhet and began broadcasting against the coup on "Radio Savannakhet," using a transmitter supplied by the United States.[111] "Radio Savannakhet" was monitored by USIS and the transcripts of its broadcasts were distributed to correspondents.[112] Kong Le was accused of being used by the Communists, and opposition troops were mobilized.

Phoumi and Souvanna Phouma temporarily avoided an open conflict by arranging for the National Assembly to meet in Luang Prabang, thereby legitimizing the new government, and installing Phoumi as the Minister of Interior. Phoumi, however, did not attend the formal installation ceremonies; instead he returned to Savannakhet, allegedly because of a report delivered through American channels of a threat to his life.[113] The *New York Times* claimed that Phoumi had been persuaded to refuse his post by CIA and United States military officers in Laos.[114]

Once again reports of Vietnamese invasions were issued, although they were as unfounded as those of 1959. These reports permitted the Thais to raise the specter of Vietnam-

ese aggression and to openly support Phoumi. Alliances
were forming, with Prince Boun Oum siding with Phoumi
and the generals, while the Pathet Lao looked to Souvanna
Phouma, with whom they had signed a cease-fire agreement
on September 7.

> For its part, the Bureau of Far Eastern Affairs in Washington
> considered Kong Le a probable Communist and looked with
> dubiety on the neutralist solution. Nowhere was the pure
> Dulles doctrine taken more literally than in this bureau. . . .
> (The Director) in 1959 was the J. Graham Parsons who had
> been applying those principles so faithfully in Laos. . . . As
> for the Defense Department, it was all for Phoumi.[115]

Air America, the CIA airline in Southeast Asia, flew supplies to Phoumi's forces at Savannakhet, while PEO sent
200 Lao paratroopers from Bangkok where they had been
trained.[116]

Souvanna Phouma's difficulties in establishing the new
government on a sound basis were compounded by Thailand's economic boycott of Vientiane, a move based on
Marshal Sarit's fear that Souvanna would negotiate with the
Pathet Lao. The Thai boycott backfired. Vientiane sought
petroleum, of which Thailand had supplied 26 per cent,
from the Soviet Union.[117] In September the establishment of
a Soviet Embassy was announced in Vientiane; the Royal
Lao Government then proceeded to resume negotiations
with the Pathet Lao on forming a coalition government.
Such acts disturbed the State Department.[118] Although
Ambassador Brown appeared somewhat sympathetic to
Souvanna Phouma, Washington continued to assure Thailand that its so-called anti-Communist efforts were not in
vain.[119] Souvanna soon came to understand that, Ambassador Brown notwithstanding, Washington intended to support the Rightists.[120] The Pentagon and the CIA continued
to build up Phoumi Nosavan by supplying aid *directly* to
Royal Lao army units, with the exception of Kong Le's
troops. Economic aid to Vientiane, however, was temporarily continued, via Vientiane, for the United States had

recognized the Souvanna Phouma government in September. Roger Hilsman finds euphemisms for American political cynicism:

> Souvanna could be supported, as head of the legally constituted government of Laos, but at the same time it would be United States policy to attempt to persuade him to abandon his policy of 'true' neutralism and the effort to form a government of national union and to adopt instead the pro-Western neutralism so long advocated by Phoui Sananikone and the United States.[121]

Souvanna's pursuit of genuine neutralism alarmed those in Washington who felt that an anti-Communist Laos was vital to American interests in Southeast Asia. Accordingly, DOD and State Department advisers, including J. Graham Parsons, urged a military solution and support of Phoumi Nosavan as the best way to maintain the United States position. The American Embassy suggested in vain full support of Souvanna Phouma and a political solution, even if it involved Pathet Lao participation in the government—a "risk" which would have to be taken. Britain and France concurred with Ambassador Brown's view that a military solution would either fail or invite intervention on the part of a major Communist power. While Souvanna remained virtually powerless, Washington, more opposed than ever to neutrality, suspended economic aid on October 7, just three days after negotiations had resumed.

UNITED STATES PRESSURE ON SOUVANNA

FIVE DAYS LATER, on October 12, Assistant Secretary of State for Far Eastern Affairs Parsons traveled to Laos to offer Souvanna Phouma a bargain: resumption of cash-grant aid in exchange for compromise with Washington. Otherwise, aid would be permanently withheld.

Parsons' conditions were that: (1) Souvanna end negotiations with the Pathet Lao; (2) Souvanna guarantee that he would negotiate with Phoumi; (3) Souvanna move the capital from Vientiane to Luang Prabang, because, as Dommen notes, "Washington felt that there the King would exert a conservative influence on the government."

Souvanna Phouma considered all of Parsons' points unacceptable; the Prime Minister declared, "My political position has not changed since 1956. The United States is free to make its choice and if United States aid is not continued, the Lao government will get it somewhere else." Ambassador Brown suggested to Souvanna that no patriotic Lao would want the Pathet Lao to take over Laos while the neutralists and rightists argued with each other. If Souvanna would agree to America's supplying military equipment to the Phoumists, the policy of cash-grant aid to Vientiane would be reinstated.[122] United States demands on Souvanna were then scaled down, for a different and "better" solution was in sight.

On November 22, Souvanna Phouma pointed out to the United States that its continued military aid to Phoumi undercut the authority of the very government Washington purported to recognize. The Embassy pretended not to understand until November 30, when it announced the suspension of military hardware to the rebels in Savannakhet. This "suspension" must have caused hollow laughter in Vientiane, for by that time Phoumi was prepared to march.[123] Once again the United States, not by accident but by design, was supporting the subversion of a legal government with which it maintained diplomatic relations.

FALL OF SOUVANNA AND ENTRANCE OF THE SOVIET UNION

"PRINCE SOUVANNA PHOUMA'S position was desperate. He had never ceased in his efforts to come to an agreement with

Phoumi. The only response he had received was to be called a Communist. . . ."[124] In December Russian planes began to deliver military equipment and oil to Souvanna's Royal Lao Government.[125] Quinim Pholesena, Souvanna's remaining senior cabinet minister, asked the Russians for help. But by then, December 9, Souvanna had fled in despair to Cambodia. "The Eisenhower administration, by rejecting the neutralist alternative had driven the neutralists into reluctant alliance with the Communists and had provoked (and in many eyes legitimized) open Soviet aid to the Pathet Lao."[126]

Soviet intervention in the form of military aid and air transport was not forthcoming until it was requested to counter the American intervention which included control of the Laotian economy, army, support for a conservative elite which lacked a popular base, and foreign exchange and governmental manipulation. Exiled in Cambodia, Souvanna Phouma stated:

> What I shall never forgive the United States for is the fact that it betrayed me, that it double-crossed me and my government . . . the Assistant Secretary of State (Parsons) is the most nefarious and reprehensible of men. He is the ignominious architect of the disastrous American policy towards Laos. He and others like him are responsible for the recent shedding of Lao blood.[127]

Washington destroyed the neutralist coalition in Laos; the Eisenhower administration was unwilling to accept a negotiated settlement except on its own terms. In January, 1960, the State Department turned down an appeal from India to support reactivation of the ICC in view of the increased military activity and general chaos.[128] Prince Sihanouk's proposal for an international conference on Laos to be attended by the participants in the 1954 Geneva Conference, ICC nations, Burma, and Thailand was similarly ignored in Washington.[129]

Just before leaving office, on January 7, 1961, the outgoing Eisenhower administration presented its "revised" view on Laos policy: (1) The United States should promote international understanding of the "true nature" of Communist intentions in Laos; (2) America must try to avoid escalation and commitment of its troops, and (3) should "maintain the independence of Laos through whatever means seem most promising."[130] The Eisenhower statement indicated little more than a re-evaluation of tactics, implying that the Kennedy administration should find a way out while preserving the United States goal—a government serving American interests and staunchly anti-Communist.

WASHINGTON: THE ADVENT OF KENNEDY

By the end of 1960, the Laotian conflict had changed from a civil struggle into a major power confrontation, with both Washington and Moscow actively engaged. The precedent of intervention had been established by the United States, and the Soviet air lift seemed a logical, if limited, response to American actions. The opportunity to end the war no longer lay in Laotian hands.

Thus, when he came to the presidency in January, 1961, John F. Kennedy faced a situation created by the United States: a Laos polarized into right and left, with a vacuum in the center, a vacuum caused by the deliberate American eradication of a genuine neutral alternative. According to the analysis of Kennedy's policy planners, the geographic significance of Laos lay in the fact that it provided one of the four "roads" from China through Southeast Asia, although the route was only potential.[131] United States intervention continued to justify itself with the containment of China. The Laos situation, indeed, presents in microcosm the basic identity of policy from Eisenhower to Kennedy, from Dulles to Rusk. Although he would occasionally complain to his friends that he had been saddled with the Indochinese involvement, Kennedy's preoccupations with "stopping China" did not differ from those of his predecessor. In accusing the Russians and Chinese of interfering in Laos, Kennedy lied. In his increasing conviction that "insurgency" had taken the place of the Russian "threat," he led the way for American *counter-revolutionary* activity ranging from B-52 raids against "guerrilla strongholds" to the assassination of key individuals or "neutralization," as it was known by the creators of the Phoenix program in South Vietnam. Kennedy's celebrated grace should not disguise his leadership in the continuum of Cold-War politics and practices.

Arthur Schlesinger, whose efforts to present Kennedy's "clear historical view of Laos" are considerable, quoted the new President as saying that Laos was not a land "worthy of engaging the attention of the great powers." Nonetheless, although Kennedy remained convinced of the importance of Laotian neutrality,

> . . . he knew that the matter was not that simple any longer. The effort had been made, American prestige was deeply involved, and extrication would not be easy . . . it was essential to convince the Pathet Lao that they could not win and to dissuade the Russians from further military assistance.[132]

Schlesinger's analysis contains much unintended irony: his own description of the Eisenhower period makes plain the role of the United States in provoking the Pathet Lao and the Russians, both of whom had been willing to recognize the neutralist government overthrown by Washington.[133] The New Frontier furnished only more elegant rhetoric for what by now was fixed policy.

FAILURE AND ESCALATION

IN EARLY JANUARY 1961, in the wake of false reports of Viet Minh aggression, American AT-6 Harvard trainer aircraft outfitted as fighter-bombers arrived for Phoumi Nosavan.[134]

Kennedy's decision at the same time to replace the PEO advisers with 400 Special Forces personnel (White Star Mobile Training Teams) from Okinawa was more important in terms of escalating the conflict. This decision is an early indication of the counter-insurgency theories propounded by John F. Kennedy and others who held that by using Mao Tse-tung's *techniques* either side in a civil war should be able to win.[135] As in Vietnam in 1961, the impending embarassment of a weak ally's defeat provoked in Washington a drive to enlarge the struggle.

Arthur Schlesinger and Roger Hilsman present a picture of a frantic administration badly informed, desperate for success—or at least to avoid failure—and buffeted by conflicting advice.[136] Although at his first press conference President Kennedy declared that Laos should be free of great power intervention, he took heart from CIA reports in February that Phoumi would soon drive Kong Le and the Pathet Lao from the Plain of Jars. With Phoumi's defeat, however, the President decided to accept Ambassador Brown's more favorable evaluation of Souvanna Phouma. But Souvanna's recent trips to Hanoi, Peking, and Moscow confirmed certain long-held views in Washington. "The State Department, having driven him to the Communists, now flourished his itinerary as proof of his perfidy."[137] Souvanna in fact was desperately continuing his search for support of a neutralist regime.

Both the Americans and the Russians were by now deeply engaged. In late February and March the Pentagon, frustrated by the dismal performances of the Royal Lao Army, put forward bold schemes for landing a division of Marines on the Plain of Jars ("We can get them in all right," said General Lemnitzer, "It's getting them out that worries me."), or sending up to 60,000 into the area south of Vientiane, to hold the lower Mekong. These plans were ultimately dismissed by the President.[138]

Kennedy, although determined to avoid "any visible

humiliation over Laos," questioned "why we have to be more royalist than the king."[139] His oldest British friend, David Ormsby Gore, told him in February that:

> The United States . . . had done its best to destroy Souvanna Phouma, who represented the best hope of a non-Communist Laos, and instead was backing a crooked, right-wing gang; the impression of Washington always rushing about to prop up corrupt dictators in Asia could not have happy consequences.[140]

Nonetheless, on March 23, Kennedy told a press conference that peace was dependent on a "cessation of the present armed attacks by externally supported Communists," and that "security of all of Southeast Asia will be endangered if Laos loses its neutral independence."[141]

> In Washington the President saw Gromyko at the Rose Garden (in March), took him to a bench in the Rose Garden, and observing that too many wars had arisen from miscalculation said that Moscow must not misjudge the American determination to stop aggression in Southeast Asia.[142]

What Kennedy seems never to have admitted was that the United States was playing the aggressive role. American policy-makers habitually use American "defensive" rhetoric to disguise intervention.

On March 29, Averell Harriman, who earlier than most Americans saw the need for a negotiated settlement, reported to Kennedy that the optimum plan would be to afford at least conditional support to Souvanna Phouma, and the best settlement for Laos was neutralization by international agreement, guaranteed by both the West and the Soviet Union.[143] Kennedy's strategy of force and conciliation at this time was reflected in his March decision to alert the Seventh Fleet and send five hundred additional troops to northeast Thailand, thirty-five miles from Vientiane, while at the same time endorsing the British proposal for negotiations.[144] The Kennedy decision conflicted with the March 27th SEATO refusal, based primarily on French opposition, to endorse an American plan for multi-national intervention.[145]

By the middle of April, Kennedy underwent the Cuban humiliation, and fearful that the Russians (and the American voters) might judge him weak yet again, instructed American advisers to wear uniforms in the field with the Royal Lao Army. Both Hilsman and Schlesinger make plain the President's reasons for escalating United States activities in Laos: his failure at the Bay of Pigs, which he feared would make him appear irresolute. Although Richard Nixon remembers him saying, "I don't see how we can make any move in Laos, which is 5,000 miles away, if we don't make a move in Cuba, which is only 90 miles away,"[146] the President did not avoid further penetration into Laotian affairs. Despite his wish to play a decisive role in Laos, Kennedy grew increasingly aware of the dangers of the Pentagon, which after its initial reluctance seemed ever-prepared to land thousands of troops with no certainty of their safety thereafter. For the military, afraid of the "no-win" potentialities of counter-insurgency, even nuclear intervention appeared attractive. At a National Security Council meeting in April, General Lemnitzer stated: "If we are given the right to use nuclear weapons, we can guarantee victory." Kennedy's later judgment on this advice was "Since he couldn't think of any further escalation, he would have to promise us victory."[147] This Schlesinger anecdote is one of many which attempt to demonstrate the President's sagacity. But what Kennedy feared—especially after Cuba—was humiliation and *loss*. In May, while preparing to send ten thousand Marines to the Laotian theater, Kennedy recalled the French debacle at Dienbienphu: "I can't take a 1954 defeat today."[148] He therefore told Khrushchev in Vienna that "the [Laos] commitments had been made before he became President, why they were undertaken was not an issue here."[149] Kennedy revealed the shallowness of his regard for the people of Laos, and the depth of his determination to avoid admissions of error. At best Kennedy could recognize miscalculation—in Cuba or in Laos—but he remained obdurately fastened to the broad lines laid down by his predecessors.

GENEVA: 1961–62

IN A SPEECH at the United Nations in September, 1960, Prince Sihanouk proposed that Laos and Cambodia should form a guaranteed neutral zone to safeguard themselves from foreign interference. Souvanna Phouma concurred with this proposal.[150] On December 15, Nehru suggested to Britain and the Soviet Union that the ICC should be re-activated in view of the renewed fighting after Kong Le's coup and the great amount of foreign intervention.[151] Seven days later, the Soviet Union proposed a reconvening of the 1954 Geneva Conference[152] but gained no support from the Western powers. New Year's Day, 1961, brought another appeal by Prince Sihanouk for a conference on Laos to be attended by the original Geneva members, the ICC nations, Thailand, and Burma.[153] Finally, on April 24, Britain and the Soviet Union called for a cease-fire and subsequent conference to settle the Laotian problem.

GENEVA CONVENES

BY MAY 3, 1961, all three parties in Laos had subscribed to the cease-fire, and eight days later the newly reactivated ICC confirmed the armistice. With the guns silent, on May 16, 1961, the Conference convened.

The seating of a Laotian delegation created immediate difficulties when the three factions could reach no agreement on coalition formulae. It was finally agreed that until a coalition government was formed representatives from Laos would be seated if sponsored by other powers.[154] The Phoumi-backed government under its Premier, Boun Oum, refused to participate when the Soviet Union sponsored a delegation headed by Souvanna Phouma and Quinim Pholsena, while China supported Souphanouvong and NLHX Central Committee member, Phoumi Vongvichit. After the three princes met in June at Zurich in a futile attempt to resolve their differences, Vientiane sent as representatives Phoui Sananikone and Pheng Norindr.[155]

The idea of partitioning Laos according to the Vietnamese model was not considered, owing to the existence of a middle faction in the Laotian dispute (absent in the 1954 Vietnamese situation), and to the general desire for a neutral coalition government.[156]

On June 3 and 4, during the Geneva Conference, John F. Kennedy and Nikita Khrushchev met in Vienna. In what was otherwise a thoroughly unpleasant and acrimonious series of exchanges, both men agreed on the importance of a neutral Laos.[157]

CHINA

AT GENEVA 1954, and Bandung 1955, China had spoken in favor of Lao neutralism.[158] Peking was reluctant to involve herself in the Laotian crisis until Phoumi took control in Vientiane in January, 1960. During the Spring of 1960, the Chinese criticized the North Vietnamese and Pathet Lao for placing any faith in the April elections. When the United States-backed CDNI triumphed, Peking's analysis of American manipulation appeared justified.[159] Nonetheless, Peking declared its intention to keep good relations with the new Vientiane government of Tiao Somsanith, who in turn pledged to respect the Geneva Accords—a gesture repudiating the anti-Geneva position of his predecessor Phoui Sananikone.[160]

Although in late fall of 1960, Souvanna Phouma again led the Royal Lao Government, by October Ambassador Parsons' pressure showed that the United States continued to support the Rightists. Peking, in turn, offered its support to the Royal Lao Government.[161] The November 18 agreement between Vientiane, Peking, and Hanoi made plain that Washington's policies had finally achieved the very polarity in Lao politics which American statesmen had claimed to dread.

In December, when Souvanna Phouma felt compelled to flee to Cambodia, the civil war increased in severity. Peking rightly perceived an escalation in American military influence on China's borders.[162] Furthermore, Russia's aid to Kong Le posed an additional threat of Soviet influence in the Chinese sphere. The Chinese on December 19 cautioned Washington against what they termed "a serious menace."[163] In the same communiqué, the Chinese nevertheless avoided threats of counter-intervention, calling instead for a reconvening of the 1954 Geneva powers.

On December 28, in a note to Britain and the Soviet Union, China stated its "sacred duty" to uphold the Geneva Accords, as well as its intention of "taking measures to safeguard its own security." At this time Peking called for the ICC to reconvene and to deal with Souvanna Phouma. The Chinese contended that the ICC could not work with the Boun Oum–Phoumi Nosavan government, which was illegal and supported by "United States armed intervention," without violating the Geneva Accords.[164]

China's terms for the reactivation of the ICC, like the Soviet Union's, were unacceptable to Washington. It increasingly became apparent to the Chinese that Washington not only did not desire to see the ICC reactivated in its present form, but intended, by its dispatch of the Seventh Fleet, to increase its military commitment in the area.[165] In February, 1961, as Britain and the USSR were negotiating for a renewed ICC, Chou En-lai, in a letter to Prince Sihanouk, argued that the ICC, authorized only to deal with the provisions of the 1954 Accords, could not operate in the present situation, and must receive new instructions from the proposed conference.[166] Peking favored a neutral buffer state rather than an imposed Communist one, for the latter would certainly precipitate United States military intervention.

No substantial evidence supports the American charges of aggressive Chinese intervention in Laos,[167] but Peking was at work establishing diplomatic and other ties. On October 7, 1961, a Chinese Consul General was established in Phong Saly (part of the Pathet Lao cease-fire area), and on November 5, a Chinese economic-cultural delegation set off for Laos[168] to deal with Souvanna Phouma.[169]

In the Chinese "Military Papers" the Chinese Army presented an accurate evaluation of the situation in Laos, stating that

> the Laotian revolutionary strength is greater now (1961) than before and there is a strong desire to have a government that wants peaceful neutrality. If we support this government we are actually supporting the revolutionary strength.[170]

On the basis of such an analysis, prepared for top-level internal use, it is plain that Peking did not intend to upset the negotiations for a neutral coalition. China's willingness to neglect the Pathet Lao appears in this statement:

> At the same time, whether it is the International Conference or the International Commission, they must deal directly with the Phouma *de jure* government.[171]
>
> . . . the Chinese conception of neutrality, which literally means in Chinese language to "stand in the middle" . . . accorded top priority to strict military non-alignment with either bloc—freedom from alliance, bases, or protection by alliance, and to political independence and the absence of external interference.[172]

LAOS DURING THE GENEVA CONFERENCE (1961)

ALTHOUGH THE DISAGREEMENTS between Laotian factions in the summer of 1961 were primarily confined to the political arena, Kong Le, on June 6, led neutralist forces against Meo tribesmen who had been organized by Phoumi Nosavan and the CIA, were supplied entirely by air, and were accompanied by American advisers. Kong Le considered the presence of these hostile forces in his area, together with supply flights over his positions, provocative.[173] American supply flights and Special Forces teams helped destroy the cease-fire.

A situation of this sort might have been foreseen. On May 20, the ICC described the fragility of the cease-fire. Their report stated that it seemed difficult to determine what constituted a provocation, but that flights over the territory of an opposition group were always regarded as hostile acts.[174] On June 6, 1961, Kong Le routed the Meos, causing a five-day suspension of the Geneva talks. Continued outbreaks of military activity in Laos were to plague the conference to the end.

WASHINGTON

PRESIDENT KENNEDY, increasingly disillusioned with Phoumi and relying on Harriman's recommendations began to look to Souvanna Phouma to act as a "third force." And Souvanna, though supported by the Soviet Union and by Peking, had not spurned the West.[175] Dean Rusk outlined the American position addressing the Geneva delegations on May 17, 1961.[176] To ensure a "genuinely neutral Laos," he maintained, three main points demanded settlement. First, the Conference needed to draw up an acceptable definition of neutrality—"more than mere nonalignment" —while also insisting on the withdrawal of all foreign military personnel, and "free choice" for the Laotians.

Rusk next advocated the creation of a strong ICC, with full access to all parts of Laos. This constituted Washington's most substantive demand at the Conference. Finally, Rusk called for an economic and technical aid

program "administered by neutral nations from the area."[177]
What this position amounts to is Washington's definition
of "neutralism." Schlesinger attempts to contrast the Dulles
view with Kennedy's: "Thus, where Dulles saw neutralism
as immoral, Kennedy felt that the new states . . . were
naturally . . . indifferent to the 'moral issues' in the
cold war. . . ." The new President, however, did not share
this indifference. "He felt . . . that the third world had
now become the critical battleground between democracy
and communism." What then did Kennedy offer the new
nations? ". . . By making national independence the crucial question [he] invited the neutrals to find common interest with us in resisting communist expansion."[178]
Throughout, the New Frontier rhetoric of Kennedy, Rusk,
Hilsman, and Schlesinger conceives of neutralist countries
joining an American crusade to save the world from Communism, with Washington providing the muscle and
wherewithal while the neutrals looked on approvingly and
made no deals with the other side. A genuine independence
which also leaned to the Left appeared as inconceivable
to the graceful Kennedy circle as to the messianic Dulles.
Schlesinger points out: "The new policy brought clear
gains. The Kennedy strategy ended the alliance between
the neutralists and the Pathet Lao."[179]

LAOS: ATTEMPTS TO UPSET THE CEASE-FIRE

IN LAOS ON OCTOBER 18, the King appointed Souvanna
Phouma to form a new government. His appointment followed the agreement reached by the three princes at Zurich
four months earlier, on June 22.[180] The agreement, however, proved meaningless when in December Phoumi
Nosavan's representative. Boun Oum, twice withdrew his
endorsement and ultimately refused to participate in further formal discussions.[181]

Phoumi Nosavan, increasingly sensitive to his growing disfavor in Washington, mounted a series of probing actions into neutralist territory beginning in October. By January of 1962 his drive collapsed.[182] His tactics were designed, however, not to win ground but to tear apart the fragile cease-fire, upset the Geneva discussions, and force the hand of the United States.[183] In these actions he was almost certainly encouraged by the CIA.[184] Hilsman fancifully describes American policy at this time as "properly ambiguous . . . if it was Phoumi . . . who broke the cease-fire, the United States would probably intervene." Yet it was American assistance which afforded Phoumi his power.[185]

By the end of 1961, after Harriman's trip to Laos, Washington, which wanted reliable allies, began to apply the kind of economic pressure to the Rightists it had hitherto used to destroy Souvanna Phouma.[186] In February, 1962, United States economic aid to the Phoumi-Boun Oum government was stopped. Phoumi, desperate to retain his power, set up the old cry of Viet Minh aggression, charging that now Chinese and Russian troops were operating in Laos. As in the past, these reports proved false.[187] Washington, although not taken in by Phoumi's maneuvers, continued to send him military aid.[188]

Harriman's persuasion eventually was augmented by Phoumi's cousin, Marshal Sarit of Thailand. Sarit, who had opposed efforts for a neutral coalition in Laos, had received assurances from Washington. In March, 1962, the Thai Foreign Minister conferred for a week with Dean Rusk over Laos and Thailand. On March 6 the two issued the now famous communiqué which significantly altered the official United States–SEATO commitment to Thailand. America promised to come to Thailand's aid in a case of "Communist aggression," without the "prior agreement" of other SEATO members. In other words, Washington guaranteed unilateral intervention in Thailand, an arrangement which guaranteed future American intervention in Thai affairs.[189]

Although on March 24 Sarit, in the presence of Harriman, recommended to Phoumi that he join the coalition, Phoumi remained reluctant. Harriman, also at the meeting, cautioned Phoumi that the Rightists were almost "finished in Laos." The meeting produced no tangible result.[190]

Hilsman and Schlesinger strive to show that Kennedy wanted a neutral solution, but it is in fact clear that this awakening came only from the incapacity of the Rightists, not through a genuine desire for an uncommitted Laos.[191] (Such a change in policy again became necessary when Nixon became president in 1969, unwilling to bring peace to Vietnam but painfully aware of the incapacity of our Saigon ally.) The unwillingness of Kennedy to cut loose from the Right in Laos led inevitably to the near-catastrophe of Nam Tha.

NAM THA

WHILE IN GENEVA diplomats were drafting most of the Conference resolutions, the Rightists prepared their final military effort in Laos. Phoumi had moved more than 5,000 troops including CIA-sponsored KMT troops from Burma into the northwest city of Nam Tha, situated in a valley, fifteen miles from China. Phoumi appeared to be using Nam Tha for a show of his own strength and as a test of DOD and CIA commitment to him.[192] As Pathet Lao forces advanced in the direction of Nam Tha, taking over the Phoumist supply airstrip at Muong Sing, reports came from Laos charging that Chinese troops were aiding the Pathet Lao. Although United States military sources confirmed these reports, State Department officials called the charges false.[193]

On May 6, 1962, Pathet Lao forces launched a limited counter-offensive against Phoumi's recently assembled Nam Tha garrison. The Rightists and the American Special Forces team fled.

Colonel Edwin Elder, the Commander of the Nam Tha MAAG detachment, immediately warned with the coolness of the professional soldier that there was "no evidence that the Chinese or (North) Vietnamese had participated in the attack."[194]

Nonetheless, rumors of foreign invasion spread.

The State Department charged the Pathet Lao with violating the cease-fire. However, Washington sources privately asserted that, even though Phoumi was warned by Washington that his aggressive build-up was dangerous, he continued his maneuvers and thus "provoked" the Nam Tha battle.[195] Furthermore, the Pathet Lao had issued several warnings through Souvanna Phouma, stating that unless Phoumi's build-up stopped, they would counterattack.[196]

While the State Department charged a cease-fire violation and on May 8 urged Moscow to restrain the Pathet Lao[197] (as if the Kremlin controlled the Laotian leftists), Phoumist troops were fleeing across the Mekong into Thailand, and Secretary of Defense Robert McNamara, conferring with Thai leaders in Bangkok, heard from Defense Minister Thanom Kittikachorn that the fall of Nam Tha posed a threat to Thailand, while Premier Sarit assured McNamara that Thailand possessed sufficient troops along the border to meet any emergency.[198]

In his May 9 news conference, President Kennedy called the Pathet Lao action a "clear breach of the cease-fire." In the President's view there were two courses open to the United States: (1) successful negotiations; (2) military intervention. As he told reporters, "Let's not think there's some great third course."[199] As Kennedy advisers met constantly, the situation in Laos became more chaotic. Fleeing Phoumist troops infected the garrison of Houei Sai on the Thai border with such panic that "Ban Houei Sai was announced as having fallen into Communist hands at 0300 on May 11, 1962, *while in actual fact no organized enemy unit was within thirty miles of the town.*"[200]

Max Frankel reported in the *New York Times,* "The United States has written off the Right-wing Laotian Army as useless against the pro-Communist forces and is therefore losing interest in supporting the army's leaders politically."[201] He further stated that Kennedy and State and Defense Department aides had concluded that only "the credibility of United States power" could help the West's bargaining position in Geneva.[202]

The "threat" perceived by the Kennedy administration, then, was not the new "crisis" in Laos, but the possibility of diminished American influence in Southeast Asia. Washington, still hoping to undermine a genuinely neutralist solution, translated Phoumi's provocation of the Pathet Lao into a Communist attack,

> a large-scale probe, a major, although still-limited, violation of the cease fire . . . and as they went up the ladder, the pace of military encroachments (by the Communists) would accelerate toward a military take-over of the whole country.[203]

The pattern of American escalation following a marked failure emerged once more. Again a crisis developed in Laos, again the agents of the United States appear chiefly responsible, and through it the Kennedy strategists eventually found an opportunity to cement America's military position in Southeast Asia.

Although by now the *New York Times* and the *Washington Post* (to name only two) had made clear the manufactured nature of the Nam Tha "crisis," the administration split along "political" and "military" lines. Hilsman, who appears unaware to this day that no aggression had taken place, discusses the "political" thinking of the State Department:

> What we needed was a package of moves that would signal to the Communists that if they continued on a military course, we would occupy the Mekong lowlands and the territory held by the Royal Lao Government up to the cease-fire line.[204]

America's intentions according to the "political advocates" should be indicated by ordering the Seventh Fleet to the Gulf of Siam and dispatching troops to Thailand. This view was presented to Kennedy before the National Security Council met on May 10, 1962. Only Hugh Toye points out that the Rightists had been successful:

> Phoumi had worked for the Nam Tha and Ban Houei Sai fiasco, bizarre even by Laotian standards, because after the suspension of American aid, his only hope had been to lose a Mekong town and thus involve the West militarily on his side. . . . The West . . . was obliged to consider the effects in Siam of the abandonment of Ban Houei Sai, which is immediately across the Mekong from Siamese territory.[205]

The Pentagon's counter-proposal (the "military") recommended, in addition to diplomatic maneuvers and moving the Seventh Fleet, American support for Phoumi and the use of military force either all-out, *including nuclear attacks on China,* or not at all.[206] From 1958 the Pentagon had expressed its fear of bogging down in a limited Laotian action, a fear dating back to the Korean War which the Generals viewed as "limited." This policy found support from ex-President Eisenhower, who advocated putting American troops into Laos. (What is noteworthy about the Eisenhower proposal is Kennedy's conviction that such support would make it "easier to send troops at least to Thailand."[207] Kennedy ordered the Seventh Fleet to deploy in Southeast Asian waters. Yet, although Thailand had not publicly expressed concern for her security,[208] Washington remained determined to use the situation in Laos to expand American military power into yet another Southeast Asian nation. Thailand, while always eager to enlist military aid from Washington (particularly in issues involving —even indirectly—sensitive Northeastern Thailand), also often adopted the appearance of independence from United States strategic planning. Therefore the absence in Bangkok of a public outcry for United States assistance is not surprising. Nevertheless, as indicated below, the war in Vietnam accelerated the pace by which other countries in the area were brought within the American sphere.

The National Security Council met on May 12, with McNamara and General Lemnitzer, just returned from Thailand, present. Both supported troop movements, supplemented by communications and supply improvements in Thailand. Kennedy accepted this plan,[209] although he would later claim that the United States moved into Thailand "at the decision of the Thai government."[210]

Walt Rostow advocated bombing North Vietnam.[211] McNamara, in meetings on May 13 and after, sided with the military view, asserting that if troops were to be used, they should occupy the panhandle of Laos all the way to North Vietnam. The McNamara group held that unless the Communists surrendered immediately, North Vietnam should be bombarded by land, sea, and air. In the case of Chinese intervention, nuclear retaliation would probably be the American course.[212] It should be remembered that a public policy of cease-fire, negotiations, and neutrality underlay these apocalyptic projections.

The "political" view held that intervention beyond the cease-fire line would gather no international support, "Thus, the 'political' proposal came down to occupying the Mekong lowlands." The Rand Corporation drew up a logistical survey of the routes through Laos, which supported the "political" view. The chances of a Chinese military response seemed slimmest with this strategy. The "political" plan appeared sound in Washington for several reasons: most ethnic Lao lived in this agriculturally and commercially central region, while militarily, the lowlands offered the most secure position. Finally, from them the United States could most easily defend Thailand.[213] Since Thailand was not under attack, these maneuverings underline the wider opportunities seen in the Nam Tha affair.

Hilsman's terms "political" and "military" provide an initial illusion of subtle manipulation vs. heavy-handed intervention. Actually, both schemes called for an American military commitment greater than at any time since Korea. Hilsman's position at first seems realistic: "The real issue is whether there is to be an accommodation . . . between the Communist and especially the Chinese Communist world and the non-Communist world or a final showdown in which only one emerges dominant. . . ." But Hilsman then manifests his own unwillingness to characterize the second alternative as lunacy: "A final showdown would present a test of will and require a grim determination in picking the time and the place . . ."[214] It was at least doubtful whether there was a crisis anywhere but in Washington.[215] Vital to an understanding of policy formulation is Hilsman's own summation of this course of action: "What the United States would do if the Chinese Communists intervened was not spelled out, but the general impression was that the recommendation would be to retaliate on the mainland with nuclear weapons."[216] What emerges from the Hilsman and Schlesinger accounts of the events surrounding Nam Tha is that there was *no evidence at all* for Vietnamese or Chinese involvement; nonetheless, the National Security Council, the members of which should have known of Colonel Elder's report or have read the *New York Times* or *Washington Post,* acted as if an international Communist force was threatening Thailand. Vietnamese and Chinese specters are used continuously in Laos to justify American intrusion. Laos had become linked to the increasing United States counter-insurgency in South Vietnam and the establishment of American influence in Thailand. To protect these interests, the United States, unprovoked, almost initiated a nuclear war. The situation and evaluation pushing Washington toward a nuclear attack exist today.

The Seventh Fleet moved to action stations on May 12, 1962. A few days later 1,000 United States Marines on SEATO maneuvers in Thailand proceeded towards the Lao border. On May 15, Washington announced the dispatch of 4,000 more troops to Thailand. By May 16, the first detachment arrived in Bangkok, followed shortly by small groups from Great Britain, Australia, and France.

Although President Kennedy declared the troop movements were intended "to help insure the territorial integrity of this peaceful country," justifying the intervention on the basis of the SEATO treaty, the Rusk-Khoman agreement, and the United Nations Charter, not only was Thailand in no danger, but Bangkok, as shown above, did not publicly request American troops until after General Paul Harkins, the American military commander in South Vietnam, met secretly with Marshal Sarit to persuade him to agree to the American deployment. On May 13 Washington still awaited the Thai approval.[217]

By means, then, of the March 6, 1962, agreement which permitted unilateral United States action in Thailand, and the spurious Nam Tha "crisis," Washington managed to position its first official combat troops on the mainland of Southeast Asia. The day of the Thai landing, Secretary McNamara announced the creation of a new United States Military Assistance Command–Thailand, to be headed by General Harkins, who retained his post as commander in Vietnam. In the words of Deputy Defense Secretary Roswell Gilpatric, the establishment of this new foothold in Asia was "not just a show, not just a demonstration of force." It soon became evident that regardless of events in Laos, American combat troops—including crack counterguerrilla units—were in Thailand to stay.

The Chinese announced that the American deployment in Thailand threatened their borders and endangered the Geneva talks.[218] But the "crisis" was over. On May 25, Premier Khrushchev declared again his support of neutralism, while on the same day Souvana Phouma reported from Paris his agreement to participate in new negotiations. At the Geneva negotiations from June 7 to June 12, Boun Oum, Souvanna Phouma, and Souphanouvong conferred on the Plain of Jars, determining a new government including Phoumi and Souphanouvong as Vice-Premiers.[219] But a settlement in Vientiane had been delayed while the world teetered on the atomic brink, and America hammered another link into its chain surrounding Vietnam and China.

GENEVA 1962

THE GENEVA CONFERENCE reconvened on July 2. Three weeks later on July 23, the Declaration was signed.[220] What might have been accomplished two years earlier had been made much more difficult by persistent United States manipulation and intervention.

On July 9, Quinim Pholsena presented the new government's Declaration of Neutrality, which was incorporated into the Conference declaration. An important article from the standpoint of Washington, it prohibited not only military alliances and foreign bases, but "the protection of any alliance or military coalition, including SEATO."[221]

Such explicit censure of SEATO was very significant, for it was the threat of United States military intervention from Thailand in 1961, presumably under SEATO auspices, which helped to prolong the Rightist regime. Laos had never been presented with a choice in the matter of the SEATO "umbrella." As Souvanna Phouma stated in August, 1956, "we cannot subscribe to SEATO, because its provisions concerning us were decided without our participation. Moreover, it is not in accordance with the Geneva agreements that we should join this organization."[222] The delegations at Geneva in 1962 concurred, finally deciding that SEATO "protection" proffered by the United States and by Thailand in particular, conflicted with the goal of neutrality.

But "neutralism" ran directly counter to Washington's over-all Asian posture[223] and Lao non-alignment appeared "risky" to American policy-makers. Although the failure of America's ally had forced Kennedy to negotiate, the

United States would continue to undermine any neutral solution.

POST-SCRIPT

ALTHOUGH THEY FALL OUTSIDE the scope of this study, the reader should have a few guide-posts to point the way to more recent events.

On March 6, 1970, President Nixon presented his administration's view of the Laotian situation. In his summation he offered a variation on an old theme: "Our support efforts have the one purpose of helping prevent the recognized Laotian government from being overwhelmed by larger Communist forces dominated by the North Vietnamese."

But even in mid-1970, the American people have yet to be told the extent of their government's involvement in Laos, although it is known by every call-girl in Vientiane and every refugee from the Plain of Jars. Senators expressed shock during the Hearings of October, 1969, at the extent of the entanglement which by April, 1970, had yet to be made public. While the CIA base at Long Cheng awaited attack, and "General" Vang Pao's CIA-sponsored army dwindled, the public was told that the Pathet Lao walked out of the Geneva-established 1962 coalition and have been causing trouble ever since. The facts, as usual, lead elsewhere.

The 1962 accords legally ratified the political and military position of the Pathet Lao. They recognized Pathet Lao control of large "liberated areas," unified the National Army with participants from Right, Center, and Left, and gave the Neo Lao Hak Xat four portfolios in the new government; the Souvanna Phouma group received seven. Among other items the agreements precluded any foreign military bases including SEATO. (On July 9, the provisional coalition announced that Laos would not accept the "protection of any alliance or military coalition, including SEATO."[224] It is this exclusion that makes illegal President Nixon's statement that Thai troops ferried by CIA planes to Long Cheng were fulfilling a SEATO obligation. As a signatory of the Geneva 1962 accords the United States was obligated to *prevent* just such action.)

Although more than 600 United States troops left Laos after the Geneva meeting, the CIA supported KMT troops (used at Nam Tha by Phoumi Nosavan) remained, as did Thai and South Vietnamese elements. In February, 1963, Peking charged the United States with reinforcing Phoumi's army and dropping arms, via the CIA, to the Meo tribesmen (headed by Vang Pao). Further, the Chinese claimed that hundreds of American soldiers had changed into civilian clothes and were now attached to the Embassy— a fact which, although denied by Washington, has been attested to by newsmen for years.

In April, 1963, Foreign Minister Quinim Pholsena, sympathetic to the Pathet Lao, was murdered in Vientiane, as was his colleague Colonel Kanthy Siphantong. Following the killings, the neutralist alliance in the Plain of Jars broke into two parts with Kong Le momentarily joining the Phoumists.

The murders and political schisms led to the departure from Vientiane of Souphanouvong and another NLHX Minister, leaving two behind. For them the situation seemed akin to the events in 1959 when they were imprisoned in Vientiane by Phoui Sananikone. They joined the other leaders of the Pathet Lao in Khang Khay.

By the beginning of 1964, a movement had begun between Souvanna Phouma and Souphanouvong to restore the Geneva *modus vivendi,* a movement halted by the coup d'état of April 19 which saw two Rightists, including the head of Phoumi Nosavan's secret police, place under house arrest Souvanna Phouma (who had recently traveled to Peking). Souvanna was released after a visit to Vientiane by Assistant Secretary of State William Bundy, who persuaded Souvanna to reorganize his government along

Rightist lines, with "personalities qualified to participate in the government." One of his first acts, in May, was to accept American airstrikes against the Leftist headquarters at Khang Khay and other targets on the Plain of Jars, during which two American aircraft were shot down. Addressing Congress on August 5, 1964, in the wake of the Tonkin Gulf incidents (which were, we now know, largely fabricated by the Americans), President Johnson utilized the situation in Laos to help justify escalation of the Vietnam War, charging "direct attack" by "communists" in Laos on "armed forces of the United States."[225] These "attacks" were Pathet Lao fire against American bombers (until recently euphemistically called reconnaissance planes). Following the Tonkin crisis United States planes bombed Laos more heavily; the bombing of the "liberated areas" (not only the Ho Chi Minh Trail) reported for the first time in full by Decornoy in *Le Monde* (July 1968), by 1969 had reduced one third of the Lao to the status of refugee.

In early 1965 General Kouprasith Abhay, who had led the 1964 coup, drove Phoumi Nosavan into exile in Thailand, and, clearly in charge in Vientiane, fabricated an election from which the Left was excluded.

During this same period, following the United States bombing of North Vietnam, Vietnamese troops appeared in increasing numbers in Laos on their way south. After President Johnson called off the bombing of North Vietnam in 1968, the raids were shifted to Laos, increasing to 1,200 strikes per month, with a plane loss of over a hundred. The devastation of Laos clearly constituted the military's price for the halt in activity over North Vietnam. Nonetheless, despite American charges to the contrary, and despite the CIA's creation of General Vang Pao's Secret Army (Vang Pao, like most American collaborators, most recently Lon Nol of Cambodia, is a French veteran), Vietnamese involvement, at the height of the 1969–70 clashes in the Plain of Jars, appeared minimal, amounting in March 1969 to a maximum of 400 troops.[226]

The airlifting by CIA planes of Thai troops into Long Cheng involved the Thais further in the Lao conflict. The *New York Times* of March 26 indicated that Thais had been supporting the CIA for some time, obtaining the same kind of counter-insurgency training experienced by the frequently rotated Thai battalions in Vietnam—experience useful for Thai operations in their own Northeast. Once again Vietnamese specters were being invoked to justify American escalation. According to *Le Monde* of October 1, 1969, "North Vietnam was more heavily bombed than Korea; Laos is now being bombed more heavily than North Vietnam. This battering has been going on for more than five years." An American diplomat in Vientiane summed up for Decornoy: "For this country to make progress it will be necessary to level everything. The people will have to go back to zero and lose their traditional culture which blocks everything."

CONCLUSIONS

LAOS EXISTED for several years near the Cold War's cutting edge in Asia. Although a nation of uncertain cohesion itself, it might have served as a buffer between hostile forces. The present study of American policies in Laos from 1945 to 1962 suggests a number of conclusions, some of which may encourage further investigation.

1. A genuine coalition between 1958 and 1962 in Laos would have alleviated considerable strain between Thailand and North Vietnam. Support of the Rightists by Bangkok and of the Pathet Lao by Hanoi indicates the importance of a strong neutral government in Vientiane.

2. A neutral coalition would also have eased one of the strains between China and the United States.

3. The elimination of Laos as a possible buffer began when the French, as early as 1947, persuaded the United States that the Indochinese war, far from being colonial,

should be viewed as a skirmish in the Cold War. In 1954, Dulles, unwilling to accept neutrality at Geneva, included Laos under SEATO protection, another step toward instability and American intervention as was eventually recognized by the Laos Protocol in 1962.

4. Washington's weaker allies—sometimes called "puppets"—can, under certain conditions, exercise significant influence over its policies. Thailand's anxieties concerning events in Laos, especially during the Sarit regime, on several occasions stimulated large-scale American activity, while the maneuvering of Phoumi Nosavan, encouraged by the CIA, nearly brought the United States to attack China with nuclear weapons. Washington's actions vis-à-vis Thailand were motivated less to reassure an ally, it seems, than to ensure a base for future military operations.

A subsidiary aspect: the influence of a weak ally such as Phoumi Nosavan can be directly proportional to the contempt in which Washington holds him. Moreover, scorn for Lao official corruption and military ineptness merged, as is now the case in Vietnam, into grudging respect for the "enemy." Hilsman's regard for Prince Souphanouvong is a case in point.

5. "Experts." As Kennedy found at the Bay of Pigs (an episode he admitted prevented him from full intervention in Laos), the authorities on Laos were also unqualified. Ironically, the Pentagon's initial reluctance to become involved with the Royal Lao Army proved sound, but the CIA backed Phoumi while the State Department attacked Souvanna. No one, it seems, after the initial enthusiasm of the OSS, ever considered anything but hostility to Souphanouvong. Ambassador Parsons' promise of a Rightist victory in the 1958 elections constitutes only the most glaring miscalculation.

6. The capacity of "experts" to turn an unpromising situation into a full catastrophe manifested itself in Laos. The Pentagon sent ever more useless supplies to the miserable Royal Lao Army, the Embassy increasingly bolstered

the failing commodity import schemes, and the CIA supported Phoumi's boundless but inept ambitions to the end. The juggernaut quality seen in the entire Laos commitment is epitomized by General Lemnitzer's promise of victory if permitted a nuclear strike.

7. One might imagine that unsuccessful covert operations or clearly lunatic military proposals would lead to a "hands-off" policy. Such is not the case. Arthur Schlesinger states:

> One quick effect of the Laos crisis was to lead the President to take up an old preoccupation from Senate days . . . the problem of countering guerrilla attack. . . . By the Autumn of 1961 a Counter-Insurgency Committee under General (Maxwell) Taylor set itself to developing the nation's capability for unconventional warfare.[227]

President Kennedy was fundamentally hostile to a neutralist solution which would obstruct the United States from keeping control of Laotian affairs. The recommendations that "next time" the United States should be "unconventional" is explicitly made in both Hilsman and Dommen, whose own accounts of the war should lead to an opposite suggestion.

8. All authorities stress the destruction of the social and physical fabric of Laos by American aid and, latterly, military action. United States aid programs quickly produced corruption, profiteering, and careerism, while the 1968 accounts by Jacques Decornoy in *Le Monde* make plain what our Air Force can achieve when political penetration fails.

9. "National interest" seems useless as an aid to understanding United States policy in Laos. Fear of failure, of public humiliation, motivated Americans whether in Vientiane or the White House and caused escalation to follow failure. The opinions of the Lao were not even formally considered when SEATO was established. President Kennedy, *knowing* the role of the Eisenhower administration in wrecking Souvanna Phouma's hopes for neutralism, publicly castigated the Russians (who were out

of the picture until 1960) and privately considered all-out war with China. In the most "pragmatic" sense, the contemplation of direct confrontation with Peking over Laos in 1962 appears aberrant.

10. The Pathet Lao, like the National Liberation Front in South Vietnam, clearly constitutes one of the positive forces in Laos. From descriptions of Souphanouvong in his early periods of resistance, or from the recent series in *Le Monde,* we can discern that in Laos as elsewhere the United States chose almost at the outset to suppress a proto-nationalist movement. The particular irony in Laos is that Washington chose also to destroy the meaningful non-Communist alternative. If Laos survives, the final victory will probably now go to the Pathet Lao because American policy long ago emasculated the neutralists, whom even Peking, as late as 1961, was willing to support.

11. American anti-Communism in Laos has for years subordinated Lao nationalism to Washington's "interests." Our endless miscalculations must not be confused with "mistakes," with a policy which meant well but took the wrong path. America, in Dean Rusk's phrase, "has not learned to leave her neighbors alone." Neighbors?

Notes

The authors thank the Dartmouth East Asia Language and Area Center for a summer research grant.

1. Partial text of interview in the *New York Times,* January, 5, 1969.
2. *Le Monde,* July 4, 1968.
3. An easily accessible bibliography may be found in Hugh Toye's *Laos: Buffer State or Battleground* (London, Oxford Univ. Press, 1968). Certain American participants in the Laos affair from 1961 to 1962 have recorded the manipulations of American political and military figures in the Dulles period but their praise for John Kennedy, despite his own interference in Laos, blinds them in their final judgments. Hilsman and Schlesinger are the main examples. Their analyses are criticized throughout this study.

4. For a description of this elite, see Joel Halpern, *Government, Politics and Social Structure in Laos* (New Haven, Yale Univ. Press, 1964), p. 5ff. The following summary is drawn from S. Simmonds, "Independence and Political Rivalry in Laos, 1945–1961," in Saul Rose (ed.), *Politics in Southern Asia* (London, Macmillian, 1963), pp. 164–199; Hugh Toye, *Laos: Buffer State,* pp. 53ff.; Katay Sasorith, *Le Laos* (Paris, Berger-Levrault, 1953), pp. 59ff.

5. For Japan's intentions regarding independence movements in Southeast Asia, see W. H. Elsbree, *Japan's Role in Southeast Asian Nationalist Movements* (Cambridge, Harvard Univ. Press, 1953).

6. For Souvanna Phouma and Souphanouvong, see A. J. Dommen, *Conflict in Laos* (New York, Praeger, 1964), ch. 5, *passim;* Roger Hilsman, *To Move A Nation* (New York, Doubleday, 1967), pp. 107–108; Toye, pp. 77ff.

7. Michael Caply, *Guérilla au Laos* (Paris, Presses de la Cité, 1966), pp. 105ff.

8. For insights into the attitude of these forerunners of the CIA, many of whom were sympathetic to the Vietnamese nationalists, see *Brig. General Phillip Gallagher Papers,* Office of the Chief of Military History, U.S. Army, and U.S. Office of Strategic Service, Research and Analysis Branch, declassified papers, National Archives, Modern Military Records. We are grateful to Miss Linda Robbins for this reference.

9. Dommen, pp. 26–28; for OSS attitudes towards the French, see Donald Lancaster, *The Emancipation of French Indochina* (London & New York, Oxford, 1961), p. 125; Peter Kemp, *Alms for Oblivion* (London, Cassell, 1961), pp. 49ff. De Gaulle, *Memoirs de guerre* (Paris, Plon. 1959), p. 213.

10. Toye, *Laos: Buffer State,* p. 78.

11. Bernard Fall, *The Two Vietnams* (New York, Praeger, 1964), p. 121.

12. For a discussion of the Pathet Lao from various points of view, see Smith, "Laos," in Kahin (ed.), *Government and Politics of Southeast Asia,* Second Edition (Ithaca, Cornell Univ. Press, 1964), p. 538, note 30; Bernard Fall, "The Pathet Lao: A 'Liberation' Movement," in Robert Scalapino (ed.), *The Communist Revolution in Asia* (Englewood Cliffs, N.J., Prentice-Hall, 1965), pp. 173–197; Toye, *Laos: Buffer State,* pp. 85ff.; Halpern, *Government, Politics,* pp. 12ff.; Dommen, *Conflict in Laos,* ch. 5. Fall's account is perhaps the most complete. He analyzes both the Pathet Lao power structure and operational mechanisms and its role in Laos until 1965. Dommen's account is the most cynical,

stressing Viet Minh manipulation. His sources are almost wholly Western; when Lao, they are drawn either from Sisouk na Champassak, who is anti-Pathet Lao, or from Royal Lao Government documents. For an alternative view see W. Burchett, *Mekong Upstream* (Berlin, Seven Seas, 1959). Almost all sources agree on Souphanouvong's excellent personal qualities, including his honesty and ability during his later service in the Royal Lao Government. A series of eyewitness accounts of the Liberated Areas of Laos by the experienced *Le Monde* journalist, Jacques Decornoy, reveals a good deal about Pathet Lao administration, contrasting it favorably with those parts of Laos still under Royal Lao Government control. *Le Monde,* July 3 to 7, 1968.

13. For a detailed survey of the period 1941–46 we are indebted to the study, "What Ever Happened to the Vietnam Trusteeship for Indochina?" prepared for an N.Y.U. seminar by Miss Linda Robbins.

14. For the background of events leading up to the Bao Dai recognition see Joseph Buttinger, *Vietnam: A Dragon Embattled* (New York, Praeger, 1967), vol. 2, ch. 8.

15. Dept. of State *Bulletin* (Washington, D.C., July 3, 1950), p. 5.

16. Frank C. Darling, *Thailand and The United States* (Washington, D.C., Public Affairs Press, 1965), p. 101.

17. See Jules Roy, The Battle of *Dien Bien Phu* (New York, Harper & Row, 1965); Bernard Fall, *Hell in a Very Small Place* (New York, Lippincott, 1967); Vo Nguyen Giap, *The Battle of Dien Bien Phu* (Hanoi, 1966); Mirsky, "Two Sides to the Dien Bien Phu Story," *The Nation,* June 27, 1966.

18. *American Foreign Policy 1950–55,* Dept. of State Publication No. 6446, December 1957, pp. 2373–81.

19. *New York Times,* April 18, 1954.

20. Victor Bator, *Vietnam, A Diplomatic Tragedy* (Dobbs Ferry, N.Y., Oceana, 1965), chapters 3 & 4; and A. Eden, *Full Circle* (Boston, Houghton Mifflin, 1960), *passim.*

21. Eden, *Full Circle,* pp. 132f.

22. Text, in *Background Information Relating to Southeast Asia and Vietnam,* (4th Revised Ed.), Committee on Foreign Relations, U.S. Senate, 1968, p. 100.

23. Section 14; text in *Background Information,* p. 92.

24. Smith, "Laos," pp. 540–41.

25. Burchett, *Furtive War* (New York, International Pubs., 1963), pp. 161ff.

26. *First Interim Report of the International Commission for Supervision and Control in Laos,* Cmd. 9445, (London, HMSO, 1955), p. 45.

27. Lord Avon, letter to the London *Sunday Times,* April 19, 1964, quoted in Toye, *Laos: Buffer State,* p. 106.

28. Text of protocol, *Background Information,* p. 105.

29. Chae Jin Lee, *Chinese Communist Policy in Laos: 1954–1965,* Ph.D. Dissertation (Ann Arbor, Mich., Univ. Microfilms, #67-1088, 1967), pp. 59–78, esp. p. 72.

30. Darling, *Thailand and the United States,* p. 81.

31. *Economic Cooperation Agreement Between the United States of America and Laos,* Dept. of State, Treaties and Other International Acts Series No. 3664 (Washington, GPO, 1956).

32. *United States Aid Operation in Laos: Seventh Report by the Committee on Government Operations,* June 15, 1959 (Washington, 1959), pp. 8–9; hereafter, *Hearings* II.

33. *Hearings* II, p. 8.

34. *Hearings* II, p. 8.

35. *Hearings* II, p. 8.

36. *United States Aid Operation in Laos, Hearings before a Sub-Committee of the Committee on Government Operations,* House of Representatives, 86th Congress, 1st Session, Washington, 1959, pp. 40 and 50; hereafter, *Hearings* I.

37. Hilsman, *To Move a Nation,* p. 112.

38. Smith, "Laos," p. 542.

39. Committee on Armed Services, Senate, *Military Cold War Education and Speech Review Policies: Hearings Before the Special Preparedness Subcommittee* (Washington, 1962), p. 2371.

40. Dommen, *Conflict in Laos,* pp. 101–103; agency rivalry is discussed at length in Hilsman, Schlesinger, and Halpern.

41. *Hearings* I, p. 40.

42. Hilsman, *To Move a Nation,* p. 113.

43. Arthur Schlesinger, *A Thousand Days* (New York, Fawcett, 1967), p. 304.

44. George Modelski, *SEATO: Six Studies* (Melbourne, F. W. Cheshire, 1962), p. 147.

45. E. H. S. Simmonds, "The Evolution of Foreign Policy in Laos Since Independence," *Modern Asian Studies,* Vol. II (1968), p. 8. The Lao relationship with Thailand was a complicated one. Parts of northeast Thailand were once Lao and presently contain perhaps three times as many Lao as Laos itself. The possibility of a "Greater Laos," Laos as a buffer between Thailand and Vietnam—or perhaps China—and the accompanying pressures from Bangkok on Washington to take Thailand's side are themes ably discussed by Toye, *Laos: Buffer State, passim,* and Halpern, *Government, Politics,* pp. 25–27.

46. Kahin (ed.), *The Asian-African Conference* (Ithaca, Cornell Univ.

Press, 1956), p. 27; Lee, *passim,* and J. Chester Cheng (ed.), *The Politics of the Red Chinese Army* (Stanford, Cal., Hoover, 1966), p. 368.

47. Modelski, *SEATO,* p. 148.

48. Sisouk na Champassak, *Storm Over Laos* (New York, Praeger, 1961), pp. 52, 63.

49. *Third Interim Report of the International Commission for Supervision and Control in Laos,* Cmd. 314 (London, HMSO, 1957), pp. 5–7.

50. *New York Times,* May 31, 1957; Smith, "Laos," p. 543.

51. During the 1959 Laos hearings, a State Department official was asked: ". . . as I understand your testimony, the State Department opposed this coalition on any terms?" The official answered: "Yes, we opposed anything which was not in accordance with the Geneva Accords, and a coalition giving cabinet positions to the Pathet Lao without elections was certainly completely outside the Geneva Accords." *Hearings* I, p. 40. The Geneva Accords, however, nowhere explicitly exclude Pathet Lao members from holding any governmental posts.

52. Texts of the agreements can be found in ICC Fourth Interim Report, Cmd. 541 (London HMSO, 1958), pp. 59–69.

53. Champassak, *Storm Over Laos,* p. 60.

54. E. H. S. Simmonds, "The Evolution of Foreign Policy in Laos Since Independence," p. 8.

55. *New York Times,* November 21, 1957.

56. *New York Times,* January 25, 1958.

57. Hilsman, *To Move a Nation,* p. 108.

58. *Hearings* I, p. 195.

59. *Hearings* II, p. 47.

60. *Hearings* I, pp. 230–232.

61. Dommen, *Conflict in Laos,* p. 107.

62. *Hearings* I, p. 229. Representative Porter Hardy appears as an early and almost unique opponent of the Laos involvement.

63. Halpern, *Government, Politics,* pp. 46, 60.

64. *Hearings* I, p. 229.

65. Hilsman, *To Move a Nation,* p. 114; it must not be supposed that the Congressional investigations of 1958 ended ICA corruption. For a succinct account of later developments see Smith, "Laos," p. 548, note 60.

66. Schlesinger, *Thousand Days,* p. 304. That the CIA helped form the CDNI and played a significant role in right-wing Lao politics thereafter is explicitly stated by Smith, Dommen, Toye, Schlesinger, and Hilsman, all of whom were in a position to know.

67. Toye, *Laos: Buffer State,* p. 120; Champassaks, *Storm Over Laos,* p. 67.
68. It had been a disputed frontier since the French colonial period, at which time Huong Lap formed part of Vietnam; North Vietnam continued to govern it following the French departure, and, although it appeared on the map of Laos, no Lao official ever visited the area nor had a Royal Lao Army military post ever been established. Toye, *Ibid.,* p. 121.
69. Toye, *Ibid.,* p. 123.
70. Smith, "Laos," p. 549, note 62, and Toye, *Ibid.,* p. 122.
71. Schlesinger, *Thousand Days,* p. 305.
72. See Darling, *Thailand and the United States* and David Wilson, *Politics in Thailand* (Ithaca, N.Y., Cornell Univ. Press, 1960 & 62), for details on Sarit's consolidation of his autocratic power over Thailand, which corresponds to Phoui Sananikone's rise and Phoumi Nosavan's later ascent.
73. *New York Times,* January 25, 1959.
74. *New York Times,* February 13, 1959; Toye, *Laos, Buffer State,* pp. 123–124.
75. Toye, *Ibid.,* p. 123.
76. S. Simmonds, "Independence," p. 184.
77. *Documents Relating to British Involvement in the Indo-China Conflict 1945–1965,* Cmnd. 2834 (London, HMSO), pp. 135ff.
78. There are numerous indications that Washington was actively seeking Lao abrogation of the Geneva Accords, especially in regard to direct U.S. military aid. See, for instance, *Hearings* I, pp. 9 and 54.
79. Miscellaneous No. 20 (1954), *Further Documents Relating to the Discussion of Indo-China at the Geneva Conference,* June 16–July 21, 1954, Cmnd. 9234, p. 42. The Laotian Government could justifiably have taken only that position or repudiate Geneva. Article Six of the agreements on Laos permitted only the French mission, and the introduction of any other foreign military personnel would violate the terms of the cease-fire. *Background Information,* p. 90.
80. Halpern, *Government, Politics,* p. 90.
81. Champassak, *Storm over Laos,* p. 78.
82. See Bernard Fall, *Street Without Joy,* Revised (London, Pall Mall, 1964), p. 333.
83. For the full report, see *Hearings* II.
84. S. Simmonds, "Independence," p. 186.
85. *New York Times,* August 18, 1959.
86. Toye, *Laos: Buffer State,* p. 129.

87. Fall, *Street Without Joy*, pp. 301–5, 334–336.
88. Dommen, *Conflict in Laos*, p. 123.
89. *Report of the Security Council Sub-Committee under Resolution of 7 September 1959*, U.N. Security Council Document 5/4236, November 5, 1959.
90. The report implied that the Pathet Lao might have received some type of support from North Vietnam; but it appeared inconclusive on this point. British correspondent Michael Field asserts that it seemed pointless to ask the UN to settle a dispute "directly involving one non-member (North Vietnam) and indirectly involving another (China)." (Michael Field, *The Prevailing Wind* [London, Methuen, 1965] p. 62). Dag Hammarskjold seemed to have perceived this fact, stating in October that UN observers should not be sent to Laos unless requested by both Laos and North Vietnam. *New York Times*, October 25, 1959.
91. Even Roger Hilsman, *To Move a Nation*, p. 121, admits this.
92. Toye, *Laos: Buffer State*, p. 132.
93. Champassak, *Storm Over Laos*, p. 132.
94. R. Smith, "Laos in Perspective," *Asian Survey*, January, 1963. Such United States involvement presents an interesting commentary on its attitude to the United Nations; Dag Hammarskjold had visited Laos one month before, advising Phoui Sananikone to emphasize economic rather than military development and once again to adopt a policy of neutrality. His advice appears to have influenced Phoui and Washington in opposite ways.
95. Toye, *Laos: Buffer State*, p. 133.
96. Hilsman, *To Move a Nation*, p. 109.
97. Schlesinger, *Thousand Days*, p. 303.
98. Dommen, *Conflict in Law*, p. 127.
99. *Ibid.*, p. 133; Hilsman, *To Move a Nation*, p. 122.
100. Champassak, *Storm over Laos*, pp. 139–140.
101. *Ibid.*, p. 141.
102. *Ibid.*, p. 141.
103. Toye, *Laos: Buffer State*, p. 135.
104. Mirsky, "The War is Over," *Ramparts*, December, 1967.
105. Toye, *Laos: Buffer State*, pp. 136–137.
106. For accounts of Kong Le's background, see Dommen, *Conflict in Laos*, pp. 142ff. and Toye, *Laos: Buffer State*, pp. 138ff.
107. Field, *Prevailing Wind*, p. 76.
108. For the texts of the August 9th Communiqués of the Paratroop Battalion, see Dommen, *Conflict in Laos*, p. 310 (Appendix IV).
109. *New York Times*, March 19, 1970.
110. Toye, *Laos: Buffer State*, p. 144.

111. Dommen, *Conflict in Laos,* p. 161.
112. Field, *Prevailing Wind,* p. 80.
113. Toye, *Laos: Buffer State,* p. 148.
114. *New York Times,* October 10, 1961.
115. Schlesinger, *Thousand Days,* p. 305.
116. Dommen, *Conflict in Laos,* p. 154.
117. *Ibid.,* p. 155.
118. Toye, *Laos: Buffer State,* p. 152.
119. *Ibid.,* p. 152.
120. The following analysis is based on accounts in Dommen, *Conflict in Laos,* pp. 158ff; Smith, "Laos," pp. 553ff., esp. p. 554, note 60; Schlesinger, *Thousand Days,* pp. 305–306; Hilsman, *To Move a Nation,* pp. 124–125; and Toye, *Laos:Buffer State,* pp. 153–155.
121. Hilsman, *To Move a Nation,* p. 124.
122. Dommen, *Conflict in Laos,* p. 160.
123. Smith, "Laos," p. 555.
124. Toye, *Laos: Buffer State,* p. 158.
125. Toye points out Dommen's error in identifying artillerymen from Hanoi; "expert examination" proved that the gunners were Kong Le's; p. 159.
126. Schlesinger, *Thousand Days,* p. 307.
127. *New York Times,* January 20, 1961.
128. Dommen, *Conflict in Laos,* p. 175.
129. See Roger Smith, "Cambodia's Neutrality and the Laotian Crisis," *Asian Survey,* 1, No. 5 (July 1961) for an account of Prince Sihanouk's concern with Laos. Also: Modelski, *International Conference on the Settlement of the Laotian Question 1961–2* (Canberra, Australian National University, 1962), p. 6.
130. Text in Department of State Press Release No. 9, January 7, 1961.
131. Hilsman, *To Move a Nation,* pp. 93–94, 129, 134; Dommen; *Conflict in Laos,* p. 202. The other three pass through Burma, Thailand and Vietnam, none of which was accessible to the Chinese.
132. Schlesinger, *Thousand Days,* pp. 307–308.
133. Hilsman, *To Move a Nation,* p. 131, supports the interventionist line: "The United States had to be fully determined to intervene if it became necessary. This in turn meant that . . . our determination had to be backed with concrete movements of troops." Hilsman writes as if U.S. policy up to 1961 had been "hands off Laos."
134. *New York Times,* January 13, 1961; for the false reports see *New York Times,* January 27, 1961.
135. See for example, Hilsman, *To Move a Nation,* pp. 415ff.
136. Schlesinger, *Thousand Days,* pp. 307ff; Hilsman, *To Move a Nation,* pp. 127ff.

137. *Ibid.,* p. 308.
138. Hilsman, *To Move a Nation,* p. 128.
139. Schlesinger, *Thousand Days,* p. 310.
140. *Ibid.,* p. 313.
141. *New York Times,* March 23, 1961.
142. Schlesinger, *Thousand Days,* p. 312.
143. *Ibid.,* p. 313; Dommen, *Conflict in Laos,* p. 204.
144. Schlesinger, *Thousand Days,* pp. 311–312; Dommen, *Conflict in Laos,* p. 192.
145. Schlesinger, *Thousand Days,* p. 312.
146. Quoted in *ibid.,* p. 314, from *Reader's Digest,* November 1964; Hilsman, *To Move a Nation,* p. 134.
147. Schlesinger, *Thousand Days,* p. 316.
148. *Ibid.,* p. 317.
149. *Ibid.,* p. 343.
150. S. Simmonds, "Independence," p. 191.
151. *Documents Relating to British Involvement in the Indo-China Conflict, 1945–1965,* Cmnd. 2834 (London, HMSO), pp. 26, 154–5.
152. *International Conference on the Settlement of the Laotian Question, May 12, 1961–July 3, 1962,* Cmnd. 1828 (London HMSO), p. 3F.
153. Cmnd. 1828, p. 4.
154. Modelski, *Conference, Laotian Question,* p. 15; A. Lall states, "Privately, all delegations were agreed that it was necessary to have all three Laotian wings represented at the Conference table." Arthur Lall, *How Communist China Negotiates* (New York, Columbia Univ. Press, 1968), p. 56.
155. Modelski, *Ibid.,* p. 15.
156. Modelski, *Ibid.,* p. 21; for a general diplomatic "appreciation" of Geneva, see Arthur Lall's study already cited, *passim.*
157. Schlesinger, *Thousand Days,* p. 340; Hilsman, *To Move a Nation,* p. 136.
158. Kahin, *Asian-African Conference,* p. 60.
159. Lee, *Chinese Communist Policy,* pp. 152–53.
160. *Peking Review,* May 17, 1960; Lee, *Chinese Communist Policy,* pp. 154–55.
161. *People's Daily,* October 17, 1960.
162. Lee, *Chinese Communist Policy,* p. 161.
163. *Ibid.,* p. 162.
164. Brian Crozier, "Peking and the Laotian Crisis: An Interim Appraisal," *China Quarterly,* July-Sept. 1961, pp. 129–130.
165. *People's Daily,* January 8, 1961.
166. Crozier, "Peking," pp. 130–1.

167. Brian Crozier, "Peking and the Laotian Crisis: A Further Appraisal," *China Quarterly*, July-Sept. 1962, p. 118.

168. *Ibid.*, p. 120.

169. *Ibid.*

170. Cheng (ed.), *The Politics of the Red Chinese Army*, p. 367.

171. *Ibid.*, p. 368; The public Chinese view, also pro-coalition, can be found in Arthur Lall's reports from the Geneva Conference, esp. p. 78.

172. Lee, *Chinese Communist Policy*, p. 186.

173. Toye, *Laos: Buffer State*, p. 177.

174. Modelski, *International Conference*, p. 61.

175. Toye, *Laos: Buffer State*, p. 176; Schlesinger, *Thousand Days*, p. 314, describes Kennedy's invitation to Souvanna; Secretary Rusk, by making himself unavailable, caused the visit to be cancelled.

176. Text in Dept. of State *Bulletin*, No. 1145, June 5, 1961.

177. Rusk's general line appears little different from that taken by Peking delegate Ch'en Yi. Although both Washington and Peking throughout insisted on neutrality, there is little evidence to support the American claim.

178. Schlesinger, *Thousand Days*, pp. 468–469.

179. *Ibid.*, p. 478.

180. Text of the Zurich Agreement in *International Conference on the Settlement of the Laos Question, May 12, 1961–July 23, 1962*, Cmnd. 1828, pp. 13–14.

181. Toye, *Laos: Buffer State*, p. 175.

182. Fall, *Street Without Joy*, Revised, p. 338.

183. Oliver E. Clubb, *The United States and the Sino-Soviet Bloc in Southeast Asia* (Washington, Brookings Inst., 1962), p. 67; Hilsman, *To Move a Nation*, p. 137.

184. Hilsman, *To Move a Nation*, and Smith, "Laos," p. 559, note 83. For an authoritative allegation of direct CIA involvement with Phoumi, see *The Times* (London), 24, 25, 31 May 1961; summarized in Toye, *Laos: Buffer State*, p. 184.

185. Hilsman, *To Move a Nation*.

186. *Ibid.*, p. 139.

187. Toye, *Laos: Buffer State*, p. 180.

188. Smith, "Laos," p. 559, note 86.

189. Darling, *Thailand and the United States*, p. 207, text in Dept. of State *Bulletin*, March 26, 1962.

190. Dommen, *Conflict in Laos*, p. 216, Hillsman, *To Move a Nation*, pp. 140–1, Toye, *Laos: Buffer State*, pp. 181–2.

191. Max Frankel, *New York Times*, May 12, 1962.

192. Smith, "Laos," p. 559, note 86.

193. *Washington Post,* May 6, 1962; *New York Times,* May 6 and May 8, 1962.

194. Fall, *Street Without Joy,* p. 339.

195. Frankel, *New York Times,* May 7, 1962; *Washington Post,* May 7, 1962.

196. *Ibid.*

197. *New York Times,* May 9, 1962.

198. *Washington Post,* May 9, 1962.

199. *New York Times,* May 10, 1962.

200. Fall, *Street Without Joy,* p. 339, italics in original; Dommen, *Conflict in Laos,* p. 218, reports the same.

201. *New York Times,* May 12, 1962.

202. *Ibid.*

203. Hilsman, *To Move a Nation,* p. 141.

204. *Ibid.,* p. 143.

205. Toye, *Laos: Buffer State,* p. 183.

206. Hilsman, *To Move a Nation,* pp. 142–147.

207. *Ibid.,* pp. 144–145.

208. *Washington Post,* May 9, 1962; *New York Times,* May 12, 1962.

209. Hilsman, *To Move a Nation,* p. 145.

210. *New York Times,* May 18, 1962.

211. Hilsman, *To Move a Nation,* p. 146.

212. Ibid., p. 147.

213. *Ibid.,* pp. 147–48.

214. *Ibid.,* p. 149.

215. James C. Thomson points out in *Atlantic,* April, 1968, the self-generating aspects of a "crisis" once it has been officially proclaimed.

216. Hilsman, *To Move a Nation,* p. 147.

217. *Washington Post,* May 14, 1962.

218. Lee, *Chinese Communist Policy,* pp. 208–209.

219. Toye, *Laos: Buffer State,* p. 186; Dommen, *Conflict in Laos,* pp. 220–221.

220. *Declaration and Protocol on the Neutrality of Laos,* Treaty Series 27, Cmnd. 2025 (London, HMSO, 1963).

221. Cmnd. 2025.

222. Modelski, *SEATO: Six Studies,* p. 148.

223. A 1966 Senate Committee on Foreign Relations report on Southeast Asian neutrality asserts that the United States has viewed unfavorably declarations of neutralism (e.g. Cambodia). Washington has maintained since John Foster Dulles that the principle of collective security, not neutrality, affords the best protection for a state's sovereignty. (Committee on Foreign Re-

lations, U.S. Senate, *Neutralization in Southeast Asia: Problems and Prospects* (Washington, 1966), p. 23.
224. Department of State Bulletin, August 13, 1962, pp. 259–261.
225. Department of State Bulletin, August 24, 1964, p. 262.
226. London *Observer,* February 28, 1970.
227. Schlesinger, *Thousand Days,* pp. 318–319.

Capitalist and Maoist Economic Development

❧ *John G. Gurley*

❧ WHILE CAPITALIST AND MAOIST processes of economic development have several elements in common, the differences between the two approaches are nevertheless many and profound. It is certainly not evident that one approach or the other is always superior, in regard either to means or to ends. What is evident, however, is that most studies by American economists of Chinese economic development are based on the assumption of capitalist superiority, and so China has been dealt with as though it were simply an underdeveloped United States—an economy that "should" develop along capitalist lines and "should" forget all that damn foolishness about Marxism, Mao's thought, great leaps, and cultural revolutions, and just get on with the job of investing the savings efficiently. This almost complete and unthinking acceptance of the view that there is no development like capitalist development has resulted in American economic studies of China that lack insight and are generally unsatisfactory. Later on, I shall briefly examine some of these weaknesses and then suggest the types of economic studies that might be undertaken if China's development efforts are to be given serious intellectual consideration. The main portion of this essay, however, is a comparison of capitalist and Maoist development processes.

I · SOME COMMON ELEMENTS

THERE IS A CORE of economic development theory, which is concerned with ways of increasing a country's national product, that would probably be accepted by both the capitalist and Maoist sides. This common core recognizes that national output consists of goods and services that are consumed (consumption) and goods that are accumulated (investment). The consumption of national output may be done by individuals, business firms, and governments; and the consumption items are generally food, clothing, housing services, household operation, and such things. The accumulation of national output—real investment or capital formation—is added to the country's capital stock, to its houses and business structures, its tools and machinery, its highways, its inventories and livestock,˙ and its military equipment. Such capital formation may be undertaken by either the private or public sectors of the economy.

Current investment yields plant and equipment and other capital goods that can be used to produce larger amounts of output in subsequent years. That is, as the capital stock builds up, a country becomes increasingly capable of enlarging the production of its goods and services. On the other hand, if national output is almost totally consumed year after year, the productive capabilities of the nation will remain depressed; consumption will continue to eat up output that might have taken the form of productive machinery, tools, and similar things.

The output capabilities of a nation, however, depend on more than the size of its capital stock. They also are affected by the size of the labor force and by the amount of available land and natural resources. A nation's capacity to produce, in other words, depends on the amount of "inputs" it has—on its capital stock, labor supply, and land. An increase in any of these factors of production will generally raise a country's output potential.

Since the amount of land is more or less fixed, the variable inputs are capital and labor. Inasmuch as output will generally grow with an increase of either, it would seem to be unimportant which one is emphasized. However, the growth of output is generally not considered as important an economic goal as is the growth of output *per capita*—that is, total output divided by the population. While an increase in population will eventually enlarge the labor force and so lead to a growth of output, the percentage rise in output will generally be smaller than the percentage increase in population. Consequently, if a nation depended solely on population gains to raise its output, it would find its output per capita declining over time, as an increasing number of workers applied themselves to the same amount of capital equipment, other capital items, and land. Total output would rise but at a diminishing rate, and so would fail to keep up with the growth of population.

Aside from some important considerations to be dealt with in a moment, an equal percentage increase in capital, labor, and land would bring about a rise in total output by the same percentage. Thus, suppose that each of the three factor inputs rose by 3 per cent in some year; then output would also rise by the same amount. Hence, output per capita would in this case remain the same, provided that population grew by the same percentage as the labor force. It is clear, then, that in the absence of other considerations an increase in output per capita can be achieved only if the percentage growth of the capital stock or of land outstrips that of the labor supply. Since, as I have said, it is usually difficult to do very much about the stock of land, the growth of output per capita depends heavily on relatively large rates of investment—on the capital stock growing faster than the labor supply. This process is called "capital deepening" because it leads to the availability of more capital per worker; and so to more output per worker.

However, output per capita may be raised not only by capital deepening but also by improvements in the *quality* of the capital stock or of the labor supply. Technical advances, achieved by inventions and innovations, will raise the quality of a given capital stock and so permit the labor supply to produce more. Capital need not grow in total amount, to raise output per capita, if it "grows" in quality.

The quality of the labor force can also be raised—by improvements in health, by job training programs, by more formal education, and by better living conditions in general. The same number of workers can produce more, even with the same capital goods, if their quality is improved, if there has been investment in the nation's human capital. In addition, the growth of output per capita may come about because of improvements in organization and management techniques—better ways of combining the factors of production and more effective ways of inspiring the labor force to greater efforts. Finally, even in the absence of increases in the quality of inputs, and even though each input grows by an equal percentage, output per capita may still rise owing to economies of scale—to inputs becoming more productive when they are combined in larger and larger amounts.

Thus, if an economy wishes to increase its output per capita, the most promising avenues to success are large investment programs to build up the capital stock rapidly; expenditures for research and development for the purpose of stimulating fast technological advances; investment in human capital by way of health, education, and in-training programs; and efforts to improve organization and management methods. These expansionary policies may then call forth economies of scale and hence additional gains in output.

II · CAPITALIST ECONOMIC DEVELOPMENT

WITHIN THE ABOVE FRAMEWORK, the theory of capitalism, as originally developed by Adam Smith almost two hundred years ago, generally holds that an economy can develop most rapidly if each and every person, whether he is an entrepreneur, a worker, or a consumer, pursues his own self-interest on competitive markets, without undue interference from government. Progress is best promoted, not by government, but by entrepreneurs owning the material means of production, whose activities, guided by the profit motive, reflect consumers' demands for the various goods and services. Labor productivity is enhanced by material incentives and the division of labor (specialization); economic progress is made within an environment of law and order, harmony of interests, and stability.

The goal of economic development, according to capitalist theory, can best be attained by the above means, and the goal itself can best be measured by the national output. There is a heavy emphasis in capitalist development, as there now is throughout most of the world, on raising the level of national output, on producing "things" in ever-increasing amounts.[1] Implicit in discussions of this goal is the view that man is mainly an input, a factor of production, a means to an end. The end is usually not the development of human beings but the development of output.[2]

The practice of capitalism has not, of course, met the ideal specification of it, and the practice itself has changed markedly over time. In practice, many markets have been more monopolistic than competitive, government has interfered in numerous and extensive ways in competitive market processes in pursuit of greater equity in income distribution, higher employment of labor, and better allocation of economic resources. Capitalism of the individualist, competitive type has given way to some extent in most parts of the industrial capitalist world to a state welfare capitalism, in which government plays a larger role and private entrepreneurs and consumers somewhat smaller ones than envisaged by Adam Smith and his disciples. Despite these departures from the ideal model of capitalism, I think it is fair to say that the main driving force of the capitalist system remains that of private entrepreneurs who own the means of production, and that competition among them is still widespread.

There is no doubt that capitalist development, whatever

importance its departures from the Smithian model have had, has been highly successful in raising living standards for large numbers of people. It has been relatively efficient in using factors of production in ways best designed to maximize the output that consumers by and large have demanded. And it has encouraged new ways of doing things—innovative activity and technological advances.

At the same time, however, capitalist development has almost always been uneven in several crucial ways: in its alternating periods of boom and bust; in enriching some people thousands of times more than others; in developing production facilities with much more care than it has devoted to the welfare of human beings and their environment; in fostering lopsided development, both in terms of geographical location within the country and, especially in low-income countries, in terms of a narrow range of outputs, such as in one- or two-crop economies. The lopsided character of capitalist development has been evident historically in those nations that today have advanced industrial economies, but it is especially evident at the present time in the underdeveloped countries (with their mixture of feudalist and capitalist features) that are tied in to the international capitalist system—that is, those countries that, by being receptive to free enterprise and foreign capital, regardless of whether they are also receptive to freedom, are in the "Free World."

Most of these poor countries are either making no progress at all or they are developing in lopsided ways, within the international capitalist system, as satellites to the advanced capitalist countries. There is a sharp division of labor within this system, by which the underdeveloped regions supply raw materials, agricultural products, minerals, and oil to the rich capitalist countries, and receive in return manufactured and processed goods as well as basic food items. Each of these poor countries is closely linked to a metropolitan region, and much more trade takes place between the underdeveloped and the advanced capitalist countries than among the underdeveloped countries themselves. The consequence is that transportation is poor across South America, that it is difficult to go from one part of Africa to another, but that, nevertheless, good highways or railroads lead from mines, from banana and coffee plantations, from oil fields to the seaports for shipment to the rich capitalist countries.

The economic development of these poor capitalist countries is lopsided in many other ways, too. A few cities in each of these countries, with their airports, hotels, nightclubs, and light industries, are often built up to the point where they resemble the most modern metropolises in advanced industrial countries; but the rural areas, comprising most of the country and containing most of the people, are largely untouched by modernization. In most of these countries, industry, culture, entertainment, education, and wealth are highly concentrated in urban centers. A traveler to most of the poor "Free World" countries, by flying to the main cities, can land in the middle of the twentieth century, but by going thirty miles from there in any direction he will be back in the Middle Ages. Education is usually for the elite and stresses the superiority of the educated over the uneducated, the superiority of urban over rural life, of mental work over manual labor. The burden of economic development, which is essentially a restraint on consumption, is shared most inequitably among the people; the differences between rich and poor are staggering, because they are nothing less than the differences between unbelievable luxury and just plain starvation.

While some of these characteristics are not peculiar to the poor countries tied in to the international capitalist system—they can be found in the Soviet socialist bloc, too—and while some are related more to feudalism than to capitalism, much of the lopsided development nevertheless is intimately connected with the profit motive. The key link between the two is the fact that it is almost always most profitable, from a private business point of view, to build on the best. Thus, a businessman locates a new factory in an urban center, rather than out in the hinterlands, in order to gain access to existing supplies, a skilled labor force, and high-income consumers; to maximize profits, he hires the best, most qualified workers; a banker extends loans to those who are already successful; an educational system devotes its best efforts to the superior students, and universities, imbued with the private business ethic of "efficiency," offer education to those best prepared, most able; promoters locate cultural centers amidst urbanites best able to appreciate and pay for them; the most profitable business firms attract the best workers and have easiest access to loanable funds; satellite capitalist countries, in the interests of efficiency and comparative advantage, are induced to specialize in cocoa or peanuts or coffee—to build on what they have always done best.

This pursuit of efficiency and private profits through building on the best has led in some areas to impressive aggregate growth rates, but almost everywhere in the international capitalist world it has favored only a relatively few at the expense of the many, and, in poor capitalist countries, it has left most in stagnant backwaters. Capitalist development, even when most successful, is always a trickle-down development.

III · MAOIST ECONOMIC DEVELOPMENT

THE MAOISTS' DISAGREEMENT with the capitalist view of economic development is profound. Their emphases, values, and aspirations are quite different from those of capitalist economists. To begin with, Maoist economic development occurs within the context of central planning, public ownership of industries, and agricultural cooperatives or communes. While decision-making is decentralized to some extent, decisions regarding investment vs. consumption, foreign trade, allocation of material inputs and some labor supply, prices of goods and factors—these and more are essentially in the hands of the State. The profit motive is officially discouraged from assuming an important role in the allocation of resources, and material incentives, while still prevalent, are down-graded.

But perhaps the most striking difference between the capitalist and Maoist views is in regard to goals. Maoists believe that while a principal aim of nations should be to raise the level of material welfare of the population, this should be done only within the context of the development of human beings and of encouraging them to realize fully their manifold creative powers. And it should be done only on an egalitarian basis—that is, on the basis that development is not worth much unless everyone rises together; no one is to be left behind—either economically or culturally. Indeed, Maoists believe that rapid economic development is not likely to occur *unless* everyone rises together. Development as a trickle-down process is therefore rejected by Maoists, and so they reject any strong emphasis on profit motives and efficiency criteria that lead to lopsided growth. Their emphasis, in short, is on man rather than on "things."[3]

A. EMPHASIS ON MAN

IN MAOIST EYES, economic development can best be attained by giving prominence to man. "In building up the . . . country, we—unlike the modern revisionists who one-sidedly stress the material factor, mechanization, and modernization —pay chief attention to the revolutionization of man's thinking and through this, command, guide, and promote the work of mechanization and modernization."[4] The Maoists' stress on this point most sharply distinguishes their thinking on the subject of economic development from that of capitalist economists. For Maoists, correct ideas can be transformed into a tremendous material force to push socialist construction to ever-higher levels. "Once Mao Tse-tung's thought is grasped by the broad masses, it will become an inexhaustible source of strength and an infinitely powerful spiritual atom bomb."[5] If, on the other hand, one concentrates on machinery, techniques, and things, economic development will proceed at a snail's pace. There can be big leaps forward only by putting man at the center, and so releasing his huge reservoir of energy, creativity, and wisdom, which up to now have been submerged by bourgeois society and by the ideas and behavior patterns it generates.

Capitalist economists have recently stressed the importance for economic growth of "investment in human capital" —that is, investment in general education, job training, and better health. It has been claimed that expenditures in these directions have had a large "pay-off" in terms of output growth. The Maoists' emphasis, however, is quite different. First of all, while they recognize the key role played by education and health in the production process, their emphasis is heavily on the transformation of ideas, the making of the Communist man. Ideology, of course, may be considered as part of education in the broadest sense, but it is surely not the part that capitalist economists have in mind when they evaluate education's contribution to economic growth. Moreover, ideological training does not include the acquisition of particular skills, or the training of specialists—as education and job training in capitalist countries tend to do. The Maoists believe that economic development can best be promoted by breaking down specialization, by dismantling bureaucracies, and by undermining the other centralizing and divisive tendencies that give rise to experts, technicians, authorities, and bureaucrats remote from or manipulating "the masses." Finally, Maoists seem perfectly willing to pursue the goal of transforming man even though it is temporarily at the expense of some economic growth.[6] Indeed, it is clear that Maoists will not accept economic development, however rapid, if it is based on the capitalist principles of sharp division of labor and sharp (unsavory, selfish) practices.

B. THE MAKING OF COMMUNIST MAN

THE PROLETARIAN world view,[7] which Maoists believe must replace that of the bourgeoisie, stresses that only through struggle can progress be made; that selflessness and unity of purpose will release a huge reservoir of enthusiasm, energy, and creativity; that active participation by "the masses" in decision-making will provide them with the knowledge to channel their energy most productively; and that the elimination of specialization will not only increase workers' and peasants' willingness to work hard for the various goals of society but will also increase their ability to do this by adding to their knowledge and awareness of the world around them.

Struggle. It is an essential part of Maoist thinking that progress is not made by peace and quietude, by letting things drift and playing things safe, or by standing for "unprincipled peace, thus giving rise to a decadent, philistine attitude. . . ."[8] Progress is made through struggle, when new talents emerge and knowledge advances in leaps. Only through continuous struggle is the level of consciousness of people raised, and in the process they gain not only understanding but happiness.

Mao sees man engaged in a fierce class struggle—the bourgeoisie against the proletariat—the outcome of which, at least in the short run, is far from certain. The proletarian world outlook can win only if it enters tremendous ideological, class struggles.

In China, although in the main socialist transformation has been completed with respect to the system of ownership, and although the large-scale and turbulent class struggles of the masses characteristic of the previous revolutionary periods have in the main come to an end, there are still remnants of the overthrown landlord and comprador classes, there is still a bourgeoisie, and the remoulding of the petty bourgeoisie has only just started. The class struggle is by no means over. The class struggle between the proletariat and the bourgeoisie, the class struggle between the different political forces, and the class struggle in the ideological field between the proletariat and the bourgeoisie will continue to be long and tortuous and at times will even become very acute. The proletariat seeks to transform the world according to its own world outlook, and so does the bourgeoisie. In this respect, the question of which will win out, socialism or capitalism, is still not really settled.[9]

Selflessness. Maoists belive that each person should be devoted to "the masses" rather than to his own pots and pans, and should serve the world proletariat rather than reaching out with "grasping hands everywhere to seek fame, material gain, power, position, and limelight."[10] They think that if a person is selfish, he will resist criticisms and suggestions and is likely to become bureaucratic and elitist. Such a person will not work as hard for community or national goals as he would for narrow, selfish ones. In any case, a selfish person is not an admirable person. Thus, Maoists de-emphasize material incentives, for they are the very manifestation of a selfish, bourgeois society.

Active Participation. While selflessness is necessary to imbue man with energy and the *willingness* to work hard, this is not sufficient, for man must also have the *ability* as well. And such ability comes from active participation—from seeing and doing. As Mao has written in a famous essay:

> If you want to know a certain thing or a certain class of things directly, you must personally participate in the practical struggle to change reality, to change that thing or class of things, for only thus can you come into contact with them as phenomena; only through personal participation in the practical struggle to change reality can you uncover the essence of that thing or class of things and comprehend them. . . . If you want knowledge, you must take part in the practice of changing reality. If you want to know the taste of a pear, you must change the pear by eating it yourself. . . . All genuine knowledge originates in direct experience. . . . There is an old

Chinese saying, "How can you catch tiger cubs without entering the tiger's lair?" This saying holds true for man's practice and it also holds true for the theory of knowledge. There can be no knowledge apart from practice.[11]

To gain knowledge, people must be awakened from their half slumber, encouraged to mobilize themselves and to take conscious action to elevate and liberate themselves. When they actively participate in decision-making, when they take an interest in State affairs, when they dare to do new things, when they become good at presenting facts and reasoning things out, when they criticize and test and experiment scientifically, having discarded myths and superstitions, when they are aroused—then "the socialist initiative latent in the masses [will] burst out with volcanic force and a rapid change [will take] place in production."[12]

I noted above that both attributes of selflessness and active participation were necessary for the making of the Communist man. For a selfish person, who has nevertheless become fully aware and knowledgeable through correctly combining theory and practice, will be given to sharp practices for his own ends and will become bureaucratic and divorced from the masses. A passive, unknowing person who has nevertheless become selfless, will be well-meaning but largely ineffective, for he will not be able to use his energies productively. In fact, it is likely that in the long run "selfless" and "active" cannot exist separately, only together. If one is not active, he will eventually revert to selfish behavior; if one is selfish, he will eventually become passive, bureaucratic, and unable to gain true knowledge.[13]

Finally, if men become "selfless," there will be discipline and unity of will, for these "cannot be achieved if relations among comrades stem from selfish interests and personal likes and dislikes."[14] If men become "active," then along with extensive democracy they will gain true consciousness and ultimately freedom, in the Marxian sense of intelligent action.[15] Together, selflessness and active participation will achieve ideal combinations of opposites:

a vigorous and lively political situation . . . is taking shape throughout our country, in which there is both centralism and democracy, both discipline and freedom, both unity of will and personal ease of mind.[16]

It is important to note the "discipline" and "unity of will." So far as the basic framework of Marxism-Leninism is concerned, Maoists believe that everyone should accept it, and they are quick to "work on" those who lag behind or step out of line. But, within this framework, the Maoists energetically and sincerely promote individual initiative, "reasoning things out and not depending on authorities or myths," "thinking for oneself," etc. Outside of this framework, an individual stands little chance; inside the framework, an individual is involved in a dynamic process of becoming "truly free," in the sense of being fully aware of the world around him and being an active decision-maker in that world. Mao's thought is meant to lead to true freedom and to unity of will based on a proletarian viewpoint. So everyone must think alike—the Maoist way—to attain true freedom!

Non-Specialization. For Marx, specialization and bureaucratization were the very antitheses of Communism. Man could not be free or truly human until these manifestations of alienation were eliminated, allowing him to become an "all-round" Communist man.[17] Maoists, too, have been intensely concerned with this goal, specifying it in terms of eliminating the distinction between town and countryside, mental and manual labor, and workers and peasants. The realization of the universal man is not automatically achieved by altering the forces of production, by the socialist revolution. Rather it can be achieved only after the most intense and unrelenting ideological efforts to raise the consciousness of the people through the creative study and creative use of Mao's thought. Old ideas, customs, and habits hang on long after the material base of the economy has been radically changed, and it takes one mighty effort after another to wipe out this bourgeois superstructure and replace it with the proletarian world outlook. This transformation of the "subjective world" will then have a tremendous impact on the "objective world."

Intellectuals, party and administrative cadres, and other mental workers are prodded into taking part in physical labor—in factories and out in the fields. This will not only

> encourage the initiative of the workers and peasants in production and uproot the ingrained habit of bureaucracy, but even more important, it can ensure that leading cadres work among the people like ordinary laborers, and opens up a way for the gradual integration of mental and manual work.

Physical labor by intellectuals will eventually get rid of men whose "four limbs do not move and [who are] unable to distinguish the five grains."[18]

And laborers should become intellectuals.

> The characteristic feature of these efforts has been, and remains, a massive attack on the notion that culture, science and technology are attributes of intellectuals . . . the widely propagated rallying cry is that the "masses must make themselves masters of science and culture." For example, the purpose of "half-work and half-study" programs is proclaimed to be to develop "red and expert socialist laborers who can grasp the principles of science and technology . . . and who are both mental workers as well as people who can go to factories and fields to engage in industrial and agricultural production," thus refuting the notions of bourgeois intellectuals who "oppose mental labor to physical labor and who hold that physical labor is the task of workers and peasants while only they themselves can engage in mental labor."[19]

C. MAOIST IDEOLOGY AND ECONOMIC DEVELOPMENT

IN MANY WAYS, then, Maoist ideology rejects the capitalist principle of building on the best, even though the principle cannot help but be followed to some extent in any effort at economic development. However, the Maoist departures from the principle are the important thing. While capitalism, in their view, strives one-sidedly for efficiency in producing goods, Maoism, while also seeking some high degree of efficiency, at the same time, in numerous ways, builds on "the worst." Experts are pushed aside in favor of decision-making by "the masses"; new industries are established in rural areas; the educational system favors the disadvantaged; expertise (and hence work proficiency in a narrow sense) is discouraged; new products are domestically produced rather than being imported "more efficiently"; the growth of cities as centers of industrial and cultural life is discouraged; steel, for a time, is made by "everyone" instead of by only the much more efficient steel industry.

Maoists build on the worst not, of course, because they take great delight in lowering economic efficiency, but rather to involve everyone in the development process, to pursue development without leaving a single person behind, to achieve a balanced growth rather than a lopsided one. If Maoism were only that, we could simply state that, while Maoist development may be much more equitable than capitalist efforts, it is surely less efficient and thus less rapid; efficiency is being sacrificed to some extent for equity. But that would miss the more important aspects of Maoist ideology, which holds that the resources devoted to bringing everyone into the socialist development process—the effort spent on building on "the worst"—will eventually pay off not only in economic ways by enormously raising labor productivity but, more important, by creating a society of truly free men, who respond intelligently to the world around them, and who are happy.[20]

IV · UNITED STATES STUDIES OF CHINESE ECONOMIC DEVELOPMENT

THE SHARP CONTRAST between the economic development views of capitalist economists and those of the Chinese Communists cannot be denied; their two worlds are quite different. The difference is not mainly between being Chinese and being American, although that is surely part of it, but rather between being Maoists in a Marxist-Leninist tradition and being present-day followers of the economics first fashioned by Adam Smith and later reformed by J. M. Keynes. Whatever the ignorance and misunderstanding on the Chinese side regarding the doctrines of capitalist economics, it is clear that many Western economic experts on China have shown little interest in and almost no understanding of Maoist economic development. Most of the economic researchers have approached China as though it were little more than a series of tables in a yearbook which could be analyzed by Western economic methods and judged by capitalist values. The result has been a series of unilluminating studies, largely statistical or institutional in method, and lacking analysis of the really distinctive and interesting features of Maoist development. But before pursuing this critical line any further it is best to turn briefly to what has been done in this area.

A. ECONOMIC RESEARCH ON COMMUNIST CHINA

LIKE SEAGULLS following the wake of a ship, economists pursue numbers. The main concentration of numbers pertaining to the economy of Communist China is in *Ten Great Years,* which was published in September, 1959, by the

State Statistical Bureau. This volume contains a wealth of data on almost all phases of economic activity, and so it has become one of the main sources for much of the empirical work on Chinese economic development. But throughout the 1950's economic data were published in hundreds of other sources—in official reports, statistical handbooks, economic books, and articles—so that altogether massive information, of varying degrees of reliability, became available on the first decade or so of China's development efforts. After 1958, however, the release of aggregate data pretty much came to a halt, which meant that little research on the 1960's has been done by economists outside of China. The data of the 1950's continue to be worked over, adjusted, and refined, though there is no longer much more that can be said about them.

Much of this research has been concerned in one way or another with China's national output: its absolute size; its rates of growth; its components, like agriculture and industrial output or consumption and investment goods; the extent to which national output has been affected by international trade and Soviet aid; and the planning methods utilized in its production. The most detailed study of the measurement of China's national output during the 1950's was made by T. C. Liu and K. C. Yeh in their *The Economy of the Chinese Mainland: National Income and Economic Development 1933–1959* (Princeton Univ. Press, 1965), but other intensive investigations have been made by Alexander Eckstein and William Hollister.[21] Two recent compilations of research work—*An Economic Profile of Mainland China,* two volumes, Joint Economic Committee of the U.S. Congress (New York, Praeger, 1968), and *Economic Trends in Communist China* (A. Eckstein, T. C. Liu, and W. Galenson [eds.] Chicago, Aldine, 1968) contain many specialized studies of agriculture, industry, investment, foreign trade and aid, manpower and natural resources, money and banking, and taxation. The most comprehensive work on Communist China's economic institutions, which carries the story well into the 1960's, is that of the Britisher, Audrey Donnithorne, *China's Economic System*.

These four works contain most of what is now known in the West about China's economy, though there have, of course, been scores of other studies, mostly of an empirical nature, on specialized aspects of the economic process. Notable among these are Kang Chao, *The Construction Industry in Communist China* (Chicago, Aldine, 1968); Charles Hoffman, *Work Incentive Practices and Policies in the People's Republic of China 1953–1965* (Albany, State University of N.Y. Press, 1967); Y. L. Wu, *The Steel Industry in Communist China* (Stanford, Cal., Hoover Institution, 1965); Sidney Klein, *Politics versus Economics: The Foreign Trade and Aid Policies of China* (Hong Kong, International Study Group, 1968); George Ecklund, *Financing the Chinese Government Budget, Mainland China, 1950–1959* (Chicago, Aldine, 1966); Dwight Perkins, *Market Control and Planning in Communist China* (Cambridge, Mass., Harvard Univ. Press, 1966); and Alexander Eckstein, *Communist China's Economic Growth and Foreign Trade* (New York, McGraw-Hill, 1966). Since data on China's foreign trade in the 1960's can be gathered from most of her trading partners, this area of research has received a great amount of attention. Finally, a few Western economists have actually visited China in recent years and have returned with much information, but mainly of a qualitative nature.

B. CRITICISM OF ECONOMIC RESEARCH

ECONOMIC RESEARCH on China suffers from an ailment common to most of economics: a narrow empiricism. Thus, most of the research studies of the Chinese economy deal with very small segments of the development process, and within these tiny areas the researchers busy themselves with data series: adding up the numbers, adjusting them in numerous ways, deflating them for price changes, and doing a lot of other fussy statistical work. Each economist tills intensively his small plot, gaining highly specialized knowledge in the process, finally ending up an expert in his cramped quarters. There are not many economists in the China field who try to see Chinese economic development as a whole, as "the comprehensive totality of the historical process." If the truth is the whole, as Hegel claimed, most economic experts on China must be so far from the truth that it is hardly worthwhile listening to them.

Moreover, it is often painful. Even a casual reader of the economic research on Communist China cannot help but notice that many of the researchers are not happy—to say the least—with the object of their investigation. This catches one's attention right away because it is so very unusual in economics. Ordinarily economists are utterly fascinated and almost in love with their special areas of study—even with such an esoteric one as "Game Theory Applied to Non-linear Development." But not so our China experts! Indeed, it is quite apparent that many of them consider China to be, not The Beloved, but The Enemy. And in dealing with The Enemy, their research often reveals very strong biases against China.

These biases show up in a variety of ways, from such trivial things as changing Peking to Peiping (à la Dean Rusk), which reveals a wish that the Communists weren't there; to the frequent use of emotive words (e.g., the Communists are not dedicated but "obsessed"; leaders are "bosses"; a decision not to release data is described as "a sullen statistical silence"; the extension of the statistical system becomes "an extension of its tentacles farther into the economy"); to the attribution of rather sinister motives to ordinary economic and cultural policies (e.g., education and literacy are promoted for the purpose of spreading evil Marxian doctrines; economic development is pursued for the principal purpose of gaining military strength for geographical expansion— which is the theme of W. W. Rostow's book on *The Pros-*

pects for Communist China); to dire forecasts of imminent disaster which are based on little more than wishful thinking; to data manipulation of the most questionable sort.

This strong propensity to treat China as The Enemy has led, in my opinion, to some grossly distorted accounts of China's economic progress. The picture that is presented by these studies as a whole is one in which China, while making some progress for a time in certain areas, is just barely holding on to economic life. It is a picture of a China always close to famine, making little headway while the rest of the world moves ahead, being involved in irrational economic policies, and offering little reason for hope that the lives of her people will be improved. Our China experts, furthermore, know what is wrong, and that in a word is Communism. They seldom fail to pass judgment on some aspect or other of Chinese economic development, and this judgment is almost invariably capitalist-oriented. Thus, national planning and government-controlled prices cannot be good because they do not meet the criteria of consumer sovereignty and competitive markets; communes violate individualism and private property; ideological campaigns upset order and harmony; the de-emphasis on material incentives violates human nature and so reduces individual initiative and economic growth; the break-down of specialization lowers workers' productivity. This sort of thing pervades much of the economic literature on China.

Given all this—the narrow specialized studies that are sometimes useful but not often enlightening, the distortions by omission or commission, the capitalist-oriented approaches and assessments, not to mention those evaluations of Communist China that are inspired by a strong allegiance to Chiang Kai-shek—given all this, it is little wonder that a fair picture of China's economic progress seldom gets presented. Seldom, not never: Barry Richman's new book on *Industrial Society in Communist China* (New York, Random House, 1969), Carl Riskin's work, for example in *The Cultural Revolution 1967 in Review* (published by the China

Studies Center, University of Michigan, 1968), and several other research efforts are refreshingly objective, relatively free of capitalist cant, and approach Maoist economics and ideology in a serious way.

The truth is that China over the past two decades has made very remarkable economic advances (though not steadily) on almost all fronts. The basic, overriding economic fact about people in China is that for twenty years they have all been fed, clothed, and housed, have kept themselves healthy, and have educated most. Millions have *not* starved; sidewalks and streets have *not* been covered with multitudes of sleeping, begging, hungry, and illiterate human beings; millions are *not* disease-ridden. To find such deplorable conditions, one does not look to China these days but rather to India, Pakistan, and almost anywhere else in the under-developed world. These facts are so basic, so fundamentally important, that they completely dominate China's economic picture, even if one grants all of the erratic and irrational policies alleged by her numerous critics. The Chinese, all of them, now have what is in effect an insurance policy against pestilence, famine, and other disasters. In this respect, China has outperformed every underdeveloped country in the world; and, even with respect to the richest one, it would not be far-fetched to claim that there has been less malnutrition due to maldistribution of food in China over the past twenty years than there has been in the United States.[22]

If this comes close to the truth, the reason lies not in China's grain output far surpassing her population growth, for it has not, but rather in the development of institutions to distribute food evenly among the population. It is also true, however, that China has just had six consecutive bumper grain crops (wheat and rice) which have enabled her to reduce wheat imports and greatly increase rice exports. On top of this, there have been large gains in the supplies of eggs, vegetables, fruits, poultry, fish, and meat. In fact, China today exports more food than she imports. As I have indicated, the Chinese are in a much better position now than ever before to ward off natural disasters. There has been significant progress in irrigation, flood control, and water conservancy; the use of chemical fertilizers is increasing rapidly, the volume of which is now over ten times that of the early 1950's; there have been substantial gains in the output of tractors, pumps, and other farm implements; and much progress has been made in the control of plant disease and in crop breeding.

In education, there has been a major breakthrough. All urban children and a great majority of rural children have attended primary schools, and enrollments in secondary schools and in higher education are proportionately large compared with pre-Communist days. If "school" is extended in meaning to include these as well as part-time, part-study education, spare-time education, and study groups organized by the communes, factories, street organizations, the army; then there are schools everywhere in China; then China may be said to be just one great big school.

China's gains in the medical and public health fields are perhaps the most impressive of all. The gains are attested to by many recent visitors to China. For example, a Canadian doctor a few years ago visited medical colleges, hospitals, and research institutes, and everywhere he found good eqiupment, high medical standards, excellent medical care; almost all comparable to Canadian standards.[23] A member of the United States Public Health Service, a few years ago, stated that "the prevention and control of many infections and parasitic diseases which have ravaged [China] for generations" was a "most startling accomplishment." He noted, too, that "the improvement of general environmental sanitation and the practice of personal hygiene, both in the cities and in the rural areas, was also phenomenal."[24]

While all these gains were being made, the Chinese have devoted an unusually large amount of resources to industrial output. China's industrial production has risen on the average by at least 11 per cent per year since 1950, which is an exceptionally high growth rate for an underdeveloped country. And industrial progress is not likely to be retarded in the future by any lack of natural resources, for China is richly endowed and is right now one of the four top producers in the world of coal, iron ore, mercury, tin, tungsten, magnesite, salt, and antimony. In recent years, China has made large gains in the production of coal, iron and steel, chemical fertilizers, and oil. In fact, since the huge discoveries at the Tach'ing oil field, China is now self-sufficient in oil and has offered to export some to Japan.

From the industrial, agricultural, and other gains I have outlined, I would estimate that China's real GNP has risen on the average by at least 6 per cent per year since 1949, or by at least 4 per cent on a per capita basis. This may not seem high, but it is a little better than the Soviet Union did over a comparable period (1928–40), much better than England's record during her century of industrialization (1750–1850) when her income per capita grew at one-half of 1 per cent per year, perhaps a bit better than Japan's performance from 1878 to 1936, certainly much superior to France's 1 per cent record from 1800 to 1870, far better than India's 1.3 per cent growth during 1950 to 1967, and much superior to the post-war record of almost all underdeveloped countries in the world.

This is a picture of an economy richly endowed in natural resources, but whose people are still very poor, making substantial gains in industrialization, moving ahead more slowly in agriculture, raising education and health levels dramatically, turning out increasing numbers of scientists and engineers, expanding the volume of foreign trade and the variety of products traded, and making startling progress in the development of nuclear weapons. This is a truer picture, I believe, than the bleak one drawn by some of our China experts.[25]

The failure of many economic experts on China to tell the story of her economic development accurately and fully is bad enough. But even worse, I think, has been the general failure to deal with China on her own terms, within the framework of her own goals and methods for attaining those goals, or even to recognize the possible validity of those goals. Communist China is certainly not a paradise, but it is now engaged in perhaps the most interesting economic and social experiment ever attempted, in which tremendous efforts are being made to achieve an egalitarian development, an industrial development without dehumanization, one that involves everyone and affects everyone. But all those efforts seem not to have affected Western economists, who have proceeded with their income accounts and slide rules, and their free enterprise values, to measure and judge. One of the most revealing developments in the China field is the growing belief among the economic experts that further research is hardly worthwhile in view of the small amount of economic statistics that have come out of China since 1958. Apparently it does not matter that 775,000,000 people are involved in a gigantic endeavor to change their environment, their economic and social institutions, their standard of living, and themselves; that never before have such potentially important economic and social experiments been carried out; that voluminous discussions of these endeavors by the Maoists are easily available. No, if GNP data are not forthcoming, if numbers can't be added up and adjusted, then the economy is hardly worth bothering about!

V · SOME SUGGESTIONS AND CONCLUSIONS

WHAT CAN BE DONE? Probably not very much until a substantial number of younger economists become interested in China. It is a hopeful sign that many young economists are now breaking away from the stultifying atmosphere of present-day "neo-classical" economics and are trying to refashion the discipline (as it once was) into political economics, so as to take account of the actual world and not the world of highly abstract models, scholastic debates, and artificial assumptions—which all justify the existing state of things and accept, without question, the rather narrow, materialistic goals of capitalist society. This reformulation by the young will have to take place first, but once the task is well along, China is bound to be attractive to many of these "new" economists. Only then will we begin to get a substantial amount of research on China that makes sense.

The research that would make sense is any that takes Maoism seriously as a model of economic development, in terms both of its objectives and of the means employed to attain those objectives. A thoughtful consideration of Maoism means paying proper attention to Marxism-Leninism as well as to the Chinese past of the Maoists. The Maoists' Marxist-Leninist goal of the Communist man within a classless society in which each person works according to his ability and consumes according to his needs, should be taken seriously in any economic analysis of what is now going on.

I mentioned earlier, when discussing the core of development theory that would probably be accepted by both the capitalist and Maoist sides, that economic growth can be attained by increasing the amounts of labor, capital goods, and land used in production; by improving the quality of these factors of production; by combining them in more efficient ways and inspiring labor to greater efforts; and by taking advantage of economies of scale. Now, Maoism undoubtedly affects every one of these ingredients of economic growth, and often in ways quite different from the capitalist impact. For example, it is likely that Maoist ideology discourages consumption and encourages saving and investment, and so promotes the growth of the capital stock. It does this by preventing the rise of a high-consuming "middle class," by fostering the Maoist virtues of plain and simple living and devoting one's life to helping others rather than to accumulating "pots and pans."

As another example, it is possible that Maoist economic

development, by de-emphasizing labor specialization and reliance on experts and technicians, reduces the quality of the labor force and so slows the rate of economic growth. On the other hand, as Adam Smith once suggested, labor specialization, while increasing productivity in some narrow sense, is often instituted at the expense of the worker's general intelligence and understanding. For, "The man whose whole life is spent in performing a few simple operations . . . generally becomes as stupid and ignorant as it is possible for a human creature to become."[26] The difference between the most dissimilar of human beings, according to Smith, is not so much the cause of division of labor as it is the effect of it. Consequently, while an economy might gain from the division of labor in some small sense, it could lose in the larger sense of creating men who are little more than passive and unreasoning robots. A major aim of the Maoists is to transform man from this alienated state into a fully aware and participating member of society. The emphasis on "Reds" rather than experts is just one part of this transformation which, it is felt, will release "an atom bomb" of talents and energy and enable labor productivity to take great leaps.

In addition to this argument, which is based on Maoist interpretation of their own history and experience, particularly during the Yenan period,[27] it is also possible that the "universal man" in an underdeveloped economy would provide more flexibility to the economy. If most people could perform many jobs moderately well, manual and intellectual, urban and rural, the economy might be better able to cope with sudden and large changes; it could with little loss in efficiency mobilize its labor force for a variety of tasks. Further, since experience in one job carries over to others, a person may be almost as productive, in the job-proficiency sense, in any one of them as he would be if he specialized on it. A peasant who has spent some months in a factory can more easily repair farm equipment, and so on. Finally, a Maoist economy may generate more useful information than a specialist one and so lead to greater creativity and productivity. When each person is a narrow specialist, communication among people is not highly meaningful: your highly specialized knowledge means little to me in my work. When, on the other hand, each person has a basic knowledge of many lines of activity, the experiences of one person enrich the potentialities of many others.

The point is that this topic—which, I should stress, includes not only labor productivity, the development of material things by human beings, but also the development of human beings themselves—this topic of generalists vs. specialists, Reds vs. experts, the masses vs. bureaucrats, or whatever, is not a foolish concept to be laughed away, as it has been in effect by some China experts. How men, in an industrial society, should relate to machines and to each other in seeking happiness and real meaning in their lives has surely been one of the most important problems of the modern age. There is also another basic issue here: whether modern industrial society, capitalist or socialist, does in fact diminish man's essential powers, his capacity for growth in many dimensions, even though it does allocate him "efficiently" and increase his skills as a specialized input. Is man Lockean in nature, reactive to outside forces, adjusting passively to unbalancing forces from without? Or is he essentially Leibnitzian, the source of acts, active, capable of growth, and having an inner being that is self-propelled? If the latter, how are these powers released?

The Maoists claim that the powers exist and can be released. If they are right, the implications for economic development are so important that it would take a bunch of absolute dunces on this side of the Pacific to ignore them.

Notes

I should like to thank John Despres, Edward Friedman, and Mark Selden for answering my call for help.

1. This is always a main goal. However, two other goals of producing the "right" composition of goods and achieving an "equitable" distribution of income are often stipulated.

   A few of the better books on capitalist development are: Charles Kindleberger, *Economic Development;* Henry Bruton, *Principles of Development Economics;* Gerald Meier, *Leading Issues in Development Economics;* Albert Hirschman, *The Strategy of Economic Development;* and W. Arthur Lewis, *The Theory of Economic Growth.*

2. In recent years, capitalist economists have paid increasing attention to "investment in human capital." (See, for example, Gary Becker, *Human Capital.*) Although this might seem to represent a basic change in their concept of man in the development process, actually it does not. "Investment in human capital" means that economic resources are invested for the purpose of raising the educational, health, and skill levels of labor, not as an end in itself but as a means of increasing the productivity of labor. Thus, economists are concerned with the "payoff" to investment in human capital, this payoff being the profit that can be made from such an expenditure. Indeed, the very term "human capital" indicates what these economists have in mind: man is another capital good, an input in the productive engine that grinds out commodities; if one invests in man, he may become more productive and return a handsome profit to the investor—whether the investor is the State, a private capitalist, or the laborer himself. Thus, the preoccupation of capitalist economists is still with man as a means and not as an end.

3. This has been expressed by Maoists in many ways. As Mao Tse-tung has put it: "Of all things in the world, people are the most precious." ("The Bankruptcy of the Idealist Conception of History," in *Selected Works of Mao Tse-tung,* Vol. IV [Peking, Foreign Languages Press, 1961 & 1965], p. 454.) The *Peking Review* adds: "Whatever we do, we give prominence to the factor of man and put man at the centre" (November 11, 1966, pp. 19–20). And: "Chairman Mao's teaching to 'be resolute, fear no sacrifice and surmount every difficulty to win victory' means, in the last analysis, to give emphasis to the human factor." (*Ibid.*, March 17, 1967, p. 12.) With regard to national defense, Lin Piao has stated: "For our armed forces, the best weapon is not aircraft, heavy artillery, tanks or the atom bomb. It is Mao Tse-tung's thought. The greatest fighting power is the men who are armed with Mao Tse-tung's thought." (Quoted in *Peking Review*, March 17, 1967, pp. 12–13.) Mao has expressed the same idea: "Weapons are an

important factor in war, but not the decisive factor; it is people, not things, that are decisive." ("On Protracted War," in *Selected Works,* Vol. II, pp. 143–144.)

4. Mao Tse-tung, quoted in *Peking Review* (November 11, 1966), pp. 19–20.

5. *Peking Review* (December 23, 1966), p. 7.

6. For 3,000 years the Chinese have paid much more attention to human relations than to conquering nature. Mao Tse-tung, as a Chinese, *and* as a Marxist, cannot help but follow in this tradition. But, as a Chinese, he wishes to make China powerful in the eyes of the world, and, as a Marxist, through socialism. The world views power in terms of GNP and nuclear weapons, not in terms of perfection in human relations. So Mao has to go in both directions at the same time, and the two goals often conflict with one another, at least in the short run.

   This conflict was especially prominent in the latter half of the nineteenth century when some Chinese advocated using Western techniques but retaining Chinese culture and human relations. At that time and later, the adoption of Western techniques subverted Chinese culture. This conflict can perhaps be stated in terms of the "quantity of life" vs. the "quality of life."

   Mao, of course, does not wish to preserve the "old ways," but he is interested in "man" and in human relations in an industrial society. Thus, just like his nineteenth century predecessors, Mao is faced with the conflict between developing "good" human beings and attaining rapid economic development.

7. Mao Tse-tung follows Marxism-Leninism in adopting the world outlook of dialectical materialism, which is a philosophy of human and natural change and interaction. Changes in society, for example, according to Mao, are not due chiefly to external causes but instead to internal ones—to the internal contradictions between the productive forces and the relations of production, between classes, etc. There is internal contradiction in every single thing, and it is the development of the contradiction that gives rise to changes; eventually to qualitative changes. External causes by themselves could explain only changes in quantity or scale, but they could not explain qualitative or "leap" changes. "The development of things should be seen as their internal and necessary self-movement, while each thing in its movement is interrelated with and interacts on the things around it." (See Mao Tse-tung, "On Contradiction," *Selected Works,* Vol. I, p. 313.)

8. Mao Tse-tung, "Combat Liberalism," *Selected Works,* Vol. II, p. 31.

9. Mao Tse-tung, "On the Correct Handling of Contradictions Among the People," in *Quotations of Mao Tse-tung* (Peking, Foreign Languages Press, 1966), pp. 17–18.

10. *Peking Review* (March 10, 1967), p. 22.

11. Mao Tse-tung, "On Practice," *Selected Works*, Vol. I, pp. 299–300. Mao holds to the dialectical-materialist theory of knowledge, the theory of unity of knowing and doing—theory and practice. He believes that truth can be discovered by starting from perceptual knowledge, actively developing it into rational knowledge, and then going out into the world of revolutionary practice to test the knowledge. "Practice, knowledge, again practice, and again knowledge. This form repeats itself in endless cycles, and with each cycle the content of practice and knowledge rises to a higher level." *(Ibid.,* p. 308.)

12. *Peking Review* (February 24, 1967), p. 22.

13. Lenin implies that to reach the Marxian goal, "From each according to his ability, to each according to his needs," people will have to become selfless *and* highly productive. If each person is to take freely according to his needs, he cannot be selfish. If there is to be enough for everyone, people will have to be highly productive. The latter is achieved by active participation, by seeing and doing, by theory and practice. See V. I. Lenin, "The State and Revolution," in *Selected Works*, Vol. 2 (New York, International Publishers, 1967), pp. 340–41.

14. *Peking Review* (January 6, 1967), p. 13.

15. Marxian freedom is real knowledge of a subject, intelligent action. A free individual "is no longer history's pawn, no longer condemned by the blind mechanics of social and economic forces to the mere suffering of history, but one who is a maker of history, who, knowing the nature of these forces, becomes, by choice and action, a part of them, thus changing them, and changing, too, himself, thus guiding both along those paths where each may live its fullest fruitfulness and history become at last appropriate to the best that human nature can become." (Vernon Venable, *Human Nature: The Marxian View* (New York, Meridian Books, 1969), p. 204.)

16. *Peking Review* (December 23, 1966), p. 21.

17. Vernon Venable sums up the position of Marx and Engels on this point when he writes: "by forcing men into a specialization of function that becomes more and more narrow, less and less interesting, less and less inclusive of his various potentials of ability, it has had the effect of stunting him, dehumanizing him, reducing him to a mere fragment of a man, a crippled monstrosity, an appendage to a machine." (Venable, *Human Nature,* pp. 123–

24.) For further views by Marx on specialization, see *The Economic and Philosophic Manuscripts of 1844*, Struik (ed.) (New York International, 1964) pp. 110, 161; *Capital* (New York, Modern Library), pp. 397–98.

Marx saw a better day when each man could pursue not any one occupation but a variety of activities. Now a crippled fragment, man should become "the fully developed individual . . . to which the different social functions he performs are but so many modes of giving free scope to his own natural and acquired powers." (Marx, *Capital*, p. 534.)

18. Quoted in Maurice Meisner, *Ascetic Values and Utopian Goals in Chinese Communist Ideology* (Mimeo., May 1967), p. 76.

19. *Ibid.*, pp. 77–78.

20. This emphasis on man was expressed by Marx in many ways, including the following: "A critique of religion leads to the doctrine that the highest being for man is man himself, hence to the categorical imperative to overthrow all relationships in which man is humbled, enslaved, abandoned, despised." (Karl Marx, "Zur Kritik der Hegelschen Rechtsphilosophie," in Marx and Engels, *Der Historische Materialismus; Die Fruhschriften* Vol. I [Leipzig, Alfred Kroner Verlag, 1932], p. 272. Quoted in Alfred G. Meyer, *Marxism: The Unity of Theory and Practice* (Ann Arbor, Univ. of Michigan Press, 1963), p. 51.) Or, as Friedrich Engels saw man in the new society: "Man, at last the master of his own form of social organization, becomes at the same time the lord over nature, his own master—free." (Friedrich Engels, "Socialism, Utopian and Scientific," in W. O. Henderson [ed.], *Engels: Selected Writings* [Harmondsworth, Penguin, 1967], p. 225.) The aim of socialism, for Marx, was not the production of more things but the self-realization of man. It is easy to forget, Marx wrote, "that the production of too many useful things results in too many useless people." (Karl Marx, *The Economic and Philosophic Manuscripts of 1844*, p. 151.) This humanist strain, this dislike of anything that makes man a mere fragment of himself, runs through all of Marx's writings. "Marx is thoroughly and consistently humanist. A positive image of man, of what man might come to be, lies under every line of his analysis of what he held to be an inhuman society." (C. Wright Mills. *The Marxists* [New York, Dell, 1962], p. 25.)

21. Alexander Eckstein, *The National Income of Communist China* (New York, Free Press, 1962); William W. Hollister, *China's Gross National Product and Social Accounts, 1950–1957* (Glencoe, Free Press, 1958).

22. Much of the material in this paragraph was suggested by John

Despres, but he is not responsible for my interpretations of his remarks.

23. G. Leslie Willcox, "Observations on Medical Practices," *Bulletin of the Atomic Scientists* (June, 1966), p. 52. See also William Y. Chen, "Medicine and Public Health," in *Sciences in Communist China*, pp. 384, 397–99.

24. Chen, "Medicine and Public Health."

25. The above account of China's recent economic progress is largely taken from my testimony before the Joint Economic Committee. See *Mainland China in the World Economy, Hearings*, Joint Economic Committee, Washington, D.C., April 5, 10, 11 and 12, 1967, pp. 184–88.

26. Adam Smith, *The Wealth of Nations*, Book V, Ch. I, Part III.

27. See the essay in this volume by Mark Selden.

People's War and the Transformation of Peasant Society: China and Vietnam[1]

❦ Mark Selden

❦ THE CONTRIBUTIONS of the National Liberation Front of South Vietnam to the theory and practice of people's war rank among the most significant revolutionary developments of our era, yet, poring through the massive scholarly, journalistic, and official writings heralding or decrying American attempts to crush the Vietnamese resistance, one is struck by the void of information concerning the NLF and developments in the liberated areas. The enemy remains almost as elusive in the literature as is his shadowy presence in the jungles and swamps of South Vietnam. After more than a decade of fighting, the NLF is as "faceless," unknown, unfathomable as ever to the American people. Indeed, a careful search reveals not a single significant scholarly approach to the subject, not an article, no less a book.[2] In the absence of independent scholarship, the officially sanctioned work of Douglas Pike, an officer of the United States Information Service with long tenure in Vietnam has gone virtually unchallenged. Consider Pike's conclusion about the NLF:

> The social changes brought to the liberated area [of the National Liberation Front of South Vietnam] were perhaps more apparent than real. The NLF administrative liberation association was more manipulated than participational, and such an arrangement usually carries with it the seeds of its own doom. The great emphasis on communication of ideas failed to achieve its principal goal: The rural Vietnamese, lacking informational background, often failed to understand in context the meaning of the message. The rural Vietnamese

knew little about the social forces loose in his country and even less about the outside world, and he greeted NLF efforts to remedy this deficiency with indifference—the condition of parochialism in which the next village is in the other world dies hard in Asia. Finally, the effort mounted by the NLF required a type of cadre—talented, skilled, dedicated, an almost superhuman person—that did not exist in sufficient numbers to ensure success.

Yet the principles involved remain intact. The deeper one plunged into the study of the NLF the stronger became the feeling of being on the edge of a future social morass, only dimly seen. Here one felt was tomorrow's society, the beginning of 1984, when peace is war, slavery is freedom, the non-organization is the organization.[3]

If Pike's volume obscures more than it reveals of the dynamic of a movement which has successfully resisted the juggernaut of American military power, it is extremely illuminating of pervasive American attitudes toward revolutionary change. To be sure, Pike is more outspoken and explicit than many social scientists. Yet his premises are widely shared not only by scholars and officials, but by the media and the public as well. These premises may be summarized as follows: The power of mass nationalist movements rests primarily on their manipulative qualities including a large component of terror, and on the ruthless application of Leninist organizational skills. Placing a low value on human life, power considerations alone control the calculus of revolutionary leadership. This unbridled hostility toward radical and nationalist movements provides one ideological source of American military involvement in Vietnam and throughout the world.

Terror and organization are not the only weapons attributed by American officials and social scientists to revolutionary nationalists. As Chalmers Johnson has argued in his influential study of the Chinese Communist resistance, insurgent movements may be created and legitimized by an unexpected ally—the foreign invader. In this view, the Japanese invasion of 1937 destroyed indigenous Chinese leadership (the Kuomintang and the warlords) and created a leadership vacuum. Moreover, the brutality and dislocation produced by the onslaught of the invasion inadvertently mobilized the peasant population for resistance. The conclusion is inescapable: Neither the creativity nor the dedication of the resistance, but above all the windfall of peasant nationalism springing from war-induced crisis lies behind the success of revolutionary nationalist movements.[4]

An important corollary to these perspectives is the belief that the mobilization approaches characteristic of liberation wars impede the post-independence progress of transforming peasant societies into developing nation states. John Lewis, discussing the revolutionary legacy in Chinese society gives forceful expression to the dominant view:

> The militant preservation of the revolutionary mass line progressively alienated party leaders from the postrevolutionary realities of the Chinese state. Moreover, the process of alienation continues as Communist leaders equate current struggles for economic construction with the pre-1949 revolutionary military struggle. Reasoning by analogy, they stipulate that what worked as a leadership system in Yenan must be equally effective for the same leaders a decade or so later in Peking. Believing that the mass line method must "represent the interests of the masses," Communist cadres have underestimated and misunderstood the deterioration of popular morale and support. Dissatisfied with exhortation without positive economic effects, harried peasants and workers have become listless and sullen according to many reliable but unconfirmed reports.[5]

This latter perspective, endorsed by scholars across the entire political and disciplinary spectrum, represents a fundamental article of faith of contemporary Western man: faith that the developmental process is a product of rational evolution directed and controlled by a technological-managerial elite. In the emphasis on the critical role of technology, Weberians and Bolsheviks, the high priests of private enterprise and their counterparts among socialist planners, concur perfectly. And indeed, examination of the major historical models of industrializing societies—from England and Germany to the United States, Russia, and Japan—does suggest the importance of new business-managerial elites in channeling resources and skills from agriculture into the most advanced industrial channels. In this respect revolutionary and gradualist approaches need not diverge; technocratic liberalism and Bolshevism lead down converging paths.

We need not concern ourselves here with the abuses of "modernization" theory as a cynical cover for the perpetuation of neo-colonial domination and what Andre Gunder Frank calls "the development of underdevelopment." But let us be blunt about the human costs implicit in these elitist approaches to industrialization even at their most successful. In the process the populace is deliberately subordinated to the imperatives of the machine, generations are sacrificed for the future fruits of industrialization, and a new elite, the professional manipulators of advanced technology, is created. Moreover, a common side effect of the process, particularly under capitalist auspices, has been the perpetuation of endemic pockets of poverty amidst plenty, their residents overwhelmed by the challenges of a new order. Are there alternative routes to development which are less costly in human terms?

The thesis of this essay is as follows: Out of the ashes of military strife which enveloped China and Vietnam in protracted wars of liberation emerged a radically new vision of man and society and a concrete approach to development. Built on foundations of participation and community action which challenge elite domination, this approach offers hope of more *humane* forms of development and of effectively overcoming the formidable barriers to the transformation of peasant societies. In the base areas and consolidated war zones in which the movement enjoyed its fullest growth, the redefinition of community began in the resistance to a foreign invader and continued in the struggle to overcome domestic problems of poverty and oppression. People's war implies more than a popular guerrilla struggle for national independence; it impinges directly and with profoundly revolutionary consequences on the full scope of rural life. In the course of people's war, local communities defined in response to the imperatives of defense and social change may be effectively integrated in national movements. The very intensity of the war-time experience contributes to rapid development of consciousness and organization. In people's war peasants cease to be the passive pawns of landlords and officials or to fatalistically accept the verdict of a harsh natural environment. Where the primary resource of insurgent movements is man, and where active commitment is the *sine qua non* of success, the sharing of common hardships and hopes creates powerful bonds among peasant resisters and between leaders and led. In the new institutions which emerge locally in the course of the resistance, to an unprecedented degree peasants begin to secure active control of their economic and political destinies.

Partisan leadership does not merely fill a vacuum created by the flight or demise of the landlord-official class. Nor does it achieve victory by reaping the grim rewards of terror, for it can never match the ruthlessness of the "official terror" instituted by foreign forces and their puppets. Rather, at its best, it forges new bonds of unity in which the very definitions of leader and led are recast and the beginnings of a new social basis are created. In China I call this the Yenan Way after the war-time capital of the movement. The same spirit infuses the Vietnamese resistance. In the embryonic social forms created under wartime duress are important features relevant to the future of the Third World, and indeed, to possibilities for participatory social patterns everywhere.

Let us begin with China, whose war of liberation may well provide the primary revolutionary model for the second half of the twentieth century. The starting point of this analysis—one which applies equally to Vietnam and much of the Third World—is the firm rejection of idealized images of the family and village which have permeated both the literature and popular perceptions. Samuel Popkin has referred to this as the

> "myth of the village." Peasants who have no material rewards are assumed to have spiritual rewards. When a son sticks to his father for the sake of survival, it is called filial piety. . . . Somehow the necessities and/or oppressions of one era seem to have become the traditional values of the next.[6]

The poverty and exploitation in which most peasants lived even in the best of times were the central features of Chinese rural life. Built into well-articulated patterns of authority and submission were the unquestioned domination of the rich over the poor, the aged over youth, and men over women.

Yet the system, when it was functioning effectively, was not without its compensations, principally the security provided within the context of family and village, and the community of interests shared by the most humble villager and leading members of the local elite, the gentry. For if gentry were exploiters in their roles as landlords and money-lenders, and if, in the final analysis, they relied on state military power to protect their interests from the challenge of rebellious peasants, they were nevertheless united with the people in the desire to minimize government incursions on the village. The legitimation of gentry prerogatives rested primarily on their intermediary role as representative of local interests in dealing with a remote government whose primary concern was the efficient collection of taxes and the stability which that necessitated.

This balance was shattered in the chaos of the late nineteenth and early twentieth century. The demise of imperial authority undermined the aura of gentry legitimacy provided by Confucian sanction. Effective performance of brokerage roles was transformed and increasingly defined by local military force. Simultaneously the exploitative functions of the local elite were intensified and brought into public purview. First, in the absence of effective imperial rule, social control, that is the repression of rebellious peasants, fell directly to landlords and their private armies. In the absence of central authority, landlords sponsored local military forces to protect their interests. Second, particularly in South China, the development of absentee landlordism throughout the Ch'ing period (1644–1911) eliminated the social basis for a landlord-peasant community of interests. Increasingly to be found living in luxury in the towns and cities, the most prosperous of the gentry had become landlords pure and simple. Physically cut off from the village, increasingly their interest in local affairs was limited to ensuring the efficient flow of rents into the family coffers. Tensions between landlords and tenants were thus sharpened at a time when rural misery and dislocation were rising sharply.

If mounting absentee landlordism and the decline of central authority in a century of ruinous war stripped the gentry of its cloak of legitimacy, the result was no "vacuum" of leadership but rather a new power mix. Insurgents did not ineluctably replace imperial-gentry control; where they succeeded in seizing power it was only in the course of bitter struggle against entrenched interests. If the landlord-warlord local leadership of the twentieth century lacked the sanctions of time and Confucian tradition, it nevertheless offered a formidable challenge to would-be revolutionaries. At the same time, the military and political patterns which emerged out of dynastic decline, warlord ravages and foreign incursion did create and redefine opportunities for insurgents in rural China.

The proliferation of private military power included both the "legitimate" armies of landlords and warlords, and bandits roaming the hills. Both of them sapped the overstrained resources of the peasantry and both contributed to the militarization of Chinese society. The extraordinary human toll of a century of warlordism has been well analyzed in numerous studies of the era. Two tendencies seem particularly relevant to the future development of the resistance. One was the expansion of peasant horizons beyond the village or local marketing community as a result of participation in military forces, whether bandit, secret society, or official. The result was to define a defense community, to create a network of extended relationships which were vital to peasant welfare. Second, a century of military upheaval placed a premium on youthful, vigorous leadership which contrasts sharply with the mandarin style of high traditional society. In particular the military expanded opportunities for attaining power among the sons of the poor. These developments, the creation of defense communities and increasing reliance on the energies of youth and the poor, would be furthered by the war-time insurgent movement which attempted to redirect their thrust for new social and national purposes.

The critical problem confronting Communist leadership in 1937 on the eve of all-out war with Japan was this: How can a small and weak army of committed revolutionaries build a movement to resist the aggressive designs of an advanced industrial power? If the experience of guerrilla warfare during the preceding decade of civil war and land revolution provided a legacy of experience, the sobering fact was that the movement had recently been crushed and the party nearly annihilated by Kuomintang and warlord armies united if only in their opposition to social revolution. Forced by 1934 to abandon its major base areas in South and Central China, surviving Communist forces had regrouped at the conclusion of the Long March in China's remote and desolate northwest.

The Japanese invasion of 1937 posed new problems and possibilities. In place of the class war which had centered on the struggle for land, the party attempted to spearhead a *national* movement, uniting the broadest possible spectrum of Chinese in defense against foreign conquest. If that were all, there would be little to distinguish the Chi-

nese Communist movement from its counterparts strug-
gling for liberation from colonial domination throughout
the Third World, and indeed, such an explanation is
inadequate to grasp the dynamics of the wartime movement.[7] For if the Communists were not *simply* agrarian
reformers, and if radical land revolution was temporarily
shelved, their ability to respond boldly and effectively to
war-aggravated problems of rural society lies at the heart of
their extraordinary popular success during the resistance.
The response to their appeal to the peasant must be understood in the context of a comprehensive and imaginative
program of rural leadership and reform. Nationalism
generated peasant support for the resistance only in the
context of a reform program in which the peasants as a
group actively participated in the effort to resolve over
whelming social, economic, and security problems endemic
in late Ch'ing and warlord China and aggravated by the
Japanese onslaught. The new nationalism in the countryside and the commitment to engage in guerrilla resistance
are inseparable from the movement's penetration and revitalization of basic elements of the shattered social and
economic life of the village. Both in areas where local pow-
er-holders had fled either the Japanese or the Communists,
and in those in which they chose to cooperate with Com-
munist-sponsored governments, the political monopoly of
the landlord elite was challenged. For the first time the
peasantry as a group was integrated into the political process and involved in new social and economic relationships
leading to the restructuring of village life.

This point is critical in understanding the failure of the
Kuomintang to reap the nationalist benefits which accrued
from foreign invasion. The Kuomintang, as the wielder
of central government power, did mobilize substantial elite
nationalist support behind it in the early war years. Indeed,
it was primarily in terms of nationalist appeals to resist the
Japanese invader that the Kuomintang and Communists
vied for support of the rural and urban elite, including

student youth, the hotbed of twentieth-century Chinese nationalism. Such appeals, however, fell on deaf ears when directed to the peasantry. From the perspective of the Kuomintang ruling power, in the face of overwhelmingly superior invading armies and a major insurgent challenge from the Communist-led resistance, active popular support became essential for preserving the power. Neither astuteness in the manipulations of warlord and landlord coalitions, nor modernized, German-trained regular armies— basic ingredients of a decade of Kuomintang hegemony —sufficed under these circumstances. By 1938, driven from urban and coastal areas which had provided the bulwark of its strength, the Kuomintang proved helpless to secure control of the countryside.

The Kuomintang failure to confront the awesome problems of peasant misery, and its related inability to mobilize peasant support for the resistance should be viewed in the perspective of a familiar Third World problem. The Kuomintang approach exemplifies many of the major obstacles to transformation of peasant societies by "military modernizers" or other elite groups cut off despite nationalistic proclivities by training, experience, and world view from the vast majority of their people. It was not merely Kuomintang stubbornness, stupidity, or blindness (any more than it is in analogous instances in Vietnam, Thailand, Laos, and much of Latin America) which posed an obstacle in this regard. We are confronting rather a fundamental *structural* barrier implicit in the constitution of these elites. Firmly committed by power considerations as well as ideological predisposition to support of landlord hegemony, the Kuomintang was incapable of leading a popular movement which could withstand the onslaught of repeated Japanese attack and provide a base for resistance. In the final analysis the Kuomintang had little to offer the peasantry except the theft of grain, brutal seizure of young sons to man the armies of the status quo, and nationalist rhetoric which proved meaningless in the absence of a social program—in short, hunger, death, and empty words.

In attempting to lead the war-time resistance, Communist leadership faced a dilemma. On the one hand the party sought to construct a broad united front including former class enemies—landlords, rich peasants, and the bourgeoisie, linked by a common spirit of anti-Japanese nationalism. On the other its strength rested primarily on peasant support. In the interest of national unity the frontal attack on the landlord class was replaced in 1937 with a program to "reduce rent and interest" whose principal features were a rent ceiling of 37.5 per cent and reduction of all rents by 25 per cent. The critical question was whether a rent reduction movement which preserved certain landlord rights and eschewed violence could stimulate the deep peasant commitment frequently produced by the radical land upheaval of the preceding decade.

In the early 1940's, facing crippling Japanese offensives and growing tensions within the united front, rent reduction was widely and effectively implemented in the Communist-led base areas. Developed as a mass movement at the village level rather than as a routine administrative undertaking, rent reduction campaigns assumed many features of the radical movement which swept away the landlord order after 1946; the basic psychological problem in both cases was to overcome deep-seated peasant fears of landlord reprisal. In rent reduction campaigns, the goal was a direct personal challenge of landlord excesses by every peasant. At this time it was the *excesses* of the landlord system, not the system itself, which was being challenged. Rent reduction directives thus called for mass participation in curbing landlord prerogatives, while insisting on the united front principle that reduced rents continue to flow into landlord coffers. Peasants could not anticipate the total destruction of the system, the exhilarating liberation from landlord rule (*fanshen*) which was the hallmark of the later land reform.[8]

Under these circumstances, building an effective mass movement on the basis of rent reduction presented formidable difficulties. The key lay in the creation of powerful peasant associations to confront recalcitrant landlords and to provide a focus for the subsequent protection, indeed the fundamental redefinition, of peasant interests. Group consciousness and support developed through the peasant associations were crucial for allaying fears and stirring a spirit of militancy. A critical step came as peasant associations became powerful enough to guarantee tenant rights to cultivate the land and enjoin landlords from arbitrarily repossessing their land. Thus a potential threat to peasant activists was eliminated. Yet the problems were peculiarly tenacious. There are numerous accounts of peasants vigorously denouncing landlord exploitation by day only to make supplemental rental payments secretly at night. Old attitudes, fears, and insecurity did not die quickly under these circumstances. Nevertheless, the cumulative effect is clear: these campaigns provided a focus for peasant activism and release from subordination to a landlord elite. Peasant associations which spearheaded the movement became the locus of peasant power and participation, providing an effective counterweight to landlord domination. Moreover, nationalist appeals were frequently integrally related with the effort to curb landlord power. Where landlords were linked in active complicity with the Japanese, by no means an uncommon occurrence, they became the object of anti-traitor struggle movements, and their lands were subject to outright confiscation. Thus the rent reduction movement was carried to its logical conclusion in the case of landlord traitors.[9]

Rent reduction was an integral part of the drive to simultaneously liberate the peasantry and stimulate the economy, to strengthen the resistance movement, and to improve conditions of rural life. By 1941, facing critical supply problems in the face of blockade and intense repression, primitive efforts at economic development became an integral part of war-time mobilization. The creation of fraternity rather than hostility between cadres and peasants lay at the root of the problem of strengthening the resistance. It also opened avenues to stimulating the economy through the introduction of new ideas and techniques from outside the village and by experimentation within. Indeed it was in the heat of the resistance struggle that distinctive Chinese approaches to development emerged: emphasis on the paramount role of human labor and popular creativity in the absence of financial and technological resources, self-sufficiency, decentralization, and community planning. It was believed that the prospect of increased rewards realized through the rent reduction movement would stimulate the peasant's "productive enthusiasm" with positive effects on over-all output. But the task of overcoming poverty and agrarian stagnation was not left to individual enthusiasm alone. The key lay in the coordination and stimulation of fragmented and idle resources. Cooperative farming was initiated as the focus of a new village economy and a new society.

The cooperatives which spread throughout the base areas in the final years of the resistance war signified a major innovation in the approach to rural problems. Building on peasant leadership manifested in the course of guerrilla resistance and rent reduction, the cooperatives marked the first effort to create indigenous organization embedded in the economic life of the village. Cooperatives redirected peasant economic concerns from their narrow focus on the family to the larger unit of the mutual-aid group and the village itself. They also served to unify and strengthen the village as an economic and social unit, integrating it in the effort to link the resistance with new approaches to economic development throughout the base areas.

In other respects the cooperative movement marked the Party's most ambitious approach to the peasant. In contrast to movements for land redistribution or rent reduction, which had appealed by the most direct means to the needs and desires of the poor, cooperatives were unfamiliar to many peasants. Moreover they offered few immediate financial benefits, and required sustained leadership and broad commitment. In the long run, success was predicated on the creation of effective local leadership committed to cooperative principles of community and economic development. Yet unless mutual aid rapidly increased production, no amount of adept leadership could overcome peasant skepticism and resistance. Basic cooperative principles such as flexibility in adapting to local variations, decentralization, and sharply limiting the size of productive units were astutely tailored to the possibilities for organization and participation in war-time base areas. If the cooperatives were to succeed, if self-perpetuating communities committed to human and economic development were to emerge out of the chaos of war and disintegration, these principles were essential. In the numerous areas in which mutual aid successfully took root, it defined effective community channels to challenge peasant particularism, led to a basic restructuring of village economic patterns and enhanced possibilities for sustained development.

The cooperative unit was in fact a microcosm of the society envisioned by war-time leadership, embodying not only a promethean vision of man actively striving to control nature, but confronting the full scope of rural problems. In addition to their basic economic functions, cooperatives also served as guerrilla units engaging in raids and combat-support operations; they provided a focus for part-time education, education linked closely with concrete problems of war, the economy, and rural society; and they represented as well an autonomous and participatory political unit which continuously addressed itself to local grievances. Above all, cooperatives embodied the resistance spirit of sharing and self-sacrifice. Mao Tse-tung's war-time slogan captures well the simple but powerful cooperatives spirit:

> Those who have labor give labor; those who have much give much; those who have little give little; human and animal

power are put together. Thus one can avoid violating the seasons, and is able to plow in time, sow in time, hoe in time, and harvest in time.[10]

The war-time cooperatives thus embodied basic principles subsequently developed after 1958 in the commune movement. These principles, above all the emphasis on local community organization, popular creativity, and self-reliance rather than state and bureaucratic management, would constitute the heart of the Chinese challenge to Soviet practice.

The inauguration of the cooperative movement sharply posed the problem of relationships between leadership committed to radical social transformation and the peasantry. As the anthropologist, Eric Wolf, has suggested:

> In peaceful times revolutionary leaders may scour the countryside in attempts to "go to the people." . . . Yet all too frequently they still do so as outsiders, as people city-bred and city-trained, drawing their behavior patterns and cultural idioms from the dominant sector. . . . These behavior patterns and cultural idioms they must first unlearn, if they are to enter into successful contact with the peasant rebels.

What is critical, Wolf notes, is the development of

> a complex dialogue with the villagers in which the outsider learns as much, if not more about local organization and criteria of relevance, than the local inhabitants. Guerrilla warfare both speeds and deepens this learning as cadre and peasant activists synchronize their behavior and translate from one cultural idiom to the other.[11]

Preoccupation with problems of a leadership effectively integrated with the peasantry resulted in the party's first major rectification movement (*cheng-feng*) in the years 1942–44 and, simultaneously, its initial experiments in sending cadres and students to serve in the villages (*hsia-fang*) as a step toward overcoming the problems of elitist bureaucratic leadership and rural isolation. The mobilization style of leadership in the base areas required forging new relationships of solidarity between leaders and led, critical for waging a successful guerrilla struggle. As Jack Belden observed following an extensive tour of the base areas:

> . . . guerrilla warfare, which often brought the Communist cadre into the peasant's hut seeking refuge, has developed in the farmer a new sense of nearness and familiarity with government. Government has become something close to earth that the peasant can touch, shake by the hand or even slap in the face. Gone are its external trappings, the awe-inspiring uniforms, the fur-lined silk gowns of the officials, the men bearing arms before austere yamen gates. In the villages the officials dress in cotton jackets and pants like peasants, they talk like peasants, live like peasants. They are mainly peasants. There is nothing about them to distinguish them from anyone else. Nor are they any longer addressed as Officer, Old Master, or even Elder Born. Why should they be? They were elevated to office by the votes of the peasants themselves.[12]

The solidarity forged in the guerrilla movement, in the attack on rural oppression and economic stagnation, and in new popular forms of culture and education, was the hallmark of the resistance. Its success was predicated on transforming hierarchical patterns of leadership into firm egalitarian bonds constantly renewed in the struggle against the foreign enemy and the struggle against injustices of rural life.[13] These same principles have been affirmed and developed in the course of the resistance to American forces in South Vietnam.

NLF success is rooted in nationalism linked to a creative response to Vietnamese rural problems. Mounting peasant misery during recent decades is the product of the French colonial legacy, the ravages of war, and mounting scarcity of land. The closure of the delta as a frontier in the early 1930's marked the beginning of a steady downward spiral in peasant income and welfare which brought millions to the verge of subsistence. By the 1950's more than 80 per cent of the delta's population and 60 per cent of all peasants in South Vietnam were tenants. Over 7,000,000 delta tenants and hired laborers owned no land whatsoever and millions more possessed but a fraction of that required to feed their families. With increasing competition for the land, tenants faced rising rents, generally in the realm of 40–60 per cent of the crop, while rural wages declined. Throughout the decades after 1930 French and Vietnamese absentee landlordism rose steadily and agricultural productivity remained stagnant.[14] Writing in 1959 of South Vietnam's land problems, an American land reform adviser observed that

> substantial concentration of ownership has taken place in the last two decades. The area held by individuals owning more than 100 hectares has climbed from 733,800 to 1,076,000 hectares, while the absolute number of such large owners has remained approximately the same. Where one percent of the owners held 36 percent of the total rice land in 1934, they now own 44 percent of the total.[15]

The Vietnamese rural economy thus presented a stark picture of spiraling tenancy, land concentration, absentee ownership, rising rents, and declining rural wages.[16]

The NLF was quick to address itself to South Vietnam's rural crisis, always, however, in the context of the struggle against foreign domination. Indeed, NLF land policy reflects the tension between its primary commitment to liberation from American domination as a *national* movement, and the *class* effort to strengthen peasant-based resistance through land reform. Readjustments of land inequities were evaluated in light of their potential effect on the resistance.

> If we have to settle cases of restoring ownership to original owners, we should rely upon their enemy-opposing achievements in reaching a decision: only those who have scored exploits in the struggle against the enemies will be given back land.[17]

In all cases the NLF emphasized increasing village solidarity based on broad acceptance of the justice of the land redistribution. The same document lays out the complex ground rules for land reform:

The immediate duty for the time being is to carry out national union, to struggle determinedly against the war-waging and aggressive imperialists, and to overthrow the Ngo Dinh Diem ruling clique. Hence, in the land problem at present, one should on the one hand wrest back land that the peasants had gotten during resistance, limit exploitation by landlords, improve the peasant's life, and intensify solidarity among the laboring peasants' ranks, and on the other hand, continue to recognize ownership rights of landlords (with the exception of the tyrannical clique of U.S.-Diemist henchmen), recognize the right of landlords to collect land rent at a determined rate. In the countryside, our tactics at present are: solidarity between landless, poor and middle peasants, alliance with rich peasants, classification of the landlord class, winning over elements more-or-less opposing the U.S.-Diemists, neutralizing half-way elements and toppling the tyrannical clique presently serving as U.S.-Diemist lackeys.

Two basic approaches have been characteristic of NLF land policy. First, as in the analogous Chinese case, was the reduction of rent. Peasants rose to reduce landlord exactions which frequently exceeded half the crop. Characteristically, the NLF offered no uniform national guidelines as to the appropriate rent levels—these were to be decided in each area on the basis of local conditions. However, a maximum rate of 15 per cent, a mere fraction of prevailing exactions, was enforced in many areas.[18] Although the landlord system was to be preserved through the continued payment of rents, heavy emphasis was placed on restricting landlord prerogatives. A significant step lay in providing safeguards for tenants against the loss of land they were cultivating.

But in many areas NLF land policy followed a second and more radical course. Particularly where the earlier Viet Minh land reform was reversed after 1954 by the Diemist restoration of landlord power, "land to the tiller" was again proclaimed. Property which had been seized by landlords was redistributed to the peasants. In addition, communal lands and the property of traitors were expropriated and redistributed. In some cases peasants received temporary rights to cultivate the land rent-free.[19]

The importance of land policy, and its integral relationship with the anti-American struggle, are vividly articulated in a widely quoted document tracing the development of the resistance in a village in Kien Phong province. After repeated failures, the report relates how the first major inroads were made in this village:

> We awoke the people to the fact that if the American-Diem clique succeeded in permanently maintaining the organization of village notables and security, soon Mister H, the cruel landlord, and others would return to the village to seize land and collect back rent. For that reason, we said, the farmers must eliminate the influence of the village notables and sweep away the security agents. . . .
>
> As I have noted, the main interest of the farmer of XB village is in land. . . . In its political and armed struggle, in its administration of the rural area, and in other revolutionary tasks, the Party knew well how to make use of the farmers' interest in land. On it we built a mass movement. And for that reason the revolutionary movement made great progress and resulted in a great success.[20]

The NLF was not alone in viewing resolution of the land problem as a key to military victory. From the time of its intervention in Vietnam the United States has also insisted that land reform held the key to the creation of a viable government capable of resisting the inroads of insurgent movements. Wolf Ladejinsky, mastermind behind the American-sponsored agrarian reform effort in Japan and other Asian countries, as adviser to President Diem, was instrumental in introducing similar measures in South Vietnam. Since the inauguration of Diem's land reform program in 1956, American officials have continued to prod reluctant Saigon regimes to carry through land reform as the centerpiece of a program to reassert control in the countryside.[21]

Ironically, both the Diem land reform and the accompanying pacification program centering on strategic hamlets, created new opportunities for the NLF to strengthen the resistance on the twin pillars of nationalism and agrarian reform. Diem's land reform, leaving untouched the entire central region (his personal power base), was limited to the delta where large estates and absentee landlords dominated the rice economy. The land reform laws designated all estates exceeding 100 hectares for government purchase and sale to occupying tenants. Yet in practice, the amount of land which actually found its way into the possession of these former tenants represented but a small fraction of the total land legally subject to redistribution. As Bernard Fall observed, "after nearly two years of the reform program only 35,700 hectares had been transferred to 18,000 farmers."[22] Diem's land reform did nothing to alter landlord domination as the central fact of South Vietnamese rural life. The overwhelming number of landless farmers and tenants were completely bypassed by it. As one American expert put it with classic understatement:

> Any real crash program would be hotly resented in Saigon, and it would be resisted locally by the province and district chiefs whose principal sources of support remain the landlords and other wealthy classes.[23]

However, to focus discussion of the land reform on such shortcomings is to miss its real significance. In many areas it served primarily to provide the cover for wresting land from the poor and restoring it to former landlords. The American-sponsored land reform was carried out primarily in areas where the Viet Minh had earlier spearheaded a successful movement to give land to the poor and landless. The return of the Diem government meant that many who had been cultivating the land for a decade as *de facto* owners suddenly were forced to pay rent—frequently collected for a fee at gunpoint by government soldiers or officials—or they were "permitted" to purchase the land they had regarded as their own.[24] In striking contrast to

Viet Minh and NLF programs, the reform was limited exclusively to tenants on large estates. Since they alone were eligible to purchase expropriated land, the great majority of the landless and the land poor were excluded from all benefits. Moreover, even where the letter of the law was scrupulously obeyed, the Diem land reform left unchallenged the economic and political supremacy of the large landlords. Retaining the legal maximum of 100 hectares after the reform, they continued to enjoy the overpowering wealth and position to ensure the subordination of local peasants including the new purchasers of small plots of land. In short, Diem's reform bolstered the power of the landlord class, did little to assist the landless and the poor, and added new antagonisms to the festering problems of village life, antagonisms to which, as we have observed, the NLF program vigorously addressed itself.[25]

The strategic hamlet conception, implemented simultaneously with Diem's land reform, while theoretically potent from a military perspective, in practice created new avenues for the resistance to transcend class and unite all villagers. The strategic hamlets, similar to Japanese programs in Manchuria and China, were explicitly modeled on British experience in Malaya. The goal was to destroy existing scattered hamlets and herd the entire local population into camps surrounded by barbed wire in an effort to control the population, to separate the fish from the water, the people from the resistance.[26] The strategic hamlet program did take a heavy toll in Vietnamese lives. At the same time, by all accounts, the destruction of their homes and farms and forced regroupment in concentration camps under horrendous conditions provoked outrage among virtually everyone involved. An NLF report captures well the negative and unintended mobilization effect of this approach on the local population:

The creation of "prosperity centres" ushered in a new stage of the rural masses' struggle. Now, it was no longer the poor peasants alone who saw their interests threatened, nor only former resistance members who risked at any moment, being arrested, tortured, and summarily executed. The rural population as a whole, poor or rich, opponent or neutralist, and even supporters of the regime, also suffered.[27]

As in the Japanese onslaught in rural China, such policies linked with brutal repression dramatized the message of the resistance to the entire population. Frequently middle and rich peasants, least susceptible to appeals of the Front on class issues, suffered the greatest losses in the strategic hamlet program and became NLF partisans.[28]

Where a resistance movement successfully links the war effort to an attack on the problems of the disintegration and oppression of village life, the combination is a potent one. The slogan, "plow in one hand, rifle in the other," implies something beyond a contemporary Asian version of the American Revolution's minute man.[29] It symbolizes the commitment to a vision of national liberation which goes beyond repelling foreign invasion to elimination of economic stagnation and social repression. The implications of the combat villages, the NLF's response to Diem's strategic hamlets, transcended military concerns:

> To set up a strong struggling village is to defend the people's life and livelihood, to preserve the human, material and financial strength for the Revolution and realistically push forward the armed struggle.[30]

To be successful, the institutions of the resistance had also to fulfill the economic and political needs of the community.

Land reform marked the initial and key phase in the effort to redefine the economic life of the village. However, closely integrated with it were other approaches suggestive of the dimensions of a new society emerging in NLF areas. The major principles of cooperative farming—self-sufficiency, self-determination and community organization—were applied not only to production but to guerrilla activity and local politics, indeed to all facets of the rural program.

An NLF document of late 1968 describing activities in Binh Dinh province, for instance, states that

> The acceleration of production work should go hand in hand with the development of labor mutual assistance cells in order to ensure a rational utilization of manpower to serve both production work and the front line. . . .
>
> In the lowland, work exchange cells and production cells should be organized by the Farmers' Association. In the mountainous areas, cells should be established to provide labor mutual support and to guide and help one another in production work.[31]

Building on a spirit of cooperation and on expanded consciousness growing out of the resistance and anti-landlord struggles, agricultural cooperation carried these principles to the economic heart of village life.

Simultaneously self-sufficiency and self-determination were emphasized as root principles of the political and economic life of the village in the face of mounting problems posed by American destruction of crops:

> . . . the present production mission is to motivate the entire party, army and people to develop a self-sufficient spirit and to strictly implement the two-step, three-prong tactics, increase and protect production, and practice economy to quickly augment the food stock.[32]

This meant not only development of new organizational forms such as cooperatives, but involvement of the entire population, including soldiers, administrative officials and students, in production. The immediate goal was the achievement of self-sufficiency for their units or organizations and reducing the tax burden on the rural population. But here again, broader aims were involved: the breakdown of distinctions between mental and manual labor, between leadership and the mass; the awareness that within resistance communities the resolution of pressing rural problems through cooperative efforts was not only possible but a daily occurrence.

Despite desperately limited resources, hand in hand with these approaches to rural economic development, has occurred impressive expansion of education and social services. One example suggests the characteristic style of educational development and its importance in the context of the larger struggle. An NLF document relates how villagers in an area abandoned by administrators of the Saigon government petitioned their district office for a school. When their request was ignored, a movement was initiated locally to build and manage the school. The result was that

> The GVN failure then appeared to the villagers as a striking contrast to their own ability to meet the need, inspiring confidence in their own capabilities. Furthermore, activities of managing the school, such as hiring teachers, deciding on curricula, and observing and evaluating its progress were an ongoing community concern. By carrying the political struggle efforts against GVN to their logical conclusion, villagers find encouraging examples of the strengths and potential of human effort in the liberation movement and simultaneously provide services to the community, which increase the involvement of the community members in new, self-sustaining integrative interactions.[33]

It is not presently possible to document the extent to which this social vision has already been institutionalized and peasant consciousness transformed in the liberated areas of South Vietnam. What is clear is that peasant consciousness and the institutional order of rural Vietnam are being reshaped in the process of waging a people's war.[34] Even so hostile an observer as Douglas Pike suggests the egalitarian possibilities of community emerging in NLF areas:

> The liberated area may be regarded as a rudimentary society, for it was an organized collection of persons working together and communicating with one another within the framework of a common culture. . . . Probably it is safe to conclude that the group norm in the liberated area was characterized by a greater sense of equalitarianism, greater social mobility with individual merit counting for more and family

for less, and a greater awareness of strata, class consciousness or social solidarity.[35]

In its reliance on popular participation and initiative, in the emphasis on the contributions of man in a context of face-to-face human struggle, in the high value placed on performance of multiple roles as soldiers, farmers, cadres and teachers, in its egalitarian and selfless spirit embodied in every facet of the movement—in all these ways we find the Yenan spirit resurrected and developed in Vietnam today.

In the Chinese and Vietnamese resistance, emphasis on popular participation, the fundamental postulate of people's war, meant that strength and legitimacy rested primarily on active peasant support. This support in turn was contingent on the movement's ability to respond effectively to war-time political, economic, and security needs. As Franz Schurmann recently observed after a visit to bomb-shattered north Vietnam, the mobilization process cannot be grasped exclusively or even primarily in organizational terms. Rather

> the spirit of individuals and classes is the energy that makes organization work. Without that spirit, organization can function only through nonhuman technology, which means turning men into machines as well as making use of machines.[36]

Consciousness of this problem, of the danger of turning men into machines, was central to the distinctive shape of popular mobilization in China's war-time base areas as it is in the China of the cultural revolution and in Vietnam today. Under continuous crisis conditions, rigid and dogmatic tendencies toward elite domination and tight central control of war and administration were effectively challenged by populist and pragmatic impulses and the conviction that ultimate support and commitment required popular participation and initiative. This was the significance of the "mass line" style of resistance leadership with its premium on decentralization, its antagonism to bureaucratic elitism and rigidity, and its heavy reliance on popular creativity. In this spirit of involvement and participation in areas which typically had been the exclusive preserve of a remote and burdensome officialdom or a narrow local elite, in seizing the initiative to grapple with the entire range of village problems, commitment to a nationalist struggle took on an immediacy and a structure in the context of redressing fundamental grievances of peasant life. As the peasantry en masse broke the bonds of passivity and subservience, new forms of local community began to replace those eroded steadily during a century of rural disintegration, colonial and semi-colonial bondage, and war.

The resistance movements in China and Vietnam suggest significant parallels with other egalitarian rebel movements, particularly those in societies undergoing rapid change in the face of war and industrialization. The Sicilian and Andalusian peasant movements eloquently described by E. J. Hobsbawm, China's Taiping rebels, the millenarian movement in the Brazilian backlands and Zapata's Mexican peasant rebels are among the best documented of these cases.[37]

Reading of Zapata's "liberated area," for instance, one discovers a spirit strikingly akin to what we have found in the resistance:

> Community, together with personal freedom: . . . this belief that people can rule themselves without sacrificing either social welfare or personal freedom—this dream became reality in the small, enclosed *campesino* community of Morelos in 1914–15.
>
> Zapata and his chiefs, of course, were themselves villagers, field hands and sharecroppers; their authority sprang from local councils and rested on fidelity to the texts they were about to make forcefully real. On this basis a politics of confidence arose. . . .
>
> For the first time in Mexico, it was not a remote bureaucracy nor an all-too-present military authority that made decisions in the name of the people. The people themselves, through the cooperation of village leaders, fashioned the new

levers of power and the new means of livelihood from the bottom up, unhindered by rigid programs, fusing the traditional agencies of local society and the momentum of the Revolution.[38]

Zapata's movement, and those cited above, stopped short of permanently transforming their societies. They were eventually destroyed by opponents of social revolution better able to master the military, organizational, and technological forces of the contemporary world.

In contrast to Zapata, there is a quality of modernity in the dedication of Chinese and Vietnamese revolutionaries to a vision of social transformation and development carried beyond local resistance communities and embodied on a national scale. That conception reaffirms the creative contributions of men, above all of peasants, working in their own villages rather than the efforts of a remote technological elite or the bureaucratic organs of the state. It is linked with a pragmatic and practical effort implemented even while the fighting rages to advance concretely toward a day when the nation as a whole can reap the benefits of independence and development. Problems of peasant particularism, economic stagnation, and elitism cannot of course be eliminated in a single sweep. What is impressive is that the base areas of the resistance contain in embryo the possibilities for new forms of community life and growth consonant with these movement ideals. Theirs is not an anarchism reveling ultimately in the struggle of atomized individuals for private ends. Rather it is the freedom of all continually redefined by an accepted and cherished community. The cooperative effort to resist a ruthless oppressor is simultaneously directed toward overcoming natural and man-made barriers to change. The spirit of the resistance thus suggests new possibilities of human fulfillment while grappling with the formidable problems of poverty and economic stagnation which stalk the Third World.

Notes

1. I would like to thank Glen Holt, William Caspary, and the members of my Washington University seminar on imperialism and people's war for their insightful suggestions and slashing criticism.

2. Available studies have been written by government officials or under military contract for consumption by an uneasy public. Douglas Pike, *Vietcong. The Organization and Techniques of the National Liberation Front of South Vietnam* (Cambridge, Mass., M.I.T. Press, 1966). Cf. Michael Charles Conley, *The Communist Insurgent Infrastructure in South Vietnam; A Study of Organization and Strategy* (Washington, D.C., American University, Center for Research in Social Systems, 1967); CIA agent George Carver has written (anonymously of course) of "The Faceless Viet Cong," in *Foreign Affairs*, Vol. 44, No. 3 (April, 1966), pp. 347–72. Of the handful of American studies of the NLF, all of them government inspired and financed, Pike's is by far the most useful. Interestingly enough, critics of the war who have diligently and often brilliantly exposed official rationalizations and blatant lies have virtually ignored the NLF. The single most important exception is the Australian journalist Wilfred Burchett. However, his *Vietnam: Inside Story of the Guerrilla War* (New York, International Publishers, 1965), the most important account written by a visitor to the "liberated areas," provides only a sketchy account of the internal features of the movement. Cf. Katsuichi Honda, "The National Liberation Front," Committee for the English Publication of "Vietnam—A Voice from the Villages," available from Mrs. Reiko Ishida, 2-13-7, Nishikata, Bunkyo-ku, Tokyo. Mr. Honda, a reporter for the *Asahi Shimbun*, bases his report on a visit to an NLF area in the Mekong Delta in late 1967.

3. Pike, *Vietcong*, p. 382. Since this writing Richard Minear has published the first serious critique of Pike's work, "Douglas Pike and the NLF," *Bulletin of Concerned Asian Scholars*, Vol. II, No. I (October, 1969), pp. 44–47. Pike's activities inside and outside government suggest the development of a new style of official, the counterpart of the now familiar peripatetic scientists and social scientists shuttling between their university base and Washington. In the case of Pike, whose primary career is government service, official leave of absence is taken to publish—

assuring the "objectivity" of the product. Pike's "private" analysis is, of course, indistinguishable from the war-time propaganda of the American government. The convergence in recent decades of official and scholarly premises and analyses—and with it the death of critical and independent scholarship which have been noted in several essays in this volume—is thus strengthened by the professional patterns of the new scholar-official. Cf. Noam Chomsky's critique of the liberal intelligentsia in "Objectivity and Liberal Scholarship," in *American Power and the New Mandarins* (New York, Pantheon, 1969), pp. 23–158.

4. Chalmers Johnson, *Peasant Nationalism and Communist Power: The Emergence of Revolutionary China, 1937–1945.* (Stanford, Cal., Stanford Univ. Press, 1962). The book may be read as a sophisticated brief for the techniques of Special War which the United States was then initiating in South Vietnam: Its primary lesson, shortly to be ignored in Washington, is the necessity to rely on aid, advisers, and special training of native armies, and avoidance of massive commitment of American forces to crush wars of liberation.

5. John Wilson Lewis, *Leadership in Communist China* (Ithaca, N.Y., Cornell Univ. Press, 1963), pp. 99–100. This view, already dominant, has been greatly reinforced as a result of the Great Proletarian Cultural Revolution. See, for example, A. Doak Barnett, *Cadres, Bureaucracy and Political Power in Communist China* (New York, Columbia Univ. Press, 1967), pp. 38–39, 142, 437–38; Benjamin Schwartz, "Upheaval in China," in *Communism and China: Ideology in Flux* (Cambridge, Mass., Harvard Univ. Press, 1968), pp. 205–27; Tang Tsou, "Revolution, Reintegration and Crisis in Communist China: A Framework for Analysis," in Ping-ti Ho and Tang Tsou (eds.), *China in Crisis: China's Heritage and the Communist Political System* (Chicago, Univ. of Chicago Press, 1968), Vol. I, Book I, pp. 277–347, especially pp. 343–47; Lucian Pye, *The Spirit of Chinese Politics* (Cambridge, Mass., M.I.T. Press, 1968), *passim;* Jerome Cohen, "The Chinese Communist Party and 'Judicial Independence' 1949–1959," in *Harvard Law Review*, Vol. 82, No. 5 (March, 1969), pp. 967–1006.

6. Samuel Popkin, "Village Authority Patterns in Vietnam," unpublished paper presented to the Peace Research Society, June 3, 1968. A useful discussion dispatching many of these myths in the case of pre-colonial Vietnam is found in Robert Sansom, "The Economics of Insurgency in South Vietnam," unpublished Ph.D. dissertation (Oxford, 1968), pp. 519–20.

7. Johnson, *Peasant Nationalism* is the classic statement of the nationalist interpretation of the Communist rise. The position was

articulated initially by George Taylor, *The Struggle for North China* (New York, Institute of Pacific Relations, 1940).

8. William Hinton, *Fanshen. A Documentary of Revolution in a Chinese Village* (New York, Monthly Review, 1966).

9. Ch'i Wu, *I-ko ko-ming ken-chü-ti ti ch'eng-ch'ang* (The Development of a Revolutionary Base) Peking, Jen-min, 1958), pp. 118, 124, provides data on landlord complicity with the Japanese in the Shansi-Hopeh-Shantung-Honan Border area. While the effort to rectify abuses in land tenure relationships was carried out under the general banner of rent reduction, the campaign touched a broad range of other problems. Investigation of land titles during the campaign frequently unearthed large landlord holdings which had gone unregistered in the effort to evade taxes. In some cases these became subject to redistribution. In the Shensi-Kansu-Ninghsia area, the single surviving base to experience land revolution prior to the outbreak of the Resistance War, the subsequent rent reduction movement rectified instances in which landlords had illegally recovered property from peasant recipients in the earlier redistribution. These were expropriated and returned to the original recipients. Cf. *Chieh-fang Jih-pao* (Liberation Daily) (March 18, April 15, May 12, 15, June 6, July 25, 1942).

10. Quoted in Franz Schurmann, *Ideology and Organization in Communist China* (Berkeley, Univ. of California Press, 1966), p. 420.

11. Eric R. Wolf, "Peasant Problems and Revolutionary Welfare," unpublished paper presented to the Third Annual Socialist Scholars Conference, New York City, September 10, 1967, p. 9.

12. Jack Belden, *China Shakes the World* (New York, Harper & Brothers, 1949), pp. 83–84. Belden's contrast to Kuomintang officialdom living high in the midst of the catastrophic famine of 1941 highlights the significance of his comments on Communist leadership. "I was ashamed to go from one Kuomintang general to another, eating special delicacies from their well-laid tables, while peasants were scraping the fields outside the yamens for roots and wild grass to stuff into their griping stomachs. But I was more than ashamed—I was overcome with a feeling of loathing—when I learned that these same generals and the Kuomintang officials were buying up land from starving farmers for arrears in taxes and were holding it to wait tenants and rainy days." (p. 97).

13. Elsewhere I have discussed in detail the institutional developments and the transformation of leadership patterns in Communist-led resistance bases. "The Yenan Legacy: The Mass Line" in A.

Doak Barnett (ed.), *Chinese Communist Politics in Action* (Seattle, Univ. of Washington Press, 1969).

14. Sansom, "The Economics of Insurgency," pp. 462–67, 475–80, 494–500, 511, 518, 529, 537. Measured exclusively in terms of tenancy rates the Vietnamese land problem was far more acute than that in North China base areas where Communist war-time resistance centered. Cf. Eric R. Wolf, *Peasant Wars of the Twentieth Century* (New York, Harper & Row, 1969), pp. 160–78.

15. Price Gittinger, "Agrarian Reform," pp. 200–208 in Richard W. Lindholm (ed.), *Vietnam: The First Five Years* (Lansing, Michigan State Univ. Press, 1959), p. 205.

16. Sansom, "The Economics of Insurgency," pp. 462–67, 494–500. Nguyen Khac Vien, "The Peasants' Struggle (1954–1960)," pp. 50–77, *Vietnamese Studies*, No. 8, pp. 52–53. Cf. James Hendry, *The Small World of Khanh Hau* (Chicago, Aldine Publishers, 1964), pp. 133–40.

17. *Viet Cong Documents* (hereafter: *VCD*) #296. The translation is that given by Christine White in an unpublished paper, "Land Reform and Revolution: Vietnam." These and all other translated Vietnamese documents cited are available at the Chicago Central Library.

18. The fifteen per cent guideline may be found in "Resolution of the Central Office for South Vietnam" of March 1966 (Press Release of United States Mission, Saigon, August 18, 1967), pp. 43–44. *VCD* #296 suggests the following guidelines: "For a *cong* of good land whose output is 15-20 *gia*, or even 30 *gia* and above, the maximum rent shall not exceed 1-1/2 *gia* per *cong*." In this case rentals would amount to only 5–10 per cent on the best land. These criteria were designed to ensure that the rewards of increased productivity went to the tiller.

19. *Vietnamese Studies*, No. 8, pp. 157–59. The essay "In the Liberated Zones of South Vietnam," pp. 156–79, contains a full statement of NLF land policy as of 1965. Other key NLF land documents include: *VCD* #2, pp. 296, 298, 455; "Political Program of the South Vietnam National Liberation Front," United States Mission in Vietnam. for the full texts of the 1960 and 1967 NLF programs.

20. *VCD* #2, pp. 41–42. For lengthy excerpts see Denis Warner, *The Last Confucian* (New York, Macmillan, 1963). The report notes how subsequent resistance work was continually pegged to the issue of land as in the use of the following slogan: "To keep your land and prevent landowners from collecting rent, you must lay naily boards (used for village defense)." (p. 50.) It also

offers one of the fullest accounts of the over-all program including education, social services, and defense at the local level.

21. Wolf Ladejinsky, "Agrarian Reform in the Republic of Vietnam," in Wesley R. Fishel (ed.), *Problems of Freedom. South Vietnam Since Independence* (New York, Free Press of Glencoe, 1961), pp. 154–57. Recently, a number of "realists" centered in the RAND Corporation, among whom Charles Wolf, Jr., and Edward Mitchell are the most articulate spokesmen, have queried the American emphasis on land reform. Their "discovery" (as if the military had not been telling us this for years) is that the key to pacification lies not with the resolution of the land problem and other rural grievances but with the provision of effective military security. The implications of Mitchell's conclusion are clear: "From the point of view of government control the ideal province in South Vietnam would be one in which few peasants operate their own land, the distribution of land holdings is unequal, no land redistribution has taken place, large French landholdings existed in the past, population density is high, and the terrain is such that mobility or accessibility is low." Edward J. Mitchell, *Land Tenure and Rebellion: A Statistical Analysis of Factors Affecting Government Control in South Vietnam.* RAND Memorandum RM-5181-ARPA.

Mitchell's work is an extraordinary blend of the super-sophistication of social scientific computerized survey methods and the crudest abuses of elementary research techniques. His entire data base is a 1965 survey of NLF and Saigon control of individual provinces, with no indication of the definition of 'control' employed. Not only does he ignore totally historical and strategic factors in the development of the Viet Minh and NLF, but his single crude index of peasant discontent is that of tenancy rates. Moreover, Mitchell distorts entirely crucial questions of terrain. His data exclude entirely dense forests, paddy land and mountains.

The Vietnamese case, no more than that of China, supports a simple correlation between rural misery and revolutionary success; many other factors including the strength of counterrevolutionary forces and the terrain critically affect the course of insurgent movements. What is abundantly clear in both cases is that conditions of misery prevailing throughout the country provided fuel for insurgent movements. Whether or not the *most* wretched of the wretched have achieved the greatest success in overthrowing their domestic and foreign oppressors is irrelevant to proving or disproving the link between oppression and rebellion.

Unburdened by moral scruples which might impede the "pacification" effort, and armed with studies like Mitchell's, an alliance of military men and social science "realists" find the solution to counter-insurgency problems in endless military escalation regardless of the costs in human lives. The "final solution," unflinchingly carrying forward the implications of Mitchell's approach, is outlined by Samuel Huntington. The chairman of Harvard's government department blandly suggests that we continue to encourage the felicitous war-time trend toward "urbanization" by appropriate military means. In the end, Vietnamese faced with the option of migration to the city or a fiery death in the countryside cannot but choose "freedom." Since the NLF is unable to secure the cities the war will end successfully for the United States with the "depopulation" of rural areas. "The Bases of Accommodation," *Foreign Affairs,* Vol. 46, No. 3 (July, 1968), pp. 642–56. Excellent critiques of Mitchell's work may be found in Sansom, "The Economics of Insurgency," pp. 580–89; and Christine White. "Land Reform and Revolution: Vietnam" (unpublished), pp. 1–3.

22. Bernard Fall, *Vietnam Witness 1953–1966* (New York, Praeger, 1966), p. 179.

23. John Montgomery, "Land Reform as a Means to Political Development in Viet Nam," *Orbis* (Summer, 1968), p. 24.

24. Sansom, "The Economics of Insurgency," pp. 564–66; Wolf, *Peasant Wars,* pp. 197–98.

25. A devastating liberal critique of Saigon's land reform program is found in Twentieth Report of the Committee on Government Operations, "Land Reform in Vietnam," Report No. 1142, Ninetieth Congress, 2nd Session, House of Representatives. Cf. the perceptive analyses from the other side in "The Peasants' Struggle," *Vietnamese Studies,* No. 8, pp. 55–67 and Vo Nguyen and Le Tan Danh, "In the Liberated Zones of South Vietnam," *Ibid.,* pp. 156–67.

26. Chong-sik Lee, *Counterinsurgency in Manchuria: The Japanese Experience, 1931–1940.* RAND Corporation Memorandum RM-5012-ARPA, 1967. Sir Robert Thompson, the architect of British counter-insurgency strategy in Malaya, and the primary inspiration of American counter-insurgency theoreticians, headed an advisory mission to Vietnam. Thompson, today Nixon's top counter-insurgency adviser, attributed the dismal results of Diem's program to administrative "adventurism" and the squandering of resources. The Diem plan called for constructing sixteen times the number of hamlets in a fraction of the time required by the British in building strategic hamlets in Malaya. Robert Thompson, *Defeating Communist Insurgency* (London, Chatto & Windus, 1966), pp. 121–40.

27. "The Peasants' Struggle," pp. 74–75.

28. An effective critique of the theory and practice of American coun-

ter-insurgency including an analysis of its striking analogy with Japanese counter-insurgency in China, is found in Noam Chomsky, "Objectivity and Liberal Scholarship," pp. 23–158 in *American Power and the New Mandarins*, particularly pp. 37–60. Cf. the August, 1967, issue of *Asian Survey* for a multifaceted discussion of counter-insurgency in Vietnam by the social scientists and officials who design it. The single American strategic development beyond Japanese practice in China (exclusive of the application of sophisticated technology to terrorize and annihilate larger segments of the population) is the unsuccessful effort to outbid the insurgents by offering land to the tiller.

29. "In the Liberated Zones of South Vietnam." p. 162.

30. *VCD*, #45. In focusing on the relationship between people's war and social transformation I do not intend to imply that the egalitarian and participatory style characteristic of these movements can *only* emerge out of people's war, but that the revolutionary situation implicit in such struggle is highly conducive to this approach. The case of Cuba suggests that similar approaches may develop in the absence of a foreign invader and a people's war, though here, too, its spirit harks back to the heroic guerrilla tradition of the Sierra Maestra. Joseph Kahl, following a recent visit to Cuba, has sensitively captured the underlying spirit of the revolution:

> One of the key slogans on the big billboards surrounding the Plaza of the revolution José Martí . . . (literally means) "The Road of Communism is to Create Wealth through *Conciencia*." That last and key word conveys an amalgam of consciousness, conscience, conscientiousness, and commitment, and is perhaps the most repeated word in the Cuban language of revolution. The implication is that in the old society the mentality of money, and the motivation for work was the fear of poverty, but in the new society people will comprehend the need to work for the common good, and abundance will flow as a result of that understanding. Along with it will come a style of life that is cooperative and humane, and without "alienation," since work will be part of a voluntary social experience. . . .

> Society is to be reshaped in the pattern of comradeship of the guerrilla fighters of the Sierra Maestra. Some of the abstractions stem from Marx, but the Cuban color comes from the mountains.

"The Moral Economy of a Revolutionary Society," pp. 30–37, *Trans-Action* (July, 1969), pp. 31–32. As the writings of Debray and Guevara make plain, the guerrilla struggle against Batista followed substantially different lines from people's war in China and Vietnam. The Cuban campaign involved a much less intimate relationship between the guerrilla and the peasant population (peasant support was sought but no significant rural revolution was initiated prior to Batista's collapse). It followed a pattern more closely akin to that of roving armies than the creation of functioning administrative areas, and of course lacked the presence of a foreign invader. Cf. Noam Chomsky's superb account of the social vision and practice of the Spanish anarchist movement in the Spanish Civil War in "Objectivity and Liberal Scholarship," pp. 76–126, and Eric Wolf, *Peasant Wars, passim.*

31. On Economic and Financial Missions from the Present Time to Early 1969," *Vietnam Documents and Research Notes,* Document No. 49 (January, 1969), pp. 6, 9. For additional discussion of NLF development of cooperative agriculture see "In the Liberated Zones of South Vietnam," pp. 165–67 and "Missions, Policy and Methods to Increase the Agricultural Output in 1967–1968," translated in *Viet Cong Loss of Population Control* (United States Mission in Vietnam, Crimp Collection, December 16, 1968). Cf. Pike, *Vietcong,* pp. 293–94 (Pike describes these efforts as " 'red-ant' collectivization.")

32. On Economic and Financial Missions From the Present Time to Early 1969," p. 5.

33. Ellen Zweig, "The Role of Struggle in the People's War of Liberation South Vietnam," unpublished paper. *VCD, #2.* Cf. *VCD, #321.*

34. In contrast to the abundant evidence available in the case of China, it is not presently possible to document satisfactorily the extent of NLF follow-up to its successful land policies along the institutional lines indicated above. In part this undoubtedly reflects the intensity of the American attack which prevents the consolidation of secure base areas on a scale comparable to those developed during the Chinese resistance. Since I am unable to read Vietnamese, it is a product also of the present necessity to rely heavily on documents translated and selected by American government sources to support official interpretations of the enemy.

35. Pike, *Vietcong,* pp. 272–73.

36. "Our People are a Wonder," *Liberation* (April, 1968), p. 18.

37. E. J. Hobsbawm, *Primitive Rebels. Studies in Archaic Forms of Social Movement in the Nineteenth and Twentieth Centuries.* (New York, Norton, 1959); Euclides da Cunha, *Rebellion in the Backlands* (Chicago, Univ. of Chicago Press, 1944); John Womack, Jr., *Zapata and the Mexican Revolution* (New York, Knopf, 1969). An arresting American movement with strong parallels to the above is that of the struggle of Spanish-Americans under the leadership of

Reies Lopes Tijerina to secure land rights in the southwest. Cf.
Stan Steiner, *La Raza: The Mexican-Americans* (New York, Harper
& Row, 1970).

38. Carlos Fuentes, "Viva Zapata," pp. 5–11, in *The New York Review of Books* (March 13, 1969), p. 8. I do not share Fuentes'
optimistic view of the possibility for creation of a viable resistance
community which preserves "personal freedom." Not at least in
the sense of *individual* autonomy which is so valued in liberal
democracies, and not in the prerogatives traditionally enjoyed by
monied and powerful elites. The exhilarating sense of freedom
and power experienced by peasant revolutionaries is rooted in
the collectivity of participation in guerrilla units, in mutual-aid
teams, in peasant associations, etc.

Revolution and Modernization: Man and Machine in Industrializing Society, The Chinese Case

ꝰ Stephen Andors

ꝰ CONTEMPORARY CHINA is both a modernizing and a revolutionary nation. China is modernizing by dealing effectively and continuously with the economic, social, and political problems of increasing man's control over his natural environment. Unlike many other countries of the Third World, it has broken the hold of tradition and superstition over a stagnant and poverty-stricken rural society. At the same time, it has turned its metropolitan areas not into centers of conspicuous elite consumption and mass poverty but into important centers of production.

China is a revolutionary nation principally in that it seeks to transcend the structures and values of contemporary industrial society. Prolonged revolutionary struggle produced a leadership style based on egalitarian and participatory values and attitudes which is marked by a constant and generally effective struggle against selfish power seeking, arbitrary use of the symbols of power, and indeed, against some of the very symbols of status and power themselves. The influence of this revolutionary heritage has, of course, been extremely important in contemporary Chinese politics.

Apart from a legacy of revolutionary struggle, the Chinese leaders have also inherited a revolutionary philosophy of history which embodies a Promethean image of man's potential. Hence, they are not looking back with nostalgia but are looking ahead with determination to build the future. Writing more than one hundred years ago, Karl Marx described this philosophy:

> This socialism is the declaration of the permanence of the revolution, the class dictatorship of the proletariat as the necessary transit point to the abolition of class distinctions generally, to the abolition of all the relations of production on which they rest, to the abolition of all the social relations that correspond to these relations of production, to the revolutionizing of all the ideas that result from these relations.[1]

American appraisals of the validity and effectiveness of China's revolutionary experience and ideology have almost all been profoundly negative.[2] This experience and ideology are seen as key obstacles to modernization. One of the fundamental presuppositions of American scholarship, not only on China, but in the social sciences generally, is that revolution and rationality stand at opposite ends of the spectrum of political and social activity. Many scholars of modern China assume, a priori, the inevitability of a tragic and irreconcilable conflict between the political and philosophical principles of Maoism, and the structural and behavioral demands of industrial society. They feel that certain values are universal and permanent, e.g., that men can only be motivated by self-interest and not also by dedication to a collective good; that psychological satisfaction can only be assured by money, position, or power, and not by living and working for the common good. They assume that technological complexity demands strict organizational hierarchy, and that within that hierarchy, some men will administer, while other men, less deserving and talented, will obey orders and work with their hands. They reject the possibility that a complex society can decentralize power, and extend participation to all men and ultimately lead toward a fuller integration of man's physical and intellectual nature. In short, American scholars assume that history has culminated with the values and organizational forms that mark the society in which they have learned, worked, and experienced life.

This study of factory management in a modernizing, revolutionary society offers a different perspective on one of the major requirements of modernization: the need to create styles of leadership and forms of mass participation that will secure the economic, political, and psychological independence of the poor and exploited against elites that aim to preserve the status quo of privilege and power in all societies. But, to be more specific, it is an attempt to confront another problem of the contemporary age: How man can organize complex human interaction around the technology he uses to control his environment, so that he becomes the master rather than the slave of his own creations; how alienation of man from the products and processes of production can be overcome so that human aspiration becomes related to concrete human work. I take the revolutionary goals of the Chinese Communists quite seriously. I do not assume that they are doomed to failure because of a logic inherent in the industrialization or technological process, or because of incentive or authority patterns dictated by "human nature" or by "Chinese culture." In focusing on management in Chinese industrial enterprises, I assume that what is revolutionary need not be irrational or inefficient.

FACTORY MANAGEMENT AND THE LEGACY OF THE GREAT LEAP FORWARD

IT IS WIDELY BELIEVED that the policies and practices of the Great Leap Forward of 1958–1960 proved singularly disastrous for Chinese industrial development, and that, after 1960, the Chinese turned to more "rational" measures to get their economy back on its feet.[3] A close examination of developments, however, shows a much more complex relationship between the "politics in command" style of the Great Leap Forward and the "rational readjustments" of the 1960–65 period which preceded the cultural revolution. It reveals that the Great Leap period was one of tentative experimentation in China's economy and of revolutionization of the human relationships which had accompanied the modernization process in other industrialized nations.

Before describing the nature of this experimentation, it would be well to understand the meaning of "politics in command," its relationship to the goals and everyday operations of industrial enterprises and the concepts of *operations, policy* and *politics.*

Operations refers to the actual production, administrative, and technical decision-making process within the enterprise. It deals with questions of who is responsible for which jobs, how tasks are assigned in the production process, and how authority and responsibility are distributed in order to fulfill the goals set down by policy. Policy refers to the middle- and long-range goals of the industrial enterprise, i.e., fulfillment of planned targets, the formulation of enterprise plans not covered in targets handed down from higher levels, relationships with other enterprises and consumption units, and over-all efficiency in using material and human resources for the whole factory. Politics refers to human relationships and motivations in the context outlined by policy and implemented by operations. The goals of politics are the goals of the revolution: creation of a classless society where no man exploits another, the end of human alienation in the work process, and elimination of fear of material deprivation. Thus politics is operative within the production context but in another and more important sense it transcends that context, requiring not just production but *a definite form of production relationship and a specific type of authority relationship.* For the Chinese, "politics in command" implies that production embodies human relationships which are in harmony with revolutionary goals.

An understanding of the distinction between politics, policy, and operations is crucial in explaining the management strategy of the Great Leap Forward, and it was this strategy itself as much as the attempts at rationalization which followed it, which in great measure explain some of the roots of the cultural revolution.

The Great Leap Forward marked the evolution of a system of industrial management that was designed to reconcile the demands of politics, policy and operations by a strategy of radical decentralization. This decentralization took place both above the enterprise level, and within each individual factory.

In November, 1957, the State Council issued a directive outlining the basic pattern of decentralization above the enterprise level.[4] Except for defense and heavy industrial plants, which remained for the most part under the direct control of central ministries, most of China's industries were put under the control of local government and administrative authorities, from the provincial level down to municipalities, counties *(hsien)*, and eventually communes. Decentralization was designed to tap potential sources of raw materials for the manufacture of locally needed products and to do away with the cumbersome and bureaucratic nature of highly centralized planning. In short, decentralization was to increase the flexibility and speed of China's modernization process. But an obvious problem arose in relationship to planning for over-all national priorities. By raising the question of local versus national interest, or individual versus collective interest, decentralization posed a political, not simply a policy, question. The question raised by the Great Leap was not whether to decentralize, but how much and by what methods.

In order to combine the advantages of planning with decentralization, the number of mandatory, planned targets that each enterprise received from higher authorities was reduced from twelve to four. The four mandatory targets—total quantity of output, total wage bill, total number of employees, and profits—gave individual enterprises a large amount of leeway in determining crucial variables such as quality, labor utilization, cost reduction, experimental manufactures, and total value of output. These variables were in fact covered in the eight other targets which were given to the enterprise as guidelines, but were not mandatory.[5]

By January, 1960, however, it had become clear that too much local control of investment and capital construction had created grave imbalances in the national economy. Factory managers, or the Party Committees leading the factories, freed from the target and commands of the plan, had begun to make decisions in response to fluctuating market conditions in order to make profit above the amount stipulated in the plan, or they invested unwisely in plant and equipment. The planning process was upset as scarce resources were not used to best advantage to fill national development needs. Thus the Great Leap Forward saw the evolution of another strategy to deal with decentralization and planning—that of tightening central financial authority over the enterprise to tie it more closely into the national plan. This meant the exercise of greater control over funds for expansion, investment, and subsidiary production. Enterprises were allowed operational funds, but were advised that unified control by the State was essential if local decisions were not to contradict regional or national development.[6]

The main problem of decentralization, however, centered on the quality of managerial personnel. Instead of serving as cogs in an unwieldy machine, management personnel were now given the authority to make important decisions within their factories. This new independence for the enterprise had important implications for the growth of managerial power. The Chinese had inherited from the Soviet Union a system for running industrial enterprises called "one-man management."[7] Under this system, which origin-ated during the 1930's under Stalin, one man at every level in factory administration was given authority and responsi-bility for the fulfillment of all planned targets at his level. Thus, if mistakes were made, or targets were not fulfilled, one man would suffer the consequences, but along with this responsibility, he had complete control over the activities at his particular level. In this way, the system of one-man management solved the problem of managerial motivation by providing administrative sanctions (demotion, dismissal, or even imprisonment) or by offering positive material re-wards (managerial bonuses or premiums) or status benefits (power, promotion, office space, etc.).[8]

This system created a bureaucratic structure unresponsive to basic level initiative and participation. It fostered a con-servative mentality on the part of the responsible persons in each enterprise and in the industrial administrative system as a whole. Thus, it was in the interest of factory managers to keep production targets low both to avoid punishment and to gain premiums more easily. And it was in the interest of production unit leaders to exclude workers from any mean-ingful participation in the management of their units, since the leader alone was held responsible for any mistakes made by others.

This system made bonuses and premiums the most impor-tant incentive for efficient managerial performance, even more so when decentralization diminished the importance of administrative sanctions by sharply reducing the number of targets classified as mandatory.

Both the Chinese and the Russians had agreed that de-centralization was the answer to the problems of highly centralized planning. However, while the system of one-man management could be employed under decentralized as well as highly centralized planning, when it combined with de-centralization crucial political problems arose. During the Great Leap Forward, therefore, China began experimenting with other approaches in industrial organization which would deal with complexity and technology in a way closer to its revolutionary heritage and its vision of the future. In tracing the evolution of the Great Leap Forward's decentralized managerial system, the following political questions were paramount:

1. How can the division of labor, necessary in any complex organization, be fashioned so that inequalities in income, privilege, and life-style are reduced rather than widened?
2. How can the difference between mental and manual labor be reduced, so that alienation of man from the processes and products of production is minimized and eventually disappears?
3. What incentives are best both to achieve the preceding goals and to motivate people to optimal performance?
4. How can the authority necessary to coordinate the activities in a complex organization be exercised so as not to contradict goals (1) and (2), and by whom should this authority be exercised?

The euphoria of the Great Leap period, intensified by the dedication and anxieties of basic level cadres, frequently led to policies more suited to a society which had already reached these goals. But to emphasize "madness"[9] in the Great Leap is really to miss the point. For the Great Leap as a whole wasn't madness, even if parts of it were; rather, it was revolutionary, motivated as much by an assessment of the present as by a vision of the future. If some assessments proved wrong, there is ample evidence that many were effective in developing a strategy to radically change the face of the future.

To understand this strategy, one must understand the Chinese analysis of bureaucracy and the two major organizational aspects of bureaucracy which they sought to eliminate. First, the division of labor existing in bureaucratic organizations was marked by a distinct separation between production and administration. In industry, this meant specifically a separation between work in offices (paper work and sitting behind a desk) and production work (running and repairing machines and implementing technical innovation). Second, this division of labor had brought about a hierarchical pattern of authority rather than a mechanism for participatory decision-making. The Chinese leadership sought to replace hierarchy with participation. Chinese leaders did not view bureaucracy as an inevitable consequence of the division of labor, nor of increasing interdependence and complexity within organizations. Instead, the alienation and hierarchy characteristic of bureaucratic organizations were seen to grow out of a particular *attitude* of upper and lower level personnel in those organizations, marked chiefly by the belief, quite strong in traditional Chinese elite culture, that manual labor was qualitatively inferior to and less important than administrative or office work.[10] From this attitude developed authoritarian relationships marked by commands and control from higher to lower levels rather than consultation and cooperation between levels and individuals. Authority in bureaucracy depended more on symbols of status and office rather than respect for capability or ability to relate to and mobilize others as a result of personal behavior.[11]

The problem of bureaucracy, then, was interpreted primarily as an attitudinal one which had important behavioral and organizational consequences. It was these attitudes, and the political and philosophical assumptions from which they sprang which threatened to undermine the revolutionary goals and contradicted the revolutionary heritage. The Great Leap Forward represented an attempt to create organization without bureaucracy.

In April, 1958, seventy-nine leading industrial enterprises sent representatives to a national conference on industrial management. These representatives studied the experiences of five large-scale modern industrial units in Heilungkiang Province in reforming their management systems.[12] At that time, it was noted that two basic factory management systems existed. In the system which Schurmann has called "functional dualism,"[13] the factory director was responsible for administration and production planning (operations), while the Party Committee of the enterprise was responsible for the communication of planned targets to the manager, and for assuming leadership in formulating the plans of the enterprise and communicating them to the next higher controlling authority. The Party Committee also decided questions of capital investment, construction, and personnel assignments within the factory. In addition to these questions of policy, the Party was responsible for politics, e.g., ensuring that management actively contributed toward the realization of revolutionary goals. In Chinese terminology, the system of functional dualism was called "the responsibility of the factory director under the leadership of the Party Committee."

The second system of factory management noted by the April, 1958, conference was that of workers' congresses under the leadership of the Party Committee. This system was meant to encourage workers on the production line to participate in the running of the factories, and to serve as a means for management to communicate plans to the workers, and for workers to express opinions about production plans and processes. In practice the role of workers' congresses was negligible, since real authority over operations in most plants was still exercised by the old one-man management system. Therefore, besides studying the experiences of functional dualism, the representatives at this conference also studied methods of worker participation in management which had been experimentally tried by the five model units. Thus, once the principle of functional dualism was accepted, the authority patterns of one-man management were seriously questioned.

The first question which arose was whether the convening of workers' congresses by the Party or trade-union leadership was the most suitable or effective form of worker participation in management. Other questions logically followed from this basic one. What should be the role of the basic level production units in the administration and management of their units? If workers actually participated in managerial tasks, how was one to solve the problem of worker hesitancy to assume responsibility; and how would the creation of worker-managers affect their relationship to the men on the production line? Would jealousy and resentment grow and would the new worker-managers be ostracized by their companions as being representatives of the upper level control units in the factory? What about the very real problem, in China, no less than in any poor and recently illiterate population, of low levels of basic mathematical and technological skills necessary for efficient management?[14] In short, could China's workers effectively assume the burdens of responsibility formerly reserved for the managerial elite?

Closely related to the problems of worker participation in management was the question of cadre participation in labor. This principle had deep historical roots in the Chinese revolutionary experience dating back to the Yenan days. It had been a major weapon in fighting manifestations of "bureaucracy" and was regarded as a key element in creating relationships of solidarity between leaders and led. The problem was that it had never been extensively applied in modern industry. Cadre participation in labor was designed to develop basic level production teams and workshops as administrative and managerial units by enhancing the managerial capacity of the workers while providing cadres with new perspectives on human and technological problems of production. However, unless administrative and management authority was really handed to the basic levels, management personnel and technicians from the factory level and specialized functional departments who participated in production could easily be resented as company spies or as usurpers of bonuses that would go to workers for extra production now done by cadres. Thus, suspicion and conflict between cadres and workers could grow. Moreover, participation in labor meant a new daily routine for the cadre. The question naturally arose as to what proportion of time should be spent in the production units, and once there, what type of work should be done. Was work in production units the only type of labor that cadres should do in addition to their administrative tasks? And finally, and most importantly, how could participation in labor be related to the need for over-all coordination and planning for the factory?

Throughout the next year, Chinese industrial enterprises reported on their experiences in dealing with these questions. By May, 1958, the Chinghua Machine Tools Plant reported on experiments with a system whereby administrative cadres on the workshop level and in specialized functional departments (inspection, planning, repair and maintenance) devoted half of each day to labor, while leading cadres at the factory level labored on basic levels one day per week. They also reported that "under the leadership of the workshop administration, the workers on production teams were taking part in some of the administrative work of the production team."[15] By August, 1959, this factory reported further evolution in the system of workers' participation in management. Many powers had been delegated to the team, but the scope, tasks, and size of the team had to be hammered out over a one-and-a-half month period of debate and discussion. Final plans had not been completed, but elaborate preliminary plans had been drawn up.[16] The Harbin Bearings Factory reported that decentralization had been carried out by giving more power to the workshops, but problems had arisen because of the lack of people prepared to take on new responsibilities. The result was a great increase in the importance, scope, and functions of the workshop, and an intensified effort to solve problems on that level. Meanwhile, certain powers were maintained in the hands of technical experts and specialized departments, while the workshops assumed responsibility for technical innovations, repairs, and other production processes pertaining to the shop itself.[17]

Thus, by the middle of 1959, widely publicized experimentation with new systems in certain key factories had moved considerably beyond workers' congresses and one-man management. This development, however, presented the Party with a problem.

The system of responsibility of the factory director under the leadership of the Party Committee was designed to strengthen and stabilize decentralization, to ensure that the system of cadre participation in labor was enforced and that worker participation in management did not lead to chaos in planning and coordination. The Party was to act as the central coordinating body for the enterprise, but it was to leave operational decisions to the responsibility of managerial and technical personnel. The problem was to ensure that this operational decision-making had cadres both guiding and participating in decisions at the basic levels, and did not lead back to one-man management in fact, if not in theory. To do this, however, Party members had constantly to encourage workers to carry out their management tasks and suggest means to do so effectively. Thus, while the Party was not supposed to become involved in operations, but rather supervise the implementation of operations in a politically acceptable way, it was increasingly involved in operations. The Party Committee of the Shanghai Diesel Oil Engine Plant had realized this as early as November, 1958:

Especially after power is sent down, the problem of helping the small groups in good management and of raising the small groups' management level, is one that still requires a lot of work. That is to say, after power is sent down, the cadres' responsibilities not only do not become lighter, but they are increased. Hence, leadership work and especially the Party's leadership must be strengthened and experience summed up.[18]

This was not a new dilemma. Before 1953, when the system of one-man management was initiated, the Chinese had tried the system of factory director responsibility under the leadership of the Party Committee. The result was "that (Party) cadres wanted to do everything. In the process, they were becoming bureaucratized and neglected political and ideological work."[19] While the system of worker participation in management and cadre participation in labor (the "two participations") was designed to take some of the pressure toward "bureaucratization" off the Party by weakening the hierarchical nature of factory organization, it alone could not do the job. Therefore, to deal with the problem of relating politics to both production operations and policy without bureaucratizing the Party, another experiment began during the Great Leap Forward to supplement the system of "two participations." It was called the "triple combination."

The "triple combination" involved politics, policy, and operations. That is, it was designed to hasten China's modernization and, at the same time, to bring production operations into harmony with revolutionary goals. The triple combination was a system in which workers, technicians, and administrative cadres formed teams, at all levels in the factory, which made the technical decisions and proposed technical innovations. The combination of workers, technicians and administrative cadres was supposed to facilitate technical decisions by eliminating the necessity of going through elaborate channels in the bureaucratic hierarchy. It was also the task of these teams to revamp rules and regulations in the factory which were incompatible with the system of "two participations." The system was designed to reduce the differences in life style and educational level among people in the factory, and to strengthen the capabilities of the basic level units and cadres in the performance of their duties. The resultant participation by workers in decisions with important implications for their work routines was to serve an important incentive function, and develop in cadres a life style which militated against the formation of a privileged elite. Thus the triple combination was designed to take maximum advantage of scarce, technically competent cadres and skilled workers by giving them an opportunity both to teach and to learn from one another and from the workers. The level of skill and theoretical understanding of workers was to rise, while the theoretical knowledge of technicians and engineers would be geared to the actual needs and conditions of production in Chinese factories. The triple combination was also to free the Party from the danger of becoming bogged down by routine operations. By October, 1959, the system was in widespread use throughout China's major industrial centers.[20]

Whatever the theoretical merits of the "two participations and triple combination" system of management, there still remained a critical problem of practical implementation. That problem was the very fundamental one of human motivation. Thus, as part of the revolution in industrial management during the Great Leap Forward, an extensive debate took place in the summer of 1958, continuing into 1959, on the question of material incentives in Chinese industry.

The question of incentives was both a political and an economic one, and the debate sharply reflected both concerns. The economic issues revolved around piece wages, bonuses, and labor norms. There was concern that the use of piece wages and bonuses would lead workers to put all of their efforts into quantity and little or none into quality, and that the labor norms used as the standard for calculating bonuses would either be too high (in which case workers would lose interest in pursuing them) or too low (in which case they would not be a challenge and would lead to excessive wage payments). On a more theoretical level, the question was how to evaluate different kinds of labor in order to determine wage scales and pay differentials; e.g., whether there was an economic justification for paying a technician or skilled worker more than a semi-skilled or unskilled worker.

It was the political issues, however, which were central to this debate. The crucial issue was concern that an incentive system which stressed the pursuit of individual material interest would foster attitudes and life styles incompatible with the goals of the revolution. If a cadre was motivated to perform his best because of the promise of promotion, higher status, greater privilege, or larger salary, how was he at the same time to develop an attitude and live a life which embodied participation in labor and reduction of the material and psychological gap between mental and manual workers? If a worker was motivated by the promise of bonuses and rewards, how then was this to be reconciled with worker participation in management in matters concerning the inspection of his own products and the planning of his own output quotas and labor norms? And if participation was not possible, then how were workers eventually to overcome the alienation that developed in the process of mass production? Underlying the whole political debate was the fact that China was a poor country whose workers and cadres could not help but be influenced by the experiences and values of the past and the models of other industrialized nations, and who by no means were always readily able to understand the principles underlying socialist collectivism. The problem, therefore, was to develop an incentive system that took all of these problems into consideration.

The adopted solution consisted of two parts. Political education was to be pressed forward vigorously and combined with a rational system of material incentives. For industrial workers, this meant education and study of the principles and rationale for collective action, with stress on the relationship of individual effort and improvement to the collective's achievements. Emulation campaigns, model workers, and competition between production units, were all part of the political incentive program, as was the practice of participating in the actual management of one's own unit. At the same time, labor norms and production quotas were re-adjusted so that emulation campaigns and individual competition were made interesting and rewarding to the individual, producing both a sense of emotional accomplishment and material reward.[21] At one point during the Great Leap, piece wages were abolished in many industrial enterprises, but wage differentials and the wage grading system were as a rule maintained throughout the period.[22]

The incentives offered cadres and management personnel generally evolved along similar lines. In addition to ideological study and participation in labor, a detailed system of cadre ranking and wage grades was maintained among cadres,[23] and between cadres and workers. However, the differences between the highest paid cadres in a factory (usually the manager and the chief engineer) and the lowest paid worker was, and remained, slightly over a ratio of three or four to one. While absolute egalitarianism was not introduced, Chinese wage differentials (as well as consumption and patterns of life style) between workers and management were much smaller than those found not only in the United States, but in the Soviet Union and throughout the Third World.[24]

In summary, the system of industrial management called the "two participations and triple combination" that evolved during the Great Leap Forward can be seen as a series of trials and experiments which attempted to harmonize the dual goals of modernization and revolution and replace one-man management with functional dualism. The incentive policy which developed along with this management system combined material and non-material incentives but stressed the latter along with narrow income gaps. Within this system of management, the Party played the central role. The Party gave unified direction to the activities of the factory, was responsible for combining politics with policy, and saw to it that both were integral parts of actual operations. Finally, it was the Party that led the attempt to combine political and material incentives, strict responsibility with enthusiasm and participation.

With this legacy of means and ends, China moved on to apply the experiences gained from the mistakes and triumphs of the Great Leap Forward.

THE GREAT LEAP LEGACY IN OPERATION: 1960–1963

BY 1960, FUNCTIONAL dualism and the system of "two participations and triple combination" had become general policy for industrial management throughout China. But important problems remained. Many of these were aggravated by economic imbalances created by the experimental process itself, e.g., worker participation in management sometimes led to a total denial of technical and administrative control and coordination, or too much and too rapid a stress on political incentives sometimes led to worker fatigue and the breakdown of machinery, or to disinterest and absenteeism. Other problems were the result of drastic changes in China's argricultural organization and incentive systems, and still others were the result of extremely bad weather and the 1960 pull-out of Soviet technicians along with their blueprints and plans, from China's industrial centers.

After 1960, Party leadership in factories and in industrial management generally was designed to serve the revolutionary goals of the Great Leap Forward, while providing the central coordination and guidance essential to modernization and production efficiency. But it was precisely here that the trouble started. The central question raised by the Great Leap and by subsequent developments was not just Party leadership or "professional" leadership, but rather what kind of Party leadership over what kinds of organizational structures. In other words, the problem was not one of "red" versus "expert," but rather one of defining what is meant by "red."[25]

In the aftermath of the Great Leap, the Chinese Communist Party faced two major problems. The first was to restore some semblance of balance and integration to a fractured national economy. The second concerned ways to deal with problems of coordination, authority, and responsibility within the enterprise, that had not been thoroughly solved by experiments during the Great Leap or were caused by some of these experiments. The strategy adopted to deal with these two major problems was crucial to subsequent developments.

Instead of diminishing the power of the Party in management, and giving more decision-making authority to "technicians" or "professionals," there was instead an increase in the power of the Party, thus following the direction set by the Great Leap. This meant, at first, an increase in the responsibilities of Provincial and Municipal level Party Committees for questions of coordination, planning, and distribution.[26] But Party Committees at the enterprise level were also affected, not only because they had the most direct links with higher Party organizations, but because of the very logic of functional dualism itself. Hence, in the aftermath of the Great Leap, factory level Party Committees had to concern themselves more than ever with problems of labor reorganization and utilization, incentives, personnel, and inter-enterprise cooperation.

The Party's involvement in management, aside from the demands of functional dualism in more normal times, was therefore intensified as a result of the economic dislocation after 1960. This involvement was predicted on the assumption that the Party was the best vehicle for organizing economic recovery because it was the most reliable politically. The Party's policies, in short, were assumed to be politically correct. An article in *Ta Kung Pao* put the matter quite succinctly:

> We have spoken of Party leadership and of politics assuming command. This, in a very real sense, means leadership and assumption of command by the Party's policies.[27]

From the Ninth Plenum of the Eighth Central Committee (January 1961) the readjustment, consolidation, and balancing of the economy begun during the previous year became official national policy. But what probably emerged from the Ninth Plenum was the realization that very serious disagreements existed within the Party over what lessons to draw from the Great Leap Forward and the experiences of the previous three years. Emphasizing the seriousness of the disputes in the Party was the fact that at about this time, Mao was moving closer to Lin Piao and the People's Liberation Army. However, the Party was still in control, and Mao and his followers may have hoped that disagreements could be confined to questions of policy and operations without becoming questions of politics or basic philosophy. The dividing line, however, was quite thin, as the dispute over "profits" clearly illustrated.[28]

The dispute over the role of profits grew out of the need to have a mechanism for achieving economic integration and to have a motive force for managerial decision-making. Ostensibly, the dispute dealt not with absolutes (whether to use profits as a target or not) but was over a matter of degree. There were, to simplify a complex discussion, two basic positions. One advocated making profits the major target of the enterprise, the fulfillment of which would determine enterprise performance ratings and hence the quantity and quality of future investment for the enterprise and the national plan. The pursuit of profit would become the major policy goal, and hence the major motivating force, for enterprise management, which, under the system of functional dualism, meant the Party Committee as well as the factory director and his immediate subordinates.

The other position gave priority to economic planning for social and national development. It stressed the subordination of individual interests to collective interests on the grounds that only the collective could guarantee the security and well-being of everyone and advocated that profit be used along with other targets to guarantee efficiency, variety, quality, and quantity. These targets were to be fulfilled by relying on an ethic of service, a high degree of dedication to collective improvement, and technical proficiency. The needs of other consumer units (individuals or other enterprises) would be communicated not through price fluctuations which would influence the level of profit, but rather through a system of economic contracts and locally conducted market surveys. The information thus obtained would become part of the planning process at the enterprise level, and at the national or local administrative level, depending on the size and function of the enterprise.[29]

It was logical that primary reliance on the profit target might appeal to management cadres concerned with huge problems of economic coordination and balancing. It was argued that the profit target subsumed in one indicator all of the other targets of the enterprise (cost, quality, quantity, variety, technical and labor quotas) under the simple principle that he who makes the best most efficiently and cheaply gets the most business and hence the highest profit. For management cadres who realized the economic fallacy of this theory (it is based on a model of perfect competition, and competition tends to eliminate itself and produce monopoly) it could be argued that profits and planning could go together if profits were based on fixed prices. Thus, rather than reflect the vagaries of the market, prices could reflect the choices of the planning authorities, and the job of large-scale balancing, integration, and planning could be performed by big "trusts" or corporations. These trusts could be separated from local governmental or administrative control and organized around the manufacture, transportation, and marketing of related products. The management of the individual enterprises within each trust would then make decisions for that enterprise on the basis solely of profitability determined by fixed prices. Within these large corporations, management could be highly centralized in terms of administrative control over individual enterprises, or it could be operationally decentralized with coordination achieved through tight financial control over local enterprises.[30]

These were two major objections to this scheme which turned the profit debate into a question of politics and not just policy. First, as long as profit remained the major goal of the enterprise, it could not also be subject to price fixing. For an enterprise could easily produce at a profit with a given set of prices, *but unless those prices were able to change in order to reflect consumer reaction,* management could earn profits and still not meet other requirements. In short, the pursuit of profit as the major goal of the enterprise carried with it the need to create a market mechanism to obtain price flexibility and reliance on a market mechanism means that over-all economic coordination and integration are decided by individuals or groups on the basis of their own interests. To come full circle, if those interests are defined as individual aggrandizement (in the form of wealth or power) then this definition itself will influence the very goals of society, its priorities as well as the definition and distribution of its rewards. Thus, the market system stands in direct opposition to planning which sees collective interests as primary and as the basis of individual choice.

Secondly, the trust system and the profit motive meant that the chief incentive for management would be the promise of bonuses, higher salary or promotion gained as a result of fulfilling or over-fulfilling the profit target of the enterprise. Economic decisions would be based on the principle of individual benefit, and divorced from the political authority which represented collective interests. At the factory level, this would mean that management would be oriented toward administrative superiors for rewards and for models of behavior. Thus, the daily routines of workers and staff would develop in a way which accentuates rather than lessens the mental-manual labor gap and which would institutionalize status, inequality, and privilege in the factories' structure and incentive systems. Thus, the pursuit of profit and the values of personal aggrandizement implied by the trust system would sharply influence the nature of the human relationships within each factory, and it was these relationships which were seen as the substance of politics. Since the Party had become so deeply involved in management as a result of functional dualism, the disagreements symbolized by the dispute over profits were reflected in all the Party's relationships to the management system.

The Great Leap Forward had seen a great increase in the role of basic level cadres in the daily operations of each enterprise. These cadres became the force which, through representation on the factory level Party Committee, helped to unify and coordinate the activities of the sections, teams, or workshops. As the place of basic level production units became central to the concept of worker participation in management, arrangements had to be made that would ensure that their activities were both rational and efficient. Team leaders, therefore, assumed a central importance in this system. Using a leadership style based on personal relationships and friendship with the other members of the team, and ideally characterized by an ability to inspire confidence and respect through the force of example in personal and professional behavior, these team leaders were responsible for organizing production and coordinating the various management functions (accounting, planning of operations, distribution, inspection, repair and maintenance) which were assigned to various members of the team.[31] Thus, worker participation in management at the basic levels not only involved the basic level cadres more closely with the activities of management, but it also increased their power and responsibility vis-à-vis higher levels within the factory. It made the leadership ability of the team leader the key to the success of the management system within the factory as a matter of practical reality, but it also served to put forth an example to be emulated by cadres at the higher levels. The importance of the team leader and of the style of leadership that he represented was to be of crucial significance later as the period of economic consolidation got under way in earnest after the Ninth Plenum.[32]

From the middle of 1961 to the middle of 1963, the management system of "two participations and triple combination" was significantly undermined by efforts to "rationalize" parts of the system which had disrupted production as a result of the boldly innovative nature of the methods tried. In the financial operations of the enterprise, stress on the role of the basic levels in accounting and disbursements of raw and other materials changed to a stress on "three level accounting," where professional accounting personnel in the financial departments of the enterprise were to exercise much tighter hierarchical control over team activities.[33] Administrative decision-making and authority in the factory evolved in the same way. Power was taken out of basic level hands and the responsibility and authority of middle level control and coordinating units, especially functional departments (wages, inspection, repair and maintenance) was increased.[34] Technical responsibility systems also began to stress the role of middle and higher level technical control, as the "triple combination" principle was interpreted solely as a part-time control system rather than as a full-time decision-making method. A strict hierarchy was created in technical matters; the technical personnel with "high levels of accomplishment" were sent to offices at the plant level while others were stationed at appropriate administrative levels in the factory. The office of the chief engineer began to assume increasing importance, and the centrality of engineering and technical decision-making in industrial enterprises assured that this development would have crucial implications for the daily routines of both workers and cadres.[35]

All of these developments meant more than an automatic "rationalization" of worker participation in management. In practice, they served to undermine the goals of the Great Leap system of "two participations and triple combination" because they sharply influenced cadre behavior, routine, and the incentive systems within the factory. The planned targets of production, emulation, and reward became less a process that workers participated in and more a system of mandatory targets, handed down through an administrative hierarchy, whose fulfillment meant more material reward rather than immediate emotional and psychological satisfaction from the work process itself. Secondly, the ability, and more importantly, the style of team leaders were called into question. Thirdly, these developments had important implications for cadre behavior and daily routine. As hierarchy grew and as the centrality of the basic levels declined, managers were left with the purely administrative job of coordinating the coordinators, and serving as a communications link between the factory and higher levels. Instead of being concerned directly with activities at the basic levels, and of participating in the actual implementation of their own decisions and policies, cadres began to listen to the reports of the chief engineer, his immediate subordinates, and the heads of the strengthened middle level functional departments. As both policy-making and operations were handled hierarchically and a sharp division separated administration from production, the political role of the Party became very ambiguous.

The Party was still the leading coordinating and policy-making body within the enterprise. But now, Party leadership in a factory was leadership over a three-level organization organized in strict hierarchical fashion complete with accompanying functional departments of control and supervision whose duties often overlapped. Functional dualism, in spite of Party leadership, was leading back to the one-man management system.

This particular evolution in the management of industrial enterprises was based on premises which must be clearly understood. First was the assumption that basic level units were incapable of fulfilling the responsibilities of production planning and technical decision-making, and therefore needed guidance and control by a strict hierarchical chain of command. An important corollary was that the top level leadership could best carry this out by strengthening middle level control and supervisory units. This method was the most familiar and the most tested, particularly in other countries which had undergone a process of successful industrialization.

A second premise was that incentives for work were best approached by offering material rewards for the fulfillment of production and technical norms sent down through the organizational hierarchy. This assumption, in turn, was based on a belief that men are basically selfish, and can best be motivated by appeals to narrow, short-range advantage. Here, the question was not so much one of including one type of incentive at the expense of totally excluding another, but instead a belief that the most reliable and most immediate production results could be obtained through the use of material, more than other types of incentives. The stress on material incentives was a natural result not only of the basic assumption about the selfishness of "human nature" but also of a stress on hierarchical as opposed to participatory decision-making.

Still another premise concerned the relationship between ideology and practical life experience. The very premise of functional dualism was that the Party could bridge the gap between two basic sets of relationships in industrial enterprises: one, between men and machines, and the other, between men and men. The relationship between men and machines was determined by technical and material conditions, and hence the responsibility systems (i.e., the distribution of power and authority in relation to the machinery) that this technology dictated were the same under any social system at a given stage of technological development. The relations between men in these different positions of authority were, however, to be changed from an "antagonistic" relationship to one of mutual trust, cooperation, and equality, primarily by reliance on political and ideological education and understanding.[36] In short, *it was assumed that the goals of politics could be separated and abstracted from the concrete organizational forms and authority relations of everyday routine, and could develop apart from this experience of life through ideological and political education.* However, by the middle of 1963, it had become clear to the Maoists that functional dualism, one of the legacies of the Great Leap Forward, had only guaranteed the primacy of the Party as an organizational structure. But the evolution of the other legacy, the system of "two participations and triple combination" unambiguously demonstrated that it could not guarantee the primacy of politics.

1963–1966: PRELUDE TO THE GREAT PROLETARIAN CULTURAL REVOLUTION

BY JUNE, 1963, there was a marked shift in emphasis in the literature on industrial management. Attempts were again made to make politics relevant to operations and policy by revitalizing the system of functional dualism. These efforts continued throughout the nation-wide socialist education campaign, and on into 1964 and 1965. Two major trends stand out in this connection. There was a renewed emphasis on cadre participation in labor, and at the same time, on the role of the basic level production units in the management of the enterprise.

The public emphasis on cadre participation in labor began with a *Jen-min Jih-pao* editorial on June 2, 1963,[37] followed by a long editorial in *Hung Ch'i* on July 10. The *Hung Ch'i* editorial began by pointing out that a serious struggle had to be carried out against tendencies which tended to weaken the Communist Party and hence undermine the goals toward which the Party was supposed to be leading China. These tendencies were already, it was said, in the "budding stage" and hence it was necessary to have Party cadres participate in "collective, productive labor in an all around, systematic, and persistent manner." The editorial went on to note that this was a question of "supreme importance" affecting not only the relationships between people in organizations, but the goals of the organization itself. In industrial enterprises, cadre participation in labor, therefore, meant not only a struggle against bureaucracy and the need to maintain a high salaried group of middle level control cadres, but was a way to increase the rate of capital accumulation.[38]

At the same time, there was a renewed stress on the role of basic level production units in management and in carrying out political education.[39] The middle level control apparatus that had grown up during the past two years came under question, and it was said that *the key to enterprise management was a direct link between the basic levels and the factory level* and that this link was to be established through cadre participation in labor.[40]

This development posed a real dilemma for the Party. Since the Party had become deeply involved with the overall direction and leadership of the production, technical, and financial responsibility systems as they had evolved up to this time, the idea of managing factories by "maintaining a firm grip on both upper and lower levels" aimed essentially at cadres who had a vested interest in the middle level control and supervisory apparatus. Basic level cadres, who, unlike other Party members, had few or no vested interests in the middle level functional departments, began to reassert some of the authority and responsibility that they had assumed in the 1958–60 period, and which had subsequently been undermined. Thus, an organizational split developed within the Party within each factory between basic level cadres and factory level and middle level cadres; and this split was commensurate with the degree to which participation in management by basic level production units had been undermined.

On the other hand, an ideological or "attitudinal" split developed which cut across organizational levels. As the role of worker participation in management was stressed again, it became apparent that cadre participation in labor in a way relevant to the actual responsibility systems and authority patterns of the enterprise meant a much greater burden on the time and motivation of the upper level cadres. It implied a real change in the *action content* of the everyday routines and lives of all cadres. Instead of getting information by reading reports and attending meetings, the cadres were now to spend time directly involved with activity on the production floor. Instead of giving orders by way of subordinates and requiring control by these same middle level personnel, all cadres were now to participate in the implementation of their own decisions, and in that way gain the knowledge required for future decisions. Moreover, a change in the action content of the cadres' daily routine also implied a change in the concepts of status and prestige upon which the authority of these cadres rested. Instead of authority being defined in terms of the office, or of the symbols of office (salary, title, dress, speech), it was now to flow from the cadres' ability to create relationships of enthusiastic cooperation between men and from competence in technical problem-solving. In short, the team leader once again became the model for the behavior of factory and middle level cadres no matter what their educational or professional qualifications.

This ideological and organizational split had become quite clear by the spring of 1964. The legacy of the Great Leap Forward, combined with the evolution of the "two participations and triple combination" system over the 1961–63 period had made it highly probable that basic level cadres and the workers who helped them in management during the Great Leap, would resist the power of the middle level cadres and the functional departments they represented. But many workers and some basic level cadres probably gained greater emotional satisfaction from carrying out orders and getting bonuses than realizing any collective achievement, participation, and control over their daily lives. And some upper level cadres and middle level control personnel probably saw both the practical and political value of eliminating or reducing what had become a cumbersome organizational structure, an unrewarding life experience, and a threat to revolutionary goals. The precise relationship between these conflicting attitudes and vested interests was a major cause of the confusion accompanying much of the Cultural Revolution in China's industrial enterprises. However, the Party's involvement with management as a result of functional dualism and the period of economic readjustment had made it certain that these conflicts would be reflected in the Party organization itself. At any rate, the attempt to remedy this split before the Cultural Revolution took the form of a revitalization of the system of functional dualism. The call went out for "revolutionization as well as modernization" and to "apply politics to actual production processes."[41]

The immediate attempt to unite the Party and revitalize the sytem of functional dualism took two forms, and both attempted to utilize forces outside the Party to accomplish this. First was the establishment of political work departments in the fields of industry and communications to parallel the Party's organizational structure in these fields down to the enterprise level.[42] The hope was that these departments would resolve the contradictions that functional dualism had created in the Party, and would overcome Party resistance to organizing production in a way more compatible with revolutionary goals. The second approach involved a mass, nation-wide campaign to "learn from the People's Liberation Army"; to learn essentially how the PLA in its everyday routine combined politics, economics, and technology.[43] The use of the PLA, however, was a warning to Party opposition that politics was not always a matter of persuasion.

Even with the PLA in the not too distant background,

there was still little inclination to face the hard fact that to unite politics with policy and operations required more than the creation of an alter ego to the Party and more political and ideological education. Writing in June, 1964, Ma Wen-kuei, an authority on factory management, implied that "revolutionization" was not to affect organization, but rather that it was necessary to be "revolutionary in spirit and thought."[44] To be revolutionary in spirit and thought, cadres were increasingly urged to participate in labor. Manual labor not only provided a concrete method to coordinate and lead without exacerbating the contradiction between administration and production, but it also created emotional and philosophical insight into the nature of revolutionary equality, and hence it laid the preconditions for ultimately eliminating the mental-manual labor gap.[45]

In spite of these exhortations, the fact remained that a sharp contradiction still existed in varying degrees of intensity between the goals of political education and understanding and the actual organizational hierarchy in the factory. This was especially true if working within those hierarchically structured organizations and systems remained the "cadres' own regular work." A problem of revolutionary strategy that had been brought up during the Great Leap remained a major problem.

> The contradiction between labor and the cadres' own regular work must be solved according to actual conditions. . . . The solving of the ideological question (i.e., willingness and desire to participate coupled with understanding of why it was necessary) must also be followed by the solving of the question of method (i.e., how to do it rationally and well). [parenthesis added]
>
> It must be admitted that in modernized industrial enterprises, it is impossible to organize the cadres well for participation in labor if no practicable measures and methods are designed to create the necessary conditions for the cadres to undertake labor. Because even if there is some transient enthusiasm for labor, it cannot long endure. Modernized industrial enterprises in particular are characterized by production

continuity, fixed production posts, complex techniques, strict management, and other features. How to accommodate these features and make cadres participation in labor conducive to strengthening of management and increasing production is indeed an important question.[46]

The last four months of 1964 saw an intensified drive to publicize various forms of participation in labor. All implied that the problem was more than an ideological one, in spite of the emphasis on ideological elements.[47]

By the end of 1964, therefore, the relationship between revolutionization and modernization was again a major concern of industrial management. Part of the problem had been recognized. Revolutionization required attitudinal change on the part of managers, administrators, technicians, and workers, and this attitudinal change had to be based on and reinforced by the action content of daily life and routine. It was also recognized that many of the required changes would have to be based on the principles of management developed during the Great Leap, especially the system of "two participations." The problem was how to avoid some of the mistakes of the Great Leap, and how to overcome currents of opposition to change within the Party.

The question of politics posed by Ma Wen-kuei in mid-1964 had been posed by the Great Leap, and it remained a question at the end of 1964. But now, instead of "revolutionization as well as modernization," revolutionization came first. An article in *Ching-chi Yen-chiu (Economic Research)* in December emphasized the determination to find a solution to this challenge against opposition from unnamed "modern revisionists."

> The modern revisionists want only modernization but oppose revolutionization. Actually, they also want to enforce the capitalist principles. They hold that modernization is omnipotent. As to man, he can only submit to and prostrate himself before the power of modern technology and be its slave.
>
> Our viewpoint is fundamentally different from theirs. *We want modernization but we want revolutionization even more.*

The socialist industrial enterprises of China must not only be modern ones. What is more important is that they must be revolutionized ones. [emphasis added][48]

The implications of this statement were clear. Some elements within the Party had become identified with the organizational positions and life styles acquired as a result of the evolution of functional dualism. They saw those positions as a necessary part of the rational administration of complex modern industrial enterprises. Thus, while they might be willing to do some manual labor and organize political education, they remained committed to the particular responsibility systems which had evolved since the Great Leap Forward. They put "modernization" ahead of "revolutionization" and they were quite clear in their assertion that modernization required a definite organizational hierarchy. Their opponents, on the other hand, were more clear in what they were against than in what they were for. They opposed organizations characterized by status inequality and alienation based on the division of administration from production. But the specific type of organization that they favored, in short, the organizational implications of revolutionization, only became clearer as time went on. The question, it should be understood, was not "revolution *or* modernization," but rather *what kind of modernization*.

The key point in the argument of the revolutionaries was an insistence on strengthening the basic level production units (shifts, teams, or shops). At first, this meant that the "triple combination" was to be used not only for implementing decisions made by administrators and technicians at higher levels, but for the actual initiation of technical innovations. Basic level production units were to become involved in decisions concerning policy as well as operations. Workers were encouraged to take part in making and testing small-scale innovations.[49] Individual teams were also given greater responsibility for management of their own affairs, for fulfilling targets, meeting technical norms, inspection, and even for participating in drawing up rules and regulations for labor discipline, attendance, and work assignments.[50] The control function of full-time accounting personnel was lessened, and the role of full-time inspection, repair, and maintenance personnel in functional departments was played down, while the role of workers in caring for and repairing their own machinery increased.[51] While the Party Committee of an industrial enterprise was often behind the organizational reform which stressed the role of basic level groups and the reduction of the power of middle level control organs, such reforms naturally elicited differences of opinion within the Party. An editorial in *Jen-min Jih-pao* in September, 1965, clearly expressed the close relationship between basic level responsibility and the whole concept of revolutionization, as well as the fact that all were not agreed on the need for revolutionization:

> Some comrades who run enterprises stress control, but ignore reliance on the masses and ideo-political work. Because everything is dependent on "control" by the above, division of administrative work has become more and more minute and levels of control more and more complex. . . .
>
> After revolutionary changes in enterprise management have taken effect, because overlapping administrative levels are reduced and a number of unnecessary sections and sub-units merged, some factory directors and key administrative personnel may be transferred to new industrial enterprises. Some factory directors may become administrative staff, while some technicians go down to work shifts and groups to become workers . . . In regard to these revolutionary changes, we must have a correct understanding of their implications. . . .
>
> *Thus, attention should be shifted to the basic level, to shifts and groups and the worker masses. This implies the basic approach, the common principle which should be acted upon at once . . . Work shifts and groups must be strengthened politically and organizationally.* [emphasis added].[52]

Over the 1961–65 period, therefore, it had become clear that the evolution of enterprise management had created two approaches to the basic question of what type of modernization should characterize China's industrial development. One approach emphasized the principle of self-interest as a motivating force for managerial performance. It stressed the role of profit in determining the goals of the enterprise, and envisioned the creation of a market-type economy which would achieve over-all coordination and efficiency as a result of individual decisions taken on the basis of profit. Within the enterprise, this implied an increase in the use of bonuses and premiums as incentives for factory level leadership in harmony with the profit motive for the enterprise, and a consequent increase in the differences in salary, status, and daily routine between managerial and technical staff on the one hand, and workers and basic level cadres on the other. Strict control and supervision over the basic level production units would ensure that production was carried out efficiently and in line with technical requirements. As this type of responsibility system evolved away from worker participation in management, the rewards available to workers and basic level cadres would become less and less matters of participation and cooperation, and more and more questions of money for the fulfillment of assigned quotas.

The other approach to management conceived of fundamentally different goals for the enterprise, the behavior of its members, and its incentive systems. This approach relied on planning in which the principle of self-interest was to be replaced by active inquiry into, and awareness of, the needs of other individuals and enterprises. Coordination in the economy was to be achieved through economic contracts and plan fulfillment, and decisions would be based on criteria, first of service, and then of efficiency and cost. The idea of a market economy, i.e., auto-regulation based on individual interest, was rejected as not only incompatible with the principles of planning for collective interests, but as necessarily leading to unacceptable human relationships in each factory. Within the enterprise, this system implied a commitment to help improve the capability and increase the authority of basic level units, so that major incentive for workers would come from an awareness of their relationship to a greater whole, and a feeling of active participation in the making of decisions which affected not only the daily content of their own work routines, but the lives of everyone in the collective economy. Each strategy for enterprise management, therefore, implied a different role for leadership personnel at the factory and basic levels, a different role for basic level production units, a different attitude toward the function of middle level control and supervisory units, and a different estimate of human capacity and motivation.

Party involvement with production and technical management had deeply enmeshed it with these issues. As the responsibility systems evolved in management, politics was split from policy and operations, and the Party, rather than reasserting the priority of politics, was itself split along the lines described above. What had gone wrong?

The answer is more complex and subtle than a theory of technological determinism would imply. If the Party became intimately involved in an organization whose primary goal was essentially production for profit, it was logical, if not inevitable, that a conservatizing, non-revolutionary bias would find fertile soil for growth. All historical examples of successful industrialization used self-interest as one of the primary motivating forces for workers and managers, along with fear of job security, administrative sanctions, physical punishment, and the authority of traditional status symbols and relationships. These "successful" examples of industrialization and modernization had all built bureaucratic organizations where specialists made decisions, administrators provided sanctions and smoothed over conflict, and workers took orders and defined reality predominantly in terms of security and hierarchy. In China too, there were great pressures to proceed in the same direction. The educational level of most workers was very low. Technicians and graduates of technical or engineering colleges were scarce, and in great demand, thus lending to the development of the feeling that they were a special group entitled to greater status, income, and privilege. These factors were reinforced by a value system which postulated that the goals of material improvement and increased security from poverty and hunger could best be reached through the efforts of individuals working primarily for themselves or their own families. Thus, for many in the Party, these goals of modernization seemed most quickly and easily reached by accepting and working with a given set of human habits, values, and talents. In short, present reality became the only reality. While such an attitude might be described as highly pragmatic, it was certainly not revolutionary, nor even, in a strict sense, scientific. On the other hand, Mao and his followers had had a glimpse of the possible in human relations during the long years of revolutionary struggle, and this experience was the base upon which they projected their vision of the Marxist future. So in this sense, they were not pragmatic; rather they were both dynamic and dialectical. Theirs was a vision of the future determined by all the evidence of the past. It was a vision that was both revolutionary and scientific.

Thus, the question posed was simple yet crucial. In building China's industrial and technological capacity, does one utilize simply the givens of the present and the examples of "proven" methods (whatever the cost in human poverty, exploitation, alienation, and inequality) or does one build organizations based on present possibilities, past experience, and a judgment about human capacity? It was in this respect that the cadres' attitudes about themselves, and toward the basic levels, was central. As the responsibility systems became divorced from real responsibility at the basic levels, the revolutionary goals that were to be served by the system of "two participations and triple combination" became more and more divorced from the daily experiences of workers and cadres on the job. The creation of revolutionary attitudes toward the basic levels and toward one's own goals in life, however, proved to be more than a question of ideology.

It is difficult to estimate the degree to which the revolutionary goals of the Great Leap management system had been undermined by subsequent developments. Throughout the 1960–65 period, there is definite evidence of worker participation in workshop level decision-making in regard to distribution of bonuses and the enforcement of labor discipline.[53] Cadre participation in labor was also practiced on a rather wide scale, and reports by foreign visitors to Chinese factories are uniformly marked by surprise at being unable to distinguish managerial personnel from workers in dress or manner.[54] The situation obviously varied from time to time and from factory to factory. However, it can be said with assurance that by 1964, Party leadership over factories, and the system of functional dualism had openly split the Party. The implementation of a dualistic revolutionary strategy for the management of industrial enterprises, a strategy which stressed both political goals and production goals as separate but equal, proved that in organizations dedicated singlemindedly to production primarily for profit, the political goals tended to be undermined by operational methods developed from non-revolutionary attitudes. Carrying out a responsibility system which stressed the role of experts combined with the role of workers proved that, unless the experts became part of the workers' production units, they would tend to monopolize power, authority, and privilege. Implementing a system which stressed both material incentives and ideological or political incentives proved that, unless political incentives were concretely embodied in daily routines of participation and cooperation, the values and heritage of the pre-revolutionary past tended to undermine the goals of the future.

The problem then, was clear. A way must be found to make the politics of revolutionary change and the values of revolutionary society part of the practical, everyday work of production and administration. The theory of functional dualism, the legacy of the Great Leap Forward, was brought under serious question. By the end of 1965, the search was on for the "establishment of a new and scientific system of management in line with socialist principles" and based on a commitment to the basic level production unit as the nucleus of a new organizational structure.[55]

CONCLUSION: THE CULTURAL REVOLUTION AND THE EMERGING SYSTEM OF MANAGEMENT

THE BASIC CONFLICTS inherent in the system of functional dualism, and the uncertainties of implementation of the "two participations and triple combination" had shown that the organizational challenge to revolutionary modernization turned on three crucial sets of questions. One concerned the goals of the industrial enterprise. Was it to produce for profit, or to fulfill the development needs of a poor country, for it had become clear in China and elsewhere, that what was profitable was not always what was needed. Would industrial development aggravate rather than ameliorate the inequalities and alienation that had accompanied modernization and industrialization in the West and the Soviet Union? Indeed, was the exclusive purpose of the enterprise "production" in the narrow sense, or was it also to serve the purposes of education and social integration which would have positive long-range consequences for industrial development as well as for the quality of life for the Chinese people?

A second set of questions related to human participation and capacity. Would low levels of interest in work, and the pursuit of higher levels of consumption be the sole definition of people's goals in life, or would the satisfaction of participation and cooperation open the door to general human fulfillment and create the opportunity to smash the barriers of class, race, education, wealth, and status that divide and have divided one man from another? Were people to be presumed capable of undertaking the responsibilities that accompanied the attempts to break down these barriers, or was the present state of man's emotional and intellectual development assumed to be permanently fixed and inequality to be embodied in the very structure of social organization?

Another crucial set of questions concerned the matter of elites. In terms of factory management, this related to the attitudes of cadres and managers toward the capabilities and potentialities of workers, and toward themselves and the action content of their daily lives. Were they to work primarily for self-advancement, or were they to work to teach and to equalize? Were they to seek the accoutrements of status and prestige prevalent in the West and the Soviet Union (clothes, salary, educational background, living accommodations, office space), or to dedicate themselves to a life style of equality and gain human fulfillment by integrating their physical and intellectual capacities into a new definition of their daily tasks?

In a larger sense, therefore, the questions raised by factory management in China do not simply concern China, for they touch the basic question of human identity. Frantz Fanon has noted how educational or privileged elites in almost all the countries of the Third World tend to use their former or present rulers as models for their own behavior, values, and life styles.[56] They find in this imitation a way to affirm their own individual equality with their masters even while they accept the obvious material and psychological subordination of their nations' masses. Thus, their positions of privilege are maintained within their own nation. Rather than turn to their own people for a mass mobilization which, by its own logic, would mean the end of privilege and require a new definition of leadership, they talk in terms of "nationalism" even while relying on the West for standards of success, behavior, and consumption. The relevance of the Chinese revolutionary experience to the countries of the Third World lies precisely in its attack on these alien models and the elites who look to them for support and guidance. Instead, the Chinese revolution has emphasized the ability to lead by integrating oneself with the people of one's own country, to mobilize human energy toward the rapid achievement of psychological, economic, and political independence.

As China moved away from the immediate experience of national liberation and began to develop modern industry, the question of models presented itself again to China's elite. Some cadres and managers wished to emulate their Soviet or Western counterparts, thus offering individual psychological proof of China's national development toward material equality. It is important to see that identification with bourgeois patterns of behavior and symbols of success had important political and power implications in China, as it did in the Soviet Union. For the influence on human relations of these attitudes and this model was institutionalized in the organizational positions of individuals in a supremely powerful political machine.

Thus, the Cultural Revolution, which had begun as a movement to change attitudes in the abstract, soon developed into a full-scale power struggle for control over the future of the revolution. In the important area of factory management, the attempt to overcome organizational resistance to change turned into a direct attack on the entire Party position in enterprises. Previously accepted as the embodiment of revolutionary goals and methods, by 1966 the Party was seen by Mao as a chief obstacle to them. Individuals in the Party had come to symbolize a model of behavior and a style of life which was anathema to revolutionary commitment and a contradiction of the revolutionary vision. But this attack on the Party organizational structure and position was not by any means an attack on the revolutionary goals which the Party was supposed to embody; rather it was an attack on those in the Party who refused to accept the fact that to reach those goals, they had to be somehow embodied in the concrete experiences of daily life. Thus, everyone was now to judge the Party on the basis of the revolutionary political, moral, and social principles of what has become known as the "thought of Mao Tse-tung." The life style and value system implied by this body of thought was to provide the model for China's modernization and the definition of individual commitment and behavior. For factory management, this meant that the system of functional dualism, which had been the legacy of the Great Leap Forward, had to be scrapped.

What seems to be emerging as a result of the Cultural Revolution is a management system that is unified but in a radically different way from the way it was under one-man management. The following characteristics stand out in this system.

While profit will serve as a cost accounting device for the individual enterprise, it will serve neither as an incentive for management nor as the sole criterion for the allocation of investment capital. Efficiency and coordination will be achieved through planning, economic contracts, and an ethic of service, cooperation, and self-sacrifice supported by constant political study and reinforced by the social pressures of small groups and mass meetings.

A single management structure is also emerging. Decision-making and responsibility for operations will be under centralized coordination at the factory level, but based on a foundation of "multi-layer and multi-stage management" with significant powers of operations planning and production control appropriately dispersed to the levels concerned. There is less emphasis on functional departments at the middle level, and more stress on the role of the basic levels in management.[57] This means that factory level management personnel will not spend time in offices doing only administrative work, but will instead coordinate activities by direct participation in production where they will help implement their own policies. Meetings and reports will be sharply reduced in number. Communications will tend to be personal rather than mechanical. Thus, politics, policy, and operations are to be united in one administrative structure, replacing the dichotomy of the Party Committee responsible for politics and policy, and the factory director responsible for operations.

The new management organs in factories are often appropriately called "revolution and production committees." The aim of these committees is to create more direct and immediate links with basic level production units. Responsibility systems are to be changed in order to facilitate the implementation of the "triple combination" system for technical innovations and testing, with much more authority concentrated at the basic levels where the triple combination will serve as the major supervisory and control device.

As a result of the stress on more personal and direct communications between upper and lower levels, and the emphasis on the triple combination, the living styles, dress, and manner of speech of workers, technicians, and managers have become remarkably similar. Fancy office space and status symbols of dress and living quarters are more discouraged than ever before.[58] The daily routine of workers and managers is becoming less and less different. Political and non-material incentives are stressed and are backed by the actual satisfaction that can come as part of participating in the process of collective effort on a basis of equality and commitment. Material incentives are being downgraded, and although "economism" was quite strong in factories at the beginning of the Cultural Revolution in January, 1967, subsequent reports suggest that piece wages and bonuses are being eliminated, although more gradually and carefully than during the Great Leap.[59] There are also important signs of attempts to reform the system of wage grading and differentials, with the salaries of upper level officials being lowered.[60]

The emerging pattern of factory management thus embodies "politics" in the very processes of decision-making, daily routine, and motivation for workers, technicians, and administrators. A revolutionary strategy is being created to deal with the challenge of modernization. It is a strategy which places primary emphasis on the capacity of the basic level production groups and workers to learn and become more aware of problem-solving methods; a strategy which gives cadres an alternative model upon which to define their worth as individuals, and which offers different premises for self-evaluation from those which have marked individual motivation in other industrial societies. Thus, politics is in command, as it was during the Great Leap Forward. But here, politics, defined as a life style, as human values and human motivations, and as dedication to the creation of a classless, non-exploitative society, is not divorced from the realities of people's daily experiences, nor from the requirements of production and the demands of technology.

China seems to be moving in a new direction. This direction is, in significant respects, different from the Great Leap experience in its practical operations and organization. But it is based on the same exalted conception of man and the same vision of the future that underlay the experimentation of the Great Leap. Complex organizations and the technology that they control can dominate and even enslave man in advanced industrial societies. They alienate him from other men, deny him meaningful participation in the production process, and turn him either into a cog in a machine, or a consumer in an ever changing but meaningless market place. Within these organizations, and within the societies that they dominate, there is no chance of integrating the whole man, emotional, intellectual, and physical, into the routine of daily life. Technology and organization have become the masters, and man their servant. In China, new types of organizations seem to be emerging; organizations which offer the hope of participation in planning, production, and creativity to all of their members. These organizations are based on the assumption that each participant has or will attain a high degree of responsibility, capability, capacity to cooperate and innovate, and the willingness to be both a teacher and a student.

It is important to understand that the system of factory management developing in China is based on certain conceptions about the capacity of human development and of how individuals and society evolve through a process of constant struggle. Needless to say, the struggle is not over, nor has the "Maoist man" by any means been created in China as a result of the Cultural Revolution. But for those who would prejudge the struggle while sitting on the sidelines, the following quotations seem to be directly relevant.

> In the process of . . . debate (at the screening-committee meetings), almost every aspect of the business comes up for discussion. . . . The result is a dynamic working unity. . . . Formerly under the piecework incentive system, a highly skilled workman was reluctant to show a younger man the tricks of his trade. But today, the older workers are eager to teach their skills, in order to raise shop productivity.

And later, in the same reference:

> The plan has completely solved the problem of "controlled production"—that is, the policy, common to almost all labor, of holding back so that management will never know how fast a man really can work.
>
> (At one factory, the engineers voluntarily gave up their vacations to work on a new machine design.) . . . the workers . . . seem to enjoy working together and sharing the good and bad times. As one of them said, "Formerly, everyone was on his own. Now, we all work for each other." . . . a man who makes a good suggestion gets a profound satisfaction out of it; he carries the story home to his wife; he is admired and thanked by his associates. . . .
>
> Examination of modern theories of motivation points up that (the whole system) provide(s) ideal means for satisfying ego and self-actualization needs which are typically frustrated under the conditions of present-day industrial employment.

This description of efficiency, cooperation, and hard work is not from *Jen-min Jih-pao,* nor does it even describe factories in China. Rather, it is from an American study about an experimental system of management in American factories.[61] In China, this approach to management, and to man, is not an isolated experiment, but a national movement. Ultimately, however, this process of struggle and development going on in China transcends the Chinese situation, and poses critical questions of action and philosophy for all of us.

Notes

1. Karl Marx, *The Class Struggles in France*, in Lewis S. Feuer (Ed.), Marx and Engels, *Basic Writings on Politics and Philosophy* (New York, Doubleday Anchor, 1959), p. 317.
2. See for example, John W. Lewis, in T'ang Tsou and Ho Ping-ti (Eds.), *China in Crisis, China's Heritage and the Communist Political System*, Volume I. Book 2 (Chicago, Univ. of Chicago Press, 1968), pp. 449–81; and also, A. Doak Barnett, *China After Mao* (Princeton, Princeton Univ. Press, 1967), pp. 48ff.
3. For one example of this interpretation, see Franz Schurmann, *Ideology and Organization in Communist China*, especially the chapter on "Management" (Berkeley, University of California Press, 1966). Schurmann argues that post-Great Leap Forward management policies moved toward a more flexible system of management, and implies a rejection of the "non-management" of the Great Leap. I would rather emphasize that the Great Leap did indeed have a conception of management and that there was a close relationship between this conception and subsequent developments.
4. *Ibid.*, p. 260, and *Survey of the China Mainland Press* (hereafter, *SCMP*), #1665, pp. 1–6.
5. *Jen-min Jih-pao* (hereafter, *JMJP*), November 27, 1957. Also, Audrey Donnithorne, *China's Economic System* (London, Allen and Unwin, 1967), p. 159.
6. Li Hsien-nien, "Several Problems in Finance and Banking Work," *Hung Ch'i*, #1, January, 1960.
7. For an excellent survey of this management system and its transformation during the Great Leap Forward, see Schurmann, *Ideology and Organization*, pp. 220–286.

8. Joseph Berliner, *Factory and Manager in the USSR* (Cambridge, Harvard Univ. Press, 1957), introduction and *passim*.

9. Franz Schurmann and Orville Schell, *The China Reader*, Volume III, (New York, Random House, Vintage 1967), pp. 401–402. See also Robert J. Lifton, *Revolutionary Immortality* (New York, Random House, Vintage, 1968), p. 103.

10. "Take the Attitude of a Common Laborer," *JMJP* editorial, March 26, 1958.

11. Li Hung-lin, "A Brief Talk on Bureaucracy," *Hsueh-hsi*, #4, February 18, 1958, in *Extracts from China Mainland Magazines*, (hereafter *ECMM*), #126, pp. 5–11.

12. Wang Hao-feng, "Important Reform of Management of Industrial Enterprises," *JMJP*, April 26, 1958, in *SCMP*, #1774, pp. 4–13. The five enterprises studied were the Chinghua Machine Tools Plant, the Chienhua Machinery Plant, the Harbin Locomotive and Carriage Repair Works, the First Engineering Bureau of the Third Engineering Cooperative in the Northeast, and the Sunkiang Metal Works.

13. Schurmann, *Ideology and Organization*, p. 292.

14. CCP Committee, Shanghai Diesel Oil Engine Plant, "Rely on the Masses for Reforming Industrial Management," *JMJP*, November 27, 1958, in *SCMP*, #1914, pp. 2–5.

15. "An Important Beginning for Reform of Industrial Management," *JMJP*, editorial, May 7, 1958, in *SCMP*, #1774, pp. 10–14.

16. Wang Shu-jen and Liu Shu-min, "How We Consolidate the Workers' Participation in Management," *Kung-jen Jih-pao*, August 21, 1959, in *SCMP*, #2106, pp. 11–14.

17. CCP Committee, Harbin Bearings Factory, "Combine Professional Management with Participation of the Masses in Management," *Kung-jen Jih-pao*, July 19, 1959, in *SCMP*, #2080, pp. 11–16.

18. "Rely on the Masses for Reforming Industrial Management," *SCMP*, #1914, pp. 2–5.

19. Schurmann, *Ideology and Organization*, p. 263.

20. Jao Pin, "Changchun Motor Car Works Strives for an Annual Output of 150,000 Motor Cars," *Hung Ch'i*, #12, November 16, 1958, in *ECMM*, #156, pp. 43–48. See also Po I-po, "Speech at a Conference of Advanced Groups and Workers in Socialist Construction," *New China News Agency* (hereafter *NCNA*), Peking, November 27, 1959. Also, K'o Ching-shih, "On the Mass Campaigns on the Industrial Front," *JMJP*, November 1, 1959, in *SCMP*, #2133, pp. 2–12.

21. See for example, Shih Ching, "Don't Let Money Assume Command," *JMJP*, October 16, 1958, in *Current Background* (hereafter *CB*), #537, pp. 1–5. At this time, a widespread campaign

took place with the theme of abolishing piece wages in much of Chinese industry. See also Wang P'u, "There is no Negating the Principle of Material Interest," *JMJP,* January 20, 1959, in *SCMP,* #1947, pp. 1–5.

22. Charles Hoffman, *Work Incentives, Practices and Policy in the People's Republic of China, 1953–1965* (Albany, State Univ. of New York Press, 1967), pp. 103–104.

23. *Ibid.* See also Ezra Vogel, "The Regularization of Cadres," *The China Quarterly,* Volume 29 (January–March, 1967), pp. 33–60.

    Also, A. Doak Barnett, *Cadres, Bureaucracy and Political Power in Communist China* (New York, Columbia Univ. Press, 1967), pp. 38–64.

24. Hoffman, *Work Incentives,* pp. 103–104; cf., Barry Richman, "Capitalists and Managers in Communist China," *Harvard Business Review,* January–February, 1967, pp. 64–65. Although large differentials in standards of living may have existed in the government bureaucracy, there is little or no evidence to draw the same conclusions for factories. For the situation in government through the eyes of a refugee, see Professor Barnett's careful study in *Cadres, Bureaucracy, and Political Power,* pp. 38ff.

25. The fullest analysis of the red-expert conflict is found in Schurmann, *Ideology and Organization,* pp. 8, 163–72.

26. *SCMP,* #2400, pp. 1–4. Also, CCP Committee, Changchun #1 Auto Plant, "Comprehensively Utilize the Available Materials and Develop Multiple Undertakings," *Hung Ch'i,* #19, October 1, 1960, in *Survey of China Mainland Magazines* (hereafter *SCMM*), #239, pp. 25–32.

27. "Consistency of Policy With Task," *Ta Kung Pao,* January 8, 1961, in *SCMP,* #2441, pp. 1–4.

28. The controversy over the role of profit was reflected in the press at the time. It began in mid-1962, and lasted for about one year. For a good example of the discussion, see Sung Hsin-chung, "Acquire a Correct Idea of the Profit Problem of a Socialist Enterprise," *Ta Kung Pao,* July 3, 1962, in *SCMP,* #2792, pp. 15–16. Also, cf., Dwight Perkins, "Incentives and Profits in Chinese Industry. The Challenge of Economics to Ideology's Machine," *Current Scene,* Volume IV, #10, May 15, 1966. There exists an interesting study of the profit debate which was made by an analyst for the CIA, but unfortunately, it seems to have disappeared and the title has been forgotten.

    I have also depended on materials published during the cultural revolution on the question of "trusts" to reconstruct part of the previous 1962 debate on the more general question of profits. For example, there is a whole series of articles on the trust system in *Chieh-fang Jih-pao* for June and July 1967. See also, Paul Sweezy, editorial in *Monthly Review*, #12, December, 1968, for an interesting discussion of the implications of profits in socialist economies.

29. For a statement of some of the points in this position in simplified form, see "Unfolding Economic Cooperation in a Well-Planned Manner," *Ta Kung Pao*, editorial, January 30, 1962, in *SCMP*, #2689, pp. 8–10.

30. Schurmann compares these two types of management to the Ford System and the General Motors System respectively, with the Ford system resembling more the structure of one-man management and the GM system more decentralized management in terms of the economy as a whole. See Schurmann, *Ideology and Organization*, pp. 297ff. It is clear, however, that while both the Ford and GM systems are compatible with the centrality of the profit target and one-man management at the factory level, neither is compatible with the political goals of the Chinese Revolution.

31. See, for one example, an article by the Party Committee, Chengtu Measuring Instruments and Cutting Tools Factory, "The New Socialist System of Enterprise Management," *JMJP*, June 24, 1960, in *SCMP*, #2295, pp. 3–16. Also, Wang Ho-feng, "Consolidate and Develop the Two Participations, One Reform, and Triple Combination System; Raise the Standard of Enterprise Management in All Respects," *Hung Ch'i*, #15, August 1, 1960, in *SCMM*, #224, pp. 18–30.

32. Schurmann, *Ideology and Organization*, pp. 249, 261, and 294. These are references to the role of the team leader and the production team in Chinese factories during the Great Leap and before 1949.

33. The evolution of financial responsibility systems in enterprises was very complicated. For more detail, see "Satisfactorily Control and Use the Circulating Funds of Industry," *Ta Kung Pao*, editorial, June 20, 1961, in *SCMP*, #2543, pp. 5–7; Hsu Hsin-hsueh, "Strengthen Further Economic Accounting in Enterprises," *Hung Ch'i*, #18, September 16, 1961; Li Cheng-jui, and Tso Ch'un-t'ai, "Several Problems Concerning Economic Accounting in Socialist Enterprises," *Hung Ch'i*, #19, October 1, 1961, in *SCMM*, #284, pp. 20–30. Also, *SCMP*, #2887, pp. 2–3; and Tso Hai, "Mass Accounting Must Be Combined with Specialized Accounting," *Ta Kung Pao*, July 12, 1961, in *SCMP*, #2551, pp. 5–9; "Each and Every Enterprise Must Strengthen Economic Accounting," *JMJP*, December 24, 1961, in *SCMP*, #2660, pp. 1–4.

34. As we shall note later, there were essentially two directions that

the evolution of responsibility systems could take. One should not, therefore, view the developments described in this section as the only rational alternative.

35. For more detail on the evolution of technical responsibility systems, see the following: "An Important Question in Strengthening Leadership Work in Enterprises," *JMJP*, editorial, August 4, 1961, in *SCMP*, #2561, pp. 7–10; "Further Develop the Role of Technical Personnel in Industrial Enterprises," *JMJP*, editorial, November 7, 1961, in *SCMP*, #2635, pp. 4–7; T'ang Ming-ch'i, "How Our Enterprise Brings the Role of Engineering and Technical Personnel into Full Play," *Kung-jen Jih-pao*, June 26, 1962, in *SCMP*, #2787, pp. 9–11; Ch'en Mao-li, "Fulfillment of Duties and Authority," *Kung-jen Jih-pao*, July 19, 1962, in *SCMP*, #2792, pp. 6–8.

36. For a good presentation of this argument, see Fei Wu-wen, "On the Responsibiilty System of Socialist State-Owned Industrial Enterprises," *Ching-chi Yen-chiu*, #7, 1962, in *SCMM*, #333, pp. 20–41.

37. "The Great Revolutionary Significance of Participation in Labor By Cadres," *JMJP*, editorial, June 20, 1963, in *SCMP*, #3006, pp. 14–18.

38. *Hung Ch'i*, #13–14, July 10, 1963, in *SCMM*, #376, pp. 1–13.

39. Wang Shao-chuan and Chou Hsiao-p'eng, "Class Education Must Be Conducted Firmly During the Production Increase and Economy Campaign," *Chung-kuo Nung-yeh Chi-hsieh* (*Chinese Agricultural Machinery*), #7, July 10, 1963, in *SCMM*, #382, pp. 14–18. Also, "The Mass Line is a Fundamental Guarantee for the Proper Management of Enterprises," *Hua-hsueh Kung-yeh* (*Chemical Industry*), #15, August 6, 1963, and an article on the Dolomite Workshop of the Shihchingshan Iron and Steel Company, in *JMJP*, March 18, 1964, in *SCMP*, #3195, pp. 3–6.

40. "Maintain a Firm Grip on Both Upper and Lower Levels," *JMJP*, editorial, April 2, 1964, in *SCMP*, #3201, pp. 1–5.

41. Feng Tai, "The Need for Revolutionization As Well as Modernization," *Ta Kung Pao*, March 27, 1964, in *SCMP*, #3206, pp. 10–14.

42. "National Political Work Conference for Industry and Communications Resolves to Learn Firmly and Effectively from the PLA," *NCNA*, Peking, April 3, 1964, in *SCMP*, #3200, pp. 1–2.

43. *Ibid.*

44. Ma Wen-kuei, "Basic Principles Governing the Administration of Socialist State-Operated Industrial Enterprises," *JMJP*, June 3, 1964, in *SCMP*, #3245, pp. 7–14.

45. "Genuinely Take Part In Labor Like an Ordinary Laborer,"

JMJP, editorial, September 22, 1964, in *SCMP*, #3313, pp. 16–19.

46. *Ibid.*

47. For one example, see "Cadres' Participation in Labor Has Become a Regular System at Kuanghua Pharmaceutical Manufactory," *Nan-fang Jih-pao*, November 3, 1964, in *SCMP*, #3358, pp. 5–8.

48. Chung Huang, "Revolutionization and Modernization of Socialist Industrial Enterprises," *Ching-chi Yen-chiu*, #12, December 20, 1964, in *SCMM*, #459, pp. 18–30.

49. Ma Tien-shui, "Intensify Mass and Foundation Work; Promote Technical Innovation and Revolution," *Kung-jen Jih-pao*, July 14, 1965, in *SCMP*, #3521, pp. 3–10; also, Tung Yang, "Instituting the Job Responsibility System; Strengthening Management Work of Industrial Enterprises," *Ching-chi Yen-chiu*, #4, April 20, 1965, in *SCMM*, #476, pp. 40–48.

50. "Take Good Care of Machinery and Equipment as Fighters Do Their Weapons," *JMJP*, editorial, July 30, 1965, in *SCMP*, #3526, pp. 2–7.

51. CCP Committee, Kansu Metallurgical Co., "Reform Labor Organization with the Revolutionary Spirit," *JMJP*, July 7, 1965, in *SCMP*, #3513, pp. 4–10.

52. "Turning to Work Shifts and Groups, Turning to the Worker Masses for the Purpose of Serving Production," *JMJP*, editorial, September 24, 1965, in *SCMP*, #3555, pp. 2–8.

53. See, for one example, Donnithorne, *China's Economic System*, pp. 204–211.

54. Eyewitness reports of visits to Chinese factories seem to confirm this without exception. See for examples, Richman, "Capitalists and Managers," *passim*; K. S. Karol, *China, The Other Communism* (New York, Hill and Wang, 1967), pp. 220–240; Rosemary Stuart, "Managers Under Mao," *Management Today* (London, April, 1967), pp. 66–71. There are many other reports, mostly by Japanese journalists, which confirm this.

55. *SCMP*, #3555, pp. 2–8.

56. Frantz Fanon, *The Wretched of the Earth* (New York, Grove Press, 1968), *passim*, but especially the sections on the national bourgeoisie.

57. Chiang Chen-yung, "Several Related Questions Concerning Industrial and Commercial Management and Administration," *Ching-chi Yen-chiu*, #1, 1966, translated in *Chinese Economic Studies*, Winter, 1967–68, International Arts and Sciences Press, White Plains, New York.

58. "Peking General Knitwear Mill Simplifies Administration," *NCNA*, Peking, July 28, 1968, in *SCMP*, #4231, pp. 16–18.

59. Samejima, "Visit to Peking Factory," *Nihon Keizai,* in Translations From the Japanese Press, Tokyo, November 6, 1967.
60. Rosemary Stuart, "Managers Under Mao," p. 70.
61. The experimental system of management referred to is of American origin, and is known as the "Scanlon Plan." Reference was made to it in Robert A. Feldmesser, "Function and Ideology in Soviet Social Stratification," in Kurt London (ed.), *The Soviet Union: A Half-Century of Communism* (Baltimore, Johns Hopkins Press, 1968). Cf. Robert A. Walker, *Modern Technology and Civilization* (New York, McGraw-Hill, 1962).

Reference to the "Scanlon Plan" was made in connection with a study of the relationship between the ideals of Communist theory of the division of labor and the actual functioning of Soviet industry on Russian social stratification. This method of management was carried out in isolated instances in American factories, and in some way bears very close similarity both to the ideals of how the division of labor would be fashioned in a socialist society and to the Chinese system of management that seems to be emerging.

Notes on Contributors

STEPHEN P. ANDORS is teaching in the Department of Political Science of the State University of New York at Oswego and is a candidate for a Ph.D. in political science at Columbia University. He holds a Certificate from Columbia's East Asian Institute, and spent 1969 in Hong Kong on study and travel grants from the Institute's Contemporary China Committee and the National Science Foundation. He previously spent two years in Thailand as a Peace Corps volunteer.

JUDITH COBURN attended Smith College and has worked as a reporter for the St. Louis *Globe Democrat* and as Washington reporter for Pacifica Radio. She had been writing a regular column, "Seat of Government," with Jeff Cowan for the *Village Voice* and has contributed articles on science policy, national military policy, and women's liberation to *Ramparts, Science,* and *The New Republic.* She has been associated with the Institute of Policy Studies and is currently in Vietnam.

JOHN W. DOWER teaches Chinese and Japanese history at the University of Nebraska and is completing his Ph.D. thesis in history and Far Eastern languages at Harvard. He is the author of *Elements of Japanese Design.* In 1963–1965 he lived and worked in Japan as a teacher, editor, and book designer.

EDWARD FRIEDMAN, an assistant professor in the Department of Political Science at the University of Wisconsin, took an M.A. in East Asian studies and a Ph.D. in political science at Harvard. He contributed essays to *China and Ourselves, International Politics in a Nuclear Age,* and *The End of a Political Science* and is the author of *The Chinese Revolutionary Party,* to be published in 1971. A contributor to many professional journals, among them the *Journal of Asian Studies, Asian Survey, Far Eastern Economic Review,* and *China Quarterly,* he has studied and lived in Taiwan and Hong Kong and has traveled widely in Asia.

JOHN GITTINGS was educated at Oxford University, where he earned First Class Honours in Oriental studies. Now a research fellow at the London School of Economics' Centre for International Studies, he is working on a full-length study of "China and the origins of the cold war." He is the author of *The Role of the Chinese Army* and *Survey of the Sino-Soviet Dispute* and has written for *China Quarterly, Pacific Affairs, Financial Times, The Nation,* and other journals. He spent three years as a China Specialist at the Royal Institute of International Affairs in London, two years at the University of Chile helping organize an Institute of International Studies, and two years in Hong Kong as China Editor of the *Far Eastern Economic Review.*

JOHN G. GURLEY took his Ph.D. and is a professor of economics at Stanford University. He taught earlier at the University of Maryland and at Princeton, has been Senior Staff with the Brookings Institution and managing editor of the *American Economic Review*. Acquainted with almost all of Asia, he has spent time in both Korea and Indonesia.

LEIGH KAGAN has attended Smith College, Stanford University, and the Universities of California and Pennsylvania, among others, in her quest to study Chinese history and learn Chinese, and is now a Ph.D. candidate at Harvard. She lived one year in India and two years in Taiwan.

RICHARD C. KAGAN teaches at Boston State College and is a faculty member of the Cambridge-Goddard Graduate School for Social Change. He took a Ph.D. in modern Far Eastern history at the University of Pennsylvania and worked in East Harlem as a Community Development Worker with the American Friends Service Committee. He has contributed to *Dissent* and *Engage*.

JONATHAN MIRSKY is Associate Professor of History and Chinese and Co-Director of the East Asia Center at Dartmouth College. He was educated at Cambridge University, Columbia University, and the University of Pennsylvania, where he took his Ph.D. in history, and has been a Visiting Schweitzer Professor at New York University. Co-author of *Peace in Vietnam,* he contributed a chapter to *Formosa Today* and has written numerous articles and reviews for *The Nation, Ramparts, Commonweal, The New York Review of Books, China Quarterly,* and other professional journals. He has repeatedly traveled and lived in Indochina as well as Japan, Indonesia, Taiwan, and Hong Kong.

JAMES PECK did his Ph.D. work in sociology at Harvard, specializing in modern China. A teaching fellow in history and sociology, he taught a course in Chinese-American foreign policy in the Kennedy Institute at Harvard. He was a national coordinator of the Committee of Concerned Asian Scholars and is co-editor of the *CCAS Bulletin*. He is currently with the Bay Area Institute.

MARK SELDEN, an assistant professor of history at Washington University, St. Louis, is the author of *People's War and the Transformation of Chinese Society: The Yenan Way*. He took his Ph.D. at Yale in modern Chinese history and lived and studied one year in Taiwan (1964–1965) and two years in Japan (1965–1966 and 1969–1970). He is co-editor of the *CCAS Bulletin*.

STEPHEN STONEFIELD is attending the Harvard University Graduate School of Arts and Sciences, taking East Asian studies. He graduated from Dartmouth *summa cum laude* and has been awarded numerous honors and fellowships, including the Senior Fellowship at Dartmouth and a Woodrow Wilson fellowship. His educational focus has been on Asia, particularly Chinese and Vietnamese history and Chinese language.

Index